THE CARING HEIRS OF
DOCTOR SAMUEL BARD

THE CARING HEIRS OF DOCTOR SAMUEL BARD

PROFILES OF SELECTED DISTINGUISHED GRADUATES
OF COLUMBIA UNIVERSITY VAGELOS COLLEGE
OF PHYSICIANS AND SURGEONS

PETER WORTSMAN

Columbia University Press

New York

Columbia University Press
Publishers Since 1893
New York   Chichester, West Sussex
cup.columbia.edu

Library of Congress Cataloging-in-Publication Data
Names: Wortsman, Peter, author.
Title: The caring heirs of Dr. Samuel Bard : profiles of selected
distinguished graduates of Columbia University Vagelos College of
Physicians and Surgeons / Peter Wortsman.
Description: New York : Columbia University Press, [2019] | Collection of
interviews previously published in the Columbia University, College of
Physicians and Surgeons alumni journal. | Includes bibliographical references.
Identifiers: LCCN 2018041843 | ISBN 9780231191289 (hardback) |
ISBN 9780231549325 (e-book)
Subjects: | MESH: Columbia University. Vagelos College of Physicians and
Surgeons. | Physicians | United States | Interview | Collected Works
Classification: LCC R690 | NLM WZ 112 | DDC 610.69/5—dc23
LC record available at https://lccn.loc.gov/2018041843

Cover design: Lisa Hamm
Cover image: © Evgeniefimenko/Dreamstime.com

To Anke L. Nolting, PhD, who makes things happen

"No less than Life, and its greatest Blessing Health, are to be the Objects of your Attention; and would you acquit yourselves of your Consciences, you must spend your Days in assiduous Enquiries, after the Means of rendering those of others long and happy."

Samuel Bard, MD
Professor of the Practice of Medicine in King's College
Founder of The College of Physicians and Surgeons

A Discourse Upon the Duties of a Physician
Delivered Before the President and Governors
Of KING'S COLLEGE
AT THE COMMENCEMENT,
Held on the 16th of May, 1769

CONTENTS

ACKNOWLEDGMENTS

THE PUBLICATION of this book was made possible by generous contributions from Ron Cohen '81, Paul J. Maddon MD, PhD '88, and George D. Yancopoulos PhD '86, MD '87. All of the profiles previously appeared in the journal *Columbia Medicine* (formerly known as *P&S*), and are reissued by permission.

PREFACE

Taking Doctors' Histories

MY EARLIEST MEMORY of a doctor's visit involves a colossal hypodermic needle loaded with adrenalin thrust by our family physician, Dr. Goldberg, into my rump that made my legs twitch uncontrollably but brought speedy relief to my asthma. Not an easy quid pro quo for a child to fathom. The follow-up to that and subsequent visits invariably involved some bitter pill or noxious tasting liquid I was compelled to swallow. Throughout childhood and well into adulthood, I continued to associate doctors with pain and bitterness.

All of my associations with the medical profession changed in 1987 when I had the great good fortune to start work as managing editor of alumni publications for the P&S Alumni Association and alumni news writer for the journal *Columbia Medicine* (formerly called *P&S*). In that capacity it has been my privilege and my pleasure to interview and profile many of America's most distinguished physicians and surgeons, all graduates of the Columbia University Vagelos College of Physicians and Surgeons, traditionally known by the acronym P&S.

I have been taking doctors' histories now, so to speak, for some three decades. The doctors I've interviewed have charted new fields of medicine, resolved longstanding biochemical mysteries, discovered the causes and cures and established the genetic bases of diseases, developed vaccines, pioneered new surgical procedures, and helped stop devastating epidemics. Some have run hospitals, medical schools, universities, the National Institutes of Health, the National Library of Medicine, the Centers for Disease Control and Prevention, various city health departments, and major pharmaceutical concerns. Others climbed mountains and made landmark findings in high altitude physiology, flew to outer space, practiced at the White House, and conducted humanitarian missions to care for imperiled populations in the United States and abroad. Others, still, wrote pioneering papers, edited prestigious medical journals, and authored prize-winning tomes and bestselling novels. In each case, whether or not their accomplishments might be deemed strictly medical, their clinical training, the scientific thinking, rigor and thoroughness, and humanistic values inculcated at P&S had a formative influence on their thinking and practice.

The following profiles of notable alumni appeared from 1987 to 2018 in consecutive issues of *Columbia Medicine*. Some of my subjects have since moved on to other endeavors and challenges, and some, alas, have passed on. While leaving the profiles in substance as they first appeared in print, I have, when appropriate, added brief updates.

To my lasting regret, I missed out on interviewing several notable individuals, including the industrialist, philanthropist, and self-styled "citizen diplomat" Armand Hammer '21, with whom I envisioned discussing his tête-à-têtes with Vladimir Lenin and other movers and shakers of the twentieth century, and the novelist Walker Percy '41, with whom I would have loved to sip mint juleps and talk literary turkey. Both fell ill and passed away at the time I attempted to make contact. There are, no doubt, many other remarkable P&S-schooled MDs whom I've missed along the way. Given the size and scope of this book, I was ultimately obliged to select a limited number of the profiles I wrote for inclusion.

A word about my working method. At its best, if the interviewer has done his or her homework, and the respondent is sufficiently relaxed and forthcoming, the interview can be an exhilarating experience, an amalgam of a Platonic dialogue, a psychoanalytic session, and an episode of the old TV show "This Is Your Life," enlightening for both parties, and hopefully also for the reader of these profiles as a third participant after the fact. In the words of one of my distinguished subjects, child psychiatrist and Pulitzer Prize-winning author Robert Coles '54, "All interviews, one hopes, become jointly conducted."

It is my belief and my credo as an interviewer that everyone has a tale to tell and is dying to tell it, and that if in the course of your research you discover the right psychological key to unlock your subject, the story will come pouring out.

In the case of the great baby doctor-turned political activist, Benjamin Spock '29, for instance, I was struck by his attachment to the ocean, and the fact that he had always lived either near a beach or in a boat bobbing on a big body of water. When I asked what the ocean meant to him, his eyes lit up. He revealed, in a kind of free association, that his father had been a prominent railroad lawyer, and that he somehow associated boats and the ocean, the fluid world, with his mother, and by extension, with pediatrics.

Then there was the interview with P. Roy Vagelos '54, retired chair and CEO of the pharmaceutical giant Merck & Co. In doing research I discovered that the initial P. in his name stood for Pindaros. "I would like to start this interview with a poem," I paused, "an ode to healing," again I paused, "by your namesake, I believe. You were named for the poet Pindar, were you not?" Dr. Vagelos smiled. The interview went well. And Merck's head of public relations, who was also present, took me aside afterwards to say he'd learned something new.

Among my greatest thrills in the course of conducting these interviews was talking to astronaut-surgeon Story Musgrave '64, upon my request, reclining in a capsule in position for take-off at NASA headquarters in Houston; visiting the Oval Office of the White House with the late Burton J. Lee III '56, physician to President George H. W. Bush; shadowing internist Karen Kinsell '93 in her rural practice in a hard-hit hamlet in southern Georgia; and spending a day at Solano State Prison, a maximum security facility in California, interviewing lifers whose lives had been turned around by the late pediatrician-turned substance abuse specialist, Davida Coady '65.

A medical mosaic of sorts, these doctors' histories invert the stethoscope, as it were, permitting the reader to listen in on the heartbeat of American medicine at its best.

Peter Wortsman

THE CARING HEIRS OF
DOCTOR SAMUEL BARD

A NEW DEAN DIGS IN AT BOSTON UNIVERSITY SCHOOL OF MEDICINE

KAREN ANTMAN '74

Dr. Antman, an internationally recognized expert on breast cancer, mesotheliomas, and sarcomas, has been provost of the medical campus and dean of Boston University School of Medicine since 2005.

⸙

ASK KAREN ANTMAN '74, Boston University's new provost of the medical campus and dean of the School of Medicine, to reflect on the root of her lifelong commitment to academic medicine, and her memory leaps back to her third year at Muhlenberg College, in Allentown, Penn., when a classmate developed Hodgkin's disease. At around the same time, a childhood friend was diagnosed with leukemia. Her classmate benefited from what at the time was experimental treatment. Her childhood friend received the standard protocol at a local community hospital. The former survived. The latter did not. Clinical trials, she realized, can make a life and death difference.

Dr. Antman took the lesson to heart and to mind. "It is not enough for an academic medical center to provide the same care that can be obtained elsewhere," she later wrote in an article that appeared in *P&S* (now *Columbia Medicine*), "we have a responsibility to improve treatments and advance knowledge."

Renowned for the development of now standard regimens for the treatment of sarcomas and mesotheliomas, and for supportive care regimens, she trained and taught at Harvard for 16 years, and spent a decade on the faculty at P&S. There she held the Wu Chair in Medicine and Pharmacology and ran the Herbert Irving Comprehensive Cancer Center, before leaving to serve as deputy director for translational and clinical sciences at the National Cancer Center.

A past president of the American Society of Clinical Oncology and the American Association for Cancer Research, she has published widely. And when the opportunity came to head up the academic medical enterprise at one of America's leading research universities, it didn't take her long to make up her mind. Her grueling schedule notwithstanding, she's still smiling.

This profile is based on an interview conducted in September 2005, in her large, airy office overlooking the central quadrangle of the Boston University Medical Campus.

PURSUING MEDICINE, DESPITE THE TENOR OF THE TIMES

Born in New Jersey, Karen Antman grew up in Pennsylvania and attended Muhlenberg College, in Allentown, majoring in chemistry and graduating magna cum laude. Science was her primary focus from the start. And though there were no physicians in the family, her mother, a nurse, had wanted to study medicine. Dr. Antman decided at age thirteen to become a physician.

But the tenor of the times in America discouraged women from contemplating medical careers. "'You don't know what you're talking about, women just don't become doctors!'" Dr. Antman recalls being told by her high school biology teacher and many others. Then, in 1967, on summer break from college, she participated in the Experiment in International Living in Prague, in the former Czechoslovakia (now the Czech Republic). On a weekend trip to Budapest the group's assigned guide, a medical student, invited her to watch her first surgery. She learned that more than half of Hungary's doctors were women. "So it was just a cultural thing," she concluded, "of course I could do it!"

Entering P&S as one of only sixteen women in a class of 160, she found it a most hospitable environment, relishing the challenge of "a great medical school in a great city," and, coincidentally, meeting her husband-to-be, classmate Elliot Antman '74, on the very first day. "Medical school was wonderful!" she wholeheartedly affirms. Outstanding teachers like the late Dr. Bernard Weinstein in oncology, the late Dr. Harold Neu and the late Glenda Garvey '69 in infectious diseases, imparted, not only a solid grasp of the material, but also an intellectual excitement. Intrigued by both the neurosciences and oncology, she ultimately decided to pursue the latter field. "Whereas in neurological diseases, you could make the diagnosis but you couldn't do much," she reasoned at the time, "in cancer, people told me you couldn't do much either," but the memory of her college classmate's illness and recovery led her to believe that "research could indeed make a difference in cancer."

Following an internship and medical residency at Columbia Presbyterian (now New York-Presbyterian) Medical Center, she pursued clinical fellowships in medicine at Harvard Medical School and in medical oncology at the Sidney Farber Cancer Institute, in Boston, where she also simultaneously pursued a research fellowship in neoplastic disease mechanisms.

In 1979, she joined the faculty at Harvard Medical School as an instructor in medicine. She likewise took on the responsibilities as coordinator of the Sarcoma and Mesothelioma Clinical Research and Treatment Programs, and in 1984, was named clinical director of the Dana-Farber Cancer Institute/Beth Israel Solid Tumor Autologous Marrow Program.

"IT'S UP TO YOU TO DO THE RIGHT THING, WE JUST WON'T PAY FOR IT!"

It was in the course of a clinical trial on which Dr. Antman was principal investigator at Dana-Farber, testing the efficacy of ifosfamide, a new drug to treat life-threatening sarcomas, that she first fathomed the importance of medical policy issues and access to the decision-making process. The sarcoma of one twenty-four-year-old patient in the study was clearly responding well, but his insurance provider refused to cover the medical cost of administering the drug. Challenging that decision, she argued, "You covered the costs of cyclophospha-mide and we already know it doesn't work as well as ifosfamide, so why won't you cover the patient cost of administering a drug that has twice the efficacy?!" The insurance person's reply still rings in her ears many years later: "'It's up to you to do the right thing, Doctor, we just won't pay for it!'"

Dr. Antman did just that. She was the principal author of one of three pivotal papers that, together, helped make ifosfamide part of the now-standard treat-ment for soft tissue sarcomas. Not long thereafter, an editorial she coauthored, "The Crisis in Clinical Cancer Research, Third-Party Insurance and Investiga-tional Therapy," in the *New England Journal of Medicine*, in 1988, attracted con-siderable attention.

She smiled, "you then find yourself on committees at the NIH, at the Ameri-can Society of Clinical Oncology, and you start getting asked for your opinions on medical policy. When you're dealing with a disease that's going to kill people who would otherwise live, and somebody's standing in the way of better treat-ment, you have to talk about policy!"

She is also well known for groundbreaking clinical research in bone marrow transplant involving the mobilization of peripheral blood-derived stem cells and effective supportive care.

THE CALL BACK TO COLUMBIA P&S

In 1993, Dr. Antman was recruited back to her medical alma mater as professor of medicine and pharmacology and associate director for clinical research of the Columbia Presbyterian Cancer Center. Subsequently named Wu Professor of Medicine and Pharmacology, she took over the leadership of the newly named and expanded Herbert Irving Comprehensive Cancer Center, a National Can-cer Institute–designated cancer center. She played a major role in the center's reorganization and is credited with strengthening the bridge between bench research and clinical applications. Specifically, she sought to focus the research around particular cancers, not treatment modalities, so as to maximize the pos-sibilities for interdisciplinary collaboration.

"If the faculty is divided by department," she points out, "then the surgeons see patients and do research on the surgical floor and the medical oncologists do their thing on a different floor. But by putting the cancer space at one location, you start to have people working on the same diseases, working together."

During her tenure there, the cancer center's external funding increased from about $45 million to close to $115 million. She also helped build the level of private philanthropy.

Considerable as her administrative responsibilities were at Columbia, Dr. Antman always found time to teach, delivering lectures to first-, second-, and fourth-year medical students, house staff and fellows. "My secretary always said I was happiest the month I was on service." In 1994, medical residents voted her Senior Faculty Teacher of the Year.

Dr. Antman intends to start teaching at BU once she's gotten a handle on the administrative ropes. A clinical investigator and educator at heart, she insists, "How do you know what systems work at a university unless you try them out?"

TAKING HER TRANSLATIONAL SKILLS
TO BETHESDA, BOSTON—AND BEYOND

In 2004, she left Columbia to accept the position of deputy director for translational and clinical sciences at the National Cancer Institute at the NIH in Bethesda, Md. "Instead of directing a single cancer center," she summed up her responsibilities, "I had a supervisory role for the Cancer Center Program, which includes sixty-one cancer centers nationwide."

A year later, the trustees at Boston University offered her the job of provost of the medical campus and dean of the School of Medicine, heading up their medical educational enterprise. And following a "crash course in the do's and don'ts of being a dean at a 'Dean School' " organized by the American Association of Medical College, Dr. Antman rolled up her sleeves and dug in. "Just keeping all the balls in the air is complicated, like being a parent," she observes, adding, "Every academic medical center has two parents, the hospital president and the dean of the medical school. At BU, the parents have a history of getting along very well indeed."

The metaphor is particularly apt for Dr. Antman, whose daughter, Amy, and son, David, will both graduate from medical school in May, Amy from Harvard and David from P&S. Come the spring, Dr. Antman will have to prove her agility at juggling in a veritable medical three-ring circus, attending three medical school graduations, at Columbia, Harvard, and BU, where she will deliver her second commencement address. Needless to say, medical education is a family affair. Her husband, Elliot Antman '74, is professor of medicine at Harvard Medical School and distinguished cardiologist at Brigham and Women's Hospital.

Among the missions of a major academic medical center, Dr. Antman puts education first, "because first of all, we are a medical school. Education is our core mission." Discoveries come a close second. "The hospital has the leadership role in care, so the medical school has to support and protect discovery."

"A DEAN'S DILEMMA: EVERY CONSTITUENCY BELIEVES THEIR ISSUE IS THE TOP ISSUE AND MUST BE DEALT WITH TODAY."

While the wonderful thing about her job is the constant variety, "never a dull moment, with pressing financial issues, animal issues, and faculty issues, a new challenge every day," the pressure is considerable, as is the need to prioritize. "Every constituency believes that their issue is the top issue and must be dealt with today!"

As to the question of a medical school dean's major challenges, she responds without a moment's hesitation, "Space and money! Any dean or faculty person will say the same at any academic medical center in America." With the NIH budget presently "flat or worse," she insists, "we have to make our faculty much more efficient and we have to diversify our funding portfolio."

At BU, as elsewhere, the academic link with industry is a vital and mutually beneficial relationship. Like Columbia's Audubon Research Park, BU's BioSquare is not only an incubator for new therapies and ideas but also a source of much-needed revenue. "Science is expensive. We need these kinds of industry-academic collaborations," she maintains, "as long as the institution keeps a close eye on possible conflicts of interest between profit-making and educational enterprises."

Topmost among BU's current needs, in her view, is philanthropy. One major need is affordable housing for medical students in Boston's expensive real estate market. She hopes to find funding to build a student dormitory on the order of Columbia's Bard Hall.

"My decade at Columbia P&S was the best possible preparation," she says, citing the experience of her close working relationship with "visionary benefactors like Herbert Irving and Clyde Wu '56."

A GLOBAL MEDICAL SCHOOL WITH A PROUD HERITAGE

Founded in 1848, Boston University School of Medicine, the first medical institution of higher learning in America to admit women, is today one of the top twenty U.S. medical schools in total federal funding for research. It is also one of the country's most selective medical schools, currently outranking Brown and Dartmouth in *U.S. News and World Report*. A leader at home and in the world arena, BU is an international university, with campuses and offices in many countries, and," says the new dean, "we plan to continue reaching out." Her goal is nothing less than "to try to make this medical school the best possible place to learn, teach, and discover!"

A CHAMPION OF HEALTH EQUALITY
AT THE HELM OF THE NYC DEPARTMENT
OF HEALTH

MARY T. BASSETT '79

In 2018, Dr. Bassett stepped down as NYC Health Commissioner to become director of the François-Xavier Bagnoud Center for Health and Human Rights at Harvard University.

———∞———

"WE DON'T BELIEVE in a back-seat approach to protecting public health," Mary T. Bassett '79 laid it on the line at the press conference on January 16, 2014, at which Mayor Bill de Blasio announced her appointment as New York City Commissioner of Health and Mental Hygiene. Dr. Bassett went on to outline her plan of action: "Whether it is protecting a community facing the loss of a hospital, or ensuring that all neighborhoods enable healthy choices as people eat, work and play, we will meet New Yorkers where they live and ensure their health is protected." She has since been true to her words, focusing on the neighborhoods most in need, and by most accounts, effectively juggling the myriad health priorities of the teeming metropolis.

Her public profile soared in the spotlight of an Ebola scare in October, 2014, during which she leapt into action, calmly and assuredly piloting what she proudly dubbed "the leading urban health department in the world," all the while taking pains to keep the public well informed.

In a career spanning more than three decades, including seventeen years teaching and directing AIDS-prevention programs in Zimbabwe, and eight years as NYC Deputy Commissioner of Health Promotion and Disease Prevention in the Bloomberg Administration, spearheading such bold initiatives as a trans fat ban and calorie labeling in the City's fast food restaurants, Dr. Bassett has applied an unabashed activist vision of public health. "We're trying to shift the paradigm from thinking of population health as driven by individual

behavior to thinking about the decisions that are, in fact, available to people, and trying to put healthy choices within everyone's reach."

She made time in her busy schedule in March 2015 to look back on her career and share her concept of public health.

HONING HER VISION AT HARLEM HOSPITAL

Training in medicine from 1979 to 1983 at Harlem Hospital, where in her last year she served as chief resident, Dr. Bassett tried to balance the considerable health burdens of the community and the hospital's scarcity of means during a difficult time. The confluence of the heroin epidemic, the beginning of the AIDS epidemic, an economic downturn and housing abandonment, among other crises with an impact on health, made it a veritable trial by fire. She lauds the dedication of her colleagues, under the charismatic leadership of Department of Medicine Chair Dr. Gerald Thomson HON '96, the Samuel Lambert and Robert Sonneborn Professor of Medicine Emeritus at P&S. "We lacked supplies, we had very sick patients, the operating room would be shut down because they didn't have air conditioning, and I remember the night they ran out of respirators. But in spite of those really daunting conditions, Dr. Thomson inspired us all by his example, generating standards, demanding quality of care, and commanding respect."

Another Columbia faculty mentor on staff at Harlem Hospital, the late Dr. John Lindenbaum, chief of hematology/oncology, was not only "a classic Socratic teacher," but also "brought the example of being a topnotch physician-scientist to Harlem Hospital." (In April 2015, she returned to P&S to deliver the John Lindenbaum Memorial Lecture.)

"Yet as committed as the staff was to the needs of the community, it didn't take me long," she says, "to see that we were patching people up and sending them back out, that as hard as we worked in the hospital, the main things that determined their health were happening outside in their homes and on the street." That realization prompted her to pursue a master's degree in public health at the University of Washington, in Seattle.

"MY GOAL HAS ALWAYS BEEN TO BE OF USE, TO HAVE A POSITIVE IMPACT."

"My goal has always been to be of use, to have a positive impact," she affirms. A child of the 1960s, her consciousness was raised and shaped early on by her parents, the late Dr. Emmett W. Bassett, a chemist who held a PhD in dairy technology from Tuskegee Institute (now Tuskegee University), the first African American investigator in the field, and Priscilla Bassett, a dedicated librarian who venerated learning. "Together they made an incredible team." Both were activists in the civil rights and peace movements. "They taught us children the importance of commitment to community, to family, and the fact that many people paved the way for us and our opportunity for advancement." She remains haunted to this day by childhood visits to her father's native Virginia, where since interracial marriages remained against state law until the law was invalidated by a U.S. Supreme Court ruling in 1967, she had to pretend that her mother, who is white, was not her mother. "I remember being tormented by the idea that I could get it wrong," she still recalls with a catch in her throat, "when, of course, I knew it was society that was getting it wrong."

Mary Bassett grew up in Washington Heights, where her parents were a driving force for the establishment of the Community Advisory Board at Presbyterian Hospital and several neighborhood health clinics. In 2014, the stretch of 162nd Street between Edgecombe and St. Nicholas Avenues, where her parents lived for decades and where they planted trees that have since grown tall, was renamed Emmett W. Bassett Street in her father's honor.

It was in the course of a high school summer job as a census taker in West Harlem that she decided to study medicine. "I was given the privilege of going into people's homes, seeing what they put on their table for dinner, sitting down and taking information about their lives," she said. "I wanted to do more than just register statistics."

As a student at Radcliffe College, where she earned a BA cum laude, with a double major in history and science, she made time to volunteer at the Black Panther Party Franklin Lynch Free Health Center in Roxbury, Mass., one of

Boston's predominantly black, low income neighborhoods. She scheduled doctor's appointments, "badgering, bullying and cajoling" physicians from Harvard-affiliated hospitals to pitch in, and helped screen residents in the city's housing projects for sickle cell anemia, a genetic disorder with a relatively high incidence among African Americans, but largely overlooked at the time by most biomedical researchers. (Another distinguished P&S alumna, the late hematologist Helen Ranney '47, first elucidated the genetic basis of the disease.)

BACK HOME IN WASHINGTON HEIGHTS

Dr. Bassett decided to study medicine in her old stomping grounds, Washington Heights. Though she cherished interactions with Dr. Thomson and other members of the Columbia faculty, including the late Dr. Harold Neu, an internationally recognized authority on infectious diseases, and the late Dr. Mervyn Susser, a South African–born epidemiologist at the School of Public Health known for emphasizing connections between disease and social conditions, her four years at P&S were by and large not a happy time. One of only three African Americans, and the only black woman in her graduating class at P&S, she recalls "a climate laden with the expectation that black students would perform poorly." Getting involved with the Black and Latin Students Organization, she and fellow students tried to make a case with the administration for improving the diversity of the student body. She winced, meanwhile, at certain residents' off-handed derisive remarks about poor patients, many of whom were blacks and Latinos from the neighborhood. And whereas she maintained a stellar academic record, she recalled one professor's "prognosis" that "Black students have trouble with academic subjects, but do much better in later clinical years 'because they have good people skills.' " It was not an isolated attitude.

While much progress still remains to be made, the cultural climate at P&S has since changed a bit for the better. The Class of 2018 included thirty-eight underrepresented minorities (seventeen African Americans, twenty Hispanics, and one Native Hawaiian) in a class of 160, the second highest percentage among peer institutions.

FROM HARLEM TO HARARE

Dr. Bassett's training at Harlem Hospital, at the time a Columbia affiliate, was a real eye-opener. "As a first-year intern, I made home visits on my own

[. . .]," in the course of which she came to realize that "the main drivers of Harlem's excess mortality were not 'ghetto' behaviors and diseases, but the common killers that affect everyone in industrialized countries: cardiovascular disease and cancer," she wrote in a short memoir, "From Harlem to Harare," included in the book *Comrades in Health: U.S. Health Internationalists, Abroad and at Home*, 2013, edited by Anne-Emanuelle Birn and Theodore M. Brown. "I liked the practice of medicine, and you could not find a more committed group than the Department of Medicine at Harlem Hospital," she wrote, "but I suspected that if my goal was to make people healthy, I wasn't accomplishing much."

After earning an MPH at the University of Washington, School of Public Health, she accepted a position as a junior lecturer in the Department of Community Medicine at the University of Zimbabwe, in Harare, where she initially expected to spend a year or two, and turned out staying on for seventeen years, and where she also raised two daughters. It was a heady, hopeful time for the country previously known as Rhodesia, in which the black majority cast off the yoke of minority white rule.

"The thing that really strikes me," she says, looking back, "was how young the leadership was of the Zimbabwe Ministry of Health, the people who were really leading the charge to improve conditions in the country following independence." She was greatly impressed by their "practical and ambitious agenda to promote primary health care, which doesn't just mean primary medical care, as we see it in the U.S., but also means paying attention to food security, water and sanitation, environmental approaches to diseases like malaria, and providing everybody access to a primary care facility." The Ministry achieved remarkable results. "A massive expansion of rural health centers placed roughly 80 percent of the population within eight kilometers of services. Before independence," she wrote in the aforementioned memoir, "infant mortality was an estimated 120–150 deaths per 1,000 live births; by 1990 it was down to 60 deaths per 1,000 births." And contrary to World Health Organization (WHO) recommendations, the Ministry's insistence on use of a simple home-based sugar-salt solution for oral rehydration of children suffering from diarrhea helped stem fatalities. WHO officials later recognized their own error and the Ministry's effectiveness.

When the AIDS crisis hit Zimbabwe, Dr. Bassett saw countless patients suffering from the disease, but wanting to have a more widespread effect, turned her focus to epidemiological studies, education in rural high schools, and prevention programs to reduce mother-to-child transmission. She became increasingly interested in the social determinants of health.

BACK TO THE BIG APPLE

In 2002, following a one-year stint as Associate Director for Health Equity at the Southern Africa Office of the Rockefeller Foundation, she was invited to take on the position of Deputy Commissioner of Health Promotion and Disease Prevention in the NYC Department of Health and Mental Hygiene, under the direction of fellow P&S alumnus Thomas Frieden '86, in the Bloomberg Administration.

In an effort to combat obesity, then as now one of the most pressing public health problems in the city and throughout the country, she helped push through calorie postings in fast food chains and the banning of trans fats in all New York restaurants. But the Department's drive to cap the serving size of highly caloric sugary drinks was challenged in court and effectively blocked by the soft drink industry. A June 2014 decision effectively ended the Board of Health's authority in this area.

Accused by some of promoting a "nanny state," she insists on the need for government to level the playing field. "To frame chronic disease risk as a consequence of ill-conceived personal choices [. . .]," she was quoted in an article in *Capital New York*, "is a modern day version of hand washing to prevent cholera. Not wrong but tragically misguided. Government at all levels should use its regulatory tools to limit tobacco use, end the glut of salty, sugary, high-calorie food and increase physical activity." In addition, she said, "it should be bolder in seeking to check advertising that promotes tobacco use and consumption of high calorie and low nutrient foods, especially those ads directed at children."

Dr. Bassett served from 2009 to 2014 as program director of the African Health Initiative and Child Abuse Prevention Program of the Doris Duke Charitable Foundation, until taking on the reins of the NYC Department of Health in January 2014. For the record, she is the fourth woman, and the second woman of African American descent, to hold the position.

PROMOTING A NEIGHBORHOOD-BASED APPROACH TO HEALTH

Building in many areas on the work of her predecessors, Drs. Thomas Frieden '86 and Thomas Farley, she has pivoted from their largely centralized approach to promoting neighborhood-based solutions to pressing public health concerns, a lesson she learned from her time in Zimbabwe.

"Anybody who has ever worked in sub-Saharan Africa will tell you they are organized by district structures," she said. "We brought this neighborhood lens and this idea that a neighborhood is a valid unit of intervention in urban public health to our work in New York. We recognized that there are certain neighborhoods with a higher disease burden than others. These neighborhoods are disproportionately poor, predominantly Black or Latino [. . .] They do not suffer from exotic diseases, but from the same things that kill all New Yorkers and all Americans: heart disease, cancer, etc." Zeroing in on pressing local needs, the Department, under her aegis, has directed more intensive efforts at community health offices in such hard hit neighborhoods as East and Central Harlem, Central Brooklyn, and the South Bronx.

Furthermore, she has sought and fostered dialogue and engagement with the community: "You need to have a supportive policy environment, but its sustainability is often based on the fact that the people who are the intended beneficiaries embrace it."

When word spread in 2014 that a Columbia physician, Dr. Craig Spencer, who had volunteered with Doctors Without Borders, in West Africa, was diagnosed with Ebola upon his return to New York City, Dr. Bassett made sure, among other top priorities, to allay fears and stem panic by getting word out to the public on how the disease was and was not transmitted and how unlikely it was to spread in the city, "and to let the West African communities in the Bronx and Staten Island know that we were committed to protecting them from stigmatization."

HOMEGROWN HEALTH SOLUTIONS AND LESSONS LEARNED FROM THE DEVELOPING WORLD

Cognizant of "how poorly we were doing in managing many chronic diseases," including asthma and diabetes, and influenced in part by community health worker strategies effectively employed in Latin America, the Department, under Dr. Bassett's guidance, restored the practice of "public health detailing," sending advisers out into the community "to support doctors in their practice and help them engage with their patients." The Department also provides brochures and posters for doctor's waiting rooms and health clinics, and other educational materials, including a kit for diabetics, demonstrating what an ideal calorie allotment should look like, with half the plate heaped with vegetables.

Dr. Bassett is an advocate of free lunches in public schools following sound nutritional guidelines.

Shop Healthy, a program originally devised in Philadelphia, which she enthusiastically endorses, "supports the establishment and retention of stores that sell fruits and vegetables" in areas that she has labeled "food deserts," where healthy choices are otherwise unavailable. "The program is really about redesigning the retail environment, changing the offerings at the deli counter," she explains. "It has been a learning experience for us in the Department of Health, working not only with shopkeepers, but also with wholesalers and distributors." She cites the case of one bodega owner who spoke at a press conference: "'Look, I'm a businessman,' he said, 'but I can't help but notice that people are just too heavy. I wanted to give this a try, and I'm happy to report I'm helping and making more money in the process.'"

Dr. Bassett hopes to enlist the presidents of public and private hospitals to become institutional sponsors of healthy food choices in their neighborhoods.

She is a firm believer in incubating creative new ideas at community health offices and then, if they prove successful, applying them elsewhere. Health Bucks, an innovative program developed in the Bronx, provides senior citizens with subsidies in the form of vouchers to buy healthy foods at local farmers' markets. She sees it as a two-pronged effort to encourage the consumption of nutritional foods and bolster the economy. The City currently leverages $650,000 worth of healthy purchases. She hopes to up the commitment to $1 million.

When Dr. Bassett was deputy commissioner, the Department of Health experimented with a program effectively used in Mexico and Brazil, called "Condition Cash Transfer." The idea was to offer cash subsidies to the poor conditioned on the accomplishment of certain actions, like putting healthy food on the table, regular doctor visits, and making sure children attend school. Though there were problems in its initial trial run in New York, she believes the Department can learn from and modify ideas that work abroad. "We are a part of the globe and we have things to learn from the developing world," she says, "just as we have much to offer."

BLACK LIVES MATTER

In a much-cited perspective piece in the *New England Journal of Medicine*, titled "#BlackLivesMatter—A Challenge to the Medical and Public Health Communities," written in response to the widely reported wave of police killings of young black men, Dr. Bassett stated unequivocally: "As New York City's health commissioner, I feel a strong moral and professional obligation to encourage critical dialogue and action on the issue of racism." But she insists on a broader view of the insidious effects of racism.

"The burden of race," she argues, "extends beyond the burden of violence and even beyond the burden of police violence. [. . .] We have an obligation to lower that risk. [. . .] I don't question the desire for justice [. . .] Violence plays an outsized role in the black population, but it doesn't account for most of the deaths that occur prematurely. The cost of racism has to be measured in lives cut short. A bigger view of justice would take into account the outsized toll of heart disease, stroke, diabetes among African Americans."

PROUD TO SERVE UNDER A "PUBLIC HEALTH" MAYOR

"In an ideal world, I would, of course, like to eliminate poverty, it would really do wonders for health, but we can do better at delivering health to our population even within the context of poverty," she insists.

"I'm proud to serve under Mayor Di Blasio, who has really made addressing the growing income inequality a centerpiece of his administration. And though I don't know if he would describe himself as a 'public health mayor,' he most definitely is. Pre-K education, affordable housing, and living wage, among other key priorities, all are important platforms for health. And while the Health Department can't do all these things, I can lend my voice as health commissioner to stressing the link between these initiatives and the health of our people."

Dr. Bassett was one of the prime movers behind the City's "Talk to Your Baby" campaign, encouraging parents to talk, read, and sing to their babies to bolster brain development, a program in which the City's first lady, Chirlane I. McCray, has taken an active interest, and at one promotional event famously burst into song.

Apropos of singing, while not herself inclined to a cappella performances, Dr. Bassett is an avid jazz fan, in her scarce spare time slipping off to attend a concert at one of the City's many venues.

LOOKING BACK AND LOOKING FORWARD

Reflecting on her career before a group of students in 2014, Dr. Bassett said, "I feel enormously privileged to have had the opportunity to work in various settings at home and abroad. [. . .] And I feel privileged to have come of age in the Sixties, a time when the legislative landscape offered opportunities to the broadest population." As for the course of her career, she reflected, "when you're living it forward it's considerably less planned than it might look in hindsight. [. . .] Looking back, I only wish I hadn't worried as much."

"I remain totally thrilled to serve as health commissioner for New York City, the absolute best job in public health, as far as I can tell."

What lies ahead? "To do my best to help make every neighborhood a healthy neighborhood, at least that's the plan."

NEW JERSEY'S HEALTH CARE CRUSADER

STANLEY S. BERGEN, JR. '55

Retiring in 1998 as the founding president of the University of Medicine and Dentistry of New Jersey, the largest free-standing public health sciences university in the country, Dr. Bergen moved to Stonington, Me., where he remains active in issues concerning hospital ethics.

───✸───

HEALTHSTATE, THE MAGAZINE of the University of Medicine and Dentistry of New Jersey, ran a three-page photographic spread on Stanley S. Bergen, Jr. '55 in its Spring-Summer 1998 issue. The tribute was occasioned by news of his retirement, effective June 30, 1998, as president of UMDNJ, an institution he helped found in 1972 and built "from an obscure medical college operating out of a trailer" (*Sunday Star Ledger*) into the largest free-standing public university of health sciences in the nation.

It all but takes your breath away just to scan the snapshots of Dr. Bergen in action. There he is breaking ground on the Newark campus in 1972; officiating at commencement; conferring with local community leaders; lobbying state legislators on pressing health care issues; personally presenting an ever-expanding network of facilities and clinics to a virtual who's who of movers and shakers, including two U.S. presidents, three New Jersey governors, a New Jersey senator, and a mayor of Newark; and jogging at dawn, his favorite form of "relaxation."

A PRESIDENT'S PRESCRIPTION

The pictures tell another story too. Look again and you notice that while the VIPs come and go, it's in the company of the unheralded citizens of his home state that Dr. Bergen is most himself. Were it not for the cap and gown in a 1991 commencement shot of the president handing out a diploma, you'd swear he was a country doctor dispensing a prescription.

For twenty-seven years, the diploma has indeed been Dr. Bergen's prescription of choice for the health and vitality of the people of New Jersey. In graduating hundreds of doctors, dentists, nurses, and other health professionals (many, including a large number of minorities, from modest economic backgrounds), UMDNJ has simultaneously been caring for its own and stirring economic growth in the state with close to 12,000 university-related jobs. Moreover, innovative community-oriented programs, like the Violence Institute of New Jersey (one of Bergen's brainchildren), which employs educational principles to "vaccinate" against violent behavior, makes the institution what its founder likes to call "a laboratory for discovering solutions."

PHYSICIAN TO THE BONE

Dr. Bergen is an hour late for a scheduled interview. A knee injury incurred while running finally demanded diagnosis and treatment. He was scheduled for an MRI, but a child in serious condition was wheeled in at the last minute and the president emeritus gladly let himself be bumped from the head of the line. Some would call that healthcare rationing, Bergen calls it "only human." A physician to the bone, he has devoted his life to the care of others and he's not about to stop now.

As to the knee, "I may have to cut back on the running," he shrugs, a considerable sacrifice for this tall, lanky, Type A+ personality who, at sixty-nine, can't sit still.

If ever the institution sought a fitting plaque to honor its founder, an imprint of his care-worn face would tell it all. While a forehead full of well-earned wrinkles angles downward, Dr. Bergen keeps his unwavering gaze locked on his interlocutor. The expression is no-nonsense, albeit kindly, more reminiscent of an old-fashioned family practitioner in a Normal Rockwell painting than of the driven academic medical administrator he is. The paradox is telling.

In fact, he got his first taste of medicine as a young kid tagging along on week-end house calls with his revered grandfather, Elston H. Bergen (P&S 1877), a Princeton, N.J., general practitioner.—"Hurry up, Stanley, we've got to get to the hospital!" The memory still makes him raise his chin and stretch his long legs, ready for action.

Can the president of a mammoth academic medical enterprise like UMDNJ, with seven schools on five campuses in one of the country's most densely populated states, be likened to a GP with his hand on the pulse and his eyes on the big picture?

"I've always had that feeling about this institution," Dr. Bergen readily concurs, "that we were a family trying to help others. I just love it when I drive up in the morning and the guard greets me: 'Hi, Dr. Bergen, how are you today!' We're a tight-knit family working together for the community, a town within a town."

AN ADMINISTRATOR WITH A DIFFERENCE

Asked if the essential qualities required of the head of an academic health care enterprise differ from those of high level administrators in business or other fields, Dr. Bergen replies with a definite, "Yes!"

"I may be old-fashioned," he allows, "but I don't believe that either higher education or health care can be considered a business. Of course, you have to apply business principles, you've got to be held accountable for where the money goes. But people are our product at UMDNJ, graduates and patients, and people can never be commodities! This place has got to be run by somebody with a physician's instincts of caring and service, a sense of duty to give back something to the community!"

GIVING BACK TO THE COMMUNITY

New Jersey born and bred, Stanley Bergen took his undergraduate degree from Princeton before crossing the Hudson to earn his medical stripes at P&S under the aegis of the legendary Dr. Robert Loeb. "Loeb may have scared the living daylights out of many of us," he recalls, "but he had an uncanny ability to extract the best, to shape you into a precise physician who constantly had the patient's best interest on your mind and in your heart."

Interning in medicine at St. Luke's Hospital (now part of St. Luke's-Roosevelt Medical Center), where he was subsequently named chief resident and Francis S. Zabriski Fellow, Dr. Bergen became interested in diabetes and worked under Dr. Theodore Van Italie in some of the early studies of oronasal tolbutamide. He was put in charge of the hospital's diabetic clinic, his first major administrative responsibility. A fascination for the nutritional aspects of diabetes made him increasingly aware of the social side of medical care, leading him to community medicine.

Following two years of military service as an army medical officer at Fort Jay Army Hospital on Governor's Island, he became medical director of the St. Luke's Convalescent Hospital in Greenwich, Conn. In 1964 he was recruited as director of medicine at Cumberland Hospital and chief of community medicine at the Brooklyn-Cumberland Medical Center.

It was here while trying to coordinate health care in a populous inner city neighborhood, where people were often compelled to wait hours for a doctor, that he fathomed the extent of the problem. Following the passage of a legislated change in New York State's health care delivery system under Governor Nelson Rockefeller, nicknamed "The Ghetto Medicine Bill," Dr. Bergen vividly remembers an altercation with a patient, a formidable African American woman with five children who buttonholed him in the waiting room: " 'You smart guys have gone and changed the system on us again. You're just trying to make it harder for us to get care for our kids. Well, let me tell you something, Mister, it took you months to change the system, it'll take us twenty-four hours to beat it!'" He was speechless. "When people have to connive just to get the basic primary care they need," he points out, "something is very wrong with the system."

In a paper entitled "Community Medicine: Method or Myth," published in the Winter 1970 issue of the *P&S Quarterly* (the precursor of *P&S*, now *Columbia Medicine*), Dr. Bergen asked: "Why does a country so sophisticated, so technically developed, so medically knowledgeable, continually fail to succeed in improving its health status?" Almost three decades later, he sees no real improvement: "We still have the best, and in some cases, the most marginal health care in the world. It's just mind-boggling, the sophisticated technology we have to deal with the molecular basis of disease, and yet on the other hand, the fact that there are Americans today who don't receive the basic vaccinations we all take for granted." The current nationwide trend to shrink the public hospital system, in his view, is changing the situation from bad to worse.

When in 1970 New York City decided to revamp its health and hospitals administration, his administrative talents at Cumberland and levelheaded leadership as chair of a medical advisory committee for the entire City hospitals system brought him to the attention of City Hall. Named senior vice president for medical and professional affairs of the newly created New York City Health and Hospitals Corporation, under Mayor John V. Lindsay, his tenure was cut short by the offer to build an academic medical center practically from scratch across the Hudson—an offer he could not refuse.

NEW JERSEY GETS ITS OWN MEDICAL SCHOOL, AT LAST

There had been a string of unsuccessful attempts in the past (one in colonial times by Dr. Nicholas Romayne, later a member of the P&S faculty) to create a school of medicine on Jersey soil. In 1956, Seton Hall Medical and Dental School was founded as a small private Catholic institution, but soon ran into financial difficulties. Instead of bailing the school out with public funds, New Jersey Governor Richard Hughes decided to create a commission to explore the feasibility of the state taking charge. The commission, headed by Johnson & Johnson president George Smith, gave him the green light.

Based in Newark, the planned new facility faced a trial by fire in the riots of 1968. In an atmosphere of social unrest and general distrust, it wasn't easy to convince the community that the new medical center for which they forfeited land would be in their own best interests.

Dr. Bergen, who came aboard in 1971 and officiated as the first president of the College of Medicine and Dentistry of New Jersey out of a trailer, recalls the view from his window as "a cold, devastated area like one of the bombed-out cities of Europe after the War."

A decade later, the institution, comprising seven schools on four campuses, was officially upgraded by the state to the status of university. Today with an operating budget of $653 million, UMDNJ includes: the Robert Wood Johnson Medical School in Piscataway, New Brunswick and Camden; the School of Osteopathic Medicine in Stratford; and the New Jersey Medical School, Dental School, School of Nursing, School of Health Professions, and Graduate School of Biomedical Sciences, all in Newark. An eighth division offering graduate degrees in public health as well as joint degrees from Rutgers University and the New Jersey Institute of Technology opened in 1999.

Throughout Dr. Bergen's tenure, it has been difficult to distinguish the founder from the institution. Giving his all, he also took licks for his leadership style. And while he has been credited for his absolute commitment and unselfish motives, as well as a political savvy that saw the school through five governors, a profile that appeared in the *Sunday Star-Ledger* when news broke of his retirement depicted a man with an obsession and quoted one university trustee who found him "rigid and imperious."

Still no one would question the fact that Dr. Bergen's benign obsession has served the institution and the people of New Jersey. "I'm a very intense person . . . a very stubborn person at times," he acknowledges in the same profile, "but I'm also a fierce advocate for UMDNJ." A founder's fury fuels those words. Surely the institution will long bear his stamp.

Among his proudest accomplishments, as outlined in a 1994 interview in the *New York Times*, Dr. Bergen cites the school's preeminence in teaching and research (UMDNJ was subsequently ranked among the 100 top-funded research universities in the country), its leadership in educating minority physicians and dentists, and the success of the Physician's Assistant Program, which he championed. Other Bergen initiatives include the Cancer Institute of New Jersey (one of only fourteen clinical care centers designated by the National Cancer Institute); the aforementioned Violence Institute of New Jersey, an interdisciplinary experiment in combining good medicine and education with social action; and the International Center for Public Health, a world-class infectious disease research complex.

The recipient of countless encomia, including honorary degrees from the New Jersey Institute of Technology, William Patterson University, Ramapo College, Princeton University, Stevens Institute of Technology, and Bloomfield College, and the Governor's Award, The Pride of New Jersey, Dr. Bergen has weighed in on the national debate on health care reform. A board member of the American Hospital Association, he also served as an advisor to President Clinton's Health Care Reform Task Force. He is one of his home state's leading advocates of cost containment and cost-effectiveness in the delivery of health care services. Following his official retirement, he assumed the voluntary position of chair of the board of the Hastings Center, a biomedical ethics institute with which he has long been affiliated.

In his student application to P&S, Dr. Bergen described the evolution of his medical motive from a "desire to an ambition." Looking back years later in response to a P&S alumni questionnaire, he wrote: "While I occasionally long for the days of patient care, I believe that each career takes its turns, either because of subconscious desires [. . .] or forces external to our control [. . .]."

Subconsciously motivated or externally driven, now with a little more time to spend with his wife, Suzanne (a nurse he first met when he was chief medical resident at St. Luke's Hospital), Stanley Bergen continues to be a powerful force for good.

A NOBEL LAUREATE'S LIFELONG COMMITMENT TO CURIOSITY

BARUCH BLUMBERG '51

Asked in an interview in the New York Times *in 2002 what drew him to medicine, Nobel laureate Baruch Blumberg '51 replied, "There is, in Jewish thought, this idea that if you save a single life, you save the whole world." In a eulogy delivered at a memorial program following Dr. Blumberg's death, on April 5, 2011, at age eighty-five, Jonathan Chernoff, scientific director of the Fox Chase Cancer Center, Dr. Blumberg's longtime scientific home base, said, "I think it's fair to say that Barry prevented more cancer deaths than any person who has lived." In 1999, Dr. Blumberg embarked on a new journey of discovery—this one, literally, out of this world, serving as founding director of the NASA Astrobiology Institute at NASA Ames Research Center, in Moffett Field, Cal., with a bold institutional mission to study the origins of life on earth and search for life elsewhere in the universe. Life continued to be his abiding focus until death took him away.*

———— ✺ ————

CURIOSITY-DRIVEN SCIENCE may not kill the cat, but critics claim it drains the kitty, a "Capitol" crime in the current climate of fiscal austerity and managed care. If future funding for basic biomedical research is on trial, few can make a more convincing case in its favor than Baruch Blumberg '51.

The story of the discovery of the hepatitis B virus, the development of a test to detect it and a vaccine to harness its virulent effects (for which he won the 1976 Nobel Prize in Physiology or Medicine) is formidable proof of the viability and cost-effectiveness of fundamental scientific inquiry. The fact is that he and his eclectic team of researchers at the Philadelphia-based Fox Chase Cancer Center (a private cancer care and research facility that profited

handsomely from its investment in the vaccine patent) did not originally have hepatitis on their minds. They were, Dr. Blumberg insists, merely pursuing a compelling line of scientific questioning with "the faith that if you study basic problems you'll find clinical applications." In so doing, they stumbled on the resolution of a medical puzzle that had eluded generations of immunologists and virologists.

In a chapter of *Immunology: The Making of a Modern Science* (edited by Gallagher, Gilder, Nossal, and Salvatore, Academic Press, 1995), Dr. Blumberg describes the studies that "started as an esoteric exercise to identify human biochemical variation in relation to susceptibility to disease." Our approach, he says, "was that of amateurs adventuring in a field which we found to be intriguing and mysterious, but not totally familiar." Yet surely his sense of the scientific "amateur" calls into question the very notion of "professional."

HAVE MIND, WILL TRAVEL

Who was and is this captain courageous, intellectual ringleader of a hand-picked band of brilliant scientific adventurers (comprising clinicians, basic scientists, immunologists, epidemiologists, statisticians, and computer scientists) whose research took them hundreds of thousands of miles afield, from Philadelphia to the Australian outback and throughout much of Southeast Asia, testing serum samples in a portable laboratory?

Baruch Blumberg eschews easy labels and traditional categories of learning. At seventy, he is still very much the maverick thinker, ever setting out in new directions. (Agile of foot as he is of mind, he recently began rock climbing and took up botany a few years back.) His impish smile belies a childlike curiosity. He rejects the compartmentalization of knowledge. "The world is all put together," he insists, "there aren't any holes or lines! To climb the academic ladder, people feel compelled to declare loyalty to a particular discipline. So now we know more and more about less and less, until we'll soon know everything about nothing!"

Once asked by a journalist to define his approach, Blumberg replied, "The virologists say I'm not really a virologist. The geneticists say I'm not really a geneticist. Actually, I think of myself as a clinical researcher." Yet even his sense of clinical research stands outside the norm, based as it is, not on therapeutic trials, but on a broader notion of population studies.

An undergraduate physics major at Union College, in Schenectady, N.Y., he earned an MA in physics and mathematics at Columbia and captained a ship in the Navy before applying to medical school. While still ostensibly studying physics (a discipline he found too impersonal), he took a job as an orderly in the operating room at Presbyterian Hospital, where he was inspired and encouraged by the legendary Virginia Apgar '33 to apply to P&S.

In the personal statement of his student application to medical school, he explained, "The practice of medicine had often appealed to me as possessing these qualities to which I felt best suited: a scientific subject combined with constant contact with people."

Blumberg relished the intellectual ferment of P&S, the scientific rigor and clinical expertise of Dr. Robert Loeb, and the pioneering biochemistry of scientists like Dr. Karl Meyer. He found the human element he'd been looking for in a fourth-year class in parasitology taught by the legendary Dr. Harold Brown. For firsthand knowledge of the subject, Brown sent his students to the tropics, where, as Blumberg would later put it in his Nobel lecture, "nature operates in a bold and dramatic manner . . . and biological effects are profound and tragic." The experience of treating and studying a native population afflicted with filariasis (elephantiasis), among countless other ailments, in a remote corner of Surinam was to mark him for life. "There was sickness all over the place and many people who had never seen a doctor," he recalls. "I was struck by the fact that with relatively minor input you could have an enormous effect on health!"

What he also found in Surinam was a population-based approach to research and a scientific focus on inherited susceptibilities to disease.

Dr. Blumberg pursued his residency under Nobel laureate Dickenson W. Richards '23 at Bellevue's First (Columbia) Division and trained in medicine with Dr. Robert Loeb at Presbyterian, subspecializing in rheumatology under Dr. Charles Ragan.

FROM POLYMORPHISMS TO HEPATITIS B

Eager to expand the scientific base of his knowledge, he subsequently earned a PhD in biochemistry from Oxford. It was there, while completing his doctoral work, that he was first introduced to the notion of "inherited polymorphic systems," as propounded by the Oxford lepidopterist Dr. E. B. Ford. That is, as Blumberg explains, "the existence in the same region of two or more inherited forms of a trait in such numbers that the form in lowest frequency could not have been maintained by recurrent mutation."

Returning to the United States in 1957 to head up the Geographic Medicine and Genetics Section at the National Institutes of Health, Dr. Blumberg teamed up with Dr. A. C. Allison, whom he'd met at Oxford, and together they designed a new method to discover immunological inherited or acquired variation. "We were looking for common inherited traits and their distribution in populations with the hope that we could identify inherited susceptibility to disease." He later moved to Philadelphia where he was named Professor of Human Genetics at the University of Pennsylvania (to which title he would later add Professor of Anthropology) and senior member of the Fox Chase Cancer Center.

Working with Dr. Allison and later with microbiologist Dr. Irving Millman, and fellow clinical researchers Drs. W. Thomas London, Alton Slutnick, and others, Dr. Blumberg and his team studied blood sera from transfused individuals in search of inherited immunological variations.

"We reasoned," he explains, "that if people inherit different proteins, some of those proteins may be antigenic in the sense that, if exposed by a transfusion to a serum protein from another person, they will develop an antibody against it."

"In 1966," he writes in the aforementioned chapter in *Immunology: The Making of a Modern Science*, "we identified an antigen-antibody system. . . . The antiserum was found in the blood of a hemophilia patient from New York and the antigen in an Australian aborigine. . . . [and] "by 1967 we had evidence that the antigen was on the surface of one of the hypothesized hepatitis viruses and that the antibody had developed in the transfused patient as a consequence of exposure to the virus . . . Later, it was concluded that 'Australia antigen' identified HBV [hepatitis B virus] was characterized by blood-borne transmission."

Blumberg insists that they didn't start out looking for the hepatitis B virus. They were interested in a normal variation, "with the faith that if you kept [up] the search, you'd eventually find some disease connection." Find it they did.

They went on to develop a vaccine prepared from the purified blood of carriers of the disease, the first vaccine ever made from human blood. Marketed by Merck & Co., and subsequently reproduced by recombinant method, the vaccine is now used in some forty countries.

Dr. Blumberg and his team also developed an effective diagnostic technique for detecting HBV that became the first required blood test for a virus and has led to a dramatic drop in posttransfusion hepatitis around the world.

A SCIENTIFIC PROBLEM SOLVER

Yet the introduction and general acceptance of this simple and relatively inexpensive detection test created a bioethical problem by turning hepatitis B virus carriers (at the time estimated at one million in the U.S. and 100 million the world over) into a virtual new class of stigmatized persons.

Sensitive to bioethical issues, Dr. Blumberg has questioned in numerous papers the extent to which biological knowledge should be allowed to influence and control the workings of society. "Experience has shown," he wrote in his Nobel lecture, "that these bioethical considerations cannot be separated from 'science,' that answers cannot be provided on a 'purely scientific' basis, and that our technical knowledge is inseparably intertwined with bioethical concerns."

Science, as he sees it, is a dynamic process. "One of the greatest problems that scientists and technologists who apply science have to get across to the public," Dr. Blumberg insists, "is that there are no perfect solutions. And there's always this danger that a striving for perfection, the perfect, drives out the good. Yet if you're satisfied with less than perfect, you won't try to make things as good as you can."

In a paper coauthored with the medical sociologist Dr. Renée Fox, entitled "The Daedalus Effect" (*Annals of Internal Medicine*, 1985), Blumberg taps Greek mythology for the prototype of the ultimate problem solver and curiosity-based scientific thinker.

"Daedalus, you remember, first created the Labyrinth and then created wings to escape it. Every time he solved a problem he created another one," Blumberg reflects. "And then he'd solve that problem and that would create another and another. You get the sense that he was almost more interested in the problems than in the solutions."

Recognition in the form of the 1976 Nobel Prize in Physiology or Medicine and countless other encomia (including the P&S Alumni Gold Medal in Medicine in 1979 and honorary degrees from some twenty-three institutions of higher learning) have enabled Dr. Blumberg to influence the course of international health care on a wide scale. His input has been particularly important in China, where hepatitis B is more prevalent than anywhere else in the world. He has also helped start vaccination programs in New Zealand, Saudi Arabia, Jordan, and Brazil.

Dr. Blumberg has not shied away from using his influence, as a member of the Human Rights Committee of the National Academy of Sciences. As part of a delegation to Chile during the Pinochet regime, he helped identify and free imprisoned scientists.

In 1989, he was named Master of Balliol College at Oxford University, a post from which he recently retired.

He subsequently embarked on a new study, analyzing the blood sera he had collected over the last three decades and stored in deep freeze, searching for the presence of two viruses, AIDS and the HTLV1 (human T-cell leukemia virus 1), microbes that hadn't yet been identified at the time the blood was drawn.

Co-owner of a cattle farm in western Maryland, hiker, rock climber, botanist, broadcaster (he hosted a PBS TV special on "Plagues, A Selective Look at the Mysteries of Epidemics"), Baruch Blumberg is as complex and multifaceted as the science he loves. "Nature is dynamic, it keeps changing," he points out. So, it seems, does Dr. Blumberg.

BABIES' BEST FRIEND

T. BERRY BRAZELTON '43

T. Berry Brazelton '43, the spirited pediatrician and eternally youthful early child development expert who celebrated his ninety-fifth birthday in 2013 with the publication of his memoir Learning to Listen: A Life Caring for Children, *died in 2018, at age ninety-nine.*

⸺ ✴ ⸺

GROWN UP NOW, many with children of their own, they still ask after the horse, the antique carousel charger that instantly kindled their trust. A nondescript sign outside says "Doctor's Office," but the twitter of canaries, the toys scattered around the waiting room—everything about the place bespeaks the charmed precinct of childhood. Here in this cozy yellow house on a quiet street in Cambridge, Mass., generations of tykes and toddlers have commanded care and respect, and generations of parents have learned how to listen.

This is home base and headquarters for T. Berry Brazelton '43D, America's most celebrated and influential baby doctor since Benjamin Spock '29. It is here that he wrote his twenty-six books on pediatrics and child development, including the classic *Infants and Mothers*, and here that he hosts and tapes "What Every Baby Knows," the longest running show on cable TV.

"THE TALLEST TWO-YEAR-OLD"

Asked if a pediatrician needs to be in touch with the child in himself, Dr. Brazelton grins: "A friend of mine says I'm the tallest two-year-old he's ever

known!" At seventy-seven, with smile lines deep as rivers and eyes squinting with unabashed glee, he'd be a dead ringer for Rex Harrison's Dr. Doolittle but for his down-home Texas drawl.

And while the fabled Dr. Doolittle chatted up the birds and the beasts, the very real Dr. Brazelton opened the lines of communication to the most beloved and least understood being on the planet, that strange visitor from Inner Space, the newborn baby. The Neonatal Behavioral Assessment Scale he developed in 1973 (known as "the Brazelton") is now used worldwide as an evaluation tool to assess the physical and neurological responses of newborns as well as their emotional well-being. His lifelong research in early child development has helped doctors and parents realize that individuality is there right from the start and that if we listen carefully, newborns can tell us what they need and want. "That's something that I've spent my whole life aware of," says Brazelton, "I can look at a child, a newborn, and tell you just what he is trying to say without words!"

Watching T. Berry Brazelton in action, on TV or in person, one is struck by his uncanny ability to mimic and in a sense "become" whomever, big or little, he happens to be communing with at the moment. His face takes on their expression, mirroring all the nuances of an infant's fascination and fear and a parent's hope and worry. Even his hands, like finger puppets infused with a life of their own, can't help but offer a second opinion. Eschewing formality, Dr. Brazelton is not above "getting down" with his little patients—in some cases, quite literally getting down on his hands and knees, to make contact.

It should come as no surprise then to learn that as an undergraduate member of Princeton's Triangle Players, he was so evocative on stage as to attract the attention of fellow Princetonians, actor Jimmy Stewart and producer Josh Logan, who offered him the juvenile lead in a Broadway production opposite Ethel Merman.

Acting, however, was most definitely not what the folks back home in Waco, Tex., had in mind, convincing young Berry to abandon any thespian aspirations and pursue his first love, medicine.

"I was nine years old, maybe younger, when I knew I wanted to do something with babies!" he recalls. As the oldest child in an extended family (with eighty cousins still living back in Texas today), he took to heart a beloved grandmother's praise for his way with the little ones.

His mother, a dynamic woman well ahead of her time, the first woman elder in the Presbyterian Church and founder in 1940 of the first abortion clinic in Texas, was somewhat overpowering when it came to childrearing, pushing hard and all but smothering his younger brother. "She was so intense," Dr. Brazelton recalls with a shake of the head and a hint of sadness clouding his smile. "Gosh, how can passion turn so sour! I knew back then that I wanted to be the kind of person who could help change that passion into something more positive, to help parents pull back and realize that they didn't have to control their kids!"

At P&S, he credits Dr. Robert Loeb with teaching the art of observation. "He made us stand at the end of the bed and watch the patient for fifteen minutes, after which we had to tell him all kinds of details—real Agatha Christy stuff!"

After medical school, Dr. Brazelton interned in medicine at Roosevelt Hospital. Following a stint in the Navy, he pursued a medical residency at Massachusetts General Hospital, before undertaking pediatric training at Children's Hospital in Boston. Back then, however, he recalls, pediatrics was largely mired in the pathological model. And though he received a solid grounding in the diagnosis of disease and physical disorders, the normal path of child development was largely ignored. He was, moreover, allergic to what he perceived as a certain hostility to parents, the unspoken sense that "they were the reason why kids got sick and were disordered." To broaden his base of knowledge, he pursued another five years of training in child psychiatry at Mass General and the James Jackson Putnam Children's Center.

Dr. Brazelton has never been afraid to cross the lines of academic disciplines (a readiness that has led to many rich collaborations, including his later work with the Swiss child psychiatrist Dr. Bertrand Cramer, with whom he coauthored *The Earliest Relationship: Parents, Infants, and the Drama of Early Attachment*, 1990).

Eager to understand the stages of healthy child development, he undertook a fellowship with experimental psychologist Dr. Jerome Bruner at Harvard's Center for Cognitive Studies. In his foreword to the first edition of Brazelton's best known book, *Infants and Mothers: Individual Differences in Development*, 1969, Bruner subsequently praised him as "a physician who has made us better aware of the care of health in infancy and childhood, but also of the importance of opportunities for growing." Encouraged by Bruner to pursue his own path of research, Brazelton crystallized a keen appreciation of the infant as an active participant, an individual able to express himself in and through his behavior, to be affected by, and in turn, to affect his environment. Brazelton also formulated one of his fundamental theses, elaborated in *Infants and Mothers*, that there are three types of normal newborns: the average baby, the quiet baby, and the active baby—a notion that has helped ease the anxiety and bolster the confidence of countless new parents.

In 1972, he cofounded (with Dr. Edward Tronick) the Child Development Unit, a pediatric training and research center at Children's Hospital, a facility that would become the workshop and crucible for his revolutionary studies on communication in the newborn. It was here that he developed the Neonatal Behavioral Assessment Scale in 1973 and did subsequent work, including cross-cultural studies, on the rich and varied interaction between the child and his environment. Over sixty pediatricians trained here have spread his insights to academic medical centers and private practices around the country.

Other foci of his research, detailed in more than 180 scientific papers and chapters, include: the development of attachment between parent and infant, cross-cultural comparative studies of infant behavior and parenting practices, the importance of early intervention to at-risk infants and their parents, and the opportunities presented in early infancy for strengthening families.

A FRIEND OF FAMILIES

Among his many insights regarding the care of children, Brazelton came to the basic realization, expressed most succinctly in *The Earliest Relationship*, that "the parent-infant pair must be cared for as a unit . . . A baby cannot exist alone, but is essentially part of a relationship."

This insight has fueled his concern at the overwhelming pressures and stresses faced by families today. His harrowing report "Why is America Failing Its Children?" published in the *New York Times Magazine* in 1990, documented a nationwide crisis of failure and neglect. "Needy children are in double jeopardy," he wrote. "They have the most health problems, and the least access to care." Challenging politicians who tout "family values" but favor draconian cuts in federally funded social and medical programs, Brazelton insists: "We are the least family oriented society in the civilized world."

Cofounder of Parent Action, a grassroots advocacy group on behalf of parents, Dr. Brazelton has made frequent appearances before Congress in support of parental and medical leave bills. Appointed by Congress in 1989 to the National Commission on Children, he continued to speak out in support of constructive aid to disadvantaged children and families.

A further insight that "the vulnerable times in a child's development are vulnerable for families too," led him to create the Touchpoints Center at Children's Hospital. Its goal is to formulate curricula and train residents to reach out to underserved populations, to help them foster a constructive response to stress.

The Brazelton Center for Infants and Parents, another unit he founded at Harvard, trains health care professionals worldwide in the effective use of his Neonatal Behavioral Assessment Scale. To date, eight pilot centers exist in this country, two in South America, nine in Europe, and three in Asia.

As clinical professor of pediatrics emeritus at Harvard Medical School and professor of psychiatry and human development at Brown, Dr. Brazelton keeps up a tireless schedule of teaching and research.

In December 1995, Harvard recognized his outstanding achievement with the creation of the T. Berry Brazelton Professorship in Pediatrics. "Not bad for a Texas boy!" he beams. Other laurels include Princeton University's Woodrow Wilson Award for Public Service and a host of honorary degrees from universities in the United States and around the world.

WITH A NOSE FOR WHAT EVERY BABY KNOWS

A friendly fixture in America's living rooms, Dr. Brazelton dished out practical advice to parents as the host of his popular television series for the Lifetime Channel, "What Every Baby Knows," on the air from 1983 to 1995, the longest running program on cable TV. Aglow before the camera, Brazelton intersperses videotaped close-ups of infants demonstrating a particular developmental concern and interviews with their parents. A master of the media, capturing an Emmy Award in 1994, Dr. Brazelton sooths, comforts, and teaches as he entertains.

He is also a regular contributor on childcare-related issues to *Family Circle Magazine* and a weekly syndicated columnist for the *New York Times*.

Back home in Cambridge, a typical day begins with a jog around the block. From 8:30 to 9:30, he personally takes telephone calls from parents around the country and the world. By 10, he's off to the Child Development Unit at Children's Hospital to pursue his research and teaching, which may take up much of the rest of the day.

"I've been very lucky," he reflects upon his success. "I just hit it right at the right time and got a lot of credit for whatever I did. I married the right lady [the former Christina Lowell] . . . been married forty-six years and my kids are okay!"

An avowed workaholic—though in his case, "playaholic" might be more apt—the smile that seldom leaves his lips is proof that T. Berry Brazelton is still busy having the time of his life.

MUSINGS OF A UNIVERSITY
PRESIDENT EMERITUS

KEITH BRODIE '65

*After stepping down as president of Duke University in 1993, Dr. Brodie was
named professor emeritus of psychiatry and behavioral sciences at Duke
and helped pioneer the field of sports psychiatry. He also applied his considerable
leadership experience to a study of stress patterns among university presidents.
Dr. Brodie died in 2016, at age seventy-seven.*

———∞∞∞———

IT HAS been fifteen years since Keith Brodie '65, the James P. Duke Professor of
Psychiatry and President Emeritus of Duke University, left office to return to
teaching, clinical consults, writing, and research, yet his attachment to the celebrated school in Durham, N.C., and to the cause of higher education, still runs
strong. "You leave the presidency, but it never leaves you," he allows.

Dr. Brodie is a rare MD, and perhaps the only psychiatrist, to have headed
up a major American university, a position more often held by lawyers and
politicians. In his compelling book *The Research University Presidency in the Late
Twentieth Century*, a study based on in-depth interviews with eight other former
university presidents, jointly published by the American Council on Education
and Praeger, he brings the savvy of his experience at the helm and a psychiatrist's insight to the study of academic leaders and leadership in America.

MOVING HEARTS AND CHANGING MINDS

Driving around Duke's sprawling bucolic campus with a former president at
the wheel of the car gives the visitor a privileged perspective on the weal of

academe. The past rewinds in the rearview mirror, one building at a time, as the future unfurls in the fast forward of construction, bypassing the present at the speed of dreams.

Dr. Brodie takes pride in pointing out a few of the programs and projects he shepherded, like the School of the Environment, the Terry Sanford Public Policy Institute (modeled after the Woodrow Wilson School at Princeton), the Levine Science Research Center (the largest single-site interdisciplinary research facility of any American university), and the jogging trail that weaves it way through the Duke Forest, well-trodden by bipeds, bicyclists, and baby carriages. It's hard not to be dazzled by the sheer size and splendor of this intellectual oasis, a city within a city, comprising some 8,611 acres of fields, woods, and gardens—the envy of any urban university—with scattered clusters of Gothic revival, Georgian, and contemporary structures, and seemingly infinite room to grow. People wave greetings along the way and a poker-faced security guard breaks into a smile, waving us down a restricted driveway in front of the landmark Duke Chapel, where visionary speakers like Dr. Martin Luther King and Bishop Desmond Tutu moved hearts and changed minds.

A visionary in his own right, Dr. Brodie is credited during his eleven years of leadership, 1982–1993—the first three as chancellor—with having been instrumental in raising the school's academic profile from that of a respected regional contender to one of the country's top-ranked research institutions. He doubled Duke's endowment and promoted interdisciplinary research. Among other initiatives, he helped fold a sleepy School of Forestry into one of the top five Schools of the Environment, and launched the interdisciplinary Institute of Statistics and Decision Sciences. He recruited provost Phillip Griffiths from Harvard, and together they brought in such bold thinkers as Stanley Fish to chair the English Department, who, in turn, hired Henry Louis "Skip" Gates to bring an African American perspective. Keen to make the culture of the university more inclusive, Dr. Brodie pushed through a Women's Studies Program, launched a Black Faculty Initiative, championed the Program for Preparing Minorities for Academic Careers, and hired an assistant dean to help boost undergraduate minority enrollment from 3 to 9 percent. Also committed to fairness, he extended Duke's generous college tuition benefits, heretofore reserved for the children of faculty, to all employees of the university.

And in 1986, a year into his presidency, Dr. Brodie made headlines when he invited Bishop Desmond Tutu to speak and, subsequently, on the Bishop's urging, spearheaded Duke's divestment from companies doing business in South Africa.

While a few of the trustees and some alumni initially balked at his more controversial decisions, Dr. Brodie gently nudged the venerable Southern school into the national spotlight, where it has sparkled ever since. By 1993, the year he stepped down, Duke had become the nation's hottest pick for undergraduate admission. Duke's Schools of Medicine, Law, and Business are among the nation's finest. Applicants are beating their way to the door in record numbers.

EMERITUS YES, RETIRED NO

"A university presidency is a very heady, very seductive experience," Dr. Brodie, now age sixty-nine, concedes. It wasn't easy decompressing and rediscovering himself after stepping down. "The trick to thriving post-presidency is to develop other identities."

In the years since then, while continuing to advise his successors and pitch in when asked, he chaired a federally mandated commission on the behavioral aspects of AIDS, coauthored the commission's report as well as two other books, and headed up the first Durham Police Review Board. He has also served as a clinical consultant to Duke's champion Blue Devils basketball team (whose star coach Mike Krzyzewski, aka Coach K, he recruited when he was chancellor) and helped pioneer the burgeoning field of sports psychiatry, cofounding the International Society of Sports Psychiatry.

FROM THE BIOCHEMISTRY OF MENTAL ILLNESS
TO THE CHEMISTRY OF LEADERSHIP

Born in New Canaan, Conn., Dr. Brodie majored in chemistry at Princeton. At P&S he became fascinated by the biochemistry of mental illness after participating in a pioneering clinical study of lithium while on a third-year elective. He interned at the Ochsner Foundation Hospital in New Orleans—his first taste of the South—returning to Columbia-Presbyterian Medical Center and the New York State Psychiatric Institute to pursue a residency in psychiatry. Like many of his medical contemporaries, he fulfilled his selective service at the NIH, as a clinical associate at the National Institute of Mental Health, where he studied the use of lithium in manic depression. In an era in which Freudian theory and psychoanalysis dominated psychiatric inquiry, Dr. Brodie's scientific focus would prove prophetic. His emphasis on the basic biology, the genetics, the pharmacology, and the neurochemistry of debilitating conditions like bipolar disease and manic-depressive psychosis heralded a subsequent shift in the field.

In 1970, he joined the faculty in the Department of Psychiatry at Stanford, where he tested the clinical effectiveness of a newer and cleaner generation of antidepressive drugs and served as program director of the General Clinical Research Center. In this capacity, he revealed a heretofore untapped ability to reel in the egos of scientific thoroughbreds on the faculty—a sine qua non of leadership—and to foster a cooperative and productive working environment in which research in diverse disciplines thrived.

"And so then, if you do those things well, the next thing you know you're given more responsibilities. I was elected to the Faculty Council and then I was asked to chair it—which at Stanford Medical School is a big deal, because you run Admissions and Financial Aid, the key to the door."

After turning down various offers to chair departments of psychiatry at the University of Texas in Houston, Rush Medical School, and the University of Wisconsin in Madison, he came to Duke, attracted by the challenge of bringing scientific rigor to a respected, albeit largely Freudian, department and the appeal of a family friendly environment in North Carolina. (Dr. Brodie and his wife, Brenda, a graduate of the Columbia School of Nursing, have four adult children, all raised in Durham.) Streamlining the department's clinical program, he recruited biologically oriented faculty working on psychopharmacological treatments and such innovative behavioral modification methods as biofeedback, introduced brain imaging, and, in conjunction with the Department of Neurology, started a sleep disorder center.

His success brought him national attention, and in 1982, at age forty-three, he was named president of the American Psychiatric Association, the youngest president ever. During the Carter administration, he turned down an offer to head up the National Institute of Mental Health, preferring the academic life. As he put it at the time, "The challenge is in the creation of a climate wherein intellectual inquiry and scholarship can flourish."

Back at Duke, meanwhile, President Terry Sanford, the former governor of North Carolina, appointed Dr. Brodie to represent the medical center as a member of the Long-Range Planning Committee for the university. Sanford subsequently named him chancellor, with responsibilities akin to those of a chief operating officer. And when Sanford left the presidency to become a U.S. Senator, the Duke board of trustees selected Dr. Brodie to succeed him.

THE PRESIDENCY: FROM HONEYMOON TO EXIT PHASE

In his book *The Research University Presidency in the Late Twentieth Century*, coauthored with Leslie Banner, Dr. Brodie applies an Eriksonian life-cycle model to the professional path of the university president: from the "courtship" or selection process to "the honeymoon period," when he or she can do no wrong, to the "plateau or settled period of an administration," and finally, to the "exit phase."

The book reads in parts like a Ken Burns documentary, with "talking heads" like Michael Sovern, president emeritus of Columbia, and Benno Schmidt, erstwhile president of Yale (and, like Sovern, former dean of Columbia Law School) taking an "under the ivy" look at the workings of academe. Anyone who has ever wondered about the decision-making process at America's elite institutions of higher learning, and Columbia alumni in particular, will be intrigued by Sovern's revelation of the two defining moments of his presidency: the decision to open Columbia College to women, and the sale of the land under Rockefeller Center. In his interview, Schmidt recalls putting Yale under the microscope, examining everything from leaky pipes in the library to academic strengths and weaknesses, pruning where necessary. A successful fundraiser, he aroused the ire of the Yale community by opting to live in New York.

Another frank and eloquent respondent, former Brown University president Vartan Gregorian, described the perpetual intellectual balancing act of the job: "Since most trustees come from the corporate culture, presidents are forced to develop a schizoid language; they defend their [policies] to the trustees in corporate language and to the faculty and students in academic language . . . It's hard to keep the two cultures talking without telling two different things to the inhabitants of those two worlds." The composite picture Brodie paints in the book of the effective president is perhaps best exemplified by Gregorian's unapologetic decision to bypass the trustees and offer emergency aid to Brown students whose parents lost jobs in the recession of the Nineties: " . . . in my opinion, when they [the trustees] hired [me], they hired me as a leader rather than a manager."

"YOU HAVE TO HAVE A VISION."

To succeed as a university president, Dr. Brodie insists, "You have to have a vision. If you become a reactor, constantly reacting, without a sense of where you want to take the place, then you become a manager and the job runs you."

As president of Duke, he was not averse to using the bully pulpit afforded by his position. "I think university leaders still carry a certain level of respect and an aura of authority . . . They need to weigh in and exert that authority when asked to provide their views . . . I realize that, well, if I'm not going to speak, the air will be filled with someone else who will, and you don't know who that will be."

Case in point. After educating himself about the pros and cons of divestment in South Africa, he invited Bishop Desmond Tutu to speak on campus. The Bishop's historic appearance at the Duke Chapel, which drew an overflow crowd, helped persuade the president that it was the social responsibility of a great university to take a stand. At the risk of losing one of his board members—who was initially very much opposed but later conceded that it was the right thing to do—Dr. Brodie decided in favor of divestment. That decision, a calculated risk, proved a defining moment of his presidency.

His broad vision ran the gamut from academic hires and programs to bricks and mortar. The aforementioned School of the Environment, which he helped shape, taking elements of the old School of Forestry, melded with the Departments of Geology from Arts and Sciences, Toxicology from the Medical School, Environmental Law from the Law School, and Environmental Engineering from the School of Engineering, now ranks among the top five in the country. He expanded Public Policy from a department to an institute and built a building to house it. Attuned to the burgeoning field of integrative medicine, he assigned 30 acres to an Integrative Health Center that has since grown into a campus of its own.

As a psychiatrist, Dr. Brodie favored close listening. In an earlier book, *Keeping an Open Door, Passages in a University Presidency*, a collection of his commencement and other public addresses, also coauthored with Leslie Banner, his former speechwriter, Dr. Brodie characterized his own leadership style as "synergistic." "I realized," he wrote, "that a research university is far too complex an entity—too filled with individual and maverick genius—to achieve dramatic change under conditions of authoritarian control and micromanagement." Trusting his instinct, he was willing to hear all sides of an issue and to delegate leadership in specific areas to his hand-picked team of administrative appointees. And though he readily admits that, early on in his first term, "I was not well-versed in the recent developments in most fields outside the Medical Center," his listening and trust paid off. A 1993 academic survey placed eighteen of Duke's departments in the top twenty, and eight in the top ten of the country. The rise of the English Department under his tenure from twenty-eighth to fifth place (tied with Stanford) in the national rankings—a point of lasting pride to Dr. Brodie, an avid bookworm—landed Duke on the front page of the *New York Times*.

HOOP SHOTS AND HIGH-PERFORMANCE ANXIETY

Though not much of a sports buff before taking office, President Brodie became a big fan of the Blue Devils, Duke's winning basketball team, never missing a game. After he left office, Coach Mike Krzyzewski approached him for help in addressing the players' "tremendous pressure to perform" as well as their concomitant performance anxiety and related issues of stress. As a clinical consultant to the team for the last decade, Dr. Brodie has been conducting psychological profiles to find and treat problems before they got out of hand and applying visualization techniques to diffuse the players' pent-up tension. In the process, he helped pioneer a new field. Cofounder of the International Society of Sports Psychiatry, he is also associate editor of the *Journal of Sports Psychology*.

While he still attends basketball games regularly, he gets most of his own exercise these days walking his Labrador and playing tennis at his summer home in Maine.

"I GUESS THAT'S WHY THEY PUT PAINTINGS ON THE WALL."

While deeply committed to the future of Duke, Dr. Brodie wastes no time on wistfulness. Among the greatest luxuries of leaving the presidency is the free time to handwrite a personal note to or take a phone call from the many friends he made along the way.

With his tousled hair, baggy green sweater, and ever-youthful smile, the former chief executive is not one to stand on ceremony. Pointing to his own likeness in the portrait gallery on the second floor of the library—it's the only presidential portrait in shirtsleeves—he chuckles: "My wife wanted me to show you this to give you a sense of my leadership style . . . With each passing year there are fewer and fewer people who remember you. Universities are always in a state of flux, with people coming and going. I guess that's why they put paintings on the wall."

PROMOTING RESPECT FOR "OUR FUTURE SELVES"

ROBERT N. BUTLER '53

The champion of elder Americans, Dr. Butler, who counseled against retirement, and never stopped his life's work of making society appreciate and honor the aging, died on July 4, 2010, having reached the age of eighty-three.

———— ∞∞∞ ————

VINTAGE WINES are cherished. Historic buildings are accorded landmark status. But aging humans fare less well. They are sentimentalized and desexualized, ignored, scorned and sometimes abused, and finally, warehoused in substandard nursing homes until they have the decency to die. Pioneering gerontologist Robert N. Butler '53 first outlined the bleak picture in his Pulitzer-prize winning book *Why Survive? Being Old in America* (1975). "In America," he wrote, "childhood is romanticized, youth is idolized, middle age does the work, wields the power and pays the bills, and old age, its days empty of purpose, gets little or nothing of what it has already done. The old are in the way . . ."

No way! insists Dr. Butler, who has staked his career on the premise that older people not only deserve better but are also an invaluable resource society can't afford to waste. Founding director of the National Institute on Aging at the NIH, founding chair of the Department of Geriatrics and Adult Development at the Mount Sinai Medical Center (the first academic department of its kind in a U.S. medical school), and founding president and CEO of the International Longevity Center, a policy research and education center, Dr. Butler has spent his professional life proving age a rich opportunity, not a foregone defeat. In landmark research conducted at the NIH, he and his colleagues debunked the myth of the inevitability of senility as a function of aging, and thereby helped liberate an ever-growing segment of the population from the stigmas associated with age.

The following profile is based on an interview conducted with Dr. Butler in March 2005 at the Manhattan headquarters of the International Longevity Center.

A photograph on the wall of his office shows a beaming Dr. Butler down on the ground doing push-ups. Glancing from the photo to the man, an interviewer, himself well into middle age, cannot help but be struck by the youthful mien and bountiful energy of his subject. Topped by a thick white mane of hair, there is an undeniable glee and "can-do" confidence to his open face and trim physique, coupled with a fierce resolve undiminished by time, as if the years had merely put a patina on the simple truth he learned long ago from his maternal grandparents, who raised him on a chicken farm in South Jersey—that life is what you make of it at whatever age. At 78, Robert N. Butler continues to make much of it.

GRANDSON OF FEISTY CHICKEN FARMERS
CRIES FOWL ON AGEIST PREJUDICE

The sudden death of his adored grandfather troubled him deeply as a young boy. But the care and caring of a family physician, Dr. Rose, helped muffle the blow and provided a focus for the grief: "I decided that doctors do all they can to keep people alive and give them the best possible life, so I made up my mind I was going to be a doctor." Two bouts with scarlet fever, one in childhood and one as a young man, and the skill and devotion of the physicians who treated him, strengthened his resolve.

That dream survived the Depression and the loss of the family farm, thanks in large part to the fighting spirit of his grandmother, who worked at multiple jobs to put food on the table and keep hope in the heart.

"Seeing my grandmother in action," Dr. Butler recalls, "I saw the indomitable spirit and the survivability and the fact that older people are not dependent and creaky and nonfunctional, but can be very effective."

Following a tour of duty in the U.S. Maritime Service and a solid undergraduate education at Columbia College, where he relished, above all, his grounding in the great books, thanks to the Core Curriculum, he entered P&S. His grandmother lived to see him earn his MD.

OLDER PEOPLE WERE SEEN AS "ARCHIVES, MUSEUMS OF PATHOLOGY"

Spurred on and inspired by such outstanding members of the medical faculty as Dr. Robert Loeb, Dr. Butler initially leaned toward a career in hematology. But in the hospital setting, as in society at large, he found himself increasingly surprised and dismayed by the general attitude toward older people. "When we did see older patients, sometimes in Group Clinic, but more often in the chronic disease hospital, Goldwater," he winces at the memory, "we saw them as archives, museums of pathology." Lamenting the thickness of their medical charts, insensitive residents would refer to them disdainfully as "crocks," or sarcastically allude to their "porcelain levels," implying that "they were more complainers than really sick."

Pursuing his internship at St. Luke's Hospital, he got to thinking: "We know very little about what makes people tick. And we know very little about aging. Why shouldn't I go into something that nobody knows much about?"

Consequently, Dr. Butler switched to psychiatry, pursuing a residency in neuropsychiatry, from 1954 to 1955, at the University of California Langley Porter Clinic. There he got involved in early research on the tranquilizers bromazine and chlorpromazine (more popularly known as Thorazine), and reserpine, a derivative of the rauwolfia root.

His work at UCSF brought him to the attention of Dr. Seymour Kety, then director of the Institutes of Neurology and Mental Health at the NIH. One of the fathers of neuroscience in the United States, Dr. Ketty was known above all for his development of a technique for measuring blood flow to and oxygen consumption in the brain. The senior scientist interviewed the young investigator in the course of a long walk up and down the hills of San Francisco, and subsequently recruited him to join what would become a landmark research project on aging in Bethesda, Md.

THE HUMAN AGING PROJECT: FIRST STINT AT THE NIH

Dr. Butler points fondly to a photograph on his office wall of Dr. Kety and Lewis Sokoloff, another scientific giant, credited with establishing the scientific basis for pet scanning, "dear friends and mentors," and fellow principal investigators on the study on aging. In yet another vintage black-and-white photograph on the wall, a very serious-looking and bespectacled Dr. Butler, age twenty-eight, is seated with colleagues beside the massive, old-fashioned, reel-to-reel tape recorder used in the study. With the aid of that robot-like device straight out of a 1950s science fiction flick, the team set out to dispel a set of insidious fictions.

The project that encompassed more than a decade, 1955–1966, was, as Dr. Butler proudly points out, "the first interdisciplinary, comprehensive, longitudinal study of healthy community-residing older persons." Earlier studies of aging had always involved ailing subjects residing in chronic disease hospitals and nursing homes, and consequently, the results were inevitably skewed by the associated factors of disease. "Our work," he says, "led to the revision of stereotypes that once had been attributed to aging, which we found had not to do with aging at all, but had to do with disease, social adversity, even personality." What the study proved beyond any doubt was that "senility is not inevitable with aging, but is, instead, a consequence of disease." The research findings were published in an influential two-volume work, *Human Aging*.

In 1961, once again skewering a negative cliché, of older people's perceived pathological obsession with the past, Dr. Butler established the importance of what he called "life review," a normal healthy process of looking back, whereby the older individual takes stock of his life.

And in 1968, he coined the term *ageism* in the course of an interview with the then-fledgling *Washington Post* reporter Carl Bernstein (later of Watergate fame). Reflecting on community resistance to a program to establish housing for older people of moderate income in Chevy Chase, a posh neighborhood bordering the District of Columbia, "I was struck," says Dr. Butler, "by the parallel to sexism and racism in terms of negative attitudes toward age. 'You know, it's really an outrage,' I told Carl, 'it's like racism, it's *ageism!*' " His outrage and the term he coined to describe it made it to a cover story in the *Post*. He subsequently wrote a paper, "Ageism, Another Form of Bigotry." The term stuck and has since found its way into the dictionary. "Of course, we still see plenty of it," he laments, "in the work place, in the health care system and elsewhere in society."

In the meantime, Dr. Butler completed his residency, dividing his training time between the National Institute of Mental Health and Chestnut Lodge, a health care facility in Maryland, and thereafter, earned his board certification in psychiatry and neurology.

While pursuing a private psychiatry practice in Washington, D.C., he taught on the faculties of Howard University School of Medicine and George

Washington University School of Medicine and served as a research psychiatrist and gerontologist at the Washington School of Psychiatry.

And then, in 1975, he was offered the job of first director of the newly created National Institute on Aging of the NIH, a position in which he served with distinction until 1982. For Dr. Butler, the year 1975 proved to be propitious.

A PULITZER PRIZE AND A SECOND STINT AT THE NIH

On his first official day on the job at the helm of the new National Institute on Aging, he was informed in a phone call from a journalist who had previously scheduled an interview on the Institute that he'd just won a Pulitzer Prize for his book *Why Survive?* "It certainly helped enhance my profile at the NIH!" Dr. Butler acknowledges with a chuckle.

He drafted a plan that he called "Our Future Selves." His first challenge was convincing the *present selves* in leadership positions at the NIH of the necessity of this new venture. Directors and other high-level scientists who had previously been skeptical of the need for an institute specifically devoted to aging, no doubt threatened by the diversion of funding, were more amenable to productive dialogue with a Pulitzer Prize winner. "Before I left the job," he reports, "I had a study or project going on with every other institute." Notable among these collaborative projects was a cancer treatment trial. Investigators had previously given lower dosages of chemotherapy to women over fifty, based on armchair estimates rather than clinical findings. The study confirmed Dr. Butler's suspicion that those older women receiving a lower dosage were not getting the same benefit. Another collaborative study identified osteoporosis as a major issue. And yet another, with the Dental Institute, created an incentive for dentists willing to learn more about the care of older patients.

Among his proudest accomplishments at the NIH was the raising of public awareness of the devastating effects of Alzheimer's disease. Thanks to interdisciplinary studies he spearheaded, and with the help of the National Alzheimer's Disease Foundation, a patient advocacy group he helped found, the disease became a household word and a national research priority.

Another photograph on the wall of his office shows Dr. Butler with his good friend and fellow activist the late Congressman Claude Pepper, of Florida, with whom he worked while at the NIH on the drafting and passage of the historic Age Determination in Employment Act.

A CALL FROM MT. SINAI TO CHAIR AMERICA'S
FIRST DEPARTMENT OF GERIATRICS

In 1982, the Mt. Sinai School of Medicine approached Dr. Butler, in his capacity as director of the National Institute on Aging, to advise them in their plans for the establishment of an Institute of Gerontology. In the course of their discussion, he suddenly blurted out, "You know, you could really make history, breakthrough history, if, instead of an institute, you created a Department of Geriatrics at Mt. Sinai!" The idea found fertile soil. That very weekend he was invited by telegram to serve as the founding chair of such a department. And though he initially declined, reluctant to leave the NIH, he ultimately leapt at "the chance to have a direct impact on medical education, in terms of curriculum development in the care of older people."

Confronting the same initial resistance from colleagues in other Mt. Sinai departments as he'd faced at the NIH, Dr. Butler held sway and ultimately built strong interdisciplinary programs and helped raise a considerable endowment for the support of research, including chairs in the molecular biology of aging, Alzheimer's disease, and the neurobiology of aging. At Mt. Sinai, he established a number of "special emphasis clinics," including the first osteoporosis clinic in the City of New York. He is particularly proud of the cadre of young clinical investigators he helped recruit and nurture, including Dr. Dan Myer, the institution's first professor of palliative care medical ethics. (This interviewer can personally attest to the wisdom and sensitivity of another outstanding recruit, Dr. Sean Morrison, a researcher in late life care, who cared for the interviewer's ninety-year-old mother.)

THE INTERNATIONAL LONGEVITY CENTER:
A "THINK *AND DO* TANK"

At Mt. Sinai in 1990, Dr. Butler founded the U.S. branch of what would later become the International Longevity Center, devoted to the study of "the impact of longevity upon society and its institutions." The Center subsequently went independent and international and now has affiliates in Tokyo, London, Paris, and Santo Domingo. In 1995, while maintaining his academic appointment, Dr. Butler relinquished the chairmanship of the Department of Geriatrics at Mt. Sinai and committed himself heart and soul to the Center as its president and CEO.

When asked about the Center's mission, he likes to quote the late nonage-narian jazz pianist Eubie Blake: "Had I known it would have taken me so long, I would have taken better care of myself!"

"I'd had the wonderful and varied experiences of working in a lab, teaching, running things, conceptualizing, pursuing my own research," he reflects. "What I felt we really needed now was an educational policy research center, a think *and do* tank, to identify the consequences of an aging population, the long-term economic, cultural, social, political, and health consequences of this unprecedented increase in longevity." In addition, the Center is committed to "mobilizing the productive capabilities of older people . . . and to optimizing the use of our resources toward that end." Another priority is "combating ageism, prejudice with respect to age."

The "Declaration of Human Rights for Older Persons," which Dr. Butler was invited to draft in 1982 for the United Nations World Assembly on Aging, has since become a widely disseminated and accepted standard worldwide, and a blueprint for the Center's efforts.

LOVE AND SEX AFTER SIXTY AND LIFE'S OTHER ENDURING PLEASURES

Meanwhile, Dr. Butler and his wife and coauthor, Dr. Myrna Lewis, kept on challenging clichés in print. Their 1976 landmark study of the vitality of the mature libido, *Love and Sex after Sixty*, for which, when it first appeared, a newspaper in Florida refused to accept an ad, was recently declared a classic by *Time Magazine*.

"Older people were regarded as sexless," Dr. Butler explains. " 'Well, we didn't find that in our studies at NIH; sex was still going on,' I said to my editor at Harper & Row. And Myrna said, 'Why don't we do a book on this and all of those vestiges of ageism?' " Among other, then deemed radical, notions, the book called for a new idea of beauty.

As Butler and Lewis eloquently put it: "The idea of beauty desperately needs to be revised to include character, intelligence, expressiveness, knowledge, achievement, disposition, tone of voice and speech patterns, posture and bearing, warmth, personal style, social skills—all those personal traits that make each individual unique and that can be found at *any* age."

Dr. Butler is currently at work on a new book, *The Longevity Revolution*, in which he weighs in on, among other hot potatoes, the issues of America's private health insurance system—"in my judgment, a true disaster!"—private pensions and Social Security. He favors a balanced economic approach, including raising the ceiling on taxable Social Security wages and, given today's longer life expectancy, recommends raising the age at which workers become eligible for benefits.

A cofounder of the Alzheimer's Disease Association, the American Association of Geriatric Psychiatry, and the American Federation for Aging Research, he is a founding fellow of the American Geriatrics Society and founding vice chair of the Alliance for Aging Research. He served as chair of the Advisory Committee to the 1995 White House Conference on Aging and continues to consult to national and international bodies, including the U.S. Senate Special Committee on Aging and the World Health Organization. Dr. Butler has received honorary degrees from the University of Gothenburg (Sweden) and the University of Southern California, and countless other encomia.

Having covered all the bases in his varied medical career, including public health, biomedical research, private medical practice, administration and management, and academe, he offers a tongue-in-cheek prognosis: "Just can't stick with anything for very long!"

Now a proud grandfather himself, Dr. Butler has, in fact, stuck through thick and thin with the firm conviction, instilled in him by his own grandparents, of the value of life at all its stages. Or as he put it in the original preface to *Why Survive?*: "When we talk about old age, each of us is talking about his or her own future. We must ask ourselves if we are willing to settle for mere survival when so much more is possible."

A NEUROSURGEON AT THE HELM
OF THE AMA

PETER CARMEL MSD '70

After serving a term as president of the American Medical Association and fifteen years as chair of the Department of Neurological Surgery, the department he founded at Rutgers New Jersey Medical School, Peter Carmel MSD '70 is once again focused on his clinical practice.

———

WHAT MADE a renowned pediatric neurosurgeon cut back on his clinical caseload and teaching responsibilities to preside over the largest and most powerful association of medical doctors and medical students in the country? "Selfish reasons," Peter Carmel MSD '70, the outgoing president of the American Medical Association (AMA), the first neurosurgeon to hold that post, affirmed with a deadpan expression before breaking into a broad smile. "To preserve my vision of American health care."

In an interview in April 2012 at his elegant apartment overlooking New York's Central Park, as the twilight cast a golden glow over the green expanse, he described that vision and outlined his priorities for preserving it.

A big man with piercing blue eyes, as he speaks the powerful hands of a surgeon move restlessly, as if competing with his no less agile tongue. His eloquence, or what he calls "a knack for schmoozing," a talent he discovered late in life, has received wide recognition. Two of his speeches were included on the prestigious online registry Vital Speeches of the Day (joining remarks by the likes of Barack Obama and Bill Clinton, and other celebrated orators). His words have swayed hearts and changed minds, boosting AMA membership, and most importantly, helping to implement the association's agenda as a pivotal player in shaping the ever-changing face of the American health care system.

Founded in 1847, as an advocate for the medical profession, physicians, and patients, the AMA has not always been in the vanguard of change. In the 1930s, the association frowned on physician participation in fledgling health maintenance organizations set up during the Depression, and was vehemently opposed to any government involvement in health insurance. In the 1950s and 1960s, it opposed Medicare. Times have changed. In 2007, the AMA launched a public information campaign, "A Voice for the Uninsured," to highlight the plight of uninsured Americans as a pressing social issue. And while the views of individual AMA members span the entire political spectrum, in 2011, with some reservations and calls for fine-tuning, the AMA House of Delegates voted to back President Obama's lynchpin legislative push for health care reform, the Affordable Care Act, including the controversial individual mandate.

"The idea of doctors being the guardians of the health care system is a very old one. But I don't think we have ever played our custodial role as well in the past as we're playing it now," Dr. Carmel insists. Having witnessed the erosion of the medical decision-making power of MDs, the outgoing AMA president passionately believes that "to uphold what we hold dear, doctors need to rally as a group to step up and contribute actively to improve our health care system, to eliminate waste, and ensure quality of care."

"I WANTED TO BE A DOCTOR SINCE I WAS THREE."

Dr. Carmel's take on medical care was shaped as a child in Brooklyn, N.Y., where he grew up, observing his father, an old-fashioned internist in private practice who was committed heart and soul to his patients and his profession. "Watching my father in action, I knew I wanted to be a doctor since I was three."

Pursuing his MD from New York University, he initially intended to become a psychiatrist but soon discovered that psychiatry did not provide the kind of hard facts and certainty he wanted. Surgery satisfied that need, only there was one problem—he fainted at the sight of blood. So he decided on neurology as an alternative, and worked as a subintern on the Neurology Service at Bellevue Psychiatric Hospital, where he performed neurological workups every third night and weekend. Becoming friendly with the then chief resident in neurosurgery, Dr. Amilcar Rojas, on some nights and weekends he would scrub in with him on operations. Fascinated by the physiology of the nervous system, he became increasingly "interested in how neurosurgeons could affect and change that physiology, in operations for Parkinson's and other movement disorders." So after a year of general surgery internship, he went to the NIH to pursue neurophysiology research, in the course of which he decided, his queasiness about the sight of blood notwithstanding, to shift to neurosurgery.

THREE DECADES AT COLUMBIA

Beginning a residency at Columbia P&S, Dr. Carmel trained under the legendary neurosurgeon J. Lawrence Pool '32. "The experience was fabulous," he recalls. "Larry Pool was one of those people whom nature smiled on. He had charm, he had grace, he had good looks, he was smart, and he had these huge hands with long, spatula-like fingers. He was a wiz in the OR. When he was 'on,' nobody could operate like Larry."

Completing his residency, Dr. Carmel was awarded an Allen Fellowship, and worked in the laboratory of Dr. Malcolm Carpenter, defining the neuroanatomy of the ventral anterior nucleus of the thalamus in primates, for which he earned an MSD in 1970.

Joining the faculty in the Department of Neurosurgery at P&S, Dr. Carmel set up and ran the Neuroendocrine Laboratory in the Institute for the Study of Human Reproduction, one of the early neuroendocrine labs in the world, which has been continuously funded by the NIH ever since. Though he, like his colleagues, was trained to perform all neurosurgical procedures, the department was then in the vanguard of a gradual national shift to surgical subspecialization. Focusing his efforts on pituitary and pediatric neurosurgery, in 1985, Dr. Carmel founded the Division of Pediatric Neurosurgery.

"CHILDREN'S BRAINS SEEM TO HAVE MORE PLASTICITY."

His choice of subspecialty was based in part on his sheer wonderment at the plasticity of the child's brain. "Kids bounce. Physically they recover from surgery much more quickly than adults. And the kid's nervous system tolerates operative shocks and operative manipulation much better than that of adults. When you take out a very large tumor, the volume displacement problem is significant. In kids the problem is very much diminished. That means, less blood loss and speedier recovery."

Working with children and their families also presented a special challenge and a special charge. "Kids are wonderful, and their families are wonderful too, bearing up under enormous emotional burdens. I'm always amazed at their bravery." And then there are those extra-special perks, like the invitation to attend the wedding of a young man he had operated on to remove a brain tumor seventeen years before. "I wouldn't have missed it for the world. You don't get that kind of an impact in many jobs."

NURTURING A DEPARTMENT OF NEUROSURGERY AT NEW JERSEY MEDICAL SCHOOL

In 1994, he was recruited by the University of Medicine and Dentistry of New Jersey to chair the then division, soon thereafter, under his aegis, to become the Department of Neurological Surgery, at New Jersey Medical School (NJMS), and to officiate as co-medical director of the Neurological Institute of New Jersey. "The biggest thing I've done in medicine is to create this department," he proudly declares, having helped to transform it into an academic powerhouse. He insisted that junior faculty all engage in research and pursue subspecialty training, based on his guiding principles: "The patient has a disease, we have an expert, that's it. We're all partners. I organized my department to maximize the talents of our faculty and to provide optimal care." A proven master in his clinical expertise, at NJMS Dr. Carmel proved no less adept at building a department and crafting the careers of generations of America's top neurosurgeons and transforming the residency training program into one of the finest in the country. The institutional political savvy and people skills he honed in the process would later come in handy.

THE CALL TO LEADERSHIP

While developing his surgical know-how and academic bona fides, Dr. Carmel also became active in his professional association, the Congress of Neurological Surgeons, serving as a member of the board. In 1985, he was called upon to represent the Congress at the House of Delegates of the AMA. A two-year stint turned into a lifetime commitment. One of his first initiatives in an organization then dominated by state medical societies was to help establish AMA bylaws for a Section for Specialties. After that he was appointed to the AMA Council on Long-Range Planning. In 2002, he was elected to the AMA Board of Trustees. At the time, a majority of the delegates still considered health care a privilege, not a right. Dr. Carmel was among those delegates who helped turn attention to the plight of the uninsured. In 2010, he won a three-man race for the presidency.

IMPROVING MEDICAL PAYMENT METHODS, EFFICIENCY, AND OTHER PRESSING PRESIDENTIAL PRIORITIES

"The AMA president does not set policy, that is done by the House of Delegates," Dr. Carmel points out. "It's the most democratic body I know. Throughout the president's three-year tenure, the first year as president-elect, second as president, and third as immediate past president, you're a spokesman, helping to articulate, enunciate, and promulgate the policies set by the House of Delegates."

Among the most pressing issues in American health care, Dr. Carmel has promoted the need to develop new methods of payment to physicians. His principal push has been to advocate for the elimination of the Sustainable Growth Rate (SGR) formula imposed on doctors who treat Medicare patients. "For physicians it's a matter of survival, it comes down to the math," he says. "The average doctor who sees a Medicare patient has a profit margin of roughly 6 percent. Based on the current formula, the SGR says that if payments to doctors in a given year go up faster than the GNP, then the difference in dollars has to be subtracted from next year's Medicare payments. Consequently, Congress plans to cut Medicare payments to doctors by 32.2 percent on January 1, 2013." According to Dr. Carmel, this would be a disaster for doctors and for Medicare. "Congress thinks American doctors are solidly behind Medicare, but, in fact, the majority of doctors are not taking any new Medicare patients, they just can't afford to."

As a time- and cost-saving measure, Dr. Carmel calls for a streamlining of paperwork. "While I do think it is fair, when the government is paying 44 percent of the tab, for the government to want to know whether it's getting value for the money, there is a thin line between checking up and instituting undue administrative hurdles. The paperwork is excessive."

In an effort to reduce the inordinately time-consuming and costly administrative burden faced by physicians, he has led the AMA's call for the repeal of implementation of the new International Compendium of Diagnostic Codes, ICD-10, introduced by the World Health Organization. "Right now we have 14,000 diagnostic codes; that number rises to 68,000 in ICD-10. Right now we have 4,000 procedural codes; that number rises to 72,000 in ICD-10." On the urging of the AMA, the Department of Health and Human Services has agreed to postpone implementation and to discuss how to diminish the administrative burden on physicians.

He has also advocated for the development of more efficient methods of delivering care. "We have to teach our physicians to practice more efficiently, to see more patients in a shorter period of time." Among possible solutions to ease the workload of MDs, the AMA advocates the use of ancillary personnel and increased use of technology.

And perhaps most worrisome for the future of American medicine, Dr. Carmel has stressed the need to address the alarming shortage of doctors in all fields: "The number of doctors we can educate is set by Medicare. Congress understands that we are already facing a shortage of primary care physicians, but we're falling short of specialists too.

"We're out there rallying physicians to stand up and defend the profession of medicine as we know it. I'm pleased to report we're winning," Dr. Carmel affirms. "AMA membership is up, and I can tell you the government is listening. We changed the face of the Affordable Care Act, and we changed the way Medicare has implemented Accountable Care Organizations [ACOs]" (the current health care model, whereby doctors and hospitals are directly accountable for care). The Department of Health and Human Services accepted almost all of the AMA's recommendations for modification of rules of participation, thereby removing the hurdles standing in the way of the creation and development of doctor-directed ACOs.

Under his tenure, the AMA has also continued to advocate for tort reform. "While the effort has gone nowhere at the federal level," Dr. Carmel says, "we have made incredible gains with the states. Eleven states have now passed caps on the reimbursement for noneconomic damages." In an effort to address the malpractice debacle, the AMA encourages pilots of many models, including medical courts with specialized judges trained to do medical litigation, and early offers of compensation.

And while the AMA agrees that among the most wasteful practices is often unnecessary medical testing due to concern about liability suits, the organization is also studying proposals that physicians who follow nationally accepted guidelines on testing should be protected in tort litigation. "The fastest-rising portion of Medicare payments is for medical testing," says Dr. Carmel." Sure, we have to consider opinions of those who say we over test, but we also have to listen to the concerns of physicians who say, I over test because I don't want to be sued."

"OUR AMERICAN HEALTH CARE SYSTEM NEEDS TO CHANGE."

"Our American health care system needs to change. There is no question about that," Dr. Carmel insists. "But we can't change just for the sake of changing. We have to have reasonable models of change. And we have to institute changes that leave the doctor-patient relationship intact. Can we do it more cheaply than we do it now? The answer is: You bet! We have to make sure that resources are available both to enable good patient care and to allow fair compensation of physicians. It's possible to do." Dr. Carmel urges continuation of a health care system organized on a mixed public and private basis.

But effective health care reform must also, in Dr. Carmel's opinion, tackle the problem of waste: "You've recently read a number of stories in the news that say that waste and fraud consume a third of our medical payments. That is, in my opinion, a modest estimate. You can quote me on that. [. . .] The bottom line is, we can and must build a better health care system. And we have to eliminate those who are taking money from the system without providing value.

"Many of us agree that universal coverage is the ultimate goal. But how do we achieve it? We don't know the answer," Dr. Carmel shrugs, "but we look to the states to be laboratories to figure out how to broaden health care as much as we can and as equitably as we can. All eyes are on the state of Vermont, where efforts are currently underway to develop a model for universal care." (P&S alumna Karen Hein '70 is a member of the newly established Green Mountain Care Board charged with creating the first single-payer health care system in the country.)

Dr. Carmel believes that America is currently facing an enormous conflict of trust in its institutions: "Do you trust the government to do the right thing? Do you trust the Congress to do anything? Do you trust the courts to equitably enforce the laws? We don't believe in our institutions anymore. It's time for us to stop complaining and get actively involved. For physicians, support of the AMA and its mission is one way to do just that."

LIFE AFTER THE PRESIDENCY

"Speaking, traveling, going, doing, representing . . ."—the presidency has proven a heady, albeit draining, experience. "It has been exhilarating to speak out on behalf of my fellow physicians, and to get such positive feedback from them."

Dr. Carmel's wife and ad hoc campaign manager, Jacqueline Bello '80, professor of clinical radiology in the Department of Radiology (Neuroradiology), professor of clinical neurological surgery, and director of the Division of Neuroradiology in the Department of Radiology at Albert Einstein College of Medicine, lauds her husband's ability to bridge divides as the secret of his success: "Peter gets it. Peter can listen to primary care people, and radiologists, he can listen to almost everyone, and if nothing else, connect with them. Even if there's not going to be an agreement at the end of the day, there is going to be a connection, and that's important. He brings people together."

Yet as much as he has relished the spotlight, Dr. Carmel sees his future back at the institution he helped build in Newark: "The major thrust of my efforts in the coming years will be to keep the New Jersey Medical School viable and growing and enlarging. [. . .] My major ambition is to create a unified institute of those departments dealing with the nervous system."

In his extra-medical life, he plans to devote more time to two abiding passions. Family comes first. "I would like to be a better husband, father, and grandfather. I have the world's best and most beautiful wife, three wonderful sons"—one of whom, Jason Carmel MD '03 PhD is assistant professor of neurology and neuroscience and assistant professor of pediatrics at Weil Cornell Medical College—"and seven terrific grandchildren. They are a constant source of pleasure, and I have to make sure they all grow up right."

Another passion is the fruit of the vine. A lifelong connoisseur of wine, Dr. Carmel recently bought a plot of land in upstate New York on which he hopes to plant a vineyard: "I'd like to be able to put a wine in the glass that's not too embarrassing."

Does he believe in the much touted virtues of resveratrol, an antioxidant found in red wine?

Dr. Carmel cracks a smile and a wink: "I don't know personally if it works, and cannot vouch for it in my official capacity as immediate past president of the AMA, but I'm not taking a chance of missing out."

A VITREORETINAL VISIONARY

STANLEY CHANG '74

DR CHANG was a co-recipient of the 2018 Wu Award in International Understanding of the Wu Family China Center for Health Initiatives.

⸺◦◦◦⸺

"THE VISIONARY starts with a clean sheet of paper and reimagines the world," wrote journalist and social commentator Malcolm Gladwell. A true visionary, Stanley Chang '74, one of the world's leading authorities on the repair of vitreoretinal disorders, works with perfluoropropane gas and perfluorocarbon liquids, and a panoramic viewing system he developed, in collaboration with Avi Grinblat, to repair retinal detachments and significantly restore or enhance the vision of countless individuals on the verge of blindness. The K. K. Tse and Ku Teh Ying Professor of Ophthalmology, former chair of the Department of Ophthalmology at P&S, and former director of the Edward S. Harkness Eye Institute, Dr. Chang took time out of his busy schedule in October 2014 to talk about his life's work.

FROM BIOENGINEERING TO RETINAL SURGERY

Born in Shanghai, China, Stanley Chang immigrated to the United States with his parents at the age of two, and grew up in the Bronx, where he attended the prestigious Bronx High School of Science. Initially following in the footsteps of his father, an engineer, he earned a BS in electrical engineering from

the Massachusetts Institute of Technology and an MS in biomedical electronic engineering from the University of Pennsylvania, before pivoting in his career path to pursue the study of medicine at P&S.

"I realized that if you become a bioengineer, you don't really understand the biologic problems," Dr. Chang reflected. "Engineering hones in on a little component of the big picture. If you want to have a global view of things, you have to be a physician to understand the problems you are going to solve with bioengineering skill. I wanted to use my aptitude for engineering but get more involved with people. Medicine seemed the perfect fit and P&S the perfect place to study it.

"Medical school was a great experience, probably one of the best times in my life," he said, crediting the influence of mentors on the faculty, including his faculty advisor, the late Dr. Donald Tapley, "so generous with his time"; the late Glenda Garvey '69, "the ultimate clinician"; cardiologist Dr. Thomas Bigger, with whom he collaborated on research while still a medical student; ophthalmologist Dr. D. Jackson Coleman, a pioneer in modern ultrasound technology; and Dr. David Abramson, a resident at the time at Presbyterian Hospital, with whom he coauthored a scientific paper, now the chief of the Ophthalmic Oncology Service in the Department of Surgery at Memorial Sloan Kettering Cancer Center.

Initially leaning toward cardiology, it was Dr. Chang's elder brother, Henry Chang, MD, a researcher in hematology at the NIH, who urged him to consider ophthalmology, because of the precision and the fine work involved. "My brother said, 'You might enjoy it.' He was right."

Dr. Chang pursued a residency in ophthalmology at the Massachusetts Eye and Ear Infirmary, a Harvard affiliate, at the time a center for innovative retinal surgery, and went on to complete a fellowship in vitreoretinal diseases at the Bascom Palmer Eye Institute at the University of Miami, where vitrectomy, removal of the vitreous as a preliminary procedure to facilitate repair of the retina, was first developed.

When his old Columbia mentor, Dr. Coleman, was named chair of the Department of Ophthalmology at Weill Cornell (formerly Cornell University Medical College), he recruited Dr. Chang to join the team of top-notch faculty, including Dr. Harvey Lincoff, a pioneer in the use of gases in the repair of retinal detachment.

MAKING THE RETINA DO THE RIGHT THING

"The eye is a sphere," Dr. Chang elucidated, "the retina sits in its lining. Neurons in the retina convert the light energy in the image into a signal that goes to the brain. The retina projects the image into the brain. The brain decodes it, and in turn, puts together an image for you. Part of the retina, the macula, the central part, gives you the sharp reading image. The peripheral retina gives you the night vision and the peripheral vision." But age and/or trauma can cause damage to this sensitive tissue. "Tears develop at the edges of the retina, which has no natural adhesive properties. A tear can progress to retinal detachment. In the case of a total retinal detachment, vision goes black."

Dr. Chang established a reputation as the go-to guy for complex retinal detachments, cases that had failed in previous surgical attempts at repair and in which there was a lot of scar tissue. "Each time the detachment occurs you lose photo receptor cells and neurons in the retina," he explained. "Our operative object was to preserve and/or restore the function of the retina after multiple detachments." At the time, he said, "the operative technology was to insert tiny tacks to try to pin the retina down against the back of the eye," which, however, can cause profuse bleeding. The patient, moreover, had to be turned upside down and operated on from below, a very cumbersome and sometimes risky practice.

Dr. Chang helped to refine the use of long-lasting perfluoropropane gas, and introduced perfluorocarbon liquids to do the job more smoothly and efficiently.

He is best known for the innovative technique of injecting perfluorooctane, a liquid heavier than water, as an intraoperative tool to flatten the retina against the back of the eye at the time of surgery, thereafter replacing it with a gas bubble or silicon oil. "The liquid," he explained, "flattens the retina, pushing all the bodily fluid out through the tear at the edges. It allows us to then apply a laser along the edges to repair the detachment."

In the past, ophthalmic surgeons working with a flat lens were only able to see some of the central part of the eye and a limited part of the retina. Working in tandem with Avi Grinblat, an optical engineer, Dr. Chang helped develop a special lens with a wide angle that increased the field of vision and permitted the surgeon to see the entire retina during the operation.

"It is a great personal satisfaction," he avows, "to see methods and tools you helped develop in the lab now used throughout the world. No more tables to turn patients upside down. No more tacks to pierce the retina and make it stay up."

Esteemed for his skill and precision, Dr. Chang is also prized for his personable rapport with patients and his sensitivity to their concerns and those of their families. "I think it's important to have good communication with the patient and to understand their worries. That's the mark of the difference between what we learned at P&S versus what was taught at other medical schools. We focused on the patient as a person, not just on repairing the eye."

Patient satisfaction is more than a statistic to him. It really matters. "I went into the field because, in general, ophthalmologists are very happy about what they do. They can really make a marked difference and help change the quality of people's lives."

In 1995, Dr. Chang was recruited back to P&S as Edward S. Harkness Professor and chair of the Department of Ophthalmology, and director of the Harkness Eye Institute, positions he held with great distinction for close to two decades. He helped boost the Institute's annual research funding from $1.5 million to more than $5 million. Under his aegis, the surgical volume increased from 1,700 cases to almost 4,000 cases annually, the ophthalmic operating rooms earned the highest patient satisfaction ratings of any unit at New York-Presbyterian, and the Department's endowment increased from $9.5 million to $45 million, including the establishment of nine endowed professorships and six named lectureships. He also helped refocus the Department's NIH-funded research to encompass the areas of macular degeneration and glaucoma.

Dr. Chang is particularly proud of having assembled an outstanding team. "What's exciting about a chair's position is that you get to hire great colleagues, mentor them, and watch them grow. It's not the chair who really counts, it's the people he brings in and the group effort."

Stepping down from the chairmanship has permitted Dr. Chang to devote more time to his own ongoing research projects. His interests include the development of vitreous replacements, the pathogenesis of retinal detachments associated with optic disc anomalies, and improving outcomes in macular and vitreoretinal surgery. He is particularly excited about "a new technology called adaptive optics, by means of which we can image the individual photo receptors in the living eye, using technology NASA used to take high-resolution pictures of the moon."

He currently sees patients three days a week, operates once a week, and devotes an entire day to academic affairs, including making the rounds with residents, meeting with research fellows, cultivating donors, and catching up with paperwork.

Dr. Chang still sees himself first and foremost as a teacher: "I came to the realization that I couldn't do every complicated detachment, and the best thing I could do was to train young people who could hopefully do things even better than I could and carry on the field. I was lucky to have great mentors, and I hope I've been a good mentor to others."

Rather than attempt to clone him, his successor at the helm of the Eye Institute, George A. Cioffi, MD, recruited his son, Jonathan Chang '09, as assistant professor in clinical ophthalmology, whose surgical specialties include macular hole surgery, epiretinal membrane surgery, vitrectomy surgery, and scleral buckling. "It has rejuvenated me to work together. Sometimes patients will say to Jonathan, 'Oh, you're a little younger than I thought!' "

Another son, Gregory, is involved in video editing and freelance video, in which capacity he has worked for Columbia.

CHAIRING THE FACULTY COMMITTEE OF THE WU FAMILY CHINA CENTER FOR HEALTH INITIATIVES

Throughout his career, Dr. Chang also made time to help foster educational dialogue with China. On his first return trip in 1979, as part of a medical mission to teach ophthalmic surgery with Project Orbis, not long after the opening of relations with the United States engineered by then Secretary of State Henry Kissinger, he found conditions to be difficult and equipment scarce. (Having long revered Dr. Kissinger, Dr. Chang was pleased to get to know him personally as a member of the advisory board of the Harkness Eye Institute.) "Times have changed, China has caught up since," said Dr. Chang. "I have visited eye hospitals much bigger than anything we have in the States, facilities with a thousand beds just for eye patients." He has in recent years perceived a dynamic shift. "China wants to become a global leader in medical technology, medical science, and biotechnology."

Dr. Chang welcomes the creation of the Wu Family China Center for Health Initiatives and is proud to serve as the inaugural chair of its Faculty Advisory Committee. In his view, Columbia has previously lagged behind other peer institutions in global outreach. "The Wu Center will do much to remedy that situation," he said, "and hopefully restore Columbia to its historic role as a global leader in the exchange of educational models and ideas. China is definitely making a major push to invest in medical education. I am sure that in whatever way my colleagues at P&S choose to get involved they and our counterparts at Zhejiang University will derive great benefit from collaborations in research, clinical care, and teaching. I would also hope that our faculty members become interested in work done over there. The Chinese do a lot in herbal medicine, acupuncture, and plastic surgery, among other areas, that we could learn from."

Proud of his Chinese heritage, Dr. Chang feels fortunate and proud to be an American as well: "The combination of Chinese and American values and work ethic is just mindboggling. It has made me succeed in my professional endeavors."

He is cognizant, however, of a relative dearth of Asian senior faculty at Columbia and other schools of similar stature, a number hardly commensurate with qualifications and accomplishments. "As Asians," he opines, "we have the tendency to not speak up and toot our own horn, but rather to be humble, do good work, and stay quiet about it. But from what I can tell," he added with a smile, "Asian chairs have been pretty good at maintaining harmony and good relations among their faculty."

EYE ON THE FUTURE

Among countless encomia, Dr. Chang is the recipient of the Hermann Wacker Prize of the Club Jules Gonin, the W. H. Helmerich Prize of the American Society of Retinal Specialists, the Lifetime Achievement Award and the Secretariat Award of the American Academy of Ophthalmology, and the Alcon Research Institute Award. He holds honorary memberships in a number of international retina societies, and was recognized as one of three National Physicians of the Year by Castle Connolly in 2008.

Ever the visionary, Dr. Chang points out that "the eye is a perfect model for regenerative medicine and stem cell therapy." He predicts that "it will probably be one of the first organs to use gene therapy effectively to treat conditions thought to be untreatable before." He is also excited about the potential of new technologies to help us "see with greater precision and resolution than the naked eye permits." But nothing, he insists, will ever replace "studied judgment and a steady hand, the ability to detect tiny tears in the retina and to repair them with minuscule instruments. It's still," he affirms, "what matters most and what gives me the greatest satisfaction."

PROTECTING IMPERILED POPULATIONS

DAVIDA COADY '65

Following a long career devoted to the care of the world's most vulnerable, including refugees, the homeless, and the incarcerated, Dr. Coady succumbed to ovarian cancer in 2018.

DAVIDA COADY '65 keeps a pin stuck to her bathroom mirror with a quote from Eleanor Roosevelt: "Do something every day that scares you." It is not the idle creed of a daredevil, but a challenge to break out of her comfort zone in fulfillment of her credo: "I believe in trying to make the world a better place and in relieving suffering."

For five decades and counting, the pediatrician-turned international health activist, turned substance-abuse specialist, has hip-hopped around the planet, often at considerable personal risk, aiding populations in dire need. In one instance, an American diplomat whisked her out of harm's way moments before she was about to be arrested by Nigerian troops who had been tipped off about her work with Biafran children. Another time, a bus driver in Honduras deliberately played dumb, calling her "just a stupid *gringa*" to save her from the clutches of soldiers who had swept her up in a dragnet on suspicion of caring for refugees from El Salvador. And despite a fear of flying, time and again she boarded flimsy aircraft flown by bush pilots under perilous conditions.

Returning from her travels in 1994, she recognized drugs and alcohol as key aggravating factors in child neglect and abuse and decided to switch gears from pediatrics to substance abuse, to promote recovery among addicts on the street and among the incarcerated in California prisons.

This interviewer spent three days in September 2015 shadowing Dr. Coady, from her home in the Berkeley Hills to halfway houses she helped create in Oakland, to the prison yard at Solano State, a maximum security prison in Vacaville, Cal., where in 2009 she and her husband, Tom Gorham, established a program to train men serving life sentences to be certified substance abuse counselors in the prisons, a program that has turned lives around.

A BREATH OF FRESH AIR IN A SUFFOCATING WORLD

The sun beats down with a merciless intensity on the prison yard. It is 105 degrees Fahrenheit out in the open and only slightly less sweltering indoors. To Randy Carter, Darryl Poole, Kenneth Davis, Curtis Abron, James Ward, and many others, Davida Coady, or "Miss Davida," as they prefer to call her, is a breath of fresh air in a suffocating world, a door that does not lock shut in their faces but opens outwards and inwards, and to which, as she has taught them, they themselves hold the key. All five men are serving life sentences at California State Prison, Solano, in Vacaville. They are all proud alumni of the Class of 2009, the first group of peer mentors she and her husband helped train.

"I'm used to being invisible," says Mr. Poole, age forty-six, a recovering addict with a record of arrests, locked up for more than twenty-seven years, who has since devoted his life to "listening to other lost children like myself in the bodies of grown men."

In the words of Mr. Carter, age fifty-two, incarcerated for thirty-four years and counting: "She taught us that we have the tools! Use your tools to help yourself and others!"

At age sixty-six, Mr. Ward, who has been behind bars for some thirty-three years, calls himself the "elder statesman" of that first crop of counselors. "I am simply a raw human being trying to do as best as I can," he said. "It takes a special kind of person to work with someone like me, to look me in the eye and tell me there's still something worth saving, and then go ahead and teach me how."

According to Vandrick Towns, now pushing forty, a graduate of the program who has since been released, after twenty-one years in prison, and currently serves as co-coordinator of the Oakland branch of Options Recovery Services, the self-help addiction recovery organization founded by Dr. Coady and Mr. Gorham, "She's got that look. She's the only person, aside from my mother, who can correct my behavior with just a look." It's a look, he adds with a chuckle, that he has since learned to turn on others as a quiet reminder to do the right thing.

And in the words of Raoul Higgins, age fifty-six, incarcerated for seventeen years and recently transferred to Solano State, who had long heard of Dr. Coady's work: "Look at the men that have been under her wing. They are the direct transformation of a miracle."

EARLY ROLE MODELS

"I believe I'm a lucky person," Dr. Coady reflected in the course of a conversation in the patio of her snug little house in the Berkeley Hills. "Where else in the world can a coal miner's daughter grow up to go to Columbia University and get to become a doctor?" Her Scottish immigrant father left a perilous existence in underwater pits in the firths off the coast of Scotland to seek a better life in America. She was inspired to pursue the study of medicine after working a summer job at a camp for diabetic children run by two pediatricians, Drs. Mary Olney and Ellen Simpson. Among other early influences was Reverend Laurance Cross, the pastor of Northbrae Community Church and former mayor of Berkeley, a man committed to civil rights and social justice, whose sermons first kindled her own desire to make a difference.

Earning her BA from the University of the Pacific, in Stockton, Cal., Dr. Coady applied and was admitted to several top medical schools. For her, the primary appeal of P&S, in addition to its stellar academic reputation, was a chance to learn about the health problems of the developing world from the revered parasitologist Dr. Harold Brown, who ran a fourth-year tropical medicine elective in Liberia. Dr. Brown remained her "mentor and hero," with whom she continued to correspond until his death in 1988. She and classmate Keith Brodie '65 honed their pedagogical and clinical skills tutoring nurses in pharmacology and other subjects and assisting with basic medical care at the Firestone Hospital in Harbel, Liberia. The two have remained fast friends. "The arc of her life is truly remarkable," Dr. Brodie, a past president of Duke University, observed. "Few people I know have contributed so much to the public good."

Contemplating various specialties in the course of her studies, including surgery and orthopedics, Dr. Coady ultimately opted for pediatrics, and completed her residency at UCLA, where she was named chief resident in her second year. Eager to learn more about the role of nutrition in child health, on Dr. Brown's advice she pursued a Certificate in International Nutrition at the Institute of Nutrition of Central America and Panama, in Guatemala City, Guatemala.

At the Institute she came into contact with Dr. Thomas Weller, then chair of the Department of Tropical Public Health at the Harvard School of Public Health, a pediatrician by training and the recipient of the 1954 Nobel Prize in Physiology or Medicine for his work in cultivating poliomyelitis virus in a test tube. Dr. Weller urged her to get a solid grounding in epidemiology at Harvard, where she earned an MPH. in 1969. Dr. Weller also got her involved as a research associate in the Harvard TB Project with the Department of Community Medicine at the Hôpital Albert Schweitzer, in Deschapelles, Haiti.

While at Harvard she also came under the influence of nutritionist Dr. Jean Mayer, the individual responsible for, among other major public health initiatives, the introduction of food stamps to supplement the diet of American households below the poverty line.

SAVING BIAFRAN CHILDREN AND
OTHER EMERGENCY AID EFFORTS

In 1968, the Igbo Tribe in Eastern Nigeria declared independence and established the short-lived nation of Biafra, an enclave promptly surrounded by Nigerian troops and threatened with starvation. Dr. Mayer and another new acquaintance, American journalist and peace activist Norman Cousins, led emergency aid efforts. From June 1969 to January 1970, Dr. Coady served as Field Director of Aid to Biafran Children, the organization founded by Cousins. Flying into Biafra, she worked in tandem with the Irish Holy Ghost Fathers, in her view the most effective group involved in the relief effort. She collaborated with Concern for Biafra, an organization that would later evolve into Concern Worldwide, to this day a powerhouse for good in some of the world's most disadvantaged countries.

On the urging of Dr. Mayer, at the time a member of the White House Conference on Food, Nutrition, and Health and a special advisor to President Richard Nixon, she reported on the dire situation and the imminent risk of mass starvation in Biafra to then National Security Advisor Dr. Henry Kissinger and to Under Secretary of State Elliot Richardson, documenting the condition of close to a million children with famine edema. Pushing for immediate emergency airlifts of food, medicine, and other necessities, she ultimately helped avert a human catastrophe.

Once the Biafran crisis subsided, Dr. Coady joined the Peace Corps, first as acting medical director, and thereafter as health program specialist, in which capacity she coordinated assistance programs in Africa and Asia. "My only regret in life is that I didn't stay with the Peace Corps," she says. But much as she relished the involvement with cadres of young volunteers and the chance to help direct effective health initiatives, the whirlwind travel schedule got to her: "Waking up every day not knowing what country I was in, I'd start talking about one project and realize I was someplace else."

Returning to her native California, she accepted a joint appointment in the Departments of Pediatrics and Preventive and Social Medicine at the School of Medicine at UCLA, where she also subsequently taught for many years in the Division of Epidemiology at the School of Public Health: "I have always told my students: Stop asking, what's going to make me happy and look to the needs of the community!"

While at UCLA, she helped to kick-start the fledgling Venice Family Clinic, a free clinic serving low-income families, at which she officiated for many years as the head of the pediatric service. The largest free clinic in the country today, it has ten sites in the greater Los Angeles metropolitan area, serving a patient pool of close to 25,000 people.

In her work, she has always sought to balance the pressing immediate needs of medicine and the long-term imperatives of public health. "Our society," she argues, "puts emphasis on curative medicine, rather than preventive medicine. Public health has always been the stepchild. When you're a doctor, people say: Oh thank you for curing me or for my surgery. But nobody thanks the public health professional for saving them from smallpox or for their clean water. So you have to be very far-sighted to go into public health, because there's no instant gratification." At the same time, she points out, "most of the people who have made real public health advances also happen to be MDs. I see myself as both. I always try to do some curative medicine along with the prevention."

CESAR CHAVEZ, MOTHER TERESA, AND OTHER FORMIDABLE FORCES FOR GOOD

While at UCLA, Dr. Coady was approached by representatives of the United Farm Workers Union. Union founder and legendary civil rights activist Cesar Chavez sought her help in creating clinics. She still vividly recalls their first meeting. "He was a totally focused, totally committed individual. 'Okay, Doctor, look,' he told me, 'I want you to understand that the health of farm workers is not going to be markedly improved by your clinics. But your clinics will increase union membership and that will bring us better health conditions, toilets in the fields, better housing, sanitation, and laws to protect us.' That totally changed my thinking," she adds. "I realized that curative medicine is a political tool to bring about better health all around."

Then in 1971, Bangladesh declared independence from West Pakistan, war broke out, and Dr. Coady was off again, taking a temporary leave of absence from teaching to help the Irish Ghost Fathers with the refugee rescue effort. In the field she crossed paths with members of the World Health Organization Smallpox Eradication Program in India. They asked her, once she had completed her mission in Bangladesh, to help in a short-term epidemiological effort that took her through rural India and the slums of Calcutta, hunting down every last case. Her team succeeded in altogether eradicating the disease there. "Whenever I look at photographs of people in India today," she smiles, "I am happy to see no smallpox scars."

It was in the course of that work that she met Mother Teresa, one of the other formative influences in her life. Dr. Coady and her colleagues sought her assistance and that of the 1,500 nuns under her tutelage in helping to locate the last cases of smallpox in impoverished neighborhoods of Calcutta. "Mother Teresa was a master organizer and a master manipulator," Dr. Coady still recalls with a note of awe in her voice. "She dealt with every person seated around a big round table one at a time. She was totally focused on whoever she was talking to. And as I sat there waiting my turn, I realized that everybody came to her asking for something and went away having promised her something. She agreed to help us and we promised, in turn, to vaccinate all the people in her feeding lines. [. . .] And when we were done with our work, Mother Teresa said: 'Oh now, Lady Doctor, can you come work for us? Don't write!' she said. 'Just come!' "

Some years later, following Dr. Coady's divorce from her first husband, friends recommended that she take a break at Club Med. Her preferred remedy to get herself out of the funk she was in was to return to Mother Teresa, as a Missionaries of Charity volunteer, and help organize their health program, including family planning, in the slums of Calcutta.

Other notable sometime partners in her efforts included the late Senator Ted Kennedy, a staunch supporter of her work with refugees, and a local parish priest, the late Father Bill O'Donnell, affiliated with St. Joseph the Worker Church, in Berkeley, whose commitment to civil rights and social justice once earned him the moniker "The High Priest of Protest." Lifelong friends, Dr. Coady and Father Bill marched together in defense of the rights of migrant farmworkers, boycotted Nestlé for promoting its newborn formula over breastfeeding in the Third World, and protested the training of Central American death squads at The School of the Americas (since renamed the Western Hemisphere Institute for Security Cooperation), at Fort Benning, Ga., among other causes.

Father Bill was also a collaborator in a number of Dr. Coady's public health initiatives, notably the Hesperian Foundation, a nonprofit health education publisher devoted to making health guides and other materials available at little or no cost to populations in need, and the San Carlos Foundation, an organization she created, and still runs as unpaid president, to "provide health and educational assistance to refugees and other people living in extreme poverty in the developing world."

Another lifelong friend is the actor Martin Sheen. In a telephone interview he fondly recalled a defining moment in their friendship. "Davida was over for dinner one night at our place, and another guest who did not know her asked what she did. 'I'm a doctor, a pediatrician,' she said. 'Where do you practice?' he inquired. 'Primarily in the Third World,' she replied. 'Why's that?' he asked. To which she replied: 'Because I think it's immoral to make money off other people's misfortunes, sickness, and suffering.' " Sheen has put his money where his mouth is in support of her work. "She's one of the most inspirational people I know," he says, "always risking her life, her medical license, and her career to save and better the lives of others."

AIDING REFUGEES IN ASIA AND
CENTRAL AMERICA

Back in the States again, shortly after she completed her work in India, another crisis beckoned. In 1978 the Vietnamese army invaded Cambodia, then under the oppressive rule of Pol Pot and the Khmer Rouge. Tens of thousands of panicked Cambodian refugees fled into neighboring Thailand, where they faced harsh conditions and severe shortages of food and medical supplies. Dr. Coady once again joined forces with Concern, in support of the efforts of the U.N. to direct the various aid groups: "Somebody needed to direct the training of these volunteers who were pouring in from all over the world, many of whom didn't know a thing about what they were doing."

At around the same time, the Nicaraguan Revolution broke out in an effort to topple the brutal dictatorship of Anastasio Somoza De Bayle. Having maintained a strong emotional tie to Central America ever since her days as a student in Guatemala, Dr. Coady connected with the exiled Nicaraguan Sandinista rebels living in the Bay Area.

When the Sandinistas overthrew the dictator in 1979, Dr. Coady pitched in to help rebuild the country's public health infrastructure. Working with the Nicaraguan Ministry of Agriculture, in an effort to address the lack of doctors and other health professionals in rural areas, among other initiatives, she helped distribute Spanish editions of a manual of basic medical advice, *Where There is No Doctor: A Village Healthcare Handbook*, published by the Hesperian Foundation, a book since translated into over 100 languages.

And when civil war broke out that same year in El Salvador, and refugees went pouring into neighboring Honduras, she once again pitched in, working under the auspices of the U.N. High Commission of Refugees to help organize the relief effort: "By this time I saw myself and was known as an authority on refugee health care." She subsequently became involved in refugee aid in the wake of an armed struggle in Guatemala and thereafter in Mexico at the time of the Zapatista-led rebellion of indigenous peoples in the southern state of Chiapas.

Her home in Berkeley became a depot for the relief effort: "Hundreds of thousands of dollars' worth of medicine went through this house on the way to Central America."

The following year found her shuttling between Uganda and neighboring Kenya, directing famine relief among the Karamojong minority in northeast Uganda in the wake of the fall of Ugandan dictator Idi Amin.

COMING UP FOR AIR AND CONSIDERING
THE NEEDS OF HER OWN COMMUNITY

"I thought I'd spend two years helping out and ended up spending the better part of a decade. When I paused to catch my breath, I figured out that I had gone on somewhere between forty-five and fifty trips to Central America and elsewhere. I decided it was time to come back home and do something in my own community."

Working part time several nights a week as a pediatrician in the Emergency Department at the Children's Hospital of the East Bay, in Oakland, Dr. Coady saw countless cases of battered or neglected children of substance abusing and alcoholic parents. Her first husband had had a drinking problem. And reflecting on her itinerant existence leaping about from crisis to crisis, acknowledging that she thrived on crisis, she was forced to face and address her own occasional binge drinking and the sometimes ill-advised personal decisions she made under the influence. After a period of soul-searching, she decided to switch specialties from pediatrics to addiction medicine: "It's not a subject this society likes to address. When I'd tell people early on that I was no longer a pediatrician, and that I was going into addiction medicine, they'd say: 'That's really sad, you were such a good pediatrician!' "

On the advice of a lawyer friend, she began working as a coordinator of the Berkeley Drug and Alcohol Treatment Court, conferring with convicted addicts and offering the option of entering a recovery program as an alternative to doing time in prison.

In 1997, she founded Options Recovery Services (ORS) to assist substance and alcohol abusers, many homeless and/or in and out of jail, to engage in effective recovery. Housed in an old Veterans Administration building in downtown Berkeley, the program is free and accessible to all. A full-service provider, ORS offers counseling, a supervised site for Alcoholics Anonymous and Narcotics Anonymous meetings, as well as such practical support as driving individuals to the Department of Motor Vehicles to get the IDs needed to enter a residential treatment program. The organization operates based on a strict model of clean and sober. Many current and former clients work for the program in various capacities, fortifying their own efforts at recovery by helping others follow suit.

Dr. Coady joined forces with her second husband, Thomas P. Gorham, MA, MFT, himself in recovery, president of the Addiction Professionals Association for California. Together they built ORS into a powerful and productive force in the Bay Area.

PEER MENTORING IN PRISON

In 2005, prisoners serving life sentences at San Quentin State Prison, in Marin County, just north of San Francisco, initiated a prisoner peer-mentoring substance abuse program. A consultant, Sol Irving, a former correctional officer turned correctional counselor with more than thirty years of experience as a peace officer, decided to set up a similar program at Solano State Prison, where he was employed at the time. Having heard of the effectiveness of ORS, Mr. Irving approached Dr. Coady and Mr. Gorham to help design the program with a focus on addressing issues of substance abuse.

The three teamed up in 2009, interviewing and selecting a core group of fifty inmates, many serving life sentences for violent crimes committed under the influence in their youth, to go through the rigorous curriculum of the Offender Mentor Certification Program. Of those first fifty, forty-seven proudly marched in cap and gown at the first graduation ceremony held in the prison gym some six months later, cheered on by their fellow inmates as officially certified drug and alcohol counselors skilled at working with their peers. A life-affirming purpose for those still serving time, it has proved a precious and marketable skill that those later released on parole have applied to build a clean life on the outside.

The curriculum is grounded in a parallel process of working on oneself while learning the skills needed to help others. As Mr. Gorham puts it: "Many of these guys made dumb decisions as young men under the influence that cost somebody's life. We demand that they grow into that adult body and start making adult decisions."

Mr. Irving says Dr. Coady is "the glue that holds it all together." His first clue that things were working was when, in an environment in which the demonstration of raw emotion is a taboo, he heard that trainees came out of sessions with her crying. Compelling prisoners to face and confront their own early trauma, which in many cases they had kept a deep dark secret, as Mr. Irving puts it, "she broke them down to build them up." Dr. Coady also teaches the pharmacology component of the curriculum, the physiological effects of alcohol and various controlled substances.

Many prisoners transfer a filial devotion, but Dr. Coady keeps a cool head about her work. "If I'm a mother figure for them, fine, great," she allows. "But I'm their doctor first and foremost, which is why they won't call me by my first name. I'm a role model. I'm the one that makes them think twice."

HOW THREE P&S ALUMNI BUCKED THE ODDS AND MADE IT BIG IN BIOTECH

RON COHEN '81, PAUL MADDON MD, PHD '88, AND GEORGE YANCOPOULOS PHD '86, MD '87

Since publication of the following collective profile, among other momentous occasions, Dr. Maddon was awarded the 2015 Columbia University Alumni Medal, Dr. Yancopoulos was named vice chair of the board of advisors of Columbia University Medical Center, and Dr. Cohen tapped his considerable theatrical talent, impersonating Dr. Samuel Bard, the founder of the College of Physicians and Surgeons, at the 2017 Alumni Reunion Gala Dinner Dance, marking the 250th anniversary of the school's founding.

⸺ ⸙ ⸺

WHEN RON COHEN '81, Paul Maddon MD PHD '88, and George Yancopoulos PhD '86, MD '87 get together, the mood is buoyant and the laughter is infectious. They swap snapshots of their respective growing offspring, compare notes on clinical trials, and reminisce about the bumpy road to success. How, in the early days, Dr. Maddon, who lacked a driver's license, relied on Dr. Yancopoulos to drive him to work. "We never got anywhere," jokes Dr. Maddon, "George couldn't drive and I had no idea where I was going." And how Dr. Cohen, way back when a member of the Princeton crew team, met Dr. Yancopoulos, who rowed (with Ron's younger brother Oren) for Columbia. "Awed by George's tremendous athletic prowess, personality, and intellect, my brother complained: 'And he's such a great guy, you couldn't even hate him!' " The camaraderie of the three P&S graduates and friends extends to family. Dr. Cohen's wife, Amy, works in corporate affairs for Dr. Maddon's company, Progenics. "So I probably see more of her than Ron does!" the latter laughs.

Rising stars in the biotech boom of the moment, each with successful FDA-approved drugs to their credit and promising candidates in the research

pipeline, their businesses are based within a two-mile radius of each other in Westchester County, N.Y., one of the fastest-growing hubs of biotech activity in the country. What all three have in common, in addition to a P&S degree, is a passion for science and medicine, a fondness for collaboration, a seemingly boundless enthusiasm and confidence, and in the words of Dr. Yancopoulos, "a willingness to embrace the risk of failure."

Seated around a table one morning in November 2011 in the conference room of the Hawthorne, N.Y., based offices of Acorda Therapeutics, Dr. Cohen's company, the three MD-entrepreneurs took time out to reflect on the paths they'd chosen, the challenges and satisfactions, and the hurdles they encountered along the way.

"IF YOU DO THIS, YOU WILL NEVER BE HEARD FROM AGAIN!"

For Dr. Maddon, former chief scientific officer and vice chair of the board of directors of Progenics Pharmaceuticals, Inc. (after serving as chair and chief executive officer for 20 years), a company he founded and first ran from his medical school dorm room, science and business have been intertwined from the start. As a Columbia College undergraduate, he perused scientific papers by the P&S professor and future Nobel laureate Richard Axel. "I was blown away by reading what we now know were the papers that delineated the dawn of molecular biology." Maddon was no less thrilled to leaf through copies of *Biotechnology News*, among the first journals and magazines to describe this new industry that was emerging in the 1980s. The combination of bench and bottom line appealed to him and something clicked: "To take a scientific discovery and make a drug out of it—I knew that this was exactly what I wanted to do."

Accepted into the MD/PhD Program at Columbia, he had the supreme confidence or gumption—call it what you will!—to insist that Dr. Axel let him know on the spot if he would let him work in his lab before he decided whether to accept or decline a coveted slot. PhD candidates generally do two years of classroom work before pursuing their research. The seasoned scientist accepted the young upstart on the spot. (The two are still close.) The same gumption served Maddon well when, upon earning his dual degree, he announced to his faculty advisors that he would not be opting for a postdoctoral fellowship in research or an internship in medicine, but would instead be venturing out on his own into the risky field of biotechnology.

His advisors were at first flabbergasted, then furious. " 'You should be ashamed of yourself!' " he was told. " 'You're wasting the education we gave you!' " But Maddon was undaunted and determined to take the leap and to succeed. He remains devoted to the university, at which he spent a total of eleven years of study. In 2008 he joined the Columbia Board of Trustees, for which he chairs the Subcommittee on Science Committee on Scientific Affairs. He is also a member of the Board of Visitors of Columbia University Medical Center.

"I remember them vilifying Paul when he took the leap and left academia," recalls Dr. Yancopoulos, who followed suit a few years later to become president of the laboratories and executive vice president and chief scientific officer of Regeneron Pharmaceuticals, which he joined shortly after its founding by his long-time business partner, Dr. Len Schleifer. Dr. Yancopoulos also served as president of Regeneron Research Laboratories. Yancopoulos and Maddon had been friends since sophomore year at Columbia College. The two shared a dream and offered each other moral and logistical support. Maddon reciprocated for the ride by lending Yancopoulos lab space. Progenics can hardly spare the elbow room nowadays. And Regeneron now occupies five buildings in two major sites, in Tarrytown and Rensselaer, and has over 1,700 employees.

But back in 1987, when Yancopoulos first accepted and then turned down a prestigious Markey Trust Research Grant and a much sought-after junior faculty position at P&S, opting instead to link his fortune to an unknown start-up biotech business, his then-mentor Dr. Fred Alt—still a close friend today—called upon his own mentor, Nobel laureate Dr. David Baltimore, to try and dissuade him. "'You have such a promising career in science,'" Dr. Baltimore told the young scientist, "'if you do this you'll never be heard from again.'"

Nevertheless, Yancopoulos, who still maintains warm ties to Baltimore, trusted his own inclination. It had been his lifelong dream to "figure out how to take basic scientific findings, apply them, and create a drug to help people suffering from a disease." His father, a Greek immigrant and ardent believer in the American dream, had had his own education and career goals interrupted by World War II and subsequent unrest in Greece. "In this country," the father said to his son, "if you do great things they will pay you a hell of a lot more than the small salary you would make as a junior faculty member." A week later Yancopoulos got a telephone call from Schleifer, a fellow MD/PhD, inviting the young man to join him as head scientist of Regeneron, a company he was in the process of founding.

For Dr. Yancopoulos at that moment something clicked. From an early age his father had told him, "If you're interested in medical research, why not be like this guy!" Whereupon he pulled out an article from a Greek-American news-paper about P. Roy Vagelos '54, then director of research, now retired CEO of the pharmaceutical giant Merck, a company he led to stellar success. "So Roy was my model from when I was about fifteen years old." Dr. Vagelos returned the favor and the confidence some years later, becoming chair of the board of Regeneron and helping to focus the company's technological know-how and scientific mission to foster drug discovery.

A DOCTOR-ACTOR CHANGES ROLES

Dr. Cohen walked a different road. He was already a practicing clinician who had pursued a residency in medicine at the University of Virginia, and had several years of clinical practice in New York behind him, when the biotech bug bit. His mother had been a concert violinist, the youngest member of the Israel Philharmonic, and his father, the late Sidney M. Cohen, MD MSD '52, a distin-guished member of the faculty in the Department of Neurology at P&S, had been an actor on the Yiddish stage in his youth. The son had always been torn between acting and medicine, opting for P&S, in part because of the school's reputation for clinical excellence, but also because of the existence of the Bard Hall Players, America's most acclaimed medical school theater group, in a number of whose productions he played leading roles: "I think P&S has always been amazing at picking people who have those kinds of mixed backgrounds, with a healthy dose of the humanities and the arts."

In the 1990s he was dividing his time in New York between a stint as medical director of a private fee-for-service clinic on Wall Street, acting classes, and auditions for roles and commercials, when he received a call from medical school friends, who put him in touch with a husband-and-wife team in the process of founding a company. First called Marrow-Tech, and initially committed to creating a bone marrow bank, the company's mission later expanded to include multiple tissue regeneration and changed its name to Advanced Tissue Science. But at that early stage of the game they were looking for a clinician "with presentational skills" to help develop their clinical trials and promote the company. For reasons he himself cannot fathom years later, Dr. Cohen agreed to sign on, on the spot.

After six and half years of helping to raise the first $5–6 million and "doing almost everything in the company and loving it," he came up for air and decided it was time for the next step. Following a one-year self-imposed sabbatical, during which he taught himself finance, Dr. Cohen had what he still thinks of as an epiphany at the UC San Diego Medical Library. Surrounding himself with every article he could find on spinal cord injury, he decided to link up labs and collaborate with top neuroscientists around the country to found Acorda, a virtual company devoted to restoring neurological function to people with spinal cord injury, MS, and other conditions.

FRUSTRATIONS AND BREAKTHROUGHS

All three MD-entrepreneurs went through their share of disappointments and frustrations before finally achieving a commercially viable breakthrough in the lab.

"The path to getting a drug approved is so complicated and so difficult to navigate, and the hurdles appear nearly insurmountable, it is amazing any drug ever gets approved," Dr. Maddon shakes his head at the sheer magnitude of the challenge. Though his company, Progenics, is devoted, among other areas, to the discovery and development of cancer therapies, and currently has a promising human monoclonal antibody-drug conjugate in phase 1 testing for the treatment of prostate cancer, they're still far from the finish line. They took a clinical detour with their first successful drug, RELISTOR®, approved in 2008 by the

FDA and by regulatory agencies in fifty other countries, for the treatment of opioid-induced constipation for patients with advanced illness cancer. The pain relief of opioids for patients with cancer and other illnesses comes at a terrible cost, effectively shutting down the body's peristalsis. RELISTOR® counteracts the effect and gets the system going again. Additional marketing regulatory approval is pending for the treatment of opioid-induced constipation in patients with suffering from chronic, noncancer pain. In this case, Progenics licensed, developed, and marketed a drug originally developed by scientists at the University of Chicago. "In this business you have to keep your finger on the pulse of what's happening with your own program and other people's programs," says Maddon, "and be able to pivot and move along alternate paths to success."

Regeneron's varied scientific portfolio, including ongoing research in oncology, ophthalmology, cardiovascular diseases, immunity and inflammation, infectious diseases, metabolic diseases and obesity, muscle disorders, pain and bone disease, is grounded in two technologies developed in-house by Dr. Yancopoulos and his associates. One is the VEGF trap, a molecular protein designed to trap cytokines and reassert control over out-of-control factors in the body that cause disease, which the French pharmaceutical giant Sanofi has signed on as a partner to codevelop. The other is the VelocImmune iMmouse, a mouse genetically engineered to have bred with a humanized immune genome, an optimal platform to generate human antibodies to combat countless disease conditions. Regeneron went through a rocky period when Procter and Gamble, which had entered into a collaborative agreement, subsequently declared the VEGF trap "clinically invalid" and left the partnership. But P&G proved dead wrong. "One problem with big-pharma, as opposed to biotech," maintains Yancopoulous, "is its aversion to risk." A few years later, when the biotech pioneer Genentech published data on a kindred technology, commercial interest was suddenly generated in Regeneron's VEGF trap. The subsequent partnership deal with Sanofi to commercialize the trap would, in Dr. Yancopoulos's words, become, "at the time, one of the biggest deals in biotech history."

Regeneron currently has two FDA-approved products on the market, EYLEA™, a drug effective in the treatment of age-induced macular degeneration, and ARCALYST®, a treatment for cryopyrin-associated periodic syndromes (CAPS), a rare hereditary condition in adults and children. There are many more medicines in the R&D pipeline at various stages of clinical trials. Dr. Yancopoulos is particularly proud that—in contrast to the industry norm—all of Regeneron's approved and pipeline products were discovered and developed by Regeneron. Those products have now led Regeneron to being one of the ten largest biotech companies (in terms of market capitalization) in the world.

Acorda's history of drug development likewise hit bumps before rebounding. Initially focusing on spinal cord injury, and after the company invested tens of millions of dollars, their lead drug, AMPYRA®, failed in phase III clinical trials. Dr. Cohen still believes "that some people with spinal cord injury might benefit from the drug, but we didn't prove it in those trials." At the same time, they conducted phase III clinical trials on the same drug for patients with MS. Those trials too failed at first. "But after deep analysis, we realized that what failed was the way we analyzed it, that, in fact, the drug had worked beautifully in a subset of patients, about 40 percent of which had had a positive response, dramatically improving their walking ability. So we designed phase III trials to prove it, and we did," says Dr. Cohen. The fruit of basic scientific research conducted at the University of Chicago in the early 1980s, AMPYRA® was first licensed by another company before Dr. Cohen saw its potential and decided to bank on it. FDA approval finally came in 2010, almost twenty-five years after the drug's discovery.

COMMITTED TO INSIGHT AND CALCULATED RISK

"If I had to start Acorda today, from exactly where I was in 1992 when I committed to it, I don't believe there's any way I would have succeeded," insists Dr. Cohen. "I don't believe this drug would have seen the light of day. Because it would have been impossible to keep investors interested long enough."

Dr. Yancopoulos concurs: "It helps to have been a little naïve. Because if you had told me it was going to take me twenty-two years to succeed, if I had known all the risks back when I started out, that I had more than a significant 50 percent chance of going out of business several times over the years, in 1995, in 1998, in 2000, and again in 2002, honestly I probably wouldn't have done this."

But for Cohen, Maddon, and Yancopoulos, and likeminded medical entrepreneurs, it's all about toying with the seemingly impossible and turning virtual failure into success.

"Ron had the insight," Dr. Maddon points out, "and he was willing to take the risk to license a product others had dropped. To someone else that drug may have been a dog, but to Ron it was a gem in the rough. Each of us is committed to insight. Each of us is willing to take risk. And each of us has developed a thick skin and is willing to risk failure."

"There is no absolute failure," Dr. Yancopoulos qualifies his friend's prognosis. "With every setback, you adapt, you figure out how to make it work and make something great out of it. And unless you keep trying, you're never going to come up with anything."

THE BEAUTY OF BRAINSTORMING

Gregarious by nature, the three entrepreneurs all agree that gathering good people and working together in a team is the key to their success and also a lot of fun.

"I think I've sort of figured out over the years how to bring a group of the right people together in a room," says Dr. Yancopoulos, "make sure the computers and the i-phones are switched off, and just brainstorm together. . . . And if you're lucky, every now and then, you hit that 'ah-hah!' moment that makes it all worthwhile."

"Some of my favorite moments in this whole process," Dr. Cohen agrees, "happen when getting together with my chief scientific officer and other team members, looking at data or thinking about data or challenging each other. We'll be talking when all of a sudden it's: Oh, my gosh! We've found the right analysis, the right direction."

"No question about it," Dr. Maddon nods, "as Ron just said, one of the greatest joys and the greatest privileges is surrounding ourselves with amazing people. They stoke the creativity, the innovation, because one person, however insightful he may be, cannot sustain a company."

Yet while all three learned to treasure team work from working for and with revered mentors at P&S, and in Dr. Cohen's case, the University of Virginia as well, where he trained, they fault America's top medical schools for, at best, turning a blind eye to the possibilities of biotech and other medically related business ventures, and at worst, discouraging their graduates from pursuing that option.

BUCKING THE ACADEMIC BIAS

"Much as I revere P&S and am profoundly grateful for the solid grounding I got there in medicine," Dr. Cohen maintains, "I would say that the three of us did what we did not because of how we were pushed at Columbia but in spite of the biases that we encountered there. There is an ethos in the academy that says: What we do here is pure, this is real science, and the stuff that goes on in industry is tainted, it's bad, it's led by the profit motive. The time has long passed for that attitude to change." Dr. Cohen believes that it is imperative for P&S and other peer institutions to incorporate course material that exposes entrepreneurially minded medical students to the possibility of applying their knowledge to industry. "We in industry often rely on the insights generated in the academy. But there is no way to turn those insights into new medicine unless you integrate industry."

"I couldn't agree more with Ron," says Dr. Yancopoulos, who favors the establishment of a guest lectureship on medicine and business at P&S. (The "Pam and Mark Grodman '77 Joint Degree Program Fund" recently established by another MD-entrepreneur, Marc Grodman '77, CEO of BioReference Laboratories, already got the ball rolling.) "P&S graduates who go into business," adds Dr. Yancopoulos, "have a different kind of drive, a different tolerance of risk. Clearly not all medical students will be so inclined, but there may be a few who have this ability and this interest and this daring, who may not even know that the possibility exists."

AN AMERICAN ODYSSEY

ROBERT COLES '54

Recipient of a Pulitzer Prize, a so-called "genius" MacArthur Foundation award, and a Medal of Freedom, the child psychiatrist, author, and defender of tender lives, has been called "a national treasure."

———⊶⊷———

"ALWAYS LIVE in a neighborhood where your neighbors teach you, that's where you do your real learning!" Robert Coles '54, the child psychiatrist cum documentary writer, advises, sweeping back an unruly tuft of graying hair over a furrowed brow. Smile lines link his eyes and ears, the seasoned tools of his trade. In a rambling life that took him clear across the country from bastions of privilege to pockets of poverty and back, from the Deep South to the Rust Belt up North, from the dusty adobe hamlets of the Southwest and the remote hollows of Appalachia to the ivied halls of Harvard, he has looked, listened, and learned. And in some sixty-five books and counting, notably his Pulitzer Prize–winning five-volume classic study, *Children of Crisis*, he has woven the wisdom gleaned into a talking patchwork quilt, a lyrical logbook of the American condition.

A widower at age seventy-four, his pace has slackened some, but the restless spirit endures. "I'd do it again without hesitating a second," Dr. Coles—"Bob!" he insists—reflects. "In fact, I'll read about something going on and I'll say to myself: If I had another life I'd be there, including, by the way, in Iraq, talking to the kids."

These days his neighbors are the trees of the Concord woods behind his old yellow frame house (the same woods that whispered their secrets to Ralph Waldo Emerson and Henry David Thoreau), the children from the school across the way, and the vivid memories of departed friends.

To enter his study is to enter a kind of secular shrine. Most walls only have ears. These walls have eyes, ears, noses, and lips and an endless string of stories to tell. They are papered with the photographs of kindred spirits to whom he pays homage, not by lighting candles, but by writing books. It's a veritable *Who's Who* of soul searchers of the twentieth century. There's Sigmund and Anna Freud, the father and daughter of psychoanalysis, the latter, a trailblazer in her work with children, his friend and mentor. Erik Erikson, another psychoanalytic pioneer focused on children, and William Carlos Williams, the great poet-doc, two more friends and influences, hang frame to frame. Down the wall a ways hang the Southern scribes, Walker Percy P&S '41, Flannery O'Connor, and James Agee, all likewise the subjects of his published reflections. Intermingled among the writers are religious thinkers and doers, Dorothy Day, cofounder of the Catholic Worker movement; Simone Weil, the French philosopher-mystic-activist; and Dietrich Bonhoeffer, the German pastor who died bravely resisting Hitler. Political activist Bobby Kennedy, with whom Bob Coles battled for the welfare of America's poorest children, has his place of honor on the wall, as does singer-songwriter Bruce Springsteen, another friend and the subject of Dr. Coles's most recent book. (Springsteen sang two benefit concerts that raised $1 million to support the documentary magazine *Doubletake*, which Dr. Coles founded and to which he is deeply committed.) It's a whispering wall, not a wailing wall, a murmuring mirror of influences.

"All interviews, one hopes, become jointly conducted," he wrote in *Doing Documentary Work*, 1997, based on lectures delivered at the New York Public Library. The scratchy tenor of his voice blends in with the squeak of his chair, the faint whir of a noninsistent clock and the chirp and chatter of birds. We're in Coles country, where listening is an art and a visitor's questions meld into the creative maelstrom.

MEETING DR. WILLIAMS

Born in Boston in 1929 into a family of some means, young Bob Coles attended the prestigious Boston Latin School and went on to Harvard, where he majored in English. A professor urged him to send a term paper he'd written on the poet William Carlos Williams to its subject. "Dear Mr. Coles," the subject promptly replied to the flabbergasted undergrad, "Thank you for your paper on me. Not bad for a Harvard student!" signed W. C. Williams, M.D., with a P.S.: "Please, if you're in the neighborhood, come by and say hello."

"Well, I went down there to Rutherford, N.J., and he was so good to me," Dr. Coles recalls. "He took me around to meet his patients." Dr. Williams's world, in which, as the poet once put it, "medicine and the poem . . . amount for me to nearly the same thing," became, for his young protégé the paradigm of the kind of life he wanted to live.

Years later, Dr. Coles had occasion to pay a literary tribute to his old mentor as the editor of *The Doctor Stories of William Carlos Williams*. He is currently literally following in Dr. Williams's footsteps in collaboration with photographer Tom Roma on a documentary project to see what became of the working-class New Jersey neighborhoods where the poet practiced and of which he wrote.

Encouraged by Dr. Williams to pursue the study of medicine, Coles was admitted to P&S. But organic chemistry and dissecting cadavers were not exactly what the doctor ordered. Medical school proved a bit of a rocky ride, lightened some by the kindness of a few professors, notably Yale Kneeland, Jr. '26, professor of medicine. A distinguished researcher in respiratory diseases, a legendary teacher, and a man of consummate culture, Dr. Kneeland sprinkled a little Tolstoy, Dostoyevsky, and Melville into his scintillating medical lectures. "You'll be alright!" he reassured the struggling English major. Rustin McIntosh, professor of pediatrics and head of Babies Hospital, another benign influence, inspired Coles to work with children.

Meanwhile, in his extra-medical life, he took the City and its environs as his expanded school and living textbook. An avid walker, like his English-born father, he combed the streets and haunted the museums, visiting Dr. Williams on weekends. Keen to mine the spiritual side of life, he audited courses taught by the noted theologian Reinhold Niebuhr at the Union Theological Seminary. He also made time to volunteer at the Catholic Worker soup kitchen on the Lower East Side, and so came to know the movement's cofounder, religious and social activist Dorothy Day. Looking back in his book *Dorothy Day, A Radical Devotion*, 1987, he wrote how she "was constantly noticing people, constantly ready to engage with them, and let them become, even for a few moments, part of her life." Dr. Coles took her wisdom to heart and put it to practice.

PICTURING PARALYSIS

Initially opting for pediatrics, he subsequently trained in child psychiatry at Children's Hospital in Boston and pursued a teaching fellowship in psychiatry at Harvard Medical School. It was the height of the terrible polio epidemic of the late 1950s, and without the aid of the vaccine later developed by Jonas Salk there was little doctors could do but listen and try to relieve the physical and psychological suffering. Finding children "paralyzed by fear as well as the polio virus," Dr. Coles introduced crayons to help break the silence, thereby facilitating the release of what he called "an inarticulate eloquence—that of visual representation." By releasing that halting eloquence, he helped his desperate little patients tap the strength to face life and the disease. For Coles, that early experience of confronting fear and paralysis later leapt to mind in the face of another kind of scourge, a social disease called segregation that would mark him forever and change the course of his life and work.

COLOR ME EQUAL: TALKING TO THE "CRAYOLA MAN"

The year was 1960. The place was New Orleans. A federal court had issued a deadline for school integration and a battle of wills was about to begin between the howling mob and a few brave children. Fulfilling his military service in the Air Force, Dr. Coles was stationed at Keesler Hospital, in Biloxi, Miss., as chief of the neuropsychiatric service and wards. He often drove into New Orleans to attend a medical conference, eat a good meal, and escape the strictures of military life.

One day, the police blocked his way. "Captain, you can't go into town!" Annoyed at the obstruction, he parked his car and walked over to where a crowd had gathered. "That was when I saw that little black girl, Ruby Bridges, six years old at the time"—he shuts his eyes and shakes his head, the smile lines stretching into psychic scars—"being practically carried into a school building by federal marshals. And I saw a mob screaming at her that they were going to kill her. She was paralyzed with fear. I kept connecting her with the kids with polio I met in the Children's Hospital and I said to myself, I'm supposed to know something about stress in children, and I thought, I'd like to meet this girl."

With the help of the local chapter of the NAACP, he eventually did meet Ruby and the three other black children, the little pioneers of school desegregation in New Orleans. And he and his late wife, Jane, a school teacher, became a part of their world. The children took to calling him "The Crayola Man," on account of the crayons he brought along to interviews along with the tape recorder. And together, the doctor and the children traded secrets and tried to unravel the tentacles of angst that held their world in a straitjacket.

"If it hadn't been for that moment and meeting Ruby and the others, my whole life would have been different," he insists. "I was lucky to be there when their world and mine changed forever. If I had studied segregation in a textbook I would have learned nothing." But luck was linked to a firm resolve and a willing ear. "I knew how to listen," he says of his ability to connect with the children, "and I knew how to make some sense of what they were saying. I never came across as a shrink, I came across, I think, as a doctor who cared about children."

Ruby Bridges put it another way. "Doctor Coles always seems as if he's just about ready to grow up!" she said to his wife Jane. "You want to know a secret, Ruby?" his wife replied. "I don't think he's ever going to grow up!" He relishes the memory, laughing out loud in the telling. "If you are going to work with children, there has to be a part of you, one hopes and prays, that's still in touch with what their lives are about." Coles later wrote a popular picture book for children called *The Story of Ruby Bridges*. In her own memoir, *Through My Eyes*, Ms. Bridges, now a lecturer, included a dedication: "To Bob Coles, who in my mind is the vessel God used to keep my story alive."

His interviews and experiences in New Orleans with black as well as white schoolchildren and their parents, and later in Atlanta, where he met with older black youths integrating high schools, formed the basis of his celebrated book *Children of Crisis*, which, he is quick to add, "I never knowingly set out to write."

A YOUNG PSYCHIATRIST LOOKS AT HIS
PROFESSION (AND SOCIETY TOO)

Back in Boston to visit family, he griped to a friend who worked for *Atlantic Monthly* magazine about the state of psychiatry. The friend urged him to "describe what he was saying." The resultant article, "A Young Psychiatrist Looks at His Profession," appeared in a special issue on Psychiatry in America. "When the heart dies, we [psychiatrists] slip into wordy and doctrinaire caricatures of life," he wrote. "Our journals, our habits of talk become cluttered with jargon . . . We embrace icy reasoning." Needless to say, the article made waves. It also loosened the fledgling author's literary floodgates. He decided then and there to forgo a medical practice, went back to the South with his wife Jane (née Hallowell) and kept on listening and writing.

"I wouldn't have done this work or lived this life if I hadn't married my wife!" he shakes his head, clearly torn between joy at her memory and abiding sadness at her loss. She died of a brain tumor in 1993. "What kind of marriage begins where the wife says to the husband, instead of let's buy a home, she says, 'You don't like a lot of things you see happening around you, so why don't you do something about it?'" A teacher of history and literature, she also collaborated with him on the two volumes of *Women of Crisis*.

It was around this time that another influence came into his life in the form of a letter. "Dear Mr. Coles," the letter said, "I understand that you're doing this work with children . . . I'd like to meet you if you're ever up in the Cambridge area." It was signed E. H. Erikson, Harvard University.

On his next trip north, the recipient did finally meet the sender, renowned child psychiatrist Erik Erikson, and the two became fast friends. Erikson encouraged Coles to gather his observations into a book.

Children of Crisis, A Study of Courage and Fear, Volume One of his celebrated five-volume study, made an immediate splash upon its appearance in 1967, lauded in the *New York Times Book Review* by novelist Walker Percy P&S '41 (later to become a friend and the subject of another book). That same year, Dr. Coles was approached by then Senator Robert Kennedy, to whom he became a trusted adviser on questions of child welfare, hunger and health, issues concerning which, on Senator Kennedy's prompting, Dr. Coles testified before Congress. Among his proudest memories is having drafted the last speech the senator delivered in his run for the Democratic nomination for president before he was assassinated.

In 1972, Dr. Coles was the subject of a *Time* magazine cover story on "America's Forgotten Children." In 1973, he received the Pulitzer Prize for the second and third volumes of *Children of Crisis*.

The previous year, he and his family moved to New Mexico, in part to escape his own newfound celebrity, and to explore new vistas. The years in the Southwest were among the happiest in his life. Fieldwork done during this period found its way into another volume of *Children of Crisis* as well as *The Old Ones of New Mexico*, a book produced in collaboration with photographer Alex Harris, which many, including Dr. Coles, consider some of his finest writing: "It's full of what I learned from these people and the dignity and beauty in their language and their land–oh my God!"

"STORYTELLING IS THE HEART AND SOUL OF MEDICINE."

Robert Coles is the rarest kind of "clinical" writer, unafraid to get personal and speak from the heart. He has alternately described himself as "a doctor, child psychiatrist, oral historian, social anthropologist, teacher, friend, storyteller, busybody, and nuisance." Avoiding academic jargon and dogmatic social theory, rejecting social stereotypes, his prose leaps across disciplines, issues, and classes, blending lyricism and an eye for the telling detail. Consider this passage from "Una Anciana," originally published as a profile for *The New Yorker* and later included in *The Old Ones of New Mexico*:

> Once he was measured as exactly six feet tall, but that was half a century ago. He is sure that he has lost at least an inch or two. Sometimes, when his wife has grown impatient with his slouch, and told him to straighten up, he does her suggestion one better and tilts himself backward. Now are you happy? He seems to be asking her, and she smiles indulgently.

This is not your typical patient history, but it is a patient history all the same. All his books can be read as compilations of patient histories alive with the words and gestures of real people with real complaints, some that show, some nestled in hidden corners of the heart that need to be coaxed out by a respectful listener. The stories themselves are the medicine, the healing ointment for the teller, the listener, and the reader.

"Healers make sense of stories, that's what a healer does," Coles insists. "A healer, after all, gets a statement from the person hoping to be healed that tells what the problem is. Healers are listeners who then tell a story back. Story-telling is not the heart and soul of the treatment of the patient, but it's the heart and soul of medicine in so far as medicine has to do with two people telling stories to one another, the patient speaking, the doctor responding."

As he has for more than four decades, he rises early every morning with the birds and still writes in longhand, filling up lined yellow pads on an old-fashioned clipboard of the sort his mother gave him when he was in elementary school "to order [his] words." In the past, with the aid of a reel-to-reel tape recorder, now mostly from memory, he spills out the voices he has gathered up. "I've spent my life becoming a voice for other people who are struggling with trying to explain who they are." He is currently at work, among other projects, compiling his Harvard lectures into a book.

A "MIGRANT TEACHER" AND "SHARE-WRITER"

Though an avowed autodidact when it comes to his working method—"I never took a course in documentary work or anthropology or social science!"—he has relished teaching. It was Erik Erikson who brought him back to Harvard, first as a research psychiatrist and an assistant in Erikson's course, later as an instructor in his own right. In 1977, Harvard Medical School named him professor of psychiatry and medical humanities. To that title Harvard University added in 1995 that of James Agee Professor of Social Ethics. He "wandered like a migrant teacher," as he likes to put it, lecturing, or rather engaging students, in almost every division of the university, including the schools of business, medicine, education, and law, as well as the Extension School. His legendary course at Harvard College, "The Literature of Social Reflection," popularly known as "Guilt 105," drew up to 1,000 registered attendees prior to his official retirement from teaching in 2003.

He also taught elementary school and high school, and more recently, invited high school teachers to visit the offices of *Doubletake*, the magazine of documentary writing and art that he created in 1995, "to amplify their formal teaching."

James Freedman, the president of Dartmouth, called him "a rare, rare American." Educator and sociologist Amitai Etzioni dubbed him "a national treasure." Encomia have flooded in from all directions. In addition to the Pulitzer Prize, he is the recipient of a John D. and Catherine MacArthur Foundation Fellowship, the National Medal of Freedom (awarded by President Clinton), the Presidential National Medal for the Humanities (awarded by President George W. Bush), the Ralph Waldo Emerson Prize of Phi Beta Kappa, the Hofheimer Award of the American Psychiatric Association, and the Gold Medal for Distinguished Achievements in Medicine of the P&S Alumni Association, to name only a few.

Author of some 65 books and counting—with five more in galleys—more than 1,500 articles and essays, father of three (an orthopedic surgeon, a pediatrician, and a teacher-photographer), grandfather of four, at age seventy-four he still likes to think of himself as a wanderer at heart.

"A *share-writer?*" hazards the visitor.

Like the fault lines of a benign earthquake, the smile lines radiate every which way as he explodes in uproarious laughter—"Well what are you going to do about this rambling guy?"

"Make a story, of course!" the visitor replies, and all the faces on his wall seem to whisper "Amen."

MEDICINE BY THE BOOK

ROBIN COOK '66

With thirty-three and counting worldwide bestsellers under his belt and sales of over one hundred million copies, inspiring close to a dozen movies and TV miniseries, the master of the medical thriller is still cooking up tantalizing plots.

COMA, OUTBREAK, *Mindbend, Mutation, Harmful Intent, Vital Signs, Fatal Cure, Foreign Body.* . . . The titles alone make you tremble. Ever since Robin Cook '66, P&S's homegrown answer to Britain's (Dr.) Sir Arthur Conan Doyle, took the publishing world by storm in 1977 with his bestselling novel *Coma*, the reading public has kept his books on the bestseller list, craving his unique brand of medicine wrapped in a plot. Hailed by the *New York Times* as "the master of the medical thriller," Dr. Cook, an ophthalmologist by training, has tackled complex medical issues like malpractice, organ harvesting, bioterrorism, cloning, and stem cell research in some twenty-eight novels to date. His latest book, *Foreign Body*, treats the controversial subject of medical tourism. Its publication was preceded by a widely viewed webcast series produced by Michael Eisner.

The interviewer caught up with the prolific author at his Boston home in September 2008.

THE HOUSES AND HOSPITALS WE HAUNT

Reflecting on the appeal of his fiction, Dr. Cook observed: "We're all going to be patients some time. You can write about great white sharks or haunted

houses, and you can say I'm not going in the ocean or I'm not going into haunted houses, but you can't say you're not going to go into a hospital." And he added, "Wrapped in the pleasure of a good read, I'm giving my readers information that actually is going to help them."

His Georgian style six-story house on Louisburg Square in Boston's historic Beacon Hill neighborhood may not be haunted, but time has put a patina on its stately façade, and Dr. Cook, an architecture and design buff, has made sure the interior is true to period. Reproductions of Attic vases and Roman friezes popular in the nineteenth century decorate the first floor. Italian landscapes and the portraits of Boston Brahmins line the second. Time tested himself, albeit still remarkably trim at sixty-seven, Dr. Cook strives for the same fidelity in his books. "I really try to stay very accurate in the scientific basis of my books."

His expression shifts from puzzlement to amusement as the interviewer pulls out a copy of his first published work, "The Effects of pO₂ Changes on Neuronal Synaptic and Antidromic Excitability (Giant Neurons of Aplysia fasciata)," coauthored with Gabriel G. Nahas and Nicholas Chalazonitis, published in the *Bulletin de l'Institut Océanographique Monaco* in 1965. The product of research conducted at the blood/gas lab he helped set up on a summer break from medical school at the Jacques Cousteau Oceanographic Institute, its tone and style are a far cry from that of his carefully crafted novels. But science is the substrate of his imagination, always informing his fiction.

Consider the following passage from the prologue to his 2005 novel *Marker*:

"Yet exactly at three-seventeen A.M., two nearly simultaneous, unrelated but basically similar, microcosmic events occurred on opposite sides of Central Park [. . .] One was on a cellular level, the other on a molecular level [. . .] The cellular level occurred in a moment of intense bliss and involved the forcible injection of slightly more than two hundred and fifty million sperm in a vaginal vault [. . .]"

The first thing that strikes one about the above passage is how entertaining it is to read: Woody Allen's *Everything You Always Wanted to Know About Sex* meets C. S. Lewis's *Lives of a Cell*. The second thing—and this is one of the astounding qualities about the work—is the solid grounding of his fiction in medical fact.

"I laugh when I write," he admits. "Of course I have a lot of fun with the language [. . .] And people have fun reading it. That's why they take my books to the beach and on planes." (His novels are on prominent display at most American airport bookstores.) "But I hope my readers get something else out of it too."

That something else is knowledge.

Marker includes an acknowledgement to "my medical school, the College of Physicians and Surgeons at Columbia University [. . .] Both my professional life and writing career have depended heavily on the foundation of knowledge and experience I learned and enjoyed at that fine institution." The tribute seeps into the fiction too. Both the lead characters, Drs. Laurie Montgomery and Jack Stapleton, a pair of medical examiners with exacting standards and a ferocious curiosity, attended P&S. The two reappear in several of his books. Dr. Stapleton, Dr. Cook avows, is a fictional alter ego.

A member on leave from the clinical faculty at Harvard Medical School, and ever the medical educator at heart, Dr. Cook is careful to underline the serious educational side of his literary pursuit. He is particularly proud of the fact that his books are taught in many high schools "because they're good for both English and science."

THE MEDICINE IS THE MESSAGE

Reading Robin Cook, one is reminded of the song from the popular musical *Mary Poppins*: "Just a Spoon Full of Sugar Makes the Medicine Go Down." For hidden beneath the mask of the entertainer is the stern face of the practitioner dashing off a prescription for his loyal readers while taking his profession to task for promises broken or unfulfilled. Every novel has an implicit warning label: Medicine can be dangerous to your health. And a caveat: To be taken with a grain of salt.

In the words of Lorena Laura Stookey, author of the book *Robin Cook: A Critical Companion*, "For Cook's readers, a friendly and familiar figure once known as 'Doc' (the bearer of the ubiquitous black bag) has faded into legend. The black bag has long since given way to medical technology, and the ancient art of healing has been broadly named—with obvious significance—the health care industry."

Dr. Cook concurs: "The most important underlying theme of my work is the fact that medicine and business got into bed together and remain much too close [. . .] People realize that medicine has really been taken over by business. And also, that some of the major changes in the practice, not necessarily for the better, that have occurred have actually come from outside the field." A physician to the bone, he adds, "I'm embarrassed at the fact that the whole health industry ignores personal health, doing healthy things, exercise, eating properly. Medicine has just been dragged along by for-profit business."

"When I was in medical school," he recalls, "my idea of medical practice was this old-fashioned very tight fiduciary relationship between the doctor and the patient. The patient was paying the doctor something he or she valued, whether it was potatoes or money or whatever. The doctor, in turn, was very conscious of the fact that this person was offering him something they held very dear, was willing to give it in exchange for expert medical advice. Both parties valued the relationship. So did the society. Things are a lot different today."

He traces part of the problem back to medical school. While he remains a loyal alumnus and a staunch supporter of P&S, an institution he reveres—he funded the refurbishing of a gym in his name at Bard Hall, among other kindnesses—his own memories of the medical school experience are not all rosy.

He faults a curriculum, which, in his day, stressed esoteric illness as opposed to common wellness. "You quickly became aware of what got you the good grades. First of all, on rounds, it made a very big difference which patient you happened to draw. If it was someone with one of those newly understood metabolic diseases you could give a little talk on [. . .] and if there were some specific treatment based on this metabolic link, you got an A. But if your patient had just the run-of-the-mill sort of problem, obesity or diabetes, you realized that nobody really cared."

Dr. Cook's diagnosis is sobering: "Medical school takes a bunch of bright students, almost invariably altruistically minded—which is a good portion of why they've gone into medicine—and somehow, somewhere along the way, injects cynicism." And while medical science has advanced at lightning speed, opening ever new horizons of knowledge, "the technology has distanced the physician from the patient and the science has raised important ethical issues."

"In my medical school days," he recalls, "there was no Department of Medical Ethics, no courses in ethics." He hopes that a proposed Robin Cook '66 Professorship in Medical Ethics at P&S may help students strive for "the high standard of medical accountability that made them want to be docs in the first place." He cites the new Physicians Charter proposed by the Internal Medicine Society as a good working model. "Its key principles, as I recall, are patient autonomy, patient well-being, and social equality." Dr. Cook is a proponent of universal tax-based single-payer health insurance.

SURGERY, SATURATION DIVING, AND LITERARY INSPIRATION

Like most doctors, he was originally motivated to pursue the study of medicine by a genuine desire to help. The desire first crystallized into a goal around a high school sports accident that he witnessed. "There was one episode in football where somebody broke their leg and I was right there. And I really wanted to help but I didn't know what to do. And I thought to myself: Wow, what a power, to know what to do! That might have been the most significant episode that pushed me toward becoming a doctor."

Valedictorian of his high school class in Leonia, N.J., he went on to attend Wesleyan University, graduating summa cum laude. He came to P&S with high hopes, admittedly "awed by the tradition of the school," and feeling "really lucky to be there."

Coming from a family of modest economic means, he had to work his way through medical school, often holding down several jobs at the same time. One of these jobs entailed running a blood/gas chemistry laboratory for the cardiac surgery team at Presbyterian Hospital, where he crossed paths with pioneering heart surgeon James R. Malm '49, professor of surgery emeritus at P&S and former chief of the Cardiac and Thoracic Surgical Service at Presbyterian Hospital. Inspired by Dr. Malm and other members of the team, Dr. Cook opted for a career in surgery, training at Queens Hospital in Honolulu. An avid surfer, he admits that the Honolulu lifestyle and the proximity of the world's best waves was part of the lure.

Following the completion of his residency training, he was drafted into the Navy, and as luck would have it, assigned to submarine school and navy diving school. Time spent on a tour of duty submerged aboard the USS Kamehameha, a ballistic missile submarine and flagship of the Pacific fleet, and thereafter as a navy aquanaut medical officer assigned to the Deep Submergence Systems Project, proved fruitful in at least two respects.

A participant in pioneering diving research, he wrote up the results in *A Medical Watch Standers Guide to Saturation Diving*, his first published book. The data is still used today.

The long periods of isolation while off duty on the submarine also offered him the occasion and the impulse to write his first literary work, *The Year of the Intern*, published in 1972. In it he formulated a critique of the human side of medical training. The book's favorable reception prompted him to try again, this time targeting the bestseller list. With the analytical skills he'd acquired in college and mastered in medical school, he carefully dissected every bestselling book on the *New York Times* list, isolating their structural strengths as well as the "active ingredients" that made them so appealing.

Writing nights, tapping the dark, heretofore unspoken, side of hospital care, he applied his flair for fiction and came up with *Coma*, a medical mystery about a scandal in organ harvesting by unscrupulous MDs. First drafting it as a screenplay, he later transformed the script into fast-paced prose. The result was a double bull's-eye, the 1977 bestselling novel and the 1978 hit movie by the same name directed by Michael Crichton.

"Most doctors are terrific," he insists, "but there are a lot of doctors who are in it for the wrong reasons and aren't necessarily very ethical. [. . .] And, in fact, when I wrote *Coma*, I think part of the real appeal of the book was that people were surprised that the bad guys were the doctors. But no doctors were surprised. We all know there are some bad apples. But nobody talks about it." The book has held up over time. Given the dearth of organs for transplantation and the growing demand, scandals abound.

Meanwhile, Dr. Cook had shifted his medical focus to ophthalmology and trained at Harvard, following the completion of which he started a private practice in ophthalmology in Marblehead, Mass., and joined the clinical faculty at Harvard Medical School. An inveterate multitasker, he simultaneously matriculated as a fulltime student at Harvard's Kennedy School of Government, and though he ultimately decided not to pursue politics as a calling, the experience kindled an interest in public health policy. He realized that his most powerful and effective tool was the pen.

While his writing eventually took precedence over his practice, Dr. Cook still sees himself first and foremost as a doctor who writes: "Sure, I've sold a lot of books, but you know, you have this idea of what a writer is like, and you know yourself too well. [. . .] I still don't think of myself as a writer."

His international readership in the millions may beg to disagree. He was the recipient of the 2002 "Author of Vision" award presented by the RP International Organization.

PROPHETIC PLOTS

In his twenty-eight books, twenty-six of which have made the bestseller list and all of which have been translated into forty languages, Dr. Cook has dramatized such pressing medical issues and emergencies as egg donation (*Shock*), therapeutic cloning (*Seizure*), concierge medicine and malpractice (*Crisis*), cancer (*Fever*), and spreading pandemics (*Outbreak*). Many of his books, like *Coma*, have remained as apropos as ever.

The ideas come from a fine-tuned feel for medicine and its discontents: "I guess I'm just sensitive about any changes in medical care that might have a detrimental effect on the public."

One book, in particular, *Vector*, 1999, on medical terrorism, proved eerily prophetic, appearing as it did three years prior to the 2001 anthrax attacks that terrorized the United States. "They started in the mail, just like in my book. It's a little unnerving," Dr. Cook acknowledges. But as he points out, he got the terrorist tactics for his novel, "what they would be using and how and even all that stuff about the skinheads," straight off the Internet.

In another book, *Fever*, 2000, one of his most popular, he wrote "about some of these companies up here in New England dumping toxic waste into the water supply [. . .] And then it all came to pass, everything came to pass within three or four years."

INFLUENCING PUBLIC OPINION AND PUBLIC POLICY

Dr. Cook takes very seriously the power of his influence on public opinion in medical matters. Active in the Republican Party, he is a personal friend of Utah senator Oren Hatch, who had him sign 650 copies of his last book, *Foreign Body*, on the dangers of medical tourism, and hand-delivered them to members of Congress.

"It's a reflection on just how bad our health care system is. 180,000 Americans go to India each year to have their operations. How bad is that! It's crazy! We're pricing ourselves out of the competition! India, a third-world country, is doing twenty-first-century medicine, competing with us, and doing better."

Dr. Cook has used his considerable influence to push causes close to his heart, including stem cell research and the reform of the American health care system, agitating for a single-payer plan: "Almost everybody agrees that we have a terrible system. We're not doing the right thing by doctors or patients. Too many people are making too much money out of it and not contributing enough. The astronomical salary paid to the CEO of a hospital or HMO is coming out of the total health care pie."

He was appointed by President George W. Bush to the Woodrow Wilson Center's board of trustees.

BACK TO SCHOOL

Meanwhile, the book ideas keep coming. Every September he researches a new subject. "September was always my favorite time of year: new school year, new course, new ideas . . ." He is currently working on a book project on issues relating to the uses and abuses of alternative medicine. "We're pushing people in the direction of alternative medicine because regular medicine is getting too expensive and people don't have insurance."

September has acquired another special meaning, now that he and his wife, Jean, have a son. It's back to school time for Cameron. At age nine, he shares his father's insatiable curiosity. The author converted his old study in the house on Beacon Hill into a bedroom for the boy, and in a touching design metaphor, had Cameron's bunk bed built around his old writing desk. Architectural design is a hobby of his. He is currently overseeing the design of new additions and modifications to his summer house on Martha's Vineyard and the interior design of a pied-à-terre in New York.

He has also of late begun to feel a tug of attachment to his medical alma mater. Dr. Cook delivered informal remarks to a packed house at the Donald F. Tapley Faculty Club as guest speaker at the September 18, 2008, P&S Alumni Council Dinner. The visit stirred up strong feelings on the part of the listeners and the speaker.

"I have a current dream, crazy as it sounds, that I'd go back to P&S and start again," he laughs. "What I'm really tempted to do, to tell you the truth, is to go back and spend a couple of weeks in each year, just to see how different it is."

A SHARED LIFE IN MEDICINE, CANADIAN STYLE

RICHARD '55 AND SYLVIA CRUESS '55

Retired from their respective positions as dean of McGill Medical School and medical director of the Royal Victoria Hospital, in Montreal, Richard and Sylvia Cruess continue as a dynamic duo leading the educational call for professionalism in medical practice.

———— ⦿⦿⦿ ————

THE DEAN of Canada's world-class medical school, McGill, and the vice president and medical director of one of Canada's finest teaching hospitals, the Royal Victoria, share a profound commitment to medicine and medical education and to universal health care coverage as provided under the Canadian system. They also share a profound commitment to each other as husband and wife.

If it is rare that two people should remain happily married for four decades and counting, it is almost unheard of for them to rise to pinnacles of leadership in the same profession while pitching in to help raise a family and run a household.

Their recipe for such success is "being willing to share and guarding our home time," says Sylvia Cruess '55, who for the past eighteen years has directed the medical administration of the Royal Victoria Hospital in Montreal, commonly known as "The Vic." The rule of thumb is simple, says her husband, Richard '55, the longest standing dean of McGill—or any Canadian medical school: "Whoever gets home first cooks." (It helps that they are gourmet cooks.)

Both tall and sturdy of build, there is something about them reminiscent of Gregory Peck and Ingrid Bergman on a downhill ski in *Spellbound*. (Skiing is another shared passion.) Their pride in each other is evident in the weave of their words punctuated periodically by a hearty laugh or the silent complicity of a smile.

Theirs is an extraordinary personal and professional partnership that began when they met as first-year medical students at P&S in 1952 and was formalized at the end of the following year when, despite family opposition, they tied the knot. Sylvia credits the wise counsel of Dr. Aura Severinghaus, then dean of students, who calmly assuaged her mother's concern. "We have found that when two students wish to get married," he said, "they do a lot better if they do than if they don't."

Richard describes their medical school experience as nothing short of "pretty wonderful." As a couple, they bonded with their classmates, many of whom have become lifelong friends. And though Sylvia was one of only twelve women in a class of 120, she doesn't remember being treated any differently. She found "the fellows fine and our own group of women particularly self-supportive."

And, like everyone else, they enjoyed access to a formidable faculty comprising many of the medical luminaries of the day. "We had the chance to hear the most exciting parts of medicine in the making, and it was up to us to pull up our socks and make the most of it," says Sylvia. Following wasn't always easy, as in the case of a complex lecture on mucopolysaccharides delivered in a thick German accent by the great biochemist, Dr. Karl Mayer—"but we learned to listen." She likewise delighted in the rigor of her medical rotation with Dr. Robert Loeb. Among the faculty, Richard most fondly recalls Virginia Kneeland Frantz '22 (mother of classmate and friend, the late Andrew Frantz '55), whose Introduction to Surgery and Surgical Pathology course was "so extremely well thought out that I came away with knowledge that's still very much with me today."

The strength of the P&S approach to medical education, in Richard's view, lay in the fact that "we were given responsibility in graduated form, with less and less supervision as we went along, so that the transition into an internship was easy." It is an approach that has been imported to McGill.

While Sylvia opted for a career in medicine, later subspecializing in endocrinology, Richard gravitated to surgery, the field of a favorite uncle. A mechanical bent and his experience with nonparalytic polio as a boy predisposed him to orthopedics.

The year 1955 was the first of the new computerized National Residency Match Plan, and, to avoid being separated at graduation, they applied to and were accepted for internships in medicine and surgery, respectively, at The Royal Victoria Hospital in Montreal. "We came and instantly fell in love with the place," recalls Richard. "We just thought that Montreal, the Vic, and McGill were absolute magic—and still do!"

Richard, then still an American citizen, was drafted and spent two years in the U.S. Navy at St. Albans. He returned to Columbia-Presbyterian to pursue orthopedic training under Drs. Frank Stinchfield and Alan DeForest Smith at the New York Orthopedic Hospital, where he also devoted a year to related basic biochemical research, an uncommon path for an orthopedist at the time.

Sylvia won an NIH fellowship to pursue postgraduate medical training, followed by a residency under Dr. Elaine Ralli, then head of New York University's Endocrine Division at Bellevue. She also took on the lion's share of raising their two sons. Her division was responsible for the prison ward and psychiatric consultations in endocrinology, responsibilities she embraced with characteristic gusto and verve. "You really get to know people and you get to see how people handle their life situations," she reflects, "which is one of the reasons this field is such fun. In endocrinology, you're treating lifelong disease. You have to teach people how to live with what they have."

Returning to Montreal, Richard joined the Department of Orthopedics at McGill, where his research on basic bone physiology and the effects of hormones on bone was funded for twenty-four consecutive years by the Medical Research Council of Canada (Canada's counterpart to the NIH). Also, in conjunction with members of McGill's large transplant program, he did the work for which he is perhaps best known, his study of avascular necrosis resulting from transplant drugs. He was the first orthopedic surgeon to make the rank of full professor at McGill, where he subsequently served as chair of the Department of Orthopedics until his appointment as dean of the Faculty of Medicine in 1981. He has been president of the Canadian Orthopedics Association and was the first Canadian to be president of the American Orthopedics Research Society. Among other key positions, he is a past president of the Canadian Association of Medical Colleges and continues to be involved in educational policy issues. He has coauthored or coedited four books and numerous papers on a wide variety of orthopedic concerns.

Sylvia's experience at Bellevue, considering what could be done for patients outside the traditional hospital environment, served her well upon her return to The Vic, where a colleague asked her to take over the administration of the Metabolic Day Centre, an outpatient endocrine clinic and the first of its kind in Canada. In 1970, the government instituted one of the first in a series of budget cuts in health care, and the metabolic center effectively took charge of all endocrine cases formerly treated on the ward. Her remarkable success as director of the center brought her to the attention of the hospital trustees, who appointed her vice president and director of professional services in 1977. She has published both in the field of endocrinology and medical administration. Among other positions, she has been a member of the board of directors of the Quebec Medical Association and currently chairs the Committee of the Directors of Professional Services of the Montreal Joint Hospital Institute.

Meanwhile, the forces of social change brought universal coverage in the form of a provincial medical system, first to Saskatchewan in 1962, then to Quebec in 1970, and later to the other provinces. Universal hospitalization was legislated in 1959.

Together, Richard and Sylvia Cruess have weathered and welcomed the rise of national health care in Canada, which Richard has hailed "the social laboratory in the North," and together they continue to champion its benefits.

"Canadians," he suggests, "have a greater faith in government and more respect for authority than is true in the U.S. It is generally recognized in Canada that government is trying to produce the best health care for the least dollars for the most people."

Sylvia adds, "Canadians are more willing than Americans to live by and with the rules of the game."

In response to criticisms of the Canadian system, notably accusations of health care rationing, Richard is adamant: "Every society in the world rations health care by some means or another. The U.S. has rationed health care by eliminating 35 million people from its system and marginally covering another 15-20 million. We ration health care by limiting access—but limiting access to everybody."

What of the suggestions of a shortage and lag in availability of advanced medical technology? Though the Cruesses agree that Canada may be a little "under-teched," as compared to the United States, they argue that their neighbors to the south may be overdependent on the costly benefits of technology and that such an overdependence may hinder good medicine. "The use of technology, which can do wonderful things," Sylvia argues, "can also distance you as a doctor in your relationship with the patient."

As to the material effects of the system for doctors—lower income levels— Richard points out that physicians are still the highest paid group of professionals in the country. And, Sylvia adds, doctors continue to enjoy the unqualified respect of their patients. As medical educators, the Cruesses are also keenly aware of the benefit of Canada's moderate medical school tuition. "Debt does not play nearly as much a role for our students as it inevitably does in the U.S.," Richard says.

"People's motives for going into medicine are probably as varied here as anywhere else," Sylvia notes, "but I think there are few for whom income is of major importance."

Critical of developments toward managed care for profit in the United States, Richard says, "When you introduce competition as a major factor in the day-to-day life of a physician, I worry where idealism is going to fit in. I see no way in which the marketplace can consider quality of care as a major determinant."

"We've both had opportunities to go somewhere else where we would have earned a great deal more money, and we chose not to," says Sylvia. "Part of it is Montreal, McGill, and our lifestyle here. We couldn't have a more enjoyable and fulfilling academic life. Cooperation far outweighs competition among researchers. It's a special atmosphere in which people really work together."

Despite two busy schedules and extensive professional travel responsibilities (including a trip to Bahrain to coordinate McGill's large resident training program for students from the Gulf States), this high-profile professional couple fiercely guard their private life. They remain close with their two grown sons in Chicago and Toronto—"both MBAs, and they're going to support us in our old age," jokes Richard. They make time for skiing, gardening, gourmet cooking, and wine tasting—Richard is a Chevalier de la Tastevin, at Clos de Vougeot, in Bourgogne, France. Committed as they are to the *Santé Publique*, it seems only apt for two doctors to close the day with a toast: *Santé*! Your health!

SURGEON-SCIENTIST TAKES
KNOWLEDGE TO THE CUTTING EDGE

PATRICIA DONAHOE '64

Dr. Donahoe's laboratory is still studying the molecular mechanisms
by which TGFB family proteins suppress growth and the molecular
mechanisms of sex differentiation.

———∞∞∞———

UP AT 5:30 A.M. to check on the progress of her eight research projects concurrently running in the lab before scrubbing in on a difficult neonatal diaphragmatic hernia operation, and subsequently returning to the lab to huddle with colleagues in preparation for an upcoming NIH site visit, Patricia Donahoe '64 is understandably peaked by the time she sits down to an afternoon interview. She will be at it a good many hours more before calling it a day.

Her voice is weary and a bit subdued. Her eyes dart about nervously. Her fingers, clearly unaccustomed to idleness, wander between a pair of glasses and a mug of coffee with the word WORKAHOLIC appropriately glazed on it. These, if not the primary tools of her trade, are the fulcrum and fuel that keep her mind and body running through the grueling 18 plus hours of a typical working day.

There is, however, nothing typical about the Marshall K. Bartlett Professor of Surgery at Harvard Medical School and chief of pediatric surgery at Massachusetts General Hospital. The first woman to be named professor of surgery at Harvard, she specializes in complex and delicate procedures, including the surgical correction of a large number of congenital abnormalities, many of which are now discovered in utero. She has, moreover, attracted national attention with her ongoing research and study of Muellerian inhibiting substance, a rare embryo protein she and her colleagues have been able to clone and purify in enhanced amounts from a cell line altered to express the protein, which she hopes will prove a viable treatment for ovarian cancer. And while the scramble for research funding is an ongoing concern, Dr. Donahoe continues to delight in the adventure of the quest. Having honed her dexterity and resilience early in life on a basketball court and lacrosse field, she concentrates on every step of the search, ever mindful of the goal.

A UNIQUE PATH TO PEDIATRIC SURGERY

A lifelong fascination with "the gorgeous anatomy of the human body" is rooted in her own firsthand experience of the body's abilities under stress. Cocaptain of all-women's sports at Braintree High School in Brookline, Mass., and destined according to the yearbook to become the "first coach of the girls' Boston Celtics," she went on to pursue a BS at the Sargent College of Physical Education at Boston University. It was here that she discovered the lure of science and "began to think more seriously about what I should do besides knocking around a basketball." Impressed by her intellectual promise, Dean George Mackechnie steered her toward medicine.

Following a brief tenure as instructor of physical education at Indiana University, where she simultaneously fulfilled her premed requirements in organic chemistry, physiology, and mathematics, she was accepted to all the medical schools to which she applied, and opted for P&S. Athletics gave her a unique perspective that would later serve her well in surgery.

Her medical school experience, she recalls, was "among the happiest periods in my life. It was like dying and going to heaven!" The intellectual ferment she found at P&S, epitomized by such outstanding faculty as her mentor Dr. David Seegal, then the chief of medicine at Roosevelt Hospital and a revered teacher of physical diagnosis, fired her imagination. While attempting to understand congenital anomalies in cardiac defects, she and classmates Will Andrew '64 and Bill Friend '64 developed an early pacemaker, for which she received a Borden Undergraduate Research Award at graduation in 1964, the first of many encomia to come. It was, however, the surgical aspect of the research project, not the technology, that thrilled her. Impressed by the skill of such outstanding P&S surgeons as Drs. Thomas Santulli, Cushman Haagensen, and Carl Feind '50, among others, she decided to pursue surgery.

"People thought I was crazy," she recalls of her resolve to enter a field heretofore by and large off limits to women. "But I was pretty naive back then," she chuckles. "I had spent a lot of time trying to find something I liked better, but I just loved surgery! Surgery, we used to say, is medicine plus: you could think like a doctor and fix like a surgeon!"

The dexterity and eye-hand coordination came easily to her, as did the sense of geometric depth. Gender-based exclusion proved a more daunting, albeit surmountable, hurdle. Not a single woman had ever been accepted into a general surgical residency program in the Boston area, where she and her husband, Jack Donahoe, returned following his assignment to a high-level position with the Ford Motor Company. Nevertheless, Dr. Donahoe applied and bucked the odds in 1969, the first woman ever appointed a surgical resident at the Tufts-New England Medical Center. She subsequently returned to research, pursuing a fellowship in the basic sciences under Dr. Judah Folkman at the Children's Hospital Medical Center, and a clinical fellowship the following year under the master surgeon Dr. W. Hardy Hendren at Massachusetts General Hospital.

In addition to her considerable responsibilities on the professional plane, she and her husband decided it was time to have children. "That was a bit of a juggle," she smiles with a sigh, hinting at the complexities of combining career and family. "My daughters are professionals today, but they're taking time off to have children!"—a choice that was not available to her, but which she wholeheartedly supports, encouraging maternity leaves and family time in her lab and on her surgical service, since "the brain does not turn off or dissolve away with motherhood."

Attracted by the "tremendous variety of surgical challenge and the chance to work with kids," she decided to further specialize in pediatric surgery. Molecular biology, she explains, "has provided us with the tools to unravel mysteries of developmental biology in ways that couldn't possibly be done before." What particularly appealed to her was the prospect of technical correction of anomalies in conjunction with an enhanced understanding of their pathophysiology, just the right mix of surgery and science. A year as senior registrar at the Alder Hey Children's Hospital and Neonatal Surgical Unit in Liverpool, England, exposed her to pioneering procedures in the field. Upon her return to the States in 1973, she joined the surgical staff at Massachusetts General Hospital (MGH) and the Department of Surgery at Harvard. She was named full professor there in 1986, the first woman ever to hold that title. Dr. Donahoe currently occupies the Marshall K. Bartlett Chair in Surgery at Harvard and heads the Pediatric Surgical Services at MGH. Since 1973, she has also been principal investigator and director of the hospital's Pediatric Surgical Research Laboratory.

A PROSPECTIVE CURE FOR OVARIAN CANCER
AT THE PATHWAY OF MALENESS

While in England, at a lecture at the Royal Liverpool Medical Society, Dr. Donahoe first heard of the work of French developmental endocrinologist Dr. Alfred Jost, who discovered Muellerian inhibiting substance (MIS), a hormone secreted in the embryo of the male that leads to the regression of the Muellerian duct, the female reproductive tract present in all embryos. Already interested in the study of growth regulators and specifically growth inhibitors, Dr. Donahoe felt an immediate surge of excitement. "I was seated in the back of the room," she recalls, "and the lights went on in my mind, the bells clanged and the whistles blew. That's it! I said." Here was a fetal inhibitor that could be studied in vitro in an assay.

"The leap of faith," she explained, "was that the receptors for these fetal inhibitors would be recapitulated in tumors that emanated from the source that responded to the inhibitor in fetal life." And just possibly, "you could treat the adult ovarian tumors with the same growth factors or growth inhibitors that influence embryonic development."

Undaunted by her lack of previous in-depth training in biochemistry and molecular biology, Dr. Donahoe boldly forged ahead, learning as she went. In research, she says, "you've got to accept a chronic amateurism to pursue a problem to its solution. There are always new unknowns. And though you never really come to the conclusive answer," she laughs, "you've got to really love the adventure of the search."

She heeded the advice of Nobel laureate Dr. John Enders, who isolated the polio virus in the very same lab (now Dr. Judah Folkman's) in which she did her research fellowship, and who one day came by to visit and told her: "There are two ways you can do research. One is to learn a skill and be better at it than anybody else in the world and look for problems to solve with that skill. The other way is to follow your nose!" For more than two decades now, Dr. Donahoe has been pursuing the latter course with great success.

The practice of surgery gives her a certain sense of fearlessness in addressing problems in the lab. Or, as she puts it, "We all put our shoes on and tie our laces the same way, don't we?!" As to the interplay of her dual roles, she firmly believes that "the research makes me a better surgeon and the surgery a better investigator, because I'm constantly looking for what a discovery might mean for my patient!"

Originally working with the minuscule amount of MIS secreted from newborn calves' testes, she and Dr. Richard L. Cate at Biogen, the Boston-based biotechnology company, soon realized that the natural source of the hormone would never suffice. In Dr. Donahoe's words, "there aren't enough bulls in the world to treat one patient." Working in collaboration, Drs. Donahoe and Cate made headlines in 1986 when they successfully grew the precious substance in the ovarian cells of a genetically engineered Chinese hamster.

Financial considerations eventually compelled Biogen to pull out of the project. Dr. Donahoe admits to a "clash of cultures" between the short-term goals of a company responsible to its shareholders and the slow, painstaking nature of biomedical research. Thanks to the ongoing support of the NIH and the NCI, her research continues. In its new Protein Production Facility, NCI is making MIS to support a long-awaited clinical trial to test the safety and early efficiency of MIS in the treatment of human ovarian cancer.

Another major area of ongoing interest is the study of lung development in the fetus, a research complement to her work in the OR treating diaphragmatic hernia.

Adamant about the team nature of research, Dr. Donahoe readily shares all credit with her colleagues: "There are many captains in this team! I think I'm just the coordinator!"

Relishing her role as a teacher, she takes a long view of the search for knowledge and the rewards and disappointments of scientific investigation. "Substantive accomplishments," she says, "often come from the people that you influence. And if you influence them in the right way, you can accomplish far more than if you did it yourself."

Recognized as a surgeon's surgeon and a world-class research scientist, she was saluted by *Ms.* magazine in 1987 as one of the Women of the Year. The coauthor of a textbook on the clinical management of intersex abnormalities, 38 book chapters, and some 168 peer-reviewed papers, her work has attracted major research funding from the NIH and the National Cancer Society. She serves on the Scientific Advisory Council of the Sophia Foundation in Rotterdam, the Netherlands, the MIT Corporation Visiting Committee, and the Board of Scientific Consultants to the Memorial Sloan-Kettering Cancer Center in New York. In 1987, she was elected a fellow of the American Academy of Arts and Sciences and, in 1991, a fellow of the Institute of Medicine of the National Academy of Science. Her long list of honors includes Boston University's Alumni Award for Distinguished Public Service in 1984; the 1990 Ortho 21st Century Women's Awards-Science Award; and the Gold Medal for Distinguished Achievements in Medicine of the P&S Alumni Association in 1995.

Such honors notwithstanding, Dr. Donahoe is a tough taskmaster on herself. In a feature profile that appeared in the *Boston Globe* in 1993, she was quoted as saying, "I am taking up space in a hospital and I have to know why I'm here." Nurturing the talent in her lab, she looks to her junior colleagues for inspiration and support. "On days when I'm not feeling particularly productive," she smiles, "I look around me at the wonderful young colleagues in the Pediatric Surgical Services and in the lab, and realize that we must be doing something right!"

With women comprising half the current class of surgical residents at MGH, Dr. Donahoe is gratified at the way things have changed: "There's a much more humanizing influence by the virtue of women being in the field."

In the little time left from her eighty-hour work week, she enjoys moments of leisure with her husband and children, now grown up and with families of their own.

Less nimble now perhaps than she once was, the lacrosse stick may have been shelved but the ball has merely been conceptualized, internalized. Now it's a molecule, an idea knocked around, a new procedure attempted, while she remains ever mindful of a more elusive goal—"my grail," she calls it, as she walks around the laboratory and asks her colleagues in jest, "Have you cured cancer yet?"

TUNING-UP THE ENGINE OF PUBLIC HEALTH IN THE MOTOR CITY

ABDUL EL-SAYED '14

Since publication of this profile, Dr. El-Sayed cast in his lot as a candidate for governor of the state of Michigan.

—◦◦◦—

"DETROIT OCCUPIES a unique space in the social conscience of America, it stands for so much of who we are as a nation," affirms Abdul El-Sayed '14, a native of Metro Detroit and the executive director since August 2015 of the Detroit Health Department. While Detroit's troubles remain formidable, Dr. El-Sayed, a self-described "optimistic realist," who also holds a DPhil in public health from Oxford University, sees a chance to make a difference where it matters and in the process, rethink health delivery for the twenty-first century. "It's a fundamental truth," he insists, "that obstacles and opportunities are almost always two sides of the same coin [. . .] The workable solutions come from the community."

At its peak population of 1,849,568, according to the 1950 Census, in the heyday of the American automobile industry, Detroit was America's fifth largest city, one of the nation's most dynamic industrial hubs, and a magnet for people from around the country and the world, including African Americans from the rural South seeking a better life. But changes in the global marketplace, the import of smaller, more fuel-efficient foreign vehicles, conflicts in the Middle East and the concomitant spike in the price of gas, and the decentralization and outsourcing of car manufacturing, among other factors, led to steady economic decline, a shrinking middle class, and urban decay. It all came to a head in 2013, when with a diminished population of some 700,000, the bottom finally fell out, and the city was compelled to file for bankruptcy.

Such dire straits took their toll on health. Among other municipal agencies, in the wake of bankruptcy the then Detroit Department of Health and Wellness Promotion was forced to suspend its activities and cede responsibility for vital health services to a private nonprofit entity. Problems multiplied. The city's infant mortality rate rose to above that of Mexico. Obesity became another pressing issue, aggravated by endemic poverty, inadequate public transportation in a sprawling urban environment, and an inequitable distribution network of fresh and healthy food. Violence soared. And worst of all, the public lost trust in city government.

Control of most public health services returned to the retooled department in 2014, shortly before Dr. El-Sayed took the wheel. The most pressing task at hand, in his view, is to lead the department's restructuring as "a paragon of effectiveness and transparency [. . .] so that it's about the people who own it," and in the process to "re-instill public confidence in the city's ability to care for its people." For the new director, it's a first step toward a long-term, more ambitious goal: "To focus on those places where health plays a role in intergenerational transmission of poverty," and thereby to "promote the healthy trajectories of future generations."

Dr. El-Sayed made time to outline the steps he is taking to realize his vision for a healthy and thriving Detroit in an on-the-go interview in April 2016, part of which was conducted, in true Motor City style, in his car en route to and from a meeting at City Hall.

COMBINING MEDICINE AND PUBLIC POLICY

At age thirty-one, Dr. El-Sayed is among the youngest, and most dynamic, individuals ever to run a department of health of a major American city. "There is," he acknowledges, "a naïve optimism you bring to your work when you're young."

The son of Egyptian immigrants, raised in Bloomfield Hills, a suburb just to the north of the city, he had what he described as "a deeply privileged life," but added that "dignifying those opportunities to me means being able to right inequities for all." A Michigander to the bone, he thrived socially and academically, playing high school football, that most American of sports, and spending summers with family in Egypt. He first experienced the sting of outright hostility as an Arab-American in the immediate wake of 9/11. After one taunt too many from a member of an opposing football team, he threw a punch. His coach took him aside and said, "You are going to be Abdul El-Sayed for the rest of your life, and you can decide to either use that as an excuse or a motivation." He took the message to heart.

Earning a BS with highest distinction from the University of Michigan (U-M), at Ann Arbor, where he double-majored in biology and political science, his plan was to become a surgeon. But public policy was never far from his mind. His father, an automotive engineer who came from modest circumstances in Alexandria, Egypt, and mother, who studied medicine there, later opting for a career as a psychiatric pediatric nurse practitioner in the United States, both outspoken opponents of the authoritarian regime in their native country, passed on a sense of social responsibility and a commitment to social change.

At U-M he came under the influence of epidemiologist Prof. Sandro Galea, who inspired him to focus on "the social factors that lead hazards to flare up into disasters." One of Professor Galea's postdocs conducted a study of the birth outcomes of Arab-American women and their infants in California following 9/11, documenting an alarming 50 percent surge in low birth weight. Troubled and intrigued, El-Sayed extended the study to Michigan, postulating that birth results would be better given the insulating presence of a large Arab-American community. (Wayne County, Mich., has the highest concentration of Arab-Americans in the country.) His premise proved correct. The public health bug bit.

Pursuing the first two years toward a combined MD/PhD in medicine and public health at U-M, he applied for and was awarded a prestigious Rhodes Fellowship to study public health at Oriel College/Nuffield Department of Population Health at Oxford University, where he earned a doctor of philosophy degree. His thesis was on "Inequalities in Obesity in England: An Agent-Based Systems Approach," a computer simulation modeling of the problem that would later come in handy back home in Detroit.

Upon his return to Michigan, after learning that his mentor, Prof. Galea, had been appointed chair of the Department of Epidemiology at the Mailman School of Public Health at Columbia University, El-Sayed applied and was admitted to the MD/PhD Program at P&S. Parallel to his medical studies, he pursued postdoctoral research in epidemiology under Prof. Galea at Mailman, still intending to pursue residency training and become a surgeon.

In 2012, he was awarded a Paul & Daisy Soros Fellowship to New Americans in support of his graduate studies.

THE PATIENT THAT TIPPED THE SCALES
TO PUBLIC HEALTH

An experience on a subinternship in internal medicine at the Allen Pavilion with one patient in particular, an older African American woman who had fallen and hit her head in a state of inebriation, proved pivotal. The house staff in the ER saw her and after putting a dressing on the wound intended to discharge her. But the young medical student suspected underlying issues. "Nope, you didn't do a fair assessment!" he protested and used various ploys to keep the patient in the hospital, including holding up on completing the patient history and physical, pending her alcohol withdrawal. Ultimately he succeeded in convincing his immediate superiors to admit the patient, who as it turned out, suffered from adrenal insufficiency brought on by HIV-AIDS. Following basic medical treatment, he arranged for her transfer to a rehabilitation facility that admitted individuals with AIDS. But on the day before her discharge, she suddenly announced that she was going home with her daughter. He urged her to try rehab, but she insisted she'd be alright. Two weeks later he found her sleeping on a bench on the subway. Disgusted by an outcome he perceived as a direct function of "systems of failure," he decided to pull his application for residency and embrace public health.

"The safety net failed her," he concluded. "She made bad decisions adversely affecting her health, but there are a lot of things that we could have done to put this person into a better decision-making mode. The best you can do at a hospital is to stabilize one patient at a time, but you're not dealing with big picture problems that are creating the health disparities. I realized that I was a lot more interested in what happens before a patient gets to the door than what happens in the hospital." While still a doctor at heart, with a surgeon's hands-on desire to intercede and make things right, he was determined to have a hand in altering the big picture.

In 2014, Dr. El-Sayed was appointed assistant professor in the Department of Epidemiology at the Mailman School of Public Health. There he pursued studies in prevention science, the social cost of psychopathology and drug use, and the health of Arab-American New Yorkers, among other areas. He taught courses in systems science and population health, systems thinking, and principles of epidemiology. "I wanted to be a researcher," he said, "because I thought research could move policy." But he grew disillusioned and frustrated with academia, writing papers, raising grants, with limited tangible results. "What I'm really interested in," he realized, "is building institutions, building ideas, making things happen."

Michigan-born friends who had returned to take jobs under the then newly elected Detroit mayor, Mike Duggan, a former director of the Detroit Medical Center, spoke of the can-do attitude and accomplishments of the new administration, including the installation of 62,000 street lights, success in fighting urban blight, and in bringing EMS response time back down from nearly an hour to eight minutes. Hearing that they were looking for a new health director, he decided to apply, and despite his youth and limited experience, he landed the job. And following "a couple of hard conversations" with his wife, Sarah Jukaku '15, then a resident in psychiatry at Cornell, who remained in New York pending her transfer to a psych residency program at U-M Ann Arbor, he took the leap, relishing "the opportunity to come back home to help rebuild the collapsed health infrastructure and make it work."

A "SOCIETAL SURGEON" INTENT ON REDRESSING
HEALTH DISPARITIES

"Sometimes I do wish that the entire field of scope of my job was entirely under my hands," says Dr. El-Sayed. "And in some ways, my role is to perform societal surgery. We know what we want to accomplish, but the task is far more complex. Rather than digging around in fascia and tissue, you're digging through the bowels of bureaucracy and social entities, coordinating various perspectives to come up with a workable solution to seek an outcome that sometimes will take a long time to accomplish and sometimes will happen immediately."

The swift solutions are, of course, the sweetest.

Case in point. When the Marathon Refinery, located in Southwest Detroit, sought permission to increase emission of sulfur dioxide, Dr. El-Sayed stepped into action. Southwest Detroit, a heavily industrial part of town and one of the city's poorest neighborhoods, was already burdened with the public health consequences of pollution. "Mayor Duggan and I recognized that this was an opportunity to advocate for a community that has been largely left in the dust," he says. With the mayor's blessing, Dr. El-Sayed drafted an op-ed piece published on the day of the company's planned public hearing. Five hundred people turned out for this and a subsequent hearing, at which the mayor and his health director were also present, and testimony of the public health consequences of higher levels of pollution was presented. As a result, Marathon rethought their plan and voluntarily invested $10 million in an effort to reduce SO_2 emissions. "That came on the back of our efforts, those of the community, the mayor and myself, and that's pretty incredible," Dr. El-Sayed said.

As a vote of confidence in the importance of public health and the effectiveness of Dr. El-Sayed's efforts, in 2016 Mayor Duggan's administration added $4 million in city funding to the department's budget.

"There are very few jobs where you actually see the fruit of your labor so quickly," he said, but conceded that there is much still to be done.

"When public health works best it develops non-stories, non-events," he adds. The introduction and maintenance of clean drinking water, for instance, one of public health's most notable accomplishments in the course of the last century, has had a prodigious effect on promoting wellness. "It's an accomplishment society tends to take for granted," he says. The Detroit Health Department, under his direction, secured a $135,000 grant to test for lead in the water in public schools, ascertaining high levels, a serious health hazard.

But clean drinking water is only one among many pressing challenges to general wellness in Detroit. Infant mortality, endemic obesity, a staggering incidence of murder and violent crime, and high rates of teen pregnancy, a significant factor in the perpetuation of poverty, continue to plague the inner city.

To address the latter issue, the Detroit Health Department, under his direction, has partnered with Wayne State University in support of a mentoring program between senior or seasoned mothers and younger pregnant women. In addition, a group prenatal care program also run out of Wayne State, called "Make Your Date," stretches sparse financial resources by having six women meet for consultation and counseling with a single doctor for an hour, instead of having each rush through a ten-minute medical consult. The Department is also committed to promoting "whoops proof" methods of contraception. "Preventing teen pregnancy is a way to save two children's lives, that of the unwanted baby and that of the teen who, if she becomes pregnant, is far less likely to finish high school. If we can't diminish teen pregnancy," Dr. El-Sayed insists, "then what we're doing is condemning a whole next generation to the poverty that the earlier generation suffered."

Another key priority is the social reintegration of seniors. "We have a large trove of wisdom that doesn't get put to good use, because we in many ways have cut off our seniors, rather than value and tap them for their store of knowledge and experience."

TOWARD THE IDEAL OF THE "TWENTY-MINUTE" NEIGHBORHOOD

While obesity plagues many parts of the country, the sprawling size of Detroit, a city built around car culture but with very little car access for many in its low-density, low-income, inner city population, aggravates the issue. The problem, according to Dr. El-Sayed, is "how to foster walkable neighborhoods and safe access to healthy food. [. . .] We're really thinking about how you can move green leafy vegetables, the kinds of foods that are part of a healthy diet, into and around the city." The Department is working closely with sustainable urban farms in Metro Detroit, but the challenge remains: "How do you transport healthy food to where the people are, how do you engage local food providers to be more thoughtful about the range of foods they offer, and how do you make it affordable?" Rather than blame people for "bad food choices," Dr. El-Sayed prefers to help foster opportunities for good choices.

"Our city is starting to coalesce around a vision of what we call a 'twenty-minute neighborhood,' that is, a neighborhood in which your daily and even weekly needs are found within 20 minutes of where you live," he explains. "That's a walkable neighborhood with immediate access to healthy food, social cohesion, and community activities."

In the 1960s at its peak, Detroit's health department was run out of one central location. But Dr. El-Sayed believes in "moving public health into the neighborhoods where Detroiters live, work, and play. The solutions must come from the community. We're going to have to use the challenges we face, to build them into the way Detroit rebuilds itself." Among the government vehicles set in place by Mayor Duggan to facilitate a productive dialogue is a district manager program, whereby locally based district managers appointed by the mayor, individuals with roots in the community, act as a direct liaison to the people.

Dr. El-Sayed also sees great promise in a departmental initiative, a health fair, at which health-related problems are aired and discussed and solutions sought at the community level.

RESHAPING THE WAY THE PEOPLE OF DETROIT THINK ABOUT THEIR HEALTH DEPARTMENT

He is proudest of his behind-the-scenes role in building a team of committed experts and programs to address such pressing issues as asthma, lead, infant mortality, teen pregnancy, and chronic disease, particularly among the elderly, and of his efforts to "rebrand and reshape the way the people of Detroit think about their health department." Though the task remains daunting and the department is still underfinanced," his job, as he sees it, "is to make sure that health is thought through as a value when government makes decisions in a way that allows for the best possible equitable and sustainable health outcomes."

An attentive reader, inveterate coffee drinker, and avid sports fan, Dr. El-Sayed works out regularly: "Can't be preaching something you don't practice."

"Health," he points out, "is uniquely something that everybody can appreciate. We all know the pain of either suffering bad health ourselves or having somebody we love suffer. We might disagree about how we go about promoting wellness, but nobody is fine with the fact that some people are really sick. And so public health creates a great spear to foster reflection about how we ought to live as a society."

THE UNRETIRING DEAN OF AMERICAN RHEUMATOLOGISTS

EPHRAIM P. ENGLEMAN '37

Still going strong until age 102, Ephraim Engleman '37, rheumatologist extraordinaire, continued to consult with selected patients, run the Rosalind Russell Medical Research Center, renamed the Rosalind Russell-Ephraim Engleman Medical Research Center for Arthritis in his honor, and stroke the strings of his prize Stradivarius. He died in 2015, at age 104.

THINK OF George Burns minus the cigar. At ninety-eight and counting, Ephraim P. Engleman '37, the dean of American rheumatologists, cautions against overexercising and early retirement. "I used to recommend retirement to my patients, but now I think it's a big mistake. It's important to keep active. As you can see from where I'm sitting"—he chuckles from his desk chair in the director's office of the Rosalind Russell Medical Research Center for Arthritis at the University of California, San Francisco (UCSF), founded in 1979—"I still run the show!"

The first rheumatologist to set up practice in the San Francisco Bay Area after World War II, in 1947 Dr. Engleman joined the clinical faculty at UCSF (where is now the oldest tenured professor) and helped shine the light of medical science on the treatment of joint diseases, a heretofore largely overlooked field. As chair in the mid-1970s of the National Commission on Arthritis, a Congressionally mandated task force, he was instrumental in the creation of the National Institute of Arthritis, Musculoskeletal and Skin Diseases. The Commission also recommended, and Congress approved, the establishment of multipurpose arthritis centers for research and education, like the Rosalind Russell Center. As president of the American Rheumatism Association (now the American College of Rheumatology), he effectively pursued

private philanthropic support for arthritis research. And as president of the International League Against Rheumatism, he led several delegations to China. Few individuals have done so much to ease the chronic ache of arthritis and other joint diseases.

Nine decades into the game, you'd think he might feel inclined to sit back and bask in the glory of past accomplishments. Not so Dr. Engleman. The Rosalind Russell Medical Research Center remains his base of operations, where he sees selected patients three days a week. Also a talented musician, he gives his nimble fingers a serious work out every Monday night on the strings of his Stradivarius (Engleman Strad II) in a local string quartet.

The interview on which this profile is based took place at his hilltop office in San Francisco in January 2009.

"ENJOY YOUR LIFE'S WORK, WHATEVER IT IS, OR DON'T DO IT!"

The bushy eyebrows bounce and the eyes sparkle as Dr. Engleman offers the interviewer, more than four decades his junior, a tried and true prescription for happy and healthy longevity: "Be sure to select parents with the right genes.

Choose the right spouse. Encourage sex. Children are an option. Enjoy your life's work, whatever it is, or don't do it."

Born in San Jose, Cal., on March 24, 1911, Ephraim P. Engleman began his professional life as a musician. A violin prodigy at age six, he became the talk of the town when, after breaking a string at his first recital, he kept his cool and went right on playing. At seventeen he landed a job playing in an orchestra in the pit of a local silent movie theater and soon graduated to master of ceremonies of a vaudeville show. Fiddling helped put him through Stanford, where he earned his bachelor's degree. But the writing was already on the wall, or rather, fading from the screen. Al Jolson's first talking picture, *The Jazz Singer*, released in 1927, soon made the movie theater orchestra an anachronism and put an abrupt end to young Eph Engleman's show business aspirations. Though he never mothballed his bow and fiddle, music became a passionate avocation and the stethoscope took center stage.

His showbiz background proved both a handicap and a boon his first year at P&S, where he initially struggled through the basic sciences. But he caught up quickly, and playing chamber music with members of the faculty, including the distinguished pathologist Dr. Hans Smetana, and the chemist Dr. Hans Clarke, helped smooth the transition. Legend has it that, not being able to find a suitable place to practice, they harmonized in the PH morgue. Among other teachers, the young Dr. Robert Loeb, then a junior member of the faculty in the Department of Medicine, made a profound impression with his diagnostic skills, his encyclopedic medical knowledge, and bedside manner: "He taught us how to listen to a heart, and listen to the patient too." Dr. Engleman firmly believes that his experience as a performer enhanced his ability to interact with patients.

His class was the first to stage a senior class show, of which he wrote and performed many of the musical numbers. (He still writes and performs in original shows for a thespian club to which he belongs.)

OF MUSICAL MURMURS AND OTHER EARLY HIGH NOTES

Returning to San Francisco to pursue his internship and residency at UCSF, Dr. Engleman thereafter went back east to Boston to train at the Joseph H. Pratt Diagnostic Hospital, then an affiliate of Tufts University. While in Boston, he heard a lecture by Dr. Walter Bauer, a pioneer in academic rheumatology at the Harvard affiliate Massachusetts General Hospital, and resolved to apply for a much sought-after fellowship.

A raconteur par excellence, Dr. Engleman tells the story with great gusto. "We weren't sitting around for more than two or three minutes when somebody came in and said, 'Dr. Bauer, ward rounds are about to start.' " Invited to participate, Dr. Engleman jumped at the chance. "We came over to a patient who had a musical heart murmur. It's a very rare thing, but when you listen to it, it's a distinct note . . . Well I happen to have had perfect pitch . . . They were doing a phonocardiograph, which measures the number of vibrations the tone makes. Now a concert A, which is what a concert violinist tunes up with, is 440 vibrations. The note I heard was a little sharper, like an A-sharp . . . And not being very shy"—Dr. Engleman smiles—"I said, 'I can predict how many vibrations are in that phonocardiogram, 500. Well I hit it right on the button. Dr. Bauer turned to me and said, 'We don't need to bother with an interview, you've got the job.' So that's the way I became a rheumatologist."

Training with Dr. Bauer, Dr. Engleman also collaborated on research. Among their most celebrated findings was the description of a condition consisting of arthritis, conjunctivitis, and urethritis first written up in Germany by Dr. Hans Reiter. Drs. Bauer and Engleman were the first in the United States to describe the malady, subsequently called Reiter syndrome. (Years later, upon learning that Dr. Reiter was a notorious Nazi doctor who conducted unconscionable experiments on concentration camp inmates, Dr. Engleman argued for the deletion of Reiter's name from the syndrome.) Dr. Engleman also coauthored (with Dr. Julius Schachter) the first studies associating chlamydia with Reiter syndrome.

When America entered World War II, Dr. Engleman immediately signed up and was assigned to the Rheumatic Fever Center at Torney General Hospital in Palm Springs, Cal., of which he subsequently became the chief. In that capacity he directed groundbreaking clinical research on adult rheumatic fever. At the time, rheumatic fever was generally regarded as a disease of children, uncommonly seen in adults. In Palm Springs he reconnected with his old P&S professor and chamber music partner, Dr. Hans Smetana, who was also stationed there. They met two or three evenings a week to play violin-piano sonatas.

RHEUMATOLOGY THEN AND NOW

In a 2005 interview published in the *Arthritis Progress Report*, the newsletter of the Rosalind Russell Medical Research Center for Arthritis, Dr. Engleman described standard treatment at Mass General for rheumatoid arthritis in 1940: "The waiting room was filled with RA patients in wheelchairs. We had little to offer them other than prolonged bed rest [. . .] and physical therapy to try to minimize deformity and preserve as much motion as possible, and a huge dose of aspirin for pain."

"Real research leading to progress of our understanding of arthritis and other joint diseases," he points out, "has only developed in the last twenty-five to thirty years."

The drug that fundamentally changed the rules of the game was, of course, cortisone, introduced by Dr. Philip S. Hench, of the Mayo Clinic, in 1949 at an historic international congress in New York hosted by the American Rheumatism Association. Dr. Engleman was present at the session and recalls the hush in the crowd and the jubilation that followed when Dr. Hench showed a film of a rheumatoid arthritis patient unable to rise out of her chair, who, twenty-four hours after being injected with cortisone, practically leapt up. "The result was startling. A standing ovation followed." Dr. Hench won the 1950 Nobel Prize in Physiology or Medicine.

An enthusiastic proponent of cortisone in moderate doses, Dr. Engleman was among the first to administer it orally to his patients with great success. "In the old days I had a bunch of cortisone, which was in vials, you know, for injection," he says. "I would lift off the cap, mix it with some fruit juice, and give it to my patients. And it worked fine."

Revolutionary procedures in orthopedic surgery proved another great boon to the field. "I think joint replacement is a really big advance in the treatment of certain types of arthritis," Dr. Engleman observes. "When I was getting my training at Mass General, it was very common to see people on gurneys or in wheelchairs at the clinic. You just don't see that anymore. And one major reason is orthopedic surgery."

The so-called "biologic" drugs introduced in the last decade have also proved very effective, he adds, though not without some potentially serious side effects, notably compromising the patient's immunity. "I see younger physicians sometimes jumping the gun and prescribing these new drugs, in my opinion, prematurely. I'm frequently criticized because I'm too conservative. That's okay. Caution comes with experience. Criticism is the province of youth."

In 1962 Dr. Engleman was named president of the American Rheumatism Association, in which capacity he actively promoted support for research. Three years later he was named clinical professor of medicine at UCSF, where he subsequently served as president and cofounder of the Association of Clinical Faculty. And in 1967 he became president of the National Society of Clinical Rheumatologists. His clinical expertise and remarkable inspirational ability to draw attention to the field soon catapulted him into the public spotlight.

CHAIRING THE "JOINT" COMMISSION AND
RUNNING THE ROSALIND RUSSELL CENTER

Dr. Engleman's single-most significant accomplishment in rheumatology was the leadership role he played as chair of the eighteen-member National Commission on Arthritis, convened in 1974 by the U.S. Congress to document "the enormous medical, social, and economic consequences of arthritis on patients and on society in general," as he wrote in an historic overview published in 1977 in the journal *Arthritis & Rheumatism*.

After holding extensive public hearings around the country, the Commission's specific recommendations for action included the creation of an NIH institute exclusively for arthritis. "We almost got it. They added on dermatology. So now we have the National Institute of Arthritis and Musculoskeletal and Skin Diseases."

Another important recommendation accepted by Congress was the creation of multipurpose arthritis centers, with research, educational and epidemiological programs, and data systems scattered at academic institutions throughout the country.

Among the first of these to be established was the Rosalind Russell Medical Research Center for Arthritis at UCSF, which Dr. Engleman has directed ever since its founding in 1979. The Center is named for the most public face of the Commission, actress Rosalind Russell, who contracted arthritis and became an outspoken and effective advocate for funding for research in rheumatology. Her signed photograph hangs on his office wall. The Center, one of the most respected in the country, has trained more than 100 rheumatology fellows. Among other research conducted here was the bench work leading to the introduction of the new drug abatacept, a powerful biological agent for treating rheumatoid arthritis. The Center also conducted important research showing striking gender differences in the diagnosis and treatment of rheumatic disease.

Dr. Engleman is particularly proud of his ability to attract philanthropic funding for the Center's programs and activities, including the establishment of three chairs in rheumatology.

Author of more than 100 professional publications, Dr. Engleman collaborated with another Commission member, Milton Silverman, the former head science writer for the *San Francisco Chronicle*, on a widely read work for the general public, *The Arthritis Book: A Guide for Patients and Their Families*.

In 1981, he was named president of the International League Against Rheumatism. In that capacity he led three medical delegations to China, where he helped establish the Chinese Rheumatism Association.

OF FIDDLES AND FAMILY

In addition to playing the violin, Dr. Engleman is a discriminating collector of rare instruments, including two Stradivarii that bear his name (the first of which he has since sold) and two prized fiddles by Giuseppe Guarneri del Jesu. The instrument dubbed Engleman Stradivarius I was on display in 1987 in Cremona, Italy, the birthplace of its maker, at an exhibit commemorating the 250th anniversary of his death. Both of Dr. Engleman's Guarneri del Jesus were included in an exhibit at the Metropolitan Museum of Art in 1994 that marked the 250th anniversary of that master's death. "I have had over the years eight or nine great violins. It's a great thrill and a great privilege for me to be able to play these instruments," he says.

Among the key factors that have helped the fiddler himself remain fine-tuned is a happy family life. Married for sixty-eight years and counting to his wife, Jean, they have three children and six grandchildren. His older son, Philip, is chief of pathology and laboratories at Santa Teresa Kaiser Hospital in San Jose. His second son, Edgar, a P&S graduate, Class of 1971, is professor of medicine and pathology at Stanford. His daughter Jill is married to a gastroenterologist, and a granddaughter, Jenny Roost, is a gastroenterologist at the Palo Alto Medical Clinic.

Best of all, Dr. Engleman reports, "we all live within thirty or forty miles of each other and meet at least once a week for dinner."

A NAMED PROFESSORSHIP AND OTHER WELL-EARNED "GOODIES"

"The longer you live the more goodies you receive," Dr. Engleman jokes. His encomia have included honorary memberships in the rheumatology societies of Australia, France, Japan, Spain, and Uruguay. He has been visiting professor at countless institutions. The American College of Rheumatology awarded him the Presidential Gold Medal, their highest honor. Back home at UCSF, he received the Medal of Honor, the school's most prestigious award, a tribute topped off by the establishment of the Ephraim P. Engleman Distinguished Professorship in Rheumatology.

His old friend and erstwhile colleague Dr. Lee Goldman, former chair of the Department of Medicine at UCSF and currently the Executive Vice President for Health and Biomedical Sciences and Dean of the Faculties of Health Sciences and Medicine at P&S, was delighted to officiate at the P&S Gala in New York at which Dr. Engleman received the 2007 Alumni Gold Medal for Excellence in Clinical Medicine.

In Dr. Goldman's words, "No one has done more for rheumatology and with more grace than Eph Engleman. Like a maestro on the violin, which he is, he has pulled the strings that have shaped modern approaches to arthritic diseases."

Those who remember the irrepressible Dr. Engleman, then a mere ninety-six, prancing to the podium with a lively spring in his step to accept the award, will be pleased to know that, aside from a little back trouble, he is still at the top of his form. His joie de vivre is infectious. "Be happy and lucky," he recommends. "And above all, keep breathing!"

FROM STUDENT TO SURGEON TO UNIVERSITY TRUSTEE—A COLUMBIA JOURNEY

KENNETH FORDE '59

Ever committed to the highest standards of medical practice and academic excellence, though retired from the practice of surgery, Dr. Forde continues to educate and advise in his capacity as trustee of Columbia University and longstanding chair of the P&S Alumni Association Honors and Awards Committee.

—◆◆◆—

"RACE," SAYS Kenneth A. Forde'59, the José M. Ferrer Professor of Surgery Emeritus at P&S, citing his great-grandmother, "is something you *run* . . . and *win*." In the course of his forty-year marathon sprint as a member of the Department of Surgery, for much of which time he was the only African American on the medical school faculty, Dr. Forde rose to the highest ranks of his field of gastrointestinal and colorectal surgery, helping to launch diagnostic and surgical endoscopy as an academic discipline and educating a generation of leaders in it along the way. Barely pausing to catch his breath following his official retirement in 2005, he took up a new torch two years later as a member of the Columbia University Board of Trustees. Dr. Forde looked back on his long career and forward to the future of his calling and the University in an interview over lunch at the Donald F. Tapley Faculty Club in September 2007.

"GO GET HIM SURGEONS!"

"It was Shakespeare who inspired me to pursue surgery," he says, only half tongue in cheek, with a telling twinkle in the eye. Born in New York City to immigrant parents from Barbados, who sent him back to the Caribbean island, then a colony

of Great Britain, for his primary and secondary schooling, he was bathed in the words of the bard. Memorizing *Macbeth* at St. George's Church Boys School, in Barbados, he heeded Duncan's call: "So well thy words become thee as thy wounds;/ They smack of honour both. Go get him surgeons." (The oratory was not lost on Dr. Forde, who is famed for keeping surgical residents on their toes with Shakespeare soliloquies and colleagues and alumni on the edge of their seat with his eloquence.) Honor would indeed come his way, but not without insidious wounds.

Returning to the States to pursue higher education, he earned a BS cum laude at the City College of New York (CCNY), while holding down two jobs, including a night stint as an orderly at New York Hospital. At CCNY he got his first taste of teaching as an assistant in biology. Fueled by the confidence instilled by his family and by the example of an ophthalmologist cousin in Canada, he was determined to pursue the study of medicine. A black clergyman, teacher and family friend counseled him "to be realistic" about his limited possibilities as a man of color. Forget about medicine, he was told, plan on becoming a teacher. He listened politely and redoubled his resolve: "I never made much of discouragement, I just worked." The same clergyman later gave him a doctor's bag with a card inside that said: "This is so you don't turn back."

But racism reared its ugly head in the OR at New York Hospital, where well-intentioned nurses had arranged for the young premed student moonlighting as an orderly to observe an operation. The illustrious surgeon took one look at his complexion and sent him out of the operating room. The pain of the memory is still evident these many years later in a downcast look and a catch in his throat. It takes a moment for the words to return: "But I learned early on that you have to know how not to accept denial of privilege, or to get caught up in confrontation or blame, but find a way to get around it and overcome it." Overcome it he did, time and again. "I lived to return to Cornell as a visiting professor!" he laughs, the twinkle back in his eyes.

Yet for all his hard work and proven academic excellence, his premedical advisor at City College discouraged him from applying to top-level schools. "Of course, once I got into P&S," he adds, "I became the darling of the City College faculty, who had only the occasional student accepted there in those years."

ANATOMY, ABSCESSES, AND OTHER THRILLS

"It was a very different Columbia that accepted him into the Class of 1959," John T. Herbert, II '73, former senior associate dean at Harlem Hospital, a former student, now colleague and friend, recalled in a book of salutes prepared on the occasion of Dr. Forde's retirement. "Very few obviously black Americans had the opportunity to apply, the nerve to compete, or the ability to succeed, but Ken had (and still has) all three."

The only African American in his class, Dr. Forde preferred to focus on the thrill of learning. In anatomy lab, he relished the instruction of a hand surgeon who came by once a week, bringing real hands-on knowledge and a whiff of the OR. "Fantastic! Fantastic! Fantastic!" Dr. Forde beams, the thrill still fresh as if it were yesterday. A subsequent surgical rotation fired his blood: "I remember the first abscess I incised and drained. That was a great thing. It's a good sign if you get excited by incisions and taking out stitches, as I've always told my students and residents."

In the Department of Surgery, he found a role model and mentor in David V. Habif '39: "I admired him, not only for his amazing technical ability but also for his ability to get involved in his patients' lives, to guide them and teach them." This pedagogical commitment profoundly impressed the young medical student. "Dr. Habif was teaching all the time, in the operating room, even at the scrub sink, wherever you saw him he was teaching. And he seemed a happy man." Following his example, Dr. Forde made teaching central to his own surgical mission: "I see surgery in a broader sphere. It's more than taking out a polyp that may or may not be cancerous. It's teaching the patient how he can adjust and accept and exploit and not be limited by challenges to his health. I'm obsessed by the idea of educating patients."

It was the physical as well as the innovative problem-solving aspect of surgery that excited Dr. Forde. "I liked tinkering, I liked manipulating things, I liked seeing results."

As a fourth-year student he did exceptionally well on a surgical rotation at St. Luke's Hospital and was encouraged by the surgical house staff to apply for an internship. But once again, a question of race—not the kind you run, but the kind that tries to run you to the ground—emerged as a factor. " 'Ken, everybody knows you've done a fantastic job here, and I'm giving you an A in the rotation,' " said the faculty member in charge of students, " 'but you know we've never had a black man on the house staff at this institution.' " And when Dr. Forde, nevertheless, showed up for the patient workup session at which internship applicants were appraised, the same professor simply dismissed him: " 'I think we know you well enough, Ken, so you don't have to stay. Goodbye!' " The memory once again triggers a catch in the throat: "Talk about humiliation!"

But again, he swallowed the pain, or rather reinvested it in fortitude, and calmly forged ahead. Seeking a mixed internship to enrich both his surgical skills and his grasp of medical principles, he applied to and was accepted at the prestigious First (Columbia) Division at Bellevue Hospital. His rotation on Medicine was under the direction of Nobel Laureate Dickinson W. Richards '23, whom he remembers as "a very kind, thoughtful, and helpful man." Upon his successful completion of the program, Dr. Richards gave him an autographed copy of his medical essays as a gift.

Dr. Forde subsequently pursued a combined residency in surgery—two years on the Columbia Division at Bellevue and two years at Presbyterian Hospital.

At Presbyterian, he scrubbed in under such luminaries as the great breast surgeon Dr. Cushman Haagensen. When one patient balked at the idea of a black surgeon working her up for surgery, Dr. Haagensen tartly replied: "He is a member of my team, and either you will be seen and examined by him or you can leave!" She left. But Dr. Haagensen held his ground.

Following two years of military service, as assistant chief of the Surgical Service at the 98th General (U.S. Army) Hospital in Neubrucke/Nahe, in Germany, Dr. Forde returned to Columbia P&S as an instructor in surgery and began his climb in the faculty ranks. His hospital appointments included positions at St. Vincent's, Bellevue, Delafield, Presbyterian, and Harlem Hospitals. At Harlem he was later named assistant director of surgery.

At Columbia-Presbyterian, he also came under the influence of Arthur B. Voorhees '46, whose discovery that synthetic tubes grafted into the dog's heart to bridge arterial gaps underwent the same endothelialization of the lumen as natural blood vessels revolutionized the field of vascular surgery. In addition to setting a sterling example in his technical perfection in the OR and meticulous record keeping, it was Dr. Voorhees who first encouraged Dr. Forde to enter the then-fledgling field of flexible endoscopy, the examination of a cavity, like the stomach or intestinal tract, with a scope.

His old mentor from medical school days, Dr. Habif, continued to play an important role in Dr. Forde's professional development at Columbia, helping him hone his endoscopic technique: "He taught me, when we did rigid sigmoid-oscopy, to position the patient and the instrument so that the endoscope falls in. Never think conceptually of pushing it, think of letting the bowel receive the instrument." Sound advice from a technical standpoint, it was also a profound lesson in humanity. "Dr. Habif was always thinking first and foremost of the patient—not how much *I*, the surgeon, can do, but how much accommodation can exist between these complicated arrangements to the comfort of the patient."

Dr. Forde would later make this kind of "accommodation" one of his guiding principles in the OR and the endoscopy suite. At each procedure he challenged himself to find the "configuration or maneuver that would allow the bowel to surrender and accept the scope." Foremost among the many "Fordeisms" known to generations of surgical residents at P&S is his famous line: "Accept the scope!" His long roster of devoted patients, many of whom still seek out his wise counsel in retirement, are proof of the quality of his care and the depth of his caring. Twice during the interview he excused himself to accept a phone call from a former patient and to offer advice.

To Dr. Forde, the patient comes first. Notwithstanding the pressures of his burgeoning practice, he always made sure to include an additional session for preprocedural discussion to educate and allay fears. One of the first surgeons to recommend a routine colonoscopy, or scoping of the large intestine, he likened it to "driving through a tunnel" to permit the patient to visualize the procedure and, so, be more relaxed. Nurses invariably marveled at the minimal sedation required by his patients, many of whom chose to watch what he was doing on the monitor.

SCOPING ON THE TODAY SHOW

Dr. Forde's growing reputation as a meticulous and caring endoscopic surgeon came to the attention of the producers of the popular NBC news program "The Today Show." Cohost Katie Couric, who had lost her husband to colon cancer, decided to educate the public to the risks of the disease with a special three-part series.

The second most-deadly condition in the United States, colon cancer is, ironically, one of the most preventable if caught and treated early on. The precancerous polyps are detectible and can be excised in a routine colonoscopy. But the idea in the popular imagination of the colon as a dirty organ and the angst aroused by the procedure keeps people from seeking out the life-saving screening.

Ms. Couric and Dr. Forde made television history when he performed a colonoscopy on her as the cameras rolled and she commented while watching him guide the scope on a monitor—thus demystifying the procedure for millions of Americans and resulting in a substantial increase in colon cancer screening.

THE ACADEMIC PRACTITIONER

An academic through and through, Dr. Forde always grounded his clinical practice in research: "I decided from the start that if I'm going to get anything out of what I was doing—I'm in a great academic medical center, after all—that I shouldn't just do it, but at the same time demonstrate whether it is useful and teach others how to do it." To that end he wrote a chapter for one of the earliest computer programs for surgical education. The coauthor of more than 125 scientific papers as well as countless abstracts and editorials, Dr. Forde was also the producer of a number of widely used educational videotapes on colonoscopy and other procedures.

He was a member of the research team that first recognized the increased prevalence of polyps in first-degree relatives of colon cancer patients, and consequently, strongly recommended screening. He coauthored two particularly provocative editorials, one that urged colonoscopy as a necessary procedure and another that stressed the lack of adequate criteria for discounting the cancerous potential of polyps. And though these papers later proved to be prophetic, they were misinterpreted by some at the time as a surgeon's attempt to push a procedure and tread on the professional turf of gastroenterologists. One of the few surgeon-members of the New York Society for Gastrointestinal Endoscopy, whose constituency comprises mostly gastroenterologists, he served as its president, and as such, helped build bridges between the disciplines.

Dr. Forde also pursued collaborative research with the late Dr. Bernard Weinstein and a young protégé in colorectal surgery, Dr. José Guillen, now at Memorial Sloan-Kettering and a professor of surgery at Cornell, examining the molecular markers for colon cancer, i.e., chemical substances released in the transformation from normal bowel to polyp and from polyp to cancer.

A VOICE FOR CHANGE

Early on in his career, Dr. Forde made it one of his educational missions to help open the gates of P&S to more qualified minority applicants. He served three terms on the P&S Admissions Committee over a span of three decades, helped screen candidates, and mentored countless members of the Black and Latino Student Organization. And while he is heartened by an evolution of consciousness in the society at large and at the University, as well as a strong commitment by President Lee Bollinger and P&S Dean Lee Goldman to bring in more talented minorities, there are still, he points out, only a handful of minorities on the faculty. He is also "disappointed that there aren't more of us in the basic sciences or in tenured positions. That's something I think the University has to catch up with, for the benefit of us all."

A former chief of the Gastrointestinal Surgery-Endoscopy Section of the General Surgery Service, among other administrative responsibilities he served for close to a decade as Vice Chair for External Affairs in the Department of Surgery.

In 1983 he was promoted to professor of clinical surgery, and in 1997 he became the José M. Ferrer '38 Professor of Clinical Surgery.

Internationally renowned, he has held visiting professorships at countless universities in the United States and abroad, and was the last visiting professor in the Department of Surgery at Pahlavi University in Shiraz, Iran, before the Shah was deposed.

SOCIETY MAN

Dr. Forde has been active outside the academy too. Committed to the importance of feasibility, safety, skill sharing, and the dissemination of knowledge in his field, he was one of the founders, and the second president, of the Society of American Gastrointestinal Endoscopic Surgeons. He also served as coeditor-in-chief of the society's journal, *Surgical Endoscopy*. In a booklet published in 1981 on the occasion of the Society's 20th anniversary, Dr. Forde was praised as "a vital force in the founding, the glue that held it together when it occasionally threatened to become uncoupled, and the force of wisdom and reason."

In 1986 he was named president of the New York Surgical Society, the second oldest surgical society in the nation. He was the first African American ever to hold that office. Dr. Forde was also a governor of the American College of Surgeons and a founding member of the American Trauma Society.

A strong believer in institutional traditions, he served as president of the John Jones Surgical Society, comprising the surgical alumni of Presbyterian Hospital, and was one of the most beloved and effective presidents of the P&S Alumni Association. As chair of the Association's Honors and Awards Committee, he has for years officiated as orator in residence at countless graduation galas and award ceremonies. As cochair of his medical school class since graduation, he has rallied their support. His ongoing devotion was recognized by a Columbia University Alumni Federation Medal and a Medal for Meritorious Service from the P&S Alumni.

A NAMED PROFESSORSHIP AND OTHER ENCOMIA

The recipient of innumerable honors, including the Townsend Harris Medal from the City College of New York, the Bohmfalk Award for Teaching, the Award for Humanism from the Arnold P. Gold Foundation, and the P&S Alumni Gold Medal for Excellence in Clinical Medicine, Dr. Forde was accorded the crowning academic compliment in 1996 when an endowed professorship in colon and rectal surgery was established in his name at Columbia.

"What really touched me about this honor," he says, "is that the initial interest and lead gift came, not from a wealthy patron, but from the Research Foundation of the American Society of Colon and Rectal Surgery," many of whose younger members he helped shepherd on their academic careers. "That was overwhelmingly meaningful." The same year he was named Practitioner of the Year by the Columbia-Presbyterian Medical Center Society of Practitioners.

In 2007, he was saluted as Alumnus of the Year by the Society of the Alumni of New York-Presbyterian Hospital/Columbia. Earlier in the year, the Columbia University Board of Trustees put their ultimate trust in him by inviting him to join their ranks. "I've gone from applicant to student, to intern, to resident, to attending and professor, and now to trustee," Dr. Forde affirms with a smile. "I'm not trying to be falsely modest, but it is indeed reassuring that the leaders of this university think I have something to contribute to its direction. We have our warts, like every other institution. But we are a great school with a solid background, a fascinating history of involvement in the nation and around the globe."

When asked to reflect on a Forde legacy, he speaks of his wife and life partner, Kay, his son, Trevor, and plucks out the photos of his two young granddaughters, with whom he plans to spend a lot more time. And then, with that inimitable twinkle in his eyes, he allows, "I hope that I have demonstrated my love for my fellow man by trying to be as informed as I could. But more than that, I hope I helped others. I have always thought that if I inspired even one person along the way, it would make it all worthwhile."

Whereupon his cell phone rings for another patient consultation.

FROM ENDOCRINOLOGY TO
ADMISSIONS, A LIFE IN MEDICINE

ANDREW G. FRANTZ '55

*Andrew Frantz '55, the longest-serving dean of admissions in the history of P&S,
who died on June 18, 2010, at age eighty, lived to see generations of physicians and
surgeons repay through their medical practice the trust he had placed in them.*

———

REFLECTING ON his role as associate dean and chair of the Admissions Committee at P&S, a position he has held for close to three decades, longer than
anyone else in the history of the medical school, Andrew G. Frantz '55 quotes
Banquo's charge to the witches in Shakespeare's *Macbeth*: "If you can look into
the seeds of time, /And say which grain will grow and which will not, / Speak
then to me . . ." His own forecasting skills have proven on the mark. "You can
often make very accurate predictions as to the trajectory of human life. You're
certainly not always right. But often you are."

OF HORMONES AND HOMER

A man of science and consummate culture, equally at home in the pituitary
gland and Plato, hormones and Homer, Dr. Frantz, professor of medicine at
P&S and former chief of the Division of Endocrinology at Presbyterian Hospital, considers each admissions interview a kind of Socratic dialogue, a potential learning experience for both the interviewee and the interviewer. While
carefully weighing a candidate's dossier, the grades, the test scores, the letters
of recommendation, and the personal statement, when in doubt he bases his

decision on whether to admit on one key question: "If *I* were sick, would I want this person to come into my room as my physician?"

A number of the "yeses" became his advisees and have since gone on to leadership positions in their chosen fields. A few became lifelong friends, among whom feelings for Dr. Frantz run strong.

One of those "accurate predictions," oncologist-writer Jerome Groopman '76, professor of medicine at Harvard Medical School, chief of experimental medicine at the Beth Israel Deaconess Medical Center, a regular contributor on medical matters to *The New Yorker* magazine, and the author of several soul-searching books, put it this way: "Andy Frantz was, and still is, a guiding light for me, as he is for so many of us fortunate to know him at P&S. He not only was a mentor in advising on classes and career but showed me the joy and fulfillment that come from the kind of doctoring that melds science with the soul in the care of every patient."

THE SCIENTIFIC SIDE OF A BIMODAL CAREER

After training in medicine at Presbyterian Hospital, where he later pursued a fellowship in endocrinology with Dr. Joseph Jailer, Dr. Frantz served for two years as a lieutenant commander in the Navy at the U.S. Naval Hospital in Memphis, Tenn. He subsequently joined the faculty in the Department of Medicine at Harvard Medical School, seeing patients and pursuing research in human growth hormone at the Endocrinology Unit at the Massachusetts General Hospital. At Harvard his lab devised a landmark radioimmunoassay on human growth hormone, helping to unravel the mystery of its physiology. Though invited to stay on in Boston, he had always envisioned his future at P&S. "I'm a New Yorker, I was born here, have family here, went to school here. I practically grew up at P&S. I always wanted to come back."

Dr. Frantz returned to New York and joined the Department of Medicine at P&S in 1966, and was named professor of medicine in 1973. In 1971, he took on the reins as the first chief of the newly established Endocrinology Division at Presbyterian Hospital, a position he held for the next seventeen years.

He is best known for the pioneering work he did on human prolactin, a heretofore neglected hormone secreted by the pituitary gland. Prolactin is involved in the generation of lactogenic activity in all mammals, including humans. Previously thought to be tied to human growth hormone, human prolactin had been ignored by researchers, some even doubting its existence as an independent entity, until Dr. Frantz's lab made the breakthrough discovery in 1970 that it is indeed present in human pituitaries and circulates in the blood as a molecule immunologically distinct from human growth hormone. Hypothesizing that the two hormones were so closely related in molecular structure that the latter might just have been missed, Dr. Frantz, working with dissected mouse breasts, devised a bioassay at least a hundred times more sensitive than the best previously existing assay, allowing for the phantom hormone's accurate measurement in human blood: "Adding a tiny amount of antihuman growth hormone antibody to the incubation mixture of sections of mouse breast in vitro, we found, would completely neutralize the activity of human growth hormone."

Some thirty years after the fact, his voice still quiets down to an intense whisper as he relives the thrill of discovery: "But it didn't tie up the lactogenic activity in the serum from nursing mothers. So, clearly, there must be something in the blood of nursing mothers which has all the properties of prolactin and is immunologically distinct from growth hormone . . . It took us about six months of testing to believe our own results," namely that he had successfully isolated and proven the existence of the missing hormone.

His paper, "Prolactin: Evidence That It Is Separate from Growth Hormone in Human Blood," coauthored with Dr. David Kleinberg, and published in the journal *Science*, took the scientific world by storm.

The discovery, it turned out, had major clinical implications. In subsequent studies, Dr. Frantz and his colleagues established the physiology of human prolactin and its role in producing pituitary tumors, of which it proved to be a dependable marker. It is the most abundant pituitary tumor in humans. Once detected, the tumor could be safely removed. This finding helped launch a new neurosurgical field and thereby improve the quality of countless lives.

Dr. Frantz's lab also established that "by giving a long-acting dopamine agonist, such as bromocriptine, we could lower prolactin to normal levels in almost all people who had too much of it, thus restoring normal menses and normal ovulation."

AT HOME IN THE LAB

Intrigued as a child by "explosions and things that smelled bad or turned green," effects he could produce with a toy chemistry set, he felt at home in the lab. "It was like being back in the nursery really, with all my playthings around me," Dr. Frantz chuckles, "I have always liked to fiddle with things." At age fourteen he wrote and typed up a short chemistry "textbook" complete with precise drawings of the apparatus involved in particularly dramatic experiments.

Science and, especially, biomedical research, were favorite subjects of conversation at the Frantz family dinner table, and P&S was the playing field. His parents had been medical school classmates, and both his father, Angus MacDonald Frantz '22, a psychiatrist-neurologist, and his mother, Virginia Kneeland Frantz '22, a surgical pathologist and the first woman to train in surgery at Presbyterian Hospital, taught on the faculty. An immensely popular professor and dynamic lecturer, she was also the coauthor of a widely used textbook, *Introduction to Surgery, Frantz and Harvey*. After his parents divorced, his mother remained a model and mentor, who "showed me how to live a fulfilled and happy life in medicine." His maternal uncle, Yale Kneeland '26, another popular member of the P&S faculty, a specialist in infectious diseases, mingled eloquence and wit with the scientific method, a mix that likewise influenced his nephew.

Espousing a humanistic approach to medicine as a science and an art, the family was also passionate about poetry and music. Dr. Frantz still plays violin and piano, protesting with a wry smile: "It was difficult for me to see why I couldn't get the piano to sound like Rachmaninoff. I don't like not being able to make the instrument sound as I know it ought to." An avid reader and rereader of the classics, Shakespeare and Plato remain his "constant close companions," from whose works he can quote at the drop of a hat, finding life-affirming wisdom in the words.

Earning his undergraduate degree at Harvard, where he majored in English, graduating magna cum laude, Dr. Frantz fondly recalls the chats he had with his mother over cocktails on Easter and Christmas breaks from college. "I still think that hour before dinner, over dry martinis, anticipating dinner and with nothing that we have to do, is one of the pleasantest times there is in life," he says. The conversation often turned to teaching and to his mother's unofficial role as a trusted counselor to students, a role he subsequently inherited upon joining the faculty. "My mother loved what she did, the research, the teaching and advising, and she communicated that passion to me." She also served on the Admissions Committee.

"I LIKE STUDENTS, AND I FEEL I'M STILL ONE AT HEART."

He still remembers his own medical student experience as if it were yesterday, including a first-year anatomy exam that initially shook his confidence and made him really dig in, henceforth rising daily at 4 A.M. to study. All the strains and thrills of student life are engraved in his mind. "For a long time I was a student in my dreams, worrying about an exam . . . waking in a cold sweat," he smiles. "I like students and I feel I'm still one at heart. This is why the admissions job has been so right for me. I can identify completely with the person sitting in that chair. I know what they're going through. And I'm also learning from them all the time."

A CALL TO ADMISSIONS

While he had served as a member of the Admissions Committee since first joining the faculty, research and teaching remained his primary focus until a fateful telephone call from the late dean of the faculty, Dr. Donald F. Tapley, in 1981 changed the course of his life. Dean Tapley informed him that the then head of Admissions had suffered a nervous breakdown, and asked if he would consider stepping in immediately as interim chair of the Admissions Committee. "You should bear in mind," Dr. Tapley pointed out, "this may well turn into something permanent."

"After thinking about it for about, I suppose, twenty milliseconds," Dr. Frantz recalls, "I said yes. It was the best thing that ever happened.

"You can always dream up experiments to confirm existing things, extend knowledge in ways that hadn't been fully explored. But I like to do the big stuff, if I can, and the new things. And I realized that a point might come when I just wouldn't have really good ideas. And I thought I could probably continue doing admissions work until I had about one neuron left."

"I KNOW I'M BEING INTERVIEWED TOO."

As dean of admissions, Dr. Frantz is in a certain sense the face of the medical school, or at least the first face many prospective candidates see: "I've learned that my job is not only picking out people, but also I'm a recruiter, I'm a salesman [. . .] But I'm not selling snake oil, I'm selling P&S. I want the admissions interview to be a positive experience, whatever the outcome. I know that I'm being interviewed too. I want the candidates to have a favorable impression of me and of this institution, because they're going to go back to whatever college and they're going to report on their experiences."

And though he has no set formula for each interview, he and his colleagues on the Admissions Committee know what they are looking for: "We want people who are certifiably smart, but we want them to have other interests and passions too. Brains alone don't make a great doctor."

He is a great proponent and supporter of the P&S Club, the oldest medical student activities organization in the country and among the most diverse, with some fifty-nine activities offered, including the Bard Hall Players, the medical school's celebrated student theatrical group: "It's a very good selling point for our school when applicants discover this wonderful resource. My gosh! There's no other school that puts on three full-scale productions every year."

Musical ability is also high on his list. "Last year there were four members of the class who had been concertmaster of the symphony orchestra at their respective universities."

One of the joys of his job has been learning to appreciate the strengths of people unlike himself, candidates from different backgrounds and with different abilities, particularly athletes. Though disinclined to toss a ball and not a fan of spectator sports, Dr. Frantz started attending P&S Rugby Team matches, and has seldom missed the annual John Wood '76 Memorial Tournament, of which P&S is a longtime champion. "The high spirits on the field are palpable," he says, the smile lines radiating from his eyes and across his forehead. "These guys are having the time of their lives."

A number of his athletically inclined picks have gone on to become national leaders in orthopedics and other fields.

So what makes an ideal P&S candidate, according to Dr. Frantz?

"There are three qualities doctors have to have. They have to be bright, of course, brighter than average. Then they have to be motivated, really motivated. But they also have to want to do good in this world."

The admissions process is arduous for both the candidate and the dean of admissions. For years Dr. Frantz put in entire weekends, reading dossiers way into the wee hours of the night. As of October 2009, he shares some of the workload with Dr. Stephen W. Nicholas, Professor of Clinical Pediatrics at P&S and Professor of Clinical Population and Family Health at the Mailman School of Public Health, the newly appointed assistant dean for admissions at P&S.

"THE WORD *DOCTOR* MEANS TEACHER IN LATIN."

The author of more than 150 papers and book chapters, Dr. Frantz is the recipient of many honors, including the Distinguished Teacher Award at P&S and the Gold Medal for Service to the Medical School and its Alumni Association, of which he is a past president.

Throughout his career, from the lab to the bedside, to the admissions office, he has embraced the educational role of the doctor. "The word *doctor* means teacher in Latin," he points out. "That's what we are trained and what we train medical students to do: to teach the patient. In the first place, we try to find out what they've got. Then we have to tell them about it. We've got to make them understand their disease or condition, but also help them to accept it, because there are still many diseases we can't cure and others we can't even alleviate."

Like his mother, he has also been devoted to the medical school and its student body. She established the Virginia Kneeland Frantz '22 Scholarship. He likewise set up a scholarship fund in his name. To Dr. Frantz, at age seventy-nine, it's not so much a matter of perpetuating his name—"What is it that Milton called *fame*? 'that last infirmity of noble minds.' "—but rather of supporting the institution to which he has given his all. Or as he put it in the title of his remarks at the first P&S Class Day in 2002: "Spirit is the Medical Center's legacy, students its future."

PRACTICING THE "ART OF THE POSSIBLE"— THE OUTGOING DIRECTOR OF THE CDC REFLECTS ON HIS TIME AT THE HELM

THOMAS R. FRIEDEN MD/MPH '86

Resigning in 2017 from his position as director of the Centers for Disease Control and Prevention, Thomas R. Frieden MD MPH '86 has since taken on the reins as president and CEO of Resolve to Save Lives, a global public health initiative committed to proven strategies of urgent action to improve health in low- and middle-income countries.

———

"PUBLIC HEALTH, like politics, is the art of the possible," according to Thomas R. Frieden MD/MPH '86, the outgoing director of the Centers for Disease Control and Prevention (CDC), America's first line of defense against threats to the health of its people. A self-described "irrational optimist," still trim and youthful at age fifty-six, Dr. Frieden is the second-longest serving director in the history of the CDC. "It certainly has been an exciting time," he allows of his tenure, 2009 to 2017, during which the Emergency Operations Center remained activated more than 90 percent of the time. Whether tackling outbreaks of such formidable microbial malefactors as H1N1, MERS, and Ebola, stopping epidemics in the making at home and abroad, confronting smoking and other key preventable causes of death, or convincing a recalcitrant Congress to allocate adequate funding to combat Zika, he has always held to the same basic credo: "Do the right thing, tell the truth, and things will come out okay."

In an interview in January 2017 at his office on the Centers' sprawling campus in Atlanta, he looked back on his eight years at the helm and considered the pressing health challenges still ahead.

FOCUS ON ACCOUNTABILITY

Among the photographs lining the wall along a corridor on the way to the director's office, two immediately catch the eye. One presents an individual covered from head to foot in yellow protective (PPE) gear being decontaminated after visiting an Ebola treatment unit in Monrovia, Liberia, with TOM scrawled in big bold letters on his hood. Another depicts a somber director touring a cemetery in Sierra Leone where safe and dignified burials are taking place. Between them they sum up the depth of Dr. Frieden's commitment to public health as a calling.

The son of a scientifically astute cardiologist, he recalls visiting his father in a nursing home toward the end of the latter's life. At the time, the younger Dr. Frieden had just been named New York City Commissioner of Health, a post to which he was appointed by then Mayor Michael Bloomberg and that he held from 2002 to 2009. "Dad," he said, "I want to be the best health commissioner." To which his father, a physician who had committed his own life to evidence-based medicine before the notion had a name, promptly replied with what would be his last words to his son: "How would you know?" The words have stuck with the son as a kind of medical mantra, a perennial call to accountability.

Ever since his first major foray into public health, 1990–1992, as an Epidemic Intelligence Service Officer assigned by the CDC to New York City, where he documented the spread of multidrug-resistant tuberculosis and then, by closely following every single case, he and his team helped cut the scourge of the dread disease by

80 percent, Dr. Frieden has tackled the big picture one patient at a time. Applying the same hands-on and doggedly systematic approach thereafter in India, 1996–2002, as a medical officer for tuberculosis control for the Southeast Asia Regional Office of the World Health Organization, on loan from the CDC, he and his team helped treat some 8 million patients, saving an estimated 1.4 million lives.

Called back to New York and sworn in January 2002 by Mayor Michael Bloomberg to head the NYC Department of Health and Mental Hygiene, he reportedly studied the City's health statistics the way an internist pores over his patient charts, on the lookout for significant data to stem preventable deaths. "We had 18,000 people under the age of sixty-five die in the City last year," he said in a previous interview conducted with this writer in 2005, "about 10,000 of them from clearly preventable causes." That was 10,000 too many fatalities for Dr. Frieden.

He initiated unprecedented health surveys to assess critical health conditions in the city, then released an ambitious, "Take Care of New York" policy to improve health. Based on verifiable data, and with Mayor Bloomberg's blessings, Dr. Frieden took the cause of preventable deaths as a public health call to arms. Among other bold initiatives, he set up a system to monitor tobacco use, pushed for an increase in the tobacco tax, produced aggressive anti-tobacco ads, promoted and ultimately helped pass the Smoke-Free Air Act of 2002, barring smoking from all work places in the City, including bars and restaurants. Based on a CDC report in 2007, such aggressive tactics paid off, leading to a significant reduction in the number of smokers, including an almost 50 percent decline in teen smokers. Under his aegis, the Health Department also launched a head-on attack against another preventable cause of death, banning all NYC restaurants from cooking with trans fats, a significant aggravating factor in heart disease.

The *New York Observer* dubbed him "a rare visionary." Mayor Bloomberg pulled out the stops in his assessment of his health commissioner's performance: "Hiring Tom Frieden was one of the best decisions I've ever made. [. . .] He is unafraid of big ideas, powerful interest groups, or impossible challenges," *Time Magazine* quoted the former mayor, including Dr. Frieden in its 2015 roster of "The 100 Most Influential People."

CONFRONTING H1N1 INFLUENZA, THE NEW CDC DIRECTOR HIT THE GROUND RUNNING

On May 15, 2009, President Barack Obama named Dr. Frieden the sixteenth director of the CDC. The new director hit the ground running, soberly assessing and leading the country's response to an impending global H1N1 influenza pandemic. "We're faced with a situation of uncertainty," he told reporters three days after officially assuming his post on June 8, 2009, in the first of many briefings, stating the facts while reassuring the public that "this is nowhere near the severity of the 1918 pandemic."

Reviewing established recommendations that favored the young as recipients of a monovalent flu vaccine, after considering the data he noted a significant health threat to fifty- to sixty-four-year-olds and subsequently modified the proposed vaccine policy to include that age group among the targeted cohort of recipients.

Dr. Frieden raised hackles at one press conference in which he was challenged to justify the delay in vaccine production contracted for by another part of the federal government. "The vaccine is grown in eggs," he calmly explained, "and even if you yell at the eggs, it won't grow any faster. We're not going to have enough vaccine when people want it. And then we'll have a lot left over after the peak of the outbreak." Reality check notwithstanding, and despite the delayed vaccine production, the CDC helped prevent an estimated one million cases, 18,000 hospitalizations, and at least 600 deaths. And whereas in retrospect some skeptics accused the director of crying wolf as to the gravity of the pandemic, Dr. Frieden soberly reminds that "there were 1,500 fatalities among children and might well have been many more had we not taken appropriate action."

"WE'RE MOST SUCCESSFUL WHEN WE'RE MOST INVISIBLE"

"Remember that big outbreak of MERS in the U.S.? No, because it didn't happen! We stopped it," he recalls with an unmistakable twinkle of pride, referring to Middle East Respiratory Syndrome Coronavirus, a potentially life-threatening illness first reported in Saudi Arabia in 2012. Two isolated cases of infected travelers from Riyadh were diagnosed and successfully treated in the United States in 2014, and the CDC helped control outbreaks in the Middle East and elsewhere. "It could have been a big outbreak," he adds, "if we didn't have diagnostics and we hadn't educated doctors and worked with the health care system to be ready."

"I sometimes get asked: Why should the CDC work on global health? Shouldn't we rely on the World Health Organization for that?" Dr. Frieden poses the question. To which he promptly replies: "Well, why do we need the Department of Defense if there are United Nations peacekeepers? The CDC works 24/7 to protect Americans from threats, whether in this county or anywhere in the world, whether those threats are infectious or environmental, natural or manmade."

In today's global environment, there is no such thing as an isolated incident. It's only a matter of time until microbes and other serious health risks cross borders. The least costly defense in lives and dollars saved is preparedness. "When you strengthen the systems that are in place, the laboratories, the doctors in the field, the monitoring and the rapid response abilities," Dr. Frieden reminds, "you can stop outbreaks there so that we don't have to fight them here. It's doing well by doing good. Public health really is a best buy."

He prizes the efficacy of established preventive stratagems like the Field Epidemiology Training Program (FETP), currently comprising some fifty-five working operations in seventy-two countries. It's a network of programs started by the CDC, many of which now function independently. This effort, greatly enhanced under his watch, has helped train some 3,000 local disease detectives to date, "so that they can do what we do." In Dr. Frieden's view, "it may well be the single most important program we run globally." Nigeria, for instance, thanks to the hard work and thoroughness of local CDC-trained field workers, is practically polio free, with the exception of a small area controlled by Boko Haram.

"We're most successful when we're most invisible," the director avows. Inevitably, however, some dire health conditions make the news.

EBOLA—"ON THE EDGE OF AN ABYSS"

"The Ebola outbreak was the most stressful and challenging threat that I've dealt with as CDC director, "Dr. Frieden reflects. "Not Ebola in the U.S.," he insists, much as the public health threat stateside was whipped up to a fever pitch by some politicians and members of the media. "We always said there could be some cases and it would be controlled, and that's exactly what happened."

It was the situation in Africa, where the CDC sent some 1,400 trained personnel, and to which he himself made four trips in the course of the epidemic, that really worried him. "I visited one Ebola hospital where there were sixty corpses of people who'd died there that couldn't be removed, so the living had to lie next to the dead. There was one doctor for 120 patients, not enough food, not enough water. It was a horrific, really an apocalyptic type of situation. But that wasn't what frightened me the most.

"When one infected individual flew from Liberia to Lagos, Nigeria, with a population of more than 20 million," he recalls with a chill, "it could have easily surged into a global catastrophe."

Following an initial incompetent handling, a new Nigerian incident manager was put in charge and members of the same CDC-trained Nigerian FETP crack team that had helped stop polio leaped into action, building an Ebola treatment unit in fourteen days. Identifying 894 contacts, they performed 17,000 home visits, found forty-three people with suspected Ebola, diagnosing nineteen cases. The same painstaking process had to be repeated again when an infected individual traveled from Lagos to Port Harcourt.

Dr. Frieden shakes his head at the memory. You can almost hear his heart pounding: "Those three or four days when we were transitioning from not-competent to excellent management, those were the most stressful days of my eight years as director of the CDC! We knew we were on the edge of an abyss. If we didn't stop it there, it would have spread all over Nigeria, all over Africa, for months and possibly years, and could have become a global catastrophe!"

Ultimately, the system functioned. "We got one laboratory up and running in Sierra Leone that worked for 421 days without a break. They set up in the field, high-throughput robotics, and performed 27,000 Ebola tests. Every worker risked infection and death." Dr. Frieden adds with unabashed awe: "The commitment of our staff and trainees is truly inspiring!"

ZIKA, A LOOMING THREAT

While the world could declare victory in the battle with Ebola, another insidious threat of infectious disease still looms elsewhere in the *Aedes aegypti* mosquito. "Zika has not been the media sensation that Ebola was, but it has been and continues to be an enormous challenge," Dr. Frieden says, remembering another bone-chilling moment in his tenure when the CDC's chief pathologist, Dr. Sherif Zaki, called him in to view stained neural tissue of infants from Brazil who had died of severe malformations. "We were able to see the Zika virus invading the neural tissue of these infants. It was really horrific!" he says. "Two days later we issued a travel warning, telling pregnant women not to go to areas where Zika was spreading."

The CDC kicked into action, engaging some 2,000 personnel in over 1,000 deployments to affected areas. They created a test, got it approved, and produced over one million test kits.

"We took the action and made a recommendation when the data was strong enough. We established an unprecedented pregnancy registry to track pregnant women with Zika in the U.S. and its territories. We recommended a modern strategy of mosquito control using ultra-low volumes of pesticide in targeted areas in Florida." In addition, "we identified sexual transmission of the disease and determined the linkage to Guillain-Barré syndrome. But there's still a lot we don't know."

Unfortunately, adequate funding was not readily forthcoming. Dr. Frieden offers a sober assessment: "The main threat is to pregnant women, and there aren't any pregnant women in Congress. And that threat is six or seven months in the future, and Congress usually thinks a week or two in the future." His successor will bear the burden of tackling Zika.

SMOKING, OBESITY, HYPERTENSION, AND OTHER WINNABLE BATTLES

While forestalling or quelling epidemics at home and abroad may have been the most dramatic of his tasks, it's the silent killers that concerned him most in his day-to-day operations. Hard-hitting anti-tobacco ads produced by the CDC in their "Tips from Former Smokers" Campaign directly influenced hundreds of thousands of Americans to stop smoking. Dr. Frieden likes to cite the assessment of a former CDC director, Dr. Bill Foege: "Public health is at its best when we see, and help others see, the faces and the lives behind the numbers."

Obesity is another pressing issue among the top of the CDC's priorities. "We don't have definitive evidence of what has caused the obesity epidemic in America," Dr. Frieden maintains, "but we do know that we're consuming more calories than we're burning." His pragmatic approach has been to focus on achievable objectives. Acknowledging that "we're much more likely to be able to prevent childhood obesity than to reverse adult obesity," at the CDC he promoted childhood programs at the national and state level. Consequently, nineteen states showed decreases in childhood obesity for the first time. And despite stiff opposition from vested interests in the soft drink industry—Atlanta is the home base of Coca-Cola—he pushed for government-mandated remedies: "It's a matter of public record that I proposed a one penny an ounce soda tax back in 2009 as being quite possibly the single most effective thing to reduce the obesity epidemic."

Dr. Frieden has written about what he calls "a health pyramid," addressing "how we can impact behavior at different levels of society." Among the key winnable battles to save lives and money outside of the traditional health care sector, he identified the need to reduce teen pregnancy as a factor in the intergenerational transmission of poverty. He is pleased to report that "we now have the lowest teen pregnancy rates ever in the U.S."

Another daunting priority he cited is hypertension control: "If you want to do one thing right in the health care system, it would be to control blood pressure. That can save more lives across the board than any other measure."

Dr. Frieden has also spoken out about the need for what he calls "a reciprocal revolution" to include improving the country's mental health in the mission of the CDC. "Depression," he points out, "remains underrecognized as a major cause of ill health."

The current epidemic in overdose deaths from opioids is another pressing concern. Prescription painkillers are a major part of the problem. Under Dr. Frieden's direction, the CDC issued new guidelines for prescribing opioid medications for chronic pain.

"DEVELOPING THE CAPACITY OF SOCIETY TO ADDRESS ITS OWN PROBLEMS"

Dr. Frieden is philosophically committed to systems that foster homegrown solutions to health concerns: "I like to develop the capacity of society to address its own problems. Public health is the organized activities of society to be healthier."

Among the programs he had a hand in creating and/or reinventing, and of which he is the proudest, is the Public Health Associates Program, whereby the CDC recruits, trains, and sends out to state health departments a cohort of what he calls "the next generation of public health leaders." Between 3,000 and 4,000 applicants with bachelor's or master's degrees vie annually for 200 positions. "We send them out to states to be in the front lines of public health. They will rejuvenate, diversify, and make even more practical our ability to protect the health of the nation. They are the future."

Self-help is part of his own personal regimen as well. In addition to eating healthy and bicycling regularly, several times a week he plays squash with friends, a vigorous, aggressive game he first took up as a student at P&S, which he describes, tongue in cheek, as his "homicide prevention program."

SO WHAT'S NEXT?

As per protocol, Dr. Frieden submitted his resignation effective January 20, 2017. So what's next?

"Being a native New Yorker, I like to quote the great philosopher Yogi Berra whenever I can: 'It's tough to make predictions, especially about the future.'" Pressed to be a bit more specific, he allows: "I've made every career decision in my life by answering the simple question: How can I save the most lives?"

MEDICINE BY BENCH, BEDSIDE, AND BOOK

JEROME GROOPMAN '76

Since being interviewed for this profile in 2000, Jerome Groopman '76 wrote three more widely read books: The Anatomy of Hope: How People Prevail in the Face of Illness, *2005;* How Doctors Think, *2008; and* Your Medical Mind: How to Decide What is Right for You, *2012.*

—⁂—

HIS LABORATORY equipment at the Harvard Institutes of Medicine includes a state-of-the-art x-ray refraction facility to image the three-dimensional structure of deadly agents, like the breast cancer protein; an automated gene sequencer to map the terra incognita of the thirteen genes discovered in his division to date; and two ultra-centrifuges with solid titanium rotors to laminate blood components based on molecular weight. High tech may be a sine qua non for his microbiological bench work. But ask Jerome Groopman '76, the Dina and Raphael Recanati Professor of Medicine at Harvard Medical School and chief of the Division of Experimental Medicine at Beth Israel Deaconess Medical Center, what his most precious tool is, and he replies without hesitation, "the human ear."

A SPECIALIST AT LISTENING

Biomedical scientists of his caliber are more likely to speak the cuneiform of genetic coding than they are to bandy such literary terms as "narrative," "metaphor," and "imagination." To Groopman, however, a man conversant in

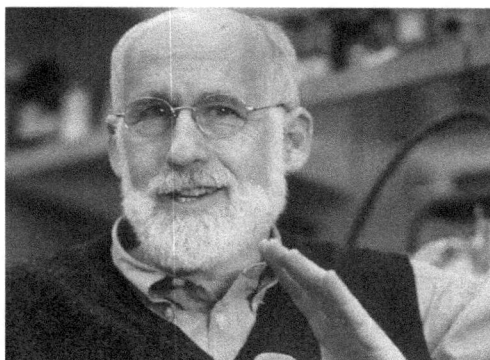

multiple disciplines (who majored in political philosophy and wrote theater criticism while deconstructing the complex jigsaw puzzle of organic chemistry as a premed at Columbia College), science and the humanities are complementary modes of thought and discourse aimed at a common end, unraveling the mysteries of life: "Human biology is miraculous, it inspires incredible awe and wonder!"

At first sight, his snow-white beard and hair make him look considerably older than his forty-eight years. But look again and a youthful verve leaps out from behind his scholarly spectacles. Endowed with the long legs and stamina of an athlete, the mental agility of a creative thinker, and the ability to get by on little sleep, Dr. Groopman straddles multiple worlds. In addition to pursuing his own ongoing basic research in hematology/oncology and HIV/AIDS; running Harvard's Division of Experimental Medicine, with its sixty-five-member team of scientists and support staff; personally directing the care of over 100 critically ill patients, many with AIDS, in the Infectious Diseases Clinic; and taking an active role, along with his wife, a busy endocrinologist, in the rearing of their three children, Dr. Groopman, miraculously, finds time to write. A staff writer (whose name appears with increasing frequency on the cover) of *The New Yorker* magazine, he is the author of two critically acclaimed books for a general audience based on the experience of his clinical practice: *The Measure of Our Days, A Spiritual Exploration of Illness*, 1997, and the recently published *Second Opinions, Stories of Intuition and Choice in the Changing World of Medicine 2001*. In a review in the *Washington Post Book World*, the Pulitzer Prize-winning author Robert Coles '54 went so far as to compare sections of the former book to Tolstoy's classic, *The Death of Ivan Ilyich*.

Listening is the stuff that holds all the disparate threads of his busy life together. As Dr. Groopman puts it in *Second Opinions*, "Careful listening is the starting point for careful thinking." Schooled in the art of attentive care, as espoused and practiced by revered mentors at P&S, like neurologist Dr. Linda Lewis (whom he cites and salutes in the book), Dr. Groopman is keenly attuned to the verbal and body language of his patients. Stories to him are two-way streets, with clinical and moral lessons for physician and patient. The science and literature fit hand in glove. "Writing," he insists, "has made me a better doctor. It forced me to explain and communicate in understandable language, freed me from jargon, and it also, actually, often acts as a platform from which to probe illness."

Adept at the use of advanced imaging and diagnostic tools, he is equally skill-ful at engaging his imaginative faculty to understand the patient's perspective. To that end, he will, in the course of consultations, extract life metaphors to build a psychological bridge and line of communication with his patients.

So, for instance, in caring for a senior intelligence officer suffering from myeloma, Dr. Groopman tapped his patient's specialized area of expertise in counterterrorism: "We'll talk about the quality of the information and intel-ligence that we have about his illness, the '*humint*' (an abbreviation for human intelligence) and the '*techint*' (an abbreviation for technological intelligence). By doing so," Dr. Groopman points out, "I'm saying to him: This is still who you are, a highly skilled professional with keen insight!" The beautiful irony, of course, is that, in medicine, as in espionage, *humint* is always more telling than *techint*. "CT scans and blood tests are invaluable," says Dr. Groopman, "but the most powerful information I obtain comes from direct interaction and observation and the patient's gut feelings."

A CV FULL OF CURRICULUM AND HEAVY ON THE VITAE

Jerome Groopman's own gut feelings about himself as a physician and a human being were nurtured early on. His father, a New York pharmacist-turned den-tist, helped instill spiritual values along with intellectual rigor. His mother, descended from a long line of Chassidic rabbis from the Carpathian Moun-tains, added a sense of the practical and an appreciation of the mysteries of life. Dr. Groopman is an observant Jew who makes time to pray daily between writing, exercising, and getting the kids ready for school. That marriage of the spiritual and the scientific is evident in his writing too: "I believe that God does provide man with the means to create miracles. The means are curiosity and intellect." (*The Measure of Our Days*) At one point he considered becoming a rabbi, but a scientific bent and desire to engage life at its "most real" made him opt for medicine.

At P&S, he came under the influence of humanistically grounded scientist-physicians, like his adviser, the late Andrew Frantz '55, professor of medicine and associate dean of admissions, with whom he enjoyed heady discussions that ran the gamut from endocrinology to T.S. Elliot's epic poem "The Wasteland"; the late Dr. Glenda Garvey '69, professor of clinical medicine, who communicated clinical rigor and complete engagement with the patient; and the late Dr. John Lindenbaum, former professor of medicine and head of the Hematology Service at Harlem Hospital, whom Dr. Groopman credited with practicing medicine at the front line, "where you get no academic kudos, doing his best for people whom society for the most part shunts aside." It was in the course of a third-year hematology elective with Dr. Lindenbaum that Dr. Groopman found his calling.

"Blood is one of the most aesthetic tissues," he writes in *Second Opinions*. "Its beauty had seduced me into choosing hematology as a first career. The cells on the slide are like dancers in a grand ball, displaying costumes of brilliant colors . . . So much can be . . . revealed in a single drop of blood."

ENCOUNTERING BEAUTY AND THE BEAST

Following a medical residency at Massachusetts General Hospital and a clinical fellowship in medicine at Harvard Medical School, Dr. Groopman "heretically broke ranks" to pursue a fellowship in the Division of Hematology-Oncology at the University of California, Los Angeles, an institution then in the vanguard of molecular research. Setting out to study the "malevolent beauty" of leukemia viruses, Dr. Groopman encountered the beast.

Called in to consult in 1981 on a curious outbreak of pneumocystis pneumonia in a group of patients who happened to be young gay men, he observed the first clinical cases of a then-unidentified disease subsequently named AIDS. The disease took the opposite course to that of the human T cell leukemia he'd been studying. While leukemia makes the T cells proliferate wildly, this new virus wiped them out. The intellectual challenge was compelling, but the specter of suffering proved wrenching. The patients, many of whom were male prostitutes, were perceived by some colleagues as social pariahs. Though far removed from their life experience, Dr. Groopman felt drawn to them and their plight. Wasted, haggard, and hollow-eyed in the late stage of this unknown disease, they reminded him of "Muselmänner," the starving "walking corpses" of Auschwitz and other Nazi concentration camps, where a number of his mother's relatives perished. Dr. Groopman committed himself to their care, inevitably in those early days of the AIDS pandemic facing down the specter of death.

The more pleasant complications of meeting and falling in love with his wife, Pam, then in training at Harvard Medical School, resulted in several hectic years of transcontinental weekend commuting between UCLA and Harvard, where he finally returned in 1983 as assistant professor of medicine and attending physician at New England Deaconess Hospital, two years later taking the reins there as chief of the Division of Hematology/Oncology. Named Dina and Raphael Recanati Professor in 1992 and professor of medicine in 1993, in 1996 he was appointed chief of the Division of Experimental Medicine at the newly merged entity of Beth Israel Deaconess Medical Center.

Dr. Groopman has continued his hematological research on human retroviruses, like HTLV, which causes leukemial lymphoma. He has simultaneously pursued pioneering work in the study of AIDS. His lab was among those that collaborated on the development of protease inhibitors, a therapeutic agent that, while not a cure, has dramatically improved the quality of life and extended the life expectancy for countless individuals. Borrowing a layman's metaphor, Dr. Groopman describes the action of the protease enzyme on the HIV virus as that of a "micro-scissor" that cuts its protein coat. Thus "the protease inhibitor is a glue that sits in the cleft of that scissor and prevents it from cutting effectively." The result translates into a virtual miracle. One of his patients, a *Wall Street Journal* columnist, who had already written and printed his own obituary, was literally compelled to take a new lease on life and, on doctor's orders, to lose a little weight. Dr. Groopman's lab is currently studying new angles of treatment, one of his foci being that part of the virus called REV, the transport that carries the invader from the nucleus into the cytoplasm of the host cell.

Hailed as an "AIDS Warrior" by the *Boston Globe*, he was the recipient of the 1988 Community Sanctity of Life Award of Brandeis University and the 1998 Presidential Citation for outstanding commitment to patient advocacy from the Massachusetts Medical Society. His writing has been recognized with the 1997 Best Wellness Book "Books for a Better Life" Award and the 1998 American Medical Writers Association Award for excellence in medical communication.

NO FRIEND OF DOCTOR DEATH

Most of his published case histories are not success stories in the traditional sense. They lack a Hollywood happy ending. Only one of the true life tales in *The Measure of Our Days* ends with a clear-cut clinical victory. Wrestling with kidney cancer, AIDS, leukemia, breast cancer, and the rare blood disorder myelofibrosis, eight individuals bare their souls and reveal their humanity.

Death is not the ultimate enemy for Dr. Groopman and his patients. Callousness and incompetence are. In *The Measure of Our Days*, the author begins with an account of the death of his own beloved father from a massive heart attack in a small community hospital in Queens, whose staff of medical professionals offered neither competent care nor compassion. Worse, Dr. Groopman, a second-year medical student at the time, felt robbed of the chance to share with his father the precious time before death.

Because of his strong feelings about the value of the end-of-life experience, Dr. Groopman is an outspoken opponent of Dr. Jack Kevorkian. "When you face your mortality," says Dr. Groopman, "it strips away what's insubstantial and it shows you what's meaningful and enduring. That's relationships, particularly of love, and the product of your work." Life's essentials, he suggests, become ever more apparent and vital as we approach our end. And while he firmly believes in "death with dignity . . . the assistance of people to not be in pain," he is reticent to cut short a precious period of life and worries, furthermore, about the questionable ethics of "death on demand."

Hardly immune to suffering, Dr. Groopman does not, however, flinch from it: "It's painful to me as a physician, but I don't run away." It is precisely the human element in medicine, the pain as well as the opportunity to help people surmount that pain, or at the very least to face it with dignity, that energizes him every day. "The laboratory research is isolated and rarified, very intellectually gratifying, and more often frustrating," he acknowledges. "But in the clinic, it's real lives you're facing. I feel blessed in what I do. I think it's extraordinary that I have met so many people with such a broad spectrum of human experience. . . . I have known salt-of-the-earth Irish accountants and hard-driving investment bankers, politicians, journalists, and I've even known the Jordanian royal family." (He was a member of the medical team that treated the late King Hussein.)

His recent book, *Second Opinions*, deals with the choices all of us, patients, physicians, family, and other loved ones, are bound to make in the changing world of American medicine. Access to the best possible care is not always readily available. Diagnoses are not always on the mark.

The book begins with Dr. Groopman's own personal ordeal as a patient and the incapacitating physical pain he endured in the wake of a botched operation on his back, the aftereffects of which he still suffers. He blames, in part, his own desire, as an impatient patient, for a quick-fix surgical solution. A subsequent chapter recounts the harrowing tale of the misdiagnosed, and later inadequately treated and almost fatal, intussusception of his first-born son. He ultimately managed to find the right surgeon to operate before it was too late and the story has a happy ending.

Dr. Groopman, who has experienced and written eloquently about both sides of the examining table, as physician and patient (as well as father, son, and grandson of a patient), seeks an informed and active participation from his patients, and by extension, from his readers: "Patients have to question and offer their intuition and their thinking. . . . A doctor is at a disadvantage when the patient does not participate in his own care."

Whether practicing medicine at the bedside or "by the book," Jerome Groopman addresses the whole person. The benefits of such an approach are manifold for the physician as well as the patient. In a lecture entitled "The Intersection of Science and the Soul," delivered at the American Association of Medical Colleges annual meeting in Washington, D.C., in October 1999, he summed up the challenge and satisfaction of a medical life: "Through this process of caring for people and trying to understand their souls we pass through an odyssey of self-discovery, we begin to understand ourselves better, our motivations, our fears, our limitations and our potential." In addition to family photos, Dr. Groopman's office walls and windowsill are alive with pictures of his shipmates on that shared odyssey, each of whom he helped reach (or at least glimpse from afar) his or her own private Ithaca. A saying tacked behind his desk says it all: "One life, it's as though you saved the whole world."

A PIONEER IN ADOLESCENT MEDICINE
COMMITTED TO HEALTH AND
WELL-BEING FOR ALL

KAREN HEIN '70

IN 2003, upon stepping down as president of the William T. Grant Foundation and moving to Vermont, "in order to be true to what I was trying to do as a doctor and a human being," Karen Hein '70 cited the words of Mahatma Gandhi: "My life is my message." It's a principle she has been applying all her life. She brought her newborn baby to introduce him to her incarcerated young patients at the Spofford Juvenile Center, an "infamous" correctional facility for adolescents in the Bronx, and hauled a spinning wheel into her office in the U.S. Senate, where she served as a health policy fellow on the professional staff of the Senate Finance Committee, to help her unwind. Her controversial campaign to buck stigmas, promote safe sex and make condoms available to New York City school kids at the height of the HIV/AIDS epidemic drew death threats and helped save lives. Her widely read book, *AIDS: Trading Fears for Facts, A Guide for Young People*, included illustrated instructions on how to use a condom. Equally at home nowadays in the company of her cashmere goats in rural Vermont and her fellow members of the Green Mountain Care Board, appointed by Vermont Governor Peter Shumlin to fulfill the state's mandate to provide all Vermonters with health coverage, Dr. Hein brings new meaning to the term "herd instinct." "It's about a sense of community," she observes. "We're all in this together."

On a morning in early March 2013, under a freshly fallen coat of snow, Dr. Hein fielded an interviewer's questions at her home in Vermont.

A CAREER OUTSIDE THE COMFORT ZONE

Her father was a Long Island family practitioner who served as the first chief of staff at North Shore Hospital. Her mother audited medical school classes, but

ultimately, given the social pressures of the time, gave up her dream of pursuing medicine to raise a family. "I think I became a doctor for my mother, who didn't get to be one," says Dr. Hein. Medicine called out to her early on. "The privilege of being a doctor had nothing to do with status or salary. For me," she affirms, "it was all about being present at the most meaningful moments of a person's life."

As a child she spent a lot of time in her father's office, intrigued by, among other things, the fetus in a jar, the anatomical models, and books on birth control. As a camp counselor, at age seventeen, she took it upon herself to have frank and open discussions about sex and contraception with her young charges. "I have always tried to look at things from a young person's perspective," she says. "My experience as an empowered young person in the 1960s continues to be my motivation now that I am in my sixties."

After completing what was at the time a two-year program at Dartmouth Medical School, she transferred to P&S, where she felt warmly welcomed by her classmates. A fourth-year subinternship at a rural bush hospital in Liberia, an experience made possible by the legendary P&S professor of parasitology and tropical medicine Dr. Harold Brown, proved "the best way to move from being a student to being a doctor." It also launched her on a career path outside her comfort zone. "Generally, I'd say, I went into what I'd call 'vacuum areas.' I have always gone, not where there was the least resistance, but where there was need, where things weren't formed and rigid yet."

As a young student activist affiliated with the Student Health Organization, she helped care for abandoned babies at Lincoln Hospital, in the South Bronx. Following a fellowship in adolescent medicine at Montefiore Hospital, she took her first job out of medical school as medical director of Spofford Juvenile Center, a facility for adolescents in trouble with the law. "You could say a prison for kids is not exactly a creative, open space," she reflects back, "but we were forced to be creative in figuring out how to give good health care to the kids in that prison." Establishing a team approach, with the help of social workers, an ethicist/lawyer, and nurses, she and her colleagues would surprise both the guards and the young detainees who sometimes came into the infirmary completely out of control, by grabbing the kid by the arm: "Oh, you've got a booboo on your hand," allowing him to de-escalate and just be a kid. "That's how we handled 'New York's most violent.' Prison health was a vacuum area in terms of people on the outside thinking about or worrying about the kids on the inside. But I found it absolutely compelling."

At Spofford, which Dr. Hein characterized as "a sentinel site for emerging issues in youth," among other kids invisible to society at large, she saw a severely ill young man, Luther Flood, age 15, with huge lymph nodes. A clinical mystery to the dermatologist who diagnosed him with a rare cancer, mycosis fungoides, Dr. Hein believes he was one of the nation's first adolescents to come down with an as yet unnamed disease subsequently called HIV/AIDS. "While others were focusing on where the HIV epidemic had surfaced," she says, "we were looking ahead to where it was going."

FOUNDED FIRST COMPREHENSIVE ADOLESCENT HIV/AIDS PROGRAM IN THE NATION

In 1987, with the help of her husband, Dr. Ralph Dell, now a professor of pediatrics emeritus at P&S, who developed mathematical models to predict how HIV was bound to be present in the adolescent population, Dr. Hein drafted a paper, "AIDS in Adolescents, a Rationale for Concern," on the basis of which she applied for and obtained a $1 million grant from the Centers for Disease Control and Prevention to establish the Adolescent Risk Reduction Program at Montefiore Hospital, the first comprehensive adolescent HIV/AIDS program in the country, of which she was founding director. Given the stigma, fear, and denial associated with the disease and those it struck, and not wanting to scare away teens or their parents, she decided not to include the word AIDS in the name, REP (Risk Evaluation Program). "We liked the kids to have cards they could carry around, and didn't want them to be stigmatized by a card with the dreaded term AIDS on it." The first of its kind, the program included HIV/AIDS education, clinical care, and clinical trials.

Initially derided by some colleagues and members of the hospital administration as the director of "The Emperor's New Clothes Clinic," Dr. Hein managed to attract the attention of U.S. Surgeon General Dr. Antonia Novello, who attended the ribbon cutting for the new facility. Dr. Hein's prognosis: "Hmmm, unintended pregnancy, wonder how many of the kids are gonna be infected with HIV!" proved right on the mark.

TEAMING UP WITH TEENS TO GET THE MESSAGE OUT

Rejecting the traditional notion of the doctor-patient relationship as a one-way street, in which the doctor spoon-feeds medicine and wisdom and the patient just swallows and obeys, Dr. Hein insists: "I always got my marching orders from my patients.

Among her many patients, one young woman, Krista Black, who had been infected with HIV/AIDS by a boyfriend with hemophilia when she was sixteen, and who contacted Dr. Hein from Ohio, proved a powerful partner in destigmatizing the disease and promoting healthy practices. "Undoubtedly, the adult medical team viewed Krista as a problem patient," Dr. Hein recalled in a chapter in a volume about pioneers in adolescent health and development (in press). "To them she was moody, difficult, hard to reach . . . a problem. What I heard on the telephone was a bright, determined young woman who was calling halfway across the country to find a doctor who would understand what she was going through."

Dr. Hein listened. They worked together for the next five years, as a team addressing Krista's concerns and those of a generation: "Krista taught me that young people are the best spokespeople for issues facing adolescents. [. . .] She taught me that answers to complex questions about illness, death, and life are best approached through teamwork, and that the team needs to include the person, or people most affected." Soon after they got to know each other, she began to include Krista in her professional presentations, public appearances, and media interviews. They shared the microphone. The eloquent young woman's pressing questions ultimately became the basis for research questions the doctor and her team began to systematically pose to their patients. Krista died at age twenty-two. Dr. Hein is still stirred when she speaks of her. "She dedicated her short, meaningful life to becoming an HIV/AIDS educator, giving a voice and a face to the wave of the epidemic that wasn't fully recognized until she died."

Then in the early 1990s, with the support of NYC Schools Chancellor Joe Fernandez, Dr. Hein helped launch a push to promote HIV/AIDS education and comprehensive sexuality education, including condom availability, among the young. Considerable uproar and death threats notwithstanding, Chancellor Fernandez and Dr. Hein and others on the AIDS Curriculum Advisory Committee together crafted an HIV/AIDS curriculum for kindergarten through twelfth grade, the most controversial part of which was raising awareness and making condoms easily available to all 450,000 high school students in the NYC public high schools. "We took it, as I always have: if you want to do a bold social experiment you want to learn from it," she says. The results were studied and written up in the *Journal of the American Medical Association*. "Researchers compared New York City schools with Chicago schools that had an AIDS curriculum but no condom availability. And low and behold, New York kids used condoms more regularly."

Dr. Hein remembers sharing her enthusiasm at having succeeded in promoting condom availability with an endocrinologist on staff at Montefiore, who merely shrugged. "That's when I realized I don't belong only in the corridors of an academic health center," she says.

Reaching out to the community at large, she addressed the concerns and questions of a generation at risk in language they could relate to in *AIDS: Trading Fears for Facts, A Guide for Young People*, published in 1989 by Consumers Union, a book coauthored with Theresa Foy Digeronimo that went on to sell more than 100,000 copies in four languages, including two versions in Spanish. With an eye-catching cover image by the late artist Keith Haring, the book dispelled false gossip and insidious rumors, and answered questions on many kids' minds, like: "Can I get HIV by sitting on the toilet in a public bathroom?" It featured a diagram of how to put on a condom over an erect penis and included a list of AIDS hotline numbers state by state and a glossary of terms with simple, straightforward definitions. The book also featured profiles of young people living with AIDS as well as noninfected kids who chose to play an active role in responding to the epidemic.

Not long after publication of the book, basketball star Earvin "Magic" Johnson made headlines with his public announcement that he had AIDS. His associates contacted Dr. Hein and she served as a member of the scientific advisory board of the foundation Johnson created.

PROMOTING CHANGE, FROM ADOLESCENT MEDICINE TO HEALTH POLICY

Throughout her career, Dr. Hein has fought to combat negative societal perceptions of young people as a danger or a threat. To her, it's a vicious circle. "Attitude drives behavior, which, in turn, drives how resources are allocated, and how health is regained or maintained." In America, she points out, "we're very positive about the military and about the Olympics, two institutions in which everybody admires young people, but in the day-to-day reality it's still obviously an image issue, especially for kids in racial minorities."

In 1993 she applied for and was awarded a Robert Wood Johnson Health Policy Fellowship, and took a sabbatical leave from Montefiore to serve on the professional staff of the U.S. Senate Finance Committee, then chaired by the late New York Senator Daniel Patrick Moynihan. She focused on assessing and recommending health insurance benefits packages, among other matters, clarifying definitions of "medically necessary care" and "medically appropriate care," and pressing the issue of mental health and substance abuse parity coverage. "The Clintons were busy, as you know, trying to achieve health care reform through the White House," she reminds, "but it's Congress that writes the laws."

Working for hours on end, for month after month, while others resorted to the treadmill, she decided to "bring sanity into my life" by setting up a spinning wheel in her Senate office.

While she admits to considerable frustration that the health reforms she worked so hard on did not, at the time, pass into law, the hard work paid off: "I am finishing the job seventeen years later as a member of the Green Mountain Board. So you just never know in your life."

Following the conclusion of her fellowship, Dr. Hein got what she refers to, tongue in cheek, as "a case of Potomac Fever. I really wanted to stay in Washington and help foster change." Considering various opportunities, she accepted the position as executive officer of the Institute of Medicine (IOM) at the

National Academies. Founded by President Lincoln, the National Academies, comprising the National Academy of Engineering, the National Academy of Science, and the Institute of Medicine, produces and disseminates informed policy reports to Congress. Among her innovations at the helm of the IOM, "I really pushed to produce one-page summaries of 500-page reports, so that Capitol Hill staffers would actually read them and not just file them away." Under the presidency of Ken Shine, MD, and her direction as executive officer, the Institute wrote the seminal report "To Err is Human," documenting the daunting statistic that medical errors account for some 98,000 deaths a year. The report has since spawned a push for medical checklists, among other institutional safeguards. Other pivotal reports produced under her watch included "The Future of Public Health," a series on "Gulf War Syndrome," and "The New Dietary Allowances for Nutritional Requirements."

After three and a half years directing the work of the IOM, she was recruited to serve as president of the William T. Grant Foundation, a major charitable organization dedicated to "using research to improve the lives of young people." She relished the responsibility of being able to direct millions of dollars to help shape research on positive youth development. Her goal as president was not just to fund research but to really try to affect the societal view of young people. Among other notable efforts under her tenure, the foundation helped fund the White House "Conference on Teenagers: Raising Resourceful and Responsible Youth," chaired by then First Lady, Hillary Rodham Clinton.

GETTING BACK TO BASICS

Upon stepping down from the presidency of the William T. Grant Foundation, Dr. Hein took a long, hard look at her life and decided she wanted to make some changes. So, instead of taking on a new position, she resolved to give up the trappings, the salary, the title, to get back to what brought her to medicine to begin with. Years ago she and her husband had bought an old farmhouse in Vermont, and had completed a major renovation in 1989. Much of the expert carpentry in the house had been done by Dr. Dell. Inspired by many trips to Mongolia, and their shared fondness for Himalayan culture, they also built themselves a yurt out back. And on a great loom upstairs Dr. Hein wove wonders, including pieces of clothing and imaginative works of art. Their children were all grown up and independent. But aside from brief family vacation breaks, they had never actually lived in the house. The time was right, they thought, to call Vermont home. Among other factors in their decision was the onset in Dr. Dell of early stage Alzheimer's disease and their desire to spend more time together. A calling card they had designed shows the two of them levitating together, two human halves of the same whole hovering in thin air.

And then there was the herd of long-haired American cashmere goats, a more recent addition to the extended Dell-Hein clan. Winter and summer, Dr. Hein tends to their needs, and thereby satisfies her own need to be closer to nature. "For me," she says, "they're a funny kind of portal, a connection between nature at large and my life among people."

Which is not to suggest that she bid humanity farewell, only that she altered the conditions of her commitment. She continues to serve as an active board member on various international NGOs. Among many other projects, she became involved with a small group of health professionals concerned about the lack of adequate training of individuals who rush to help in troubled areas in times of crisis, sometimes doing more damage than good. The group came up with a set of core competencies for humanitarian assistance, on which various international aid organizations are signing off. The move to Vermont also gave Dr. Hein the opportunity to participate in an important health care initiative and complete the work she'd begun as a health policy fellow attached to the Senate Finance Committee.

THE GREEN MOUNTAIN CARE BOARD

In May 2011, the Vermont Legislature passed and Vermont Governor Peter Shumlin signed Act 48, a landmark law that set out "to create a health care system in which all residents receive coverage from a single source, with all coverage offered equitably and health care costs contained by systematic change in the way providers of health care are compensated for their services." Dr. Hein was named by Governor Shumlin as one of five members of the Green Mountain Care Board, a body with regulatory authority to make binding decisions relating to the state's health care system in an entirely transparent process.

"System" is the key word for Dr. Hein. "It has to be a system so that all the players and parts, the 14 hospitals, the federally qualified health centers, independent practices, rural clinics, and small critical access centers, fit and function together. [. . .] What's really exciting about Vermont health care reform is that we're looking at all those moving parts and trying to get our arms around all of it, so that it isn't just a bunch of moving cogs, but adds up to an integrated health care system." In addition, she stresses, "for it to work, the people of Vermont have to feel a part of the system. They have to feel empowered enough to be sure they are getting from the system what they think is important." And finally, she adds, "the system has to be affordable, affordable to individuals, to families, and to the state."

Dr. Hein also emphasizes the need to take into account various social determinants of health, including behavior, environment, and public health. The Board is also acknowledging the role of nutritious school lunch and sex education programs run by the Department of Education, the promotion of bike helmets and building and upkeep of bike paths established by the Department of Transportation, and meaningful employment and safe working conditions monitored by the Department of Labor, among other factors affecting health. "My priority is the integration of clinical care, public health and population health," she says, i.e., "the distribution of scarce resources across the population."

The Board has furthermore accepted a broader definition of health. "Do no harm, is that it? I don't think so. It's not just the absence of disease," Dr. Hein maintains, "health also has to do with social, economic, and personal well-being. And that's what I'm hoping our system can promote."

Despite the negative perception promoted by outspoken and well-funded opponents of the law, "that we've tried this before and it never worked, [. . .] that it's just too complicated to tackle, with too much money at stake," Dr. Hein remains optimistic that the Board will surmount such attitudinal barriers and come up with a workable model. "Vermonters are very reasonable and we do work across the aisles. [. . .] We can and will engage people around issues that they really care about. Most people do not want to end up in an ICU with a million tubes and no say in the matter. We'll just naturally end up saving money and having Vermonters feel supported and in charge, not of living or dying, but of how they live and how they can feel supported when they are dying."

"There is no one single reason, no one single villain or flaw" in the present American health care system, Dr. Hein believes. "But the system has rewarded volume. Doctors and hospitals are rewarded on the basis of piecework." While the managed care model was "all about saving money," the Vermont model "is about improving health and saving money."

And whereas she hopes that Vermont may influence health care reform elsewhere in the country, she is averse to the notion that change should necessarily start at the state level. "I'm very dismayed by the way people refer to Vermont. Oh, it's just Vermont! It's such a small state! It's such a rural state! It's such a politically aligned state! It's as if these were reasons why America can't do the right thing by its people. And I believe it can."

REFLECTIONS AT THE LOOM

At age sixty-nine, Dr. Hein still wakes up at 5 A.M., as she has for most of her career. And when she's not shuttling up to Montpelier for meetings of the Green Mountain Care Board, she takes precious time out at daybreak to knit or sit by her loom weaving the combed cashmere hair of the herd. In this seeming lull of what she calls "a creative flow state" she manages to disengage the gears and just be. "That's when the big ideas or solutions really take shape.

"I believe that the incentive in American medicine as it is practiced today has gotten way out of whack. What's rewarded is not what I went into medicine to do. What's rewarded is 'fast.' What's rewarded is 'high tech.' What's rewarded are big deals that yield products with a profit. I went into medicine to be able to be there at the important moments in people's lives, to help deliver babies and sit with people as they die and create a system of support for well-being throughout life. [. . .] Being a physician has been the way I have realized my adolescent desire to be a part of change in the country and the world."

AT HOME IN HIGH PLACES

CHARLES S. HOUSTON '39

Having ascended and studied the physiological effects on humans of some of the highest places on earth, suffering from macular degeneration and waning eyesight, Charles S. Houston '39, who died in 2009, at age ninety-six, still found splendor to the last in the song of the wild birds feeding in his backyard in his beloved Vermont.

———⌀⌀⌀———

A CLOSE-UP taken at 26,000 feet shows the frost on his beard, a curl of rope attached to the cliff above his head, the white of his teeth, and an unmistakable smile on his lips. The year is 1938, the place K2, pinnacle of Central Asia's towering Karakoram Range, the second highest mountain in the world and among the most difficult to climb. Charles S. Houston '39 is in his element.

"NOT CONQUERORS, BUT PILGRIMS"

Lest anyone mistake the climber's expression for the smile of conquest, consider the lines of a poem he wrote to commemorate an earlier ascent in 1936 up the slope of Nanda Devi in India, 25,600 feet high, then the highest place on earth ever reached by man (the *American Alpine Journal*, 1995):

"Not conquerors, but pilgrims, seeking Light not fame."

Or as he would put it in his book, *Going Higher—Oxygen, Man, and Mountains* (reissued in its fourth edition by The Mountaineers, Seattle, 1998): "Enjoy the mountains; they have beauty and wisdom for us if we approach them with

humility, respect, and knowledge." Throughout his multifaceted career as mountaineer, scientist, teacher, and physician, Charles Houston, one of the world's foremost authorities on high-altitude medicine, has been gathering and disseminating the knowledge of high places as a humbling prerequisite for respect. Not a man to be easily pigeonholed, Dr. Houston is also, among a long list of accomplishments, the inventor of a mechanical heart (the forerunner of the Jarvik artificial heart), a former Peace Corps director for India, and a pioneer in group practice and community medicine. The common denominator, if there be one, is a sense of life as a great adventure.

A YANKEE IN THE COURT OF GENGHIS KHAN

The snow drifts from the living room window of his cozy home in Burlington, Vt., make a fitting backdrop. Outside, a red-headed cardinal, a velvet gray titmouse, and a gold and a purple finch flit across the whiteness, vying for seed from a freestanding feeder. Inside, the walls and shelves are covered with Himalayan, Indian, and Tibetan art and artifacts, much of a mountain theme, under the watchful and distinctly Occidental eye of an ancestor, General Charles Scott, a hero of the American Revolution, painted by Gilbert Stuart.

At eighty-six and counting, Dr. Houston is the incarnation of that odd admixture of mystery and matter of fact, Yankee, and yak. Compact and spry, flinty-eyed and gnome-like of expression, he acknowledges with a twinkle that some might find him "difficult," or as he prefers to put it, "a pusher." He carefully selects his words, footholds in the conceptual ascent, like the lifelong climber that he is. The conversation leaps from pre-Incan human sacrifice at shrines above 22,000 feet and the Chinese tradition of mountain painting, poetry and pilgrimages, to the geological substrata of mountain worship and the lack of punctuation in the Biblical Hebrew passage: "I will look to the hills from whence cometh my strength." But there is nothing misty eyed about the man. His sharp gaze immediately engages the visitor and makes of him a partner in a shared quest. The look belies a boundless curiosity filtered through the hard light of science.

MEDICINE, A CALLING THAT CAME EARLY

Science was his first love, medicine a calling that came early. The loan of a microscope by a physician friend of the family when he was ten prompted him to investigate the world around him, to dissect and study insects and dead animals. Looking back, he confirms: "I've never thought of any other career but medicine."

Earning his undergraduate degree at Harvard, Houston entered P&S, where he came under the influence of the dynamic duo Drs. Atchley and Loeb. Robert Loeb, an early role model with whom he remained lifelong friends, "was so perceptive," Houston shakes his head in admiration, "he never missed a trick. He was remorseless in pointing out things in patients we'd missed." Sixty years after the fact, Dr. Houston delights in reenacting a typical colloquy with Dr. Loeb: " 'Did you look at the fingernails?' 'What?' 'Well, look at them! Did you notice that coffee stain on the back of his hands?'" Dana Atchley, a mentor to both him and his future wife, Dorcas, then head nurse on the male ward at Presbyterian Hospital, was "exactly the opposite, quiet and very meticulous . . . Loeb was physical, physical, physical. Atchley: history, history, history—together they made an inimitable team."

THE CALL OF THE HILLS

As a Harvard undergraduate and active member of the illustrious Harvard Mountaineering Club, a brotherhood of virtuoso climbers and explorers, he'd already participated in pioneering ascents of Alaska's Mt. Crillon and the forbidding Mt. Foraker.

On two leaves of absence from P&S, young Houston made mountaineering history. First in 1936, as the member of a celebrated expedition led by the British climber H. W. Tilman up Nanda Devi in India, then the highest mountain ever climbed. And a second time in 1938, himself the leader of the First American Karakoram Expedition to K2. Though his party did not reach the summit, they climbed the cone (at 26,000 feet) and mapped a feasible route to the top subsequently followed by an Italian team in the first successful ascent in 1954. Nature's hazards and hurdles notwithstanding, as Houston reminded a P&S audience upon his return, "there is risk to mountain climbing, but there is also danger walking the streets of New York." Dean Willard Rappleye, who was on hand, called it "one of the most entertaining evenings I have had the privilege to attend," and saluted the speaker as "a man of many talents."

An ill-fated return in 1953, in which one of his teammates, Art Gilkey, perished, inspired the book, *K2—The Savage Mountain*. Gilkey contracted thrombophlebitis and had to be carried. As leader and medical member of the expedition, Dr. Houston, who himself suffered a concussion in a valiant attempt to save his friend, took the death particularly hard. It was to be his last major ascent. "When I thought about it later," he says, "it wasn't fair to my wife and children. I was close enough to my own demise. That was the end of my climbing, period!" He and the other surviving members of the team later received the David Sowles Award of the American Alpine Club for their unselfish action in going to the assistance of a fellow climber at personal risk.

In a memorable passage, Dr. Houston (who coauthored the book along with fellow climber, Robert H. Bates), gives a lyric evocation of just what it is that makes humans want to climb mountains, despite the risk:

The answer cannot be simple; it is compounded of such elements as the great beauty of clear cold air, of colors beyond the ordinary, of the lure of unknown regions beyond the rim of experience [. . . .] the thrill of danger—but danger controlled by skill [. . . .] How can I phrase what seems to me the most important reason of all? It is the chance to [. . .] strip off nonessentials, to come down to the core of life itself [. . .].

Among his other mountaineering exploits, Dr. Houston led an expedition in Nepal in 1949, whose members included his father, Oscar Houston, and H.W.

Tilman, to the foot of Mt. Everest. Scanning the south face, the first Westerners to do so, Houston's team plotted the route that would eventually be taken in 1953 by Sir Edmund Hillary and Tenzing Norgay on their successful ascent.

ADVENTURES IN HIGH-ALTITUDE MEDICINE

Following a medical internship at Presbyterian Hospital, Dr. Houston volunteered in 1941 for a commission in the U.S. Navy. Based in Pensacola, Fla., he coordinated the Navy's high-altitude training programs for aviators and directed a landmark high-altitude study called "Operation Everest." Houston argued that "if aviators were acclimatized to a moderate altitude, like 15,000 feet, they could then fly higher," a definite tactical advantage before the days of pressurization. His educated hunch proved right, and Houston earned his flight surgeon's wings. Declining the Navy's bid to sign him on as medical director of the nuclear experiments at Bikini, Dr. Houston resigned his commission and returned to civilian life.

Prior to the war, he and P&S classmate Henry Saltonstall '39 had planned to practice together in a peaceful rural setting. Following a brief stint at Bellevue Hospital, Houston joined his old friend and two other physicians in 1952 to open the Exeter Clinic, in Exeter, N.H., the third group practice in New England. There he enjoyed the life of an old-fashioned country doctor, on occasion skiing out to visit snowbound patients.

Then in 1957, an adventure of another kind lured him to Aspen, Colo. Walter Paepcke, a successful Chicago businessman, and his wife, Elizabeth, conceived the idea of the Aspen Institute for Humanistic Studies, whose grand opening included concerts and lectures by Dr. Albert Schweitzer. Recruiting Mortimer Adler to head up the humanistic program, Paepcke convinced Dr. Houston to serve as founding medical director of the Aspen Health Center. Conceived as a health refuge for America's leaders in business, labor, government, and the professions, the Center's espoused purpose was to "prevent rather than to treat illness due to stress," an idea well ahead of its time.

"The complete man," according to a prospectus written by the new medical director, "must be more than a properly nourished, well-muscled person. His mind and spirit also need stimulation [. . .]. He needs experiences outside of, as well as within, his profession. If not, he is living on his intellectual capital, and he may well become bankrupt in spirit." Dr. Houston organized a daily fitness regimen, led discussions, and lectured on health-related concerns. The Center only lasted a few years, but it helped pave the way for a new interest in preventive and holistic medicine.

Dr. Houston stayed on in Aspen, where he built up another group practice. A number of his patients suffered from advanced rheumatic heart disease. He spent his spare time in a workshop he'd set up in the garage and conceived one of the early models of an artificial heart. Attracting NIH funding, he worked with a surgeon, installing his mechanical device in experimental animals, and keeping them alive for twelve to twenty-four hours.

His rescue of a skier who'd fallen sick from what appeared to be pneumonia at 12,000 feet led to another discovery. Taken down to a hospital in Aspen, the patient quickly recovered. Baffled at first, Dr. Houston published in 1960 the first documented case of high-altitude pulmonary edema (HAPE), in the *New England Journal of Medicine*. HAPE is a life-threatening congestion of the lungs caused by a lack of oxygen.

OF POULTRY AND PEACE: ADVENTURES IN THE PEACE CORPS

A call from Washington, D.C., once again led Dr. Houston and his clan to decamp, this time for India. The Peace Corps had recently been created by President Kennedy. Its founding director, Sargent Shriver, who'd heard of Houston's Himalayan exploits, convinced him to take on operations in India. "It was unbelievable," he recalls the experience with a laugh and a gasp. "Every day there was some crisis, something different and exciting, or dangerous or frightening!" Directing a volunteer force that started with six and soon swelled to 250, with another 900 on the way, Dr. Houston oversaw programs in nursing, farming, English language instruction, well digging, farm instrument production, chicken rearing, and almost anything else under the sun. The Peace Corps' greatest benefit, he believes, was to the volunteers themselves and to America. "They've become a very distinguished sensitized segment of society," he says, citing among former volunteers, career diplomats, and college presidents. One of his sons, Robin, became a Peace Corps doctor in Nepal and continues to work in the field of international public health.

Those were the heady days of Camelot, when, for a brief moment, President Kennedy managed to infuse the nation with a rush of idealism. Remembering that moment, Dr. Houston reflects: "We believed we were going to change the world, or at least to nudge it, and in fact, we did. Though other forces pushed back the progress."

Recalled to Washington to create a Doctors Peace Corps, Dr. Houston managed, among other noteworthy accomplishments, to help create a medical school in Jalalabad, Afghanistan, before the rapidly escalating war in Vietnam put a stop to his plans.

BRINGING THE MEDICAL MESSAGE BACK HOME

Uncertain of what to do next, Dr. Houston attended a meeting of international medical educators, at which he happened to be seated next to the dean of the University of Vermont Medical School in Burlington. The dean mentioned the creation of a Department of Community Medicine for which they were seeking a chair. So the Houstons once again picked up their roots and moved to the Green Mountains.

While Dr. Houston managed to create a number of innovative programs in the course of his tenure, including a popular externship with rural practitioners, a turf conflict ensued between his department and the Department of Medicine. "I wasn't terribly diplomatic," Dr. Houston admits. Community Medicine was abolished and its erstwhile chair, who had a joint appointment in medicine, stayed on until his mandatory retirement at sixty-five.

Ever the "pusher" and doer, Dr. Houston perceived his academic role in community medicine as transcending the strict boundaries of the academy. He served on the Governor of Vermont's Commission that wrote the landmark 250 Environmental Protection Act in 1968. And from 1991 to 1992, he was a member of the Governor's Commission for Health Care Reform created to develop a viable health care system for Vermont.

MORE MEDICINE FROM ON HIGH

His primary research efforts, meanwhile, continued to focus on high-altitude medicine and physiology. From 1967 to 1979, he headed the High-Altitude Physiology Study on Mt. Logan in the Northwest Territory. The study yielded twenty papers and led to the description of a heretofore undocumented medical condition, high-altitude retinal hemorrhage, and also identified ataxia, the staggering gate, as an early warning sign of brain edema onset.

In 1975, he launched the first Mountain Medicine Symposium, subsequently expanded and renamed the International Hypoxia Symposium, the premier worldwide venue for high-altitude studies, which he cochaired until 1997.

The field of high-altitude physiology and medicine has grown immeasurably since he helped put it on the map. And while Dr. Houston, the veteran climber, decries the overcommercialization of mountaineering and an irresponsible amateurism leading to such disasters as the tragic deaths on Everest in 1996 described in Jon Krakauer's bestselling *Into Thin Air*, Dr. Houston, the high-altitude doctor, welcomes the burgeoning wealth of knowledge of high-altitude conditions. His book, *Going Higher*, is considered a classic compendium for climbers and physicians alike. In 1997, he received the coveted King Albert Medal of Merit Award for his contributions to our understanding of mountain sickness and man's acclimatization to high altitude.

A medical colleague and longtime admirer, Dr. Sam Silverstein, the John C. Dalton Professor and chair of the Department of Physiology and Cellular Biophysics at P&S, himself an avid climber, calls Dr. Houston "a true explorer in every sense of the word. In search of new challenges, he has never followed any prescribed path, always wanting to cross new ridges and see what's on the other side."

"My greatest success," Dr. Houston demurs, "is, with my wife, to have raised three wonderful children."

Advancing years have not diminished his activity. He served as a consultant to NASA on a recent Everest Expedition, an adviser to the producers of the IMAX film *Everest, Mountain Without Mercy*, and a contributor to the companion text published by the National Geographic Society.

Ever restless, Dr. Houston peers out the window. "The feeder needs refilling," he observes, donning boots and gear, trudging out into the snow to feed the birds.

AN ALL-STAR ON THE TEAM AGAINST TB

MICHAEL ISEMAN '65

A giant in the clinical care of drug-resistant tuberculosis, Dr. Iseman retired in 2006, having taught over the course of five decades the longest-running course on TB in the United States, and lectured in forty-seven states and thirty-four foreign countries. Also a natural athlete, he was a former star player of football and rugby, and describes himself as an unreformed baseball fanatic.

———

REMEMBER TB, that turn-of-the-century scourge everyone thought was long since licked? Think again! It's almost the turn of another century and tuberculosis is back with a vengeance. The dread malady once dubbed "The White Death" and the "Captain of All These Men of Death" is currently mowing mankind down at the rate of 2-3 million people a year, a rate, moreover, that's on the rise. An infinitely resourceful culprit, the tubercle bacillus, identified in 1882 by Robert Koch as the cause of the disease, has succeeded by mutation in resisting and plowing through the front line of drugs once thought invincible in combating it. Never wholly vanquished, TB has reemerged as the single most lethal infectious human affliction. For many years, Michael Iseman '65, a renowned expert on multidrug-resistant (MDR) TB, a clinician and public health consultant with his eye on the big picture, has been predicting just that. Dr. Iseman is a committed team player and tactician in the international effort to control the spread of the disease.

The National Jewish Center for Immunology and Respiratory Medicine in Denver, where Dr. Iseman holds the Girard and Madeline Beno Chair in Mycobacterial Diseases and officiates as chief of the Clinical Mycobacterial

Service, is the longest continuously running clinical facility for TB treatment in the United States. Currently, thanks to Dr. Iseman and colleagues, a medical Mecca for the treatment of MDR-TB cases elsewhere considered "incurable," National Jewish Center has reclaimed leadership in the field. The triannual course Dr. Iseman holds here in the clinical management and control of tuberculosis attracts health care professionals from around the country and the world. An official consultant to the World Health Organization (WHO), Dr. Iseman is also editor-in-chief of the prestigious publication *Tubercle and Lung Disease* (the official journal of the International Union against Tuberculosis and Lung Disease).

After sending out urgent smoke signals for years, Dr. Iseman was gratified when in 1995 WHO finally declared tuberculosis "a global emergency." Yet Iseman is too much of a realist to declare victory. "There are so many fires burning on our earth, how do you decide where to direct the limited energy and resources?" he asks. A philosophical pragmatism has kept him from discouragement at the vastness of the problem. "Those of us who work in the field think of ourselves in a kind of missionary way as 'the voice of conscience,' if you will. But there are lots of Jiminy Crickets sitting on Pinocchio's shoulder trying to get his attention!"

A LIFELONG ATHLETE MAKES MEDICINE HIS FIELD

A tiny cricket is not exactly the image to which one might liken Michael Iseman. Titan is more like it. His strength of character is matched by solid muscle. Every bit as fit and formidable of build today as when he helped trounce the opposition in football for Princeton and rugby for P&S, Iseman's stature would intimidate were it not for an open accessible smile. A gentle giant disguised by shirt and tie and a pair of tired eyes under reading glasses, this mild-mannered doctor for a great metropolitan medical center fights a never-ending battle against what Frank Ryan, in his book *The Forgotten Plague*, termed "a superbug."

Dr. Iseman is endowed with the zest and energy of a lifelong athlete, the acumen and compassion of a dedicated clinician, and the insight and savvy of a public health specialist attuned to human foibles. Add to that a sense of history (his undergraduate major at Princeton) and a grudging respect for the wiles of his microscopic adversary, "a brilliantly adaptable and subtle species."

Born in the small Midwestern town of Fremont, Neb., where his father was a local merchant and his mother a registered nurse, Iseman mastered every sport to which he ever applied his mind and body. He played baseball for Fremont High, varsity football and track at Princeton, rugby and basketball at P&S. He surfed in the Navy and took up skiing with a passion as soon as he moved to Colorado—not to mention the handball tournaments he won and the gold medal he helped the YOFRA/New Haven Rowing Club earn at the 1984 World's Veteran's Championships in Belgium.

An All-American back in high school, he once received a personal phone call from the governor of Nebraska asking him to stay home and play baseball for the University of Nebraska, a virtual stepping stone to the big leagues. But while Iseman would argue that sports is a wonderful training ground for the whole person, he had his eye on a wider field.

The inspiration to go into medicine came from his hometown doc who "helped put me back together every time I tore myself apart with some sports injury" and consequently "opened my eyes to the amazing power of this healing art." At Princeton, while already firmly committed to a career in medicine, a wide-ranging intellectual curiosity led him to major in history. He took his pre-medical requirements in summer school before applying to P&S.

Lacking the scientific grounding of other classmates, Iseman worked especially hard in his first two years of medical school and enjoyed the mutual support of a tightknit group of friends. He relished the lectures of Dr. Harold

Brown in parasitology, "who, in talking about the mechanisms of tropical infectious diseases, made us think outside the American model of medicine," and Dr. Harry Rose "whose brilliant lectures in microbiology awakened all our curiosity."

On his fourth year subinternship in medicine under Dr. Charles Ragan at Bellevue's "First (Columbia) Medical Division," Iseman had an inkling of his future. He enjoyed the human dynamic of city-county medicine and found a great esprit among the house staff. Dr. Ragan subsequently offered him an internship. "It was indeed on the chest service at Bellevue," he says, "that I began my fascination with lung diseases and tuberculosis. Nothing else that I did interested me as much."

Iseman made something of a name for himself early on when, with Dr. Ragan's support, he helped introduce fiberoptic bronchoscopy to New York and taught others at Bellevue and elsewhere how to use the new diagnostic tool. Following a stint in the Navy, he returned to New York to find that the Columbia Service had transferred to Harlem Hospital. Completing his second year of residency at Harlem, he subsequently pursued a fellowship in pulmonary medicine there under Dr. Julia Jones, "my mater, mentor, and quiet inspiration."

A CONVINCING ADVOCATE FOR
"DIRECTLY OBSERVED THERAPY"

Moving to Denver in 1972, Dr. Iseman joined the faculty of the University of Colorado School of Medicine (where he currently holds an appointment as professor of medicine) and took on the duties of associate director of the Pulmonary Service at Denver General Hospital. There he came under the influence of Dr. John Sbarbaro, head of the hospital's tuberculosis clinic. Impressed by Dr. Sbarbaro's "Machiavellian sense of medical administration" and his deep understanding of human behavior and its impact on medicine, as soon as Iseman saw Sbarbaro practice "directly observed therapy," he became a convinced "disciple."

Sbarbaro realized as far back as the early 1960s, in the wake of the closing of the major TB sanatoria, that people inevitably stop taking their medicine when they start to feel well. And since tuberculosis is spread by casual contact, by breathing the same air as a carrier of the disease, in public health terms a person with communicable TB is not a free agent.

When Iseman inherited the directorship of Denver General's TB Clinic, he not only continued the practice of "directly observed therapy," but also helped promote its virtues to public health authorities around the nation and the world.

Finding the traditional seven-day regimen of TB treatment impractical and unenforceable in the long run, Iseman authored the first official statement of the American Thoracic Society, documenting the efficacy of short-course treatment restricted to two times a week, thus making compliance a reasonable demand. At Denver General and at National Jewish, where he joined the faculty in 1982, the TB Clinic stays open all day six days a week, no appointment necessary, with a welcoming atmosphere, a nurse's listening ear, and a glass of juice to wash down the pills. Treatment is absolutely free and supervised to assure compliance. Noncompliance leads to immediate legal action.

The carrot-and-stick policy proved effective. In 1994, the American Thoracic Society and the Centers for Disease Control and Prevention officially accepted "directly observed therapy" as a model regimen. A year later, the WHO followed suit, embracing it as a global model.

New York City, where public TB treatment programs had been disbanded in the 1970s, faced a public health crisis of catastrophic proportions by the early 1980s with the simultaneous emergence of AIDS, overcrowding in city hospitals, and the prevalence of both diseases among the growing homeless population. HIV attacks the same T lymphocyte that controls TB. Stripped of their natural defenses, AIDS patients with latent TB or those who subsequently contracted the disease, died in a matter of weeks. The discovery of multidrug-resistant strains of the disease among the fatalities sent a panic call that was heard from City Hall to Albany to Washington, D.C. Rallying the support of federal, state, and city agencies, public health officials managed to turn the tide and cut the devastating losses by employing a strict regimen of "directly observed therapy."

Dr. Iseman views New York's success story with a mix of relief and dread. "What they were able to do in New York, thanks to the infusion of federal dollars," he points out, "they'll never be able to pull off in Kinshasa, Buenos Aires, Jakarta, Bangkok, where funds are lacking and AIDS and TB are far more prevalent than they ever were in New York."

An active and vocal member of the American Thoracic Society, in 1984 he was appointed associate editor of the *American Review of Respiratory Disease*, in which capacity he produced a series of editorials warning against the spread of the deadly new drug-resistant strains. Iseman thus entered the international arena and became increasingly involved with tuberculosis in the Third World.

His career in TB, as he described it in a talk at the Seventeenth Annual Alumni Reunion Weekend at P&S in 1995, "is like an inverted pyramid." From his early work dealing with individual patients at Harlem Hospital and later at Denver General, he became increasingly aware of the public health dimension.

At National Jewish, he perceived a nationwide referral pattern of multidrug-resistant cases in the 1980s. His international consultation led him to consider global patterns of the disease.

TB, STILL WITH US AND FATAL AFTER ALL THESE YEARS

A descendent of microorganisms in the primordial soil, the TB bacillus sprouted with the grass, spread to ruminant animals, from whence it was passed on to the first herders at the dawn of civilization and has been with us ever since. Traces have been found in ancient human remains from the equator to the polar circle. The disease continues to plague people old and young, men, women, and children on every continent.

"How can it be," asks Iseman, "that an illness for which we have a vaccine and a curative therapy is still rampant in the world today?"

Though the development of such wonder drugs as streptomycin, isoniazid, and para-aminosalicylic acid surely constitute "one of the modern miracles of medicine," he argues, "the bacillus outwitted us, defeating the current level of our technology to combat it." The BCG vaccination has proven flawed, offering at best a partial protection.

In 1990, 7.54 million cases of TB were estimated by the WHO to exist worldwide. With rampant HIV, Africa's component of TB is soaring. And in Southeast Asia and Latin America, where access to medical care has been fragmentary and chaotic, it is estimated that as many as 25 to 40 percent of the cases may be drug resistant. The consequences of these statistics are already spilling across the border into the United States, where the majority of MDR-TB is detected among foreign-born persons.

NEW THERAPIES AND OLD OUTMODED
TREATMENTS REAPPRAISED

At National Jewish, undaunted by the odds, Dr. Iseman and his colleagues specialize in the treatment of patients who have failed therapy elsewhere and are referred there as a last hope. He and his team are currently experimenting with thirteen different drugs that have demonstrated a degree of effectiveness against TB. In 1983, they also rediscovered an outdated mode of treatment:

surgery. Removing all or part of a damaged lung, careful to expunge all of the bacilli, their successes have exceeded their own expectations. "We're now taking and curing patients who are sick to a degree I never could have imagined any regimen able to treat. That's very gratifying," says Dr. Iseman.

"I've come a long way from Fremont, Neb.!" he beams. "Medicine has meant everything to me. It still feels kind of magical to be able to do something so worthwhile, to impart knowledge, facilitate healing, diminish suffering—what better way to spend a life!"

A few years ago, the two-time winner of the Kaiser Permanente Award for Excellence in Teaching at the University of Colorado Medical School and recipient in 1995 of the P&S Alumni Gold Medal for Excellence in Clinical Medicine, among many other honors, enjoyed a physician's ultimate affirmation. His son Matthew '98, who accompanied him on a medical mission to Africa, turned to him and asked: "Hey Dad, how do I become a doctor?"

CHAMPIONING INTELLECTUAL RIGOR
AND RISK AT THE AMERICAN UNIVERSITY
OF BEIRUT

FADLO R. KHURI '89

IN 2016 the American University of Beirut (AUB), the oldest and arguably the most respected institution of higher learning in the Middle East, celebrated its 150th anniversary, a momentous occasion for any school, but particularly noteworthy for an institution committed since its founding to free and open dialogue, critical thinking, and intellectual rigor in a region of tumult. Looking ahead, the pedagogical challenges and opportunities remain formidable, according to Fadlo R. Khuri '89, an oncologist by training and committed educator, who took office as the school's sixteenth president in September 2015. "A full half of the population in many Arab countries is under the age of twenty-five," Dr. Khuri points out. "Young people are not yet set in their ways. They're open to new ideas. The risk is that they can be turned toward ideological extremism, but they can also be influenced to do great good."

Dr. Khuri characterizes the institution, of which he is an alumnus and to which he has longstanding familial ties on both his mother's and father's side, as "a beacon of openness and transparency and secularism and a force for reason" in a country and a part of the world splintered by rivalries between conflicting religious and political factions. "What we needed to do early on in my term was to gain trust on all sides," he says. Having won that trust from trustees, faculty, students, and parents, he is seeking consensus to steer the school toward making a sustainable positive impact in the region and beyond. "As a small university," he argues, "we need to take intellectual risks and focus on courage."

Courage is definitely a required quality for any academic leader in the Middle East. One of Dr. Khuri's predecessors at AUB, Dr. Malcolm H. Kerr, an American national and the third president to be born in Lebanon, was assassinated while in office, and his successor, Dr. Calvin Plimpton MSD '51, faced an

attempted kidnapping. Among other pressing and unquestionably courageous priorities, under Dr. Khuri's aegis, AUB has focused on the needs of refugees, that in a country with a population of four million that currently hosts close to 2 million refugees. AUB's Center for Civil Society and Civic Engagement won the 2016 MacJannet Prize for global citizenship in recognition of its educational outreach to Syrian refugees. In addition, an AUB architect, Karim Najjar, designed prefab modules for schools for refugee children. The schools are leaping into action as quickly as they can be built.

Dr. Khuri made time for an interview at AUB's New York office a year into his presidency in September 2016.

GROUNDED IN CULTURES OF CARING

Born in Boston, Mass., to Lebanese émigré parents, his father a physician, his mother a mathematician, Fadlo Khuri moved back to Lebanon in 1970 and was brought up in Beirut, where he attended high school at the International College in Beirut and began his undergraduate studies at AUB. As a young man growing up during the Lebanese Civil War, a time of acute sectarian differences, he was often asked by friends: "What party do you belong to?" His parents replied: "We belong to the party of AUB."

A history buff steeped in American culture—with a reverence for Abraham Lincoln as a model leader, a lifelong allegiance to the Boston Red Sox, a taste for New England clam chowder, and a can-do attitude—he is also deeply rooted in the rich cultural diversity of Lebanon and the Arab world. As he put it in a presentation in 2016 to Alpha Omega Alpha Honor Medical Society(AOA) inductees at the AUB Medical School: "I was born a Lebanese, but raised intellectually by Koreans, Chinese, and Americans, by Christians, Moslems, Jews, atheists, and communists alike." Such diverse influences helped him understand from an early age: "There really is no 'other' when you've figured out that you yourself are part of that 'other.' [. . .] I am not some preternaturally sensitive individual," he insists. "I grew up in the truly diverse environment of AUB where people debated tough ideas and tolerance of difference was the norm." The school admitted its first women as fulltime students in the 1920s, long before Harvard, Yale, Princeton, and Columbia. His mother, Dr. Soumaya Khuri, a professor of mathematics at AUB, was and remains a vocal feminist. "When you bring different people from different backgrounds together even in a trouble spot," he argues, "that fear of the other starts to evaporate."

He returned to the United States to earn a bachelor's degree from Yale University and to study medicine at P&S.

"I went into medicine," he affirms, "because I wanted to help people," and credits the encouragement of his father, the late Raja Najib Khuri, MD, a renowned renal physiologist, professor and former chair of the Department of Physiology at AUB, who served as the school's acting president shortly after the assassination of Dr. Kerr, and from 1978 to 1987 as dean of the Medical School.

In the aforementioned speech, Dr. Khuri vividly recalled his first day on clinical rounds as a third-year medical student at P&S. Entrusted with the care of a gracious rabbinical scholar dying of pancreatic cancer, he felt compelled to dwell on the family's bitter plaint: "How could such a good man have such a cruel and unkind death?" Ultimately, he concludes, "my search for meaning in this painful event drove me into the field of cancer research."

At P&S he came under the influence of the late Dr. Bernard Weinstein, professor of medicine and director of the Comprehensive Cancer Center at Presbyterian Hospital. "Bernie was the first person to really make science thrilling for me at Columbia." Another P&S mentor, the late Leslie Baer '63, director of the Hypertension Research Program at Presbyterian, under whose guidance he pursued his third-year medical rotation, "taught me how to write a thoughtful patient history [. . .], to include my reasoning, the rationale for a diagnosis and plan of treatment."

It was also at Columbia that he met the most important person in his life, his future wife, Lamya Tannous Khuri, PhD '93 Nutrition.

Yet another distinguished member of the P&S faculty, the late Dr. John Lindenbaum, at the time vice chair of medicine, counseled him to give clinical medicine a try and recommended training in medicine at Boston City Hospital. In Boston, Dr. Khuri faced the daunting challenge of treating a growing cohort of patients in the early days of the AIDS epidemic. Grueling as it was, he "enjoyed the immediacy of taking care of patients. It's easy to feel you're working for a job your first eight hours, but after that you need to know that it's more than a job, that it's a calling.

"Anybody who tells you that the physician-patient relationship is a one-way stream, that the great, noble physician gives and the patient just takes," he adds, "they don't know medicine, they haven't practiced it." In addition to the emotional gratification of providing care, medicine offers an intellectual challenge. "There's something very rewarding about piecing together the jigsaw puzzle of disease. Even if you can't cure someone, you've eased their pain, diagnosed immediate complications, alleviated a symptom."

He subsequently completed a fellowship in hematology/medical oncology at New England Medical Center, Tufts University School of Medicine. In 1995 he joined the Department of Medicine at the University of Texas MD Anderson Cancer Center, and in 2002 he was recruited by Emory University as professor of hematology and oncology and director of the Cancer Discovery and Developmental Therapeutics Program at the Winship Cancer Institute, where he was later named Roberto C. Goizueta Distinguished Chair and assembled a dynamic research team.

A widely cited molecular oncologist and acknowledged leader in translational thought, the author of over 300 peer-reviewed articles, Dr. Khuri's clinical research has focused on the development of molecular, prognostic, therapeutic, and chemopreventive approaches to improve the standard of care for patients with lung and aerodigestive cancers. "Committed to thinking of cancer as not just end stage, but taking in the entire evolution from premalignancy in order to establish the earliest possible intervention point in the disease," he and his team at Emory were in the vanguard of what has come to be known as precision or personalized medicine.

A CALL TO SERVICE

"The real challenge in life," he reflects, "is about being able to reinvent and redefine yourself every ten to fifteen years." Upon learning that AUB was seeking a new president, Dr. Khuri, who had been contemplating a career pivot, decided to apply for the job. It was for him a chance to give back to an institution that helped shape his character and his thinking and an opportunity to have a positive impact on a country and a culture to which he feels a strong emotional tie. "We're at a tipping point in history in the Arab world. That's one of the biggest reasons I went back," he says. "I want to contribute in any way I can to the shift towards a better, sounder set of beliefs and ideologies than currently exist there."

Did a career in medical oncology help prepare him for the challenges of leading a major university?

"Yes, I most definitely think it has," he affirms. "First, it helps to understand that you often have to synthesize complex and contradictory data to make a difficult decision. Medicine prepares you to accept responsibility for that decision. It is also a very humbling profession; this is particularly the case in oncology. Even though inevitably you fail a lot, you celebrate every victory and learn from every defeat. Sometimes you don't have the answer. So learning to live with ambiguity, which I think is the hallmark of a good leader, is a very key quality."

Dr. Khuri believes that the American pedagogical model of a liberal education, as promoted by the founders of the American University of Beirut, is still viable today, though it may well be in need of updating. "We must acknowledge the successes and the failures of previous applications of the American intellectual ethos." American political policy, he points out, has not always been a force for good in the Middle East, "mistakes were made and are being made, but people in the region did not lose faith in the American intellectual agenda."

And whereas in the United States, in Dr. Khuri's view, "politicians don't take academic institutions all that seriously, except as intellectual factories to produce policy wonks, there is a respect for and a fear of academe among the political leaders in Lebanon and the Arab world, which is both exhilarating and a little frightening. They care about what we advocate.

"The university cannot replace the role of the Lebanese government," he says, "but we can step up and provide the truth, whether it's about carbon emissions or trash burning or medicine or history. As educators, we also can and must take better care of our students, so that they go out into the world more knowledgeable, more confident, more empowered to make a difference than when they came in."

As a pedagogue, Dr. Khuri is a strong believer in the ethos espoused by AUB's founding president, Dr. Daniel Bliss: "We were not anxious to appear great, but we were anxious to lay foundations upon which greatness could be built." Over the years, AUB has produced leaders in a multitude of fields, notably Ashraf Ghani, president of Afghanistan; Zaha Hadid, the first woman to win the prestigious Pritzker Architecture Prize; Ray Irani, former chair and CEO of Occidental Petroleum (a company founded by P&S alumnus Armand Hammer '21); and Charles Malik, a diplomat and former Secretary of the U.N. Commission of Human Rights, instrumental in drafting the Universal Declaration of Human Rights, among many others.

Dr. Khuri hopes to cultivate future leaders. The wave of protest movements that has come to be known as the Arab Spring awakened dreams, many of which were beaten down by oppressive regimes, but the dreams did not die. "Democracy is a very fragile entity," he posits, "it's like one of those flowers that doesn't necessarily grow in all soil unless it's really carefully tended for a long time." By his frank assessment, "statesmen and stateswomen are rare in the Arab world—we have never had a Lincoln or a Mandela, but that doesn't mean we can't help bring them to the fore tomorrow."

One of his most ambitious projects as part of the university strategic plan is the creation of a global health sciences center. More than just a traditional conglomerate of schools of medicine, nursing, pharmacy, and public health, Dr. Khuri wants AUB to take advantage of the fact that "we are at the epicenter of some major health crises, not just medical crises." He hopes the center will take a leadership role in addressing health-related issues that transcend the traditional boundaries of the health sciences to include, notably, issues related to conflict medicine.

MISSION CREATES MARGIN

In a speech titled "Legacy of Service," delivered at the 2016–2017 Opening Ceremony, Dr. Khuri challenged the role of the university. "We have strayed far too long and far too deeply on the utilitarian and professional path," he warned, a dangerous detour he perceives not just at AUB, but at universities everywhere, at which the humanities have sunk to second-rung status behind applied professional, and more obviously profitable, pursuits. To redress this perceived failing, Dr. Khuri hopes to reinvigorate the study of philosophy, Arabic, and international literature, and to restart independent fine arts, music, and theater departments, among other fields of liberal study.

"Beirut is not a tidy city, physically or intellectually," he readily admits, "but that lack of tidiness is precisely why the founding fathers of the university chose well. You want a lot of fertile dissonance in a rich academic environment, and from my perspective that dissonance is grounded in the humanities.

"Yes, we will continue to train some of the best engineers in the Middle East and the world," he affirms. But in response to parents and trustees who may question the utility of what they perceive as impractical pursuits, he argues: "I don't want to train less engineers, I just want those engineers to take more humanities courses, learn more about why we do things, as opposed to just how we do things. You really only get that chance in college, and it's currently underemphasized in the curriculum."

Dr. Khuri recalls a conversation he had some years ago with a member of the board of trustees of Emory University, an institution at which he spent more than a decade and a half on the faculty and to which he remains devoted. "No margin, no mission!" was the mantra preached by the trustee. Budgetary constraint was the common reason given for trimming the curriculum. "You've got it a 100 percent wrong," Dr. Khuri responded. "It's the mission that creates the margin! If you're no good at your educational mission and you don't believe in it, the margin's going to go away, because some other institution that does believe in their mission is going to do a better job and achieve a better margin, and they're going to make you a dinosaur!"

A NEW MARSHALL PLAN FOR THE ARAB WORLD

Energized by "a very creative and participatory faculty and staff, echoing the call of students who come in wanting to make a difference," he argues that "a university can only do so much, we can come up with the ideas, but society has to meet us halfway."

In his inaugural remarks upon taking on the mantle of the presidency, Dr. Khuri boldly proposed: "Can we at AUB become the first brick in a new Marshall Plan for the Arab world, a homegrown one?" Piloted by U.S. Secretary of State George Marshall following World War II to bolster the shattered economy of Europe, including that of a defeated Germany, the plan included a vigorous educational component. Education should be a priority of support in the Middle East, he argues, "not because of noblesse oblige, but because it's to everyone's long-term strategic advantage."

To address the rising cost of tuition, among other initiatives Dr. Khuri has proposed a national service and teaching model, whereby in exchange for debt forgiveness funded by the Lebanese government, students pledge to teach in rural areas for a set number of years. As a young man, he himself taught English, math, and science in Palestinian refugee camps and in the southern district of Beirut.

About to lead a major capital campaign, Dr. Khuri hopes to foster a meaningful sense of philanthropy in Lebanon and the Middle East. "We need to substantially increase our endowment, to spend on building our infrastructure, and most importantly on supporting our faculty and students," he says. "But I want our prospective donors to give because they truly believe in the cause. If they don't believe in it, we don't need their money."

When not promoting the cause of AUB, he flies to Atlanta, where his wife is still holding down the fort while their youngest finishes high school. Among favorite leisure activities, he follows sports, in particular the exploits of the Boston Red Sox, and takes long walks in the hills around Beirut. "Lebanon is a beautiful country, I'm very comfortable with the people I meet, from whom I learn a lot. I'm still a perpetual student."

MAKING HEALTH CARE HAPPEN,
A COMMITTED PRIMARY CARE
PRACTITIONER IN THE DEEP SOUTH

KAREN KINSELL '93

YOU CAN still find arrowheads scattered about if you know where to the look, trinkets of the Creek War of 1813–1814. Steamboats came and went, carting off cotton and leaving behind an abandoned opera house, a vintage hardware store, a cluster of reconstructed log cabins and a historic stockade, the faded traces of bygone glory. Once a hub of commerce and a strategic Confederate outpost in the War Between the States, Fort Gaines is today a picturesque memento of yore on the Chattahoochee River, county seat of Clay County, Georgia, three hours' drive south of Atlanta—a county designated by the State Office of Rural Health as the most medically underserved, and ranked last in the state health assessment for the second year in a row. With a population of 1,100, comprising 429 households, roughly 60 percent black and 40 percent white, and a median household income of $18,300, the town has one doctor.

Karen Kinsell MD/MPH '93 is presently, in fact, the only MD in the entire county, tending to the health needs of some 3,600 people. Her patient pool includes many destitute individuals, some of whom cross state lines from nearby Alabama to seek care. She regularly works ten-hour days, seeing between thirty and forty patients, including many uninsured, charging a nominal ten dollars a visit, "if they can afford it, nothing if they can't."

"I have a commitment to the community," affirms Dr. Kinsell, who also serves as vice chair of the local school board. "I think I make a difference here. If I left they would be in pretty bad shape."

It was a privilege to shadow Dr. Kinsell over two days in October 2013 for an interview on the run, conducted between her car, her office and the local nursing home, where she stopped by after hours to look in on a patient. Close to a century old, wavering in and out of consciousness, Mr. Coleman's smile upon seeing her said it all.

"I WANTED TO PRACTICE [. . .] IN A PLACE SO 'SORRY' THEY DIDN'T EVEN KNOW THEY NEEDED ME."

A feisty Indiana native not inclined to mince words, Dr. Kinsell, who faced her share of hurdles when she first came to Georgia in 1996, and is still willing to wrangle with the powers that be if the cause is right, recalls with a chuckle, "I wanted to practice in an underserved area, in a place so 'sorry' they didn't even know they needed me."

They *know*. Local feelings for her run strong. "If I could win the lottery, I would build her the finest clinic she ever had," declares the newly elected Fort Gaines mayor, Tirena Kenyon, who previously served as Dr. Kinsell's first receptionist. Absent lottery windfalls and public funding, the doctor makes do with the Clay County Medical Center, in the remodeled, albeit some-what sagging, premises of a former Tasty Freeze ice cream stand. "It has ter-mites and a tendency to slip into the ditch behind it, but the ceiling holds," Dr. Kinsell allows.

"She'll drop whatever she is doing to rush to the rescue," Mayor Kenyon says. "I don't care where she comes from, these are *her* people now. [. . .] She's one heck of a diagnostician, too, let me tell you," the mayor adds. "I'll give you an example. My husband was having severe abdominal pains. It was late at night, so I didn't want to bother her and took him to the little emergency room in the town next door. Big mistake! After writhing in agony for a day and a half, they told him to go home and take Maalox. I finally called her. 'It's his gallbladder,' she said over the phone after I described the symptoms, 'get him to the hospital in Albany right away.' He had emergency surgery that afternoon. She saved his life."

FROM THE MIDWEST TO MIDTOWN, FROM THE BRONX TO THE BACKWOODS

A graduate of Lawrence University, a liberal arts college in Appleton, Wis., Karen Kinsell initially pursued a PhD in human nutrition at Cornell before switching to a program in geriatric social work at Yeshiva University to have a more immediate impact on people's lives. After working for seven years as director of two residence facilities for homeless women, many with mental health issues, near Times Square, in the beating heart of Manhattan, she decided she needed more training and clout to really make a difference, and so revived an old idea to become a doctor.

Consequently, at age thirty-four, having been out of college for twelve years, she buckled down to make up the prerequisite premed courses, scored high on the MCATs, and was admitted to several medical schools, opting for Columbia P&S "because it was the most rigorous place I got into . . . and because it offered a dual degree MD-MPH track with the School of Public Health" (now the Mailman School of Public Health).

The second-oldest member of her class, she was "informed in no uncertain terms that by not starting medical school until age thirty-four [she] had essentially deprived society of twelve years of being a doctor," Dr. Kinsell recalls. "I know that it takes tremendous resources to train a physician. And you have a responsibility to do all you can with that education. But I still felt I had a lot to offer. My experiences before medical school helped me tremendously to be a better doctor."

Enjoying the patient contact in the clinical years and particularly relishing classes in public health, the combined experience reaffirmed her belief, as per Dr. Rudolph Virchow, 1821–1902, German physician, pathologist, pioneer in public health and social medicine, that: "Medicine is politics."

Among her teachers at P&S, the late Glenda Garvey '69—"Tough! Demanding!"—and pathologist Jay Lefkowitch '76—"Knowledgeable! Cool!"—left indelible impressions. But having decided from the start to pursue a career in primary care in an institution that clearly favored specialty training, she admits to have felt "a bit like a fish out of water." To make matters worse, she fell ill at the end of her second year and had to take a brief leave of absence, but she pulled through alright.

Dr. Kinsell pursued training as a chief resident in primary care internal medicine at Montefiore Medical Center, and its affiliate, West Central Bronx Hospital, honing her diagnostic skills treating the city's most hard-hit population.

"It was grueling and gratifying," she affirms, "but there were already a thousand fine doctors floating around in the Bronx, and they didn't need another." In addition, the murder of the Chinese restaurant owner across the street from where she lived gave her pause. That and a bad case of asthma aggravated by pollution and cold made her reconsider big-city life. "I came from a small Midwestern town, but didn't want to go back there either. I wanted an underserved area where it was warm and I could run around in shirt sleeves most of the year [. . .] So I went to the library [. . .] got a map and a book of statistics [. . .] and considered ten government-funded clinics for the poor in the Deep South."

She picked a remote corner of Georgia near the Alabama border. But the institutional culture of Albany Area Primary Health Care, an affiliate of Phoebe Putney Health Systems, in Albany, where she initially decided to practice, did not prove to be a perfect fit. Ostensibly devoted to a mission of "improving access to health care," the parent institution, Phoebe Putney—"the subject of several unflattering media portrayals [. . .] detailing the flourishing health care giant's attempts to gain control of the health care market in southwest Georgia," according to a 1998 article in *American Medical News*—paid too much attention to regulations and the bottom line for her liking. She was reprimanded for grabbing a health chart and rushing off to help a woman whose sister called in to say she was having a stroke off-site. Another time the administration chided her for making a home visit to a frail, bedridden, old woman, again contrary to institutional policy. And when, to her considerable upset, her contract was not renewed, Fort Gaines caught her eye as just the sort of place she wanted to practice. The only problem was the contract with Phoebe Putney included a "no-compete clause," according to which she agreed not to practice within a twenty-mile radius, and Fort Gaines was a mile short. After much legal wrangling, the Georgia Court of Appeals eventually found that contract to be unconstitutional, and Dr. Kinsell hung out her shingle.

"HOW DO YOU ACTUALLY MAKE THE CARE HAPPEN?"

Given the current constraints of the American health care system, such as it is, and committed as she is to affordable care, Dr. Kinsell confesses that her business model of charging uninsured patients "ten dollars or nothing" per visit is "financially completely unsustainable."

Having trained to become a Certified Application Counselor under the Affordable Care Act, she remains extremely frustrated by Georgia Governor Nathan Deal's refusal to expand Medicaid and thereby permit state residents and doctors to benefit from health insurance, despite the state's large number of uninsured. The Georgia health insurance commissioner has, furthermore, gone on record saying he would do all he could to "obstruct" enrollment. "Southwest Georgia," she points out, "has the second highest insurance rates in the state, probably a combination of poverty, ill-health, and lack of competition, with only one insurer in the region [. . .] It would make life a whole lot easier for all if there were a viable payment scheme in place."

"PEACE CORPS WITH CABLE"

Her patients often present a complex puzzle of interrelated medical, psychological, and social issues. On the afternoon this interviewer sat in on her practice with the patients' consent, Dr. Kinsell saw a self-described "germophobe," a young woman distressed about a lesion on her lip. "The presenting issue was really NOTHING, but she needed to have her ills acknowledged!" The next patient was a woman in a wheelchair who had just had a knee replacement. She complained of being "tired of just sitting there," and so had gotten up, walked around prematurely, and had fallen. Next came a young man suffering from chronic pancreatitis brought on by alcoholism, also diagnosed with a bipolar disorder, the medicine for which clearly impacted his demeanor. He found and sold precious arrowheads to supplement meager disability payments. In this case, suspecting addiction, Dr. Kinsell was skeptical of his request for additional prescription pain killers. "A lot of what I do is medical detective work," she allows.

Dr. Kinsell thinks of her practice as "doing Peace Corps work with cable. [. . .] It may not be as exotic as, say, practicing in sub-Saharan Africa, [. . .]

you've got more creature comforts, cable TV, Internet, and such. [. . .] But what makes the American Deep South any less valuable or worthy or interesting than any other culture?"

"POVERTY COLORS YOUR EXPECTATIONS OF WHAT LIFE SHOULD BE LIKE."

"In most cases you're not discovering multiple sclerosis," she says of her day-to-day practice. "Most of it is figuring out how you can treat whatever your patient walks in with in a way that's actually feasible. And that's where you need to get clever about how to get people medications they're not going to be able to pay for." Her commitment to her patients includes helping them apply for prescription assistance plans with major drug companies. Her abiding concern is, "How do you actually make the care happen?

"Of course, you have to be able to *smell* how sick your patient is, to know if he or she requires a different level of care, like treating upper lobe pneumonia. You don't want someone waiting in your office for two hours who really needs to see a specialist right away. That's one of the key challenges of practicing primary care in a remote rural setting!"

Her office walls are decorated with inspirational quotes from Christ, Gandhi, Abraham Lincoln, and the Dalai Lama, among others. "It catches people's attention and helps them and me get through the day."

"In some respects medical care is very similar to religion," she observes. "You go to see somebody dressed in white robes, in a small room, and you tell them all this private information about yourself. There is something in the human brain [. . .] a silent suffering [. . .] that needs to feel . . . acknowledged. [. . .] It's the second oldest profession, okay?" Dr. Kinsell grins. "Before there was any medicinal arsenal to change the course of biological disease, people still needed to turn to healers, shamans, medicine men. [. . .] A third of all primary care patients are clinically depressed. [. . .] Most of the people who came in this morning would not have died if I hadn't seen them. You're trying to improve the quality of their daily life. That's also what a doctor does."

Economics, she points out, is also a major factor in medicine. "Poverty causes and complicates so many conditions and diseases. If you've had a heart attack, your prognosis if you're poor is markedly worse. Your ability to afford the medications and take them correctly is compromised.

"Poverty colors your expectations of what your life should be like. I've had young people come in, and when I ask them what they're going to do, they reply dead seriously: 'Either I'm gonna go to auto-body school or else I'm gonna collect my disability.' "

THE BITTER SIDE OF SWEETNESS

Having already been interested as a graduate student of nutrition in the adverse effects of sugar consumption, every day Dr. Kinsell witnesses the bitter side of sweetness. The problem of obesity has reached epidemic proportions. Only very few of her patients are normal weight.

"Obesity causes most diabetes, a lot of hypertension, and in turn, cardiovascular disease, some cancers, depression, and a lot of arthritis," she says. "The number of middle-aged women over 250 pounds with arthritic knees is just overwhelming. People hereabouts will frequently drink a six pack of soda pop and other soft drinks a day. And not just teenagers, mothers and grandmothers too.

"I had a vastly overweight lady almost literally run me down with a shopping cart at the Dollar General the other day to tell me how excited she was to lose twenty pounds. She said it took the pressure off her knees, that she could walk again. Her mother, who is likewise obese, was in the hospital with congestive heart failure. Her son, age fifteen, drinks nothing but soft drinks. I said, 'You don't have to buy it for him.' She said, 'If we don't have it, he'll put sugar in water and drink that.'

"I was struck one day last year," Dr. Kinsell reports. "Within twenty-four hours I had three young men come in who were over 400 pounds. The first was thirty-four with congestive heart failure. The second was twenty-nine with severe hypertension. The third, age twenty-four, over 430 pounds, came in to address some other issue, but didn't think he had a problem with weight.

"Of course, lack of adequate education is a tremendous part of the problem. The high school graduation rate among adults is under 58 percent," she says. Teen pregnancy, drug and alcohol abuse, inadequate asthma prevention, an ignorance of basic preventive measures, and the absence of positive role models are among other education-related health issues. As vice chair of the local school board, she has tried to make a modest difference. In recent years she has also written an intermittent health column in the local newspaper.

"NOTHING ABOUT THIS JOB IS *EVER* BORING!"

All things considered, she relishes the opportunity to practice primary care medicine the way she wants. In a remote rural practice "you have to figure everything out for yourself [. . .] Well heck, if I had an x-ray machine, it'd be pretty easy, wouldn't it! To make an accurate diagnosis without any labs or high-tech equipment, and no second opinion from somebody down the hall, that's the primary challenge. From a professional standpoint, it's an ongoing test of your medical skills."

Dr. Kinsell has been saluted as a Lion's Club "Woman of the Year" and named a National Library of Medicine "Local Hero." But the real payoff is in the practice.

"Would I recommend this kind of lifestyle to others?" she asks aloud. "I like living in a little town and seeing people at the supermarket, seeing what they buy and knowing what they talk about. It helps me be a better doctor. It's a small enough venue so that you can really make and see a difference. Nothing about this job," she adds, "is *ever* boring! I don't have any hospital administrators to second guess what I do! I call all the shots. It's Disneyland for a doctor!" she grins, before once again reasserting a serious medical mien. "And yes, it's good to know I'm needed."

UROLOGIST, HISTORIAN, COLLECTOR, SLEUTH—A MEDICAL MAN FOR ALL SEASONS

JOHN K. LATTIMER '38

Having lived through more adventures and more diverse experiences than most, urologist-historian John K. Lattimer '38 died peacefully in 2007, at age ninety-three. Lecturing from a wheelchair a year before his passing, he brought the house down during a presentation in the P&S Alumni Auditorium at Alumni Reunion Weekend, closing with a slide of General Patton peeing into the Rhine, upon which Dr. Lattimer remarked, "He sure had a healthy prostate."

⸺⸙⸺

THROUGHOUT HIS long and fruitful career, John K. Lattimer '38 has often touched and been touched by history. Innovative academic urologist, record-setting athlete, veteran army surgeon on hand at the Normandy Invasion and the Nuremberg Tribunal, noted collector, eclectic author, ballistics expert and forensic authority on the Lincoln and Kennedy assassinations, and the recipient of more medals than a fine lapel can hold, his epic list of accomplishments fills a full fifty-nine lines of *Who's Who in the World*. His patients have included such key players in the course of events as Othar Ammann, the man who built the George Washington Bridge, Columbia University President Nicholas Murray Butler, actress Greta Garbo, U.S. President Warren Harding, aviator Charles Lindbergh, Dewitt Wallace, cofounder (with his wife, Lila) of the *Reader's Digest*, the injured survivors of the Hindenburg explosion, and the notorious defendants at the Nuremberg Tribunal. At eighty-six and counting, a hip replacement may have slowed his strut and tipped his statuesque six-foot, four-inch frame a hair, but the verve and gusto still run at full tilt, keeping an interviewer on his toes.

FROM MOUNT CLEMENS, MICHIGAN, TO MORNINGSIDE HEIGHTS

"My theory is that people's capabilities in their given fields grow from a cluster of elements, all of which have to click," Dr. Lattimer reflected in a profile that appeared in *Americana* magazine in 1981. While he was referring specifically to the art of collecting, one of his many avocational interests, his own complex elemental cluster is difficult to dissect.

As a boy stalking pesky crows on the family farm in Mount Clemens, Mich., young Lattimer learned to lock onto his wily target and stick with it until the job was done, a skill that would come in handy years later when he ran the U.S. government effort to stalk and stamp out renal TB, and later still when he applied his ballistic talents to demystify the much-touted myth of conspiracy in the assassination of President Kennedy. He inherited a healthy dose of curiosity and analytical skill from his father, an inventor-engineer and early pioneer in long-distance communication for AT&T. His maternal grandfather, a successful Michigan physician who took him along on house calls, and a long line of doctors on his mother's side predisposed him to a medical career. Moving to New York with his family, he returned to the heartland every chance he got to cut loose on the lands the Lattimers had homesteaded before the Civil War.

It was there on a Michigan country road one hot summer day that he first encountered living history in the person of a young pilot who stopped to give him and a friend a lift. "You know who that was, don't you?" said the friend, breathless with excitement. "That was Charles Lindbergh!" All summer long, John Lattimer watched his hero hone the art of skip bombing on Lake Michigan, a practice put to effective use in World War II. Dr. Lattimer delights in recounting the hilarious and hair-raising tale of how he and his friend salvaged unexploded bombs as perilous souvenirs, gingerly transporting them home via rowboat and bus, thus launching his career as a collector of the arcane. (Family heirlooms already included a set of early American silver-hilted swords, including the one brandished by a notable ancestor, Ethan Allen, at the capture of Ford Ticonderoga.) Years later, when Lindbergh, then a patient, came for dinner, Dr. Lattimer amused his guest by hauling out a vintage bomb he'd dropped.

Back in New York, where the family settled down, Lattimer attended Columbia College. In addition to the traditional course of study, he shone as an athlete, setting a record as the Columbia decathlon champion and as an Amateur Athletic Union 200-meter hurdler (a record unbroken for twelve years), and winning the 50-yard dash at the Millrose Games. During his military service, he later won the 200-meter hurdle for his unit, the 7th U.S. Army Field and General Hospitals, at the GI Olympics in Germany.

MEDICINE BECKONS, UROLOGY CALLS

It was, as Dr. Lattimer recalls, Nicholas "Miraculous" Butler, the illustrious president of Columbia University (and later a patient) who first conceived the idea in 1910 of a medical center comprising hospitals in various specialties as well as schools of medicine, dentistry, and nursing all located in the same vicinity.

Dr. Lattimer's medical student days and subsequent years of training at the Squier Urological Clinic paralleled the golden age of P&S. With legends like Dean Willard Rappleye at the helm, and the world-renowned team of Drs. Robert Loeb and Dana Atchley running the show in medicine, the patient population comprised captains of industry, international statesmen and royalty, movie stars, and star athletes. In the corridors and elevators of the medical center, Lattimer remembers bumping into the likes of the King of Siam, the Prince of Wales, the Prime Minister of Canada, Madame Chiang Kai-Shek, actor Clark Gable, and boxer Jean Tunney. Yet famous as he was, Dr. Loeb was not above ferrying the entire class of 1938 over to Seaview on Staten Island to study tuberculosis lesions. Renowned (and feared) for his keenly observant eye, Dr. Loeb also taught students a fundamental human lesson: "The patient wants a friend."—a message that Dr. Lattimer took to heart and has passed on to generations of P&S students. Dr. Atchley taught the day-to-day rigors of quality care. "When you had one of Atchley's patients in the hospital," Dr. Lattimer remembers with a chuckle and a chill, "your phone would ring at 5 A.M. 'What are you going to do with Greta Garbo today? I want to be there!' "

But of all his teachers, Lattimer was most dazzled by the competence and style of the chair of urology, J. Bentley Squier, P&S 1894, who ran the famous clinic established in his name like a gold-plated temple of excellence for all, V.I.P.s and indigent patients alike. Arriving on alternate days in a purple-paneled Bugatti Royale and a pearl gray Rolls Royce, he sent his liveried footman ahead, hat in hand, to announce his arrival. This lavish manner did not keep him from personally inspecting the floors on Sundays. Dr. Squier was famous for his surgical skill and speed at a prostatectomy (three minutes flat!) and other delicate operations, time often being a factor of life and death in the days before antibiotics and blood transfusions. Another famous member of the faculty, and chair after Squier's retirement, Dr. George Francis Cahill was a wizard at removing adrenal tumors, thus reversing hormone imbalance and the accompanying distortion of secondary sex characteristics. For a time, the department became involved in sex-change operations. Christine Jorgensen, the world's first transsexual, consulted in later years with Dr. Lattimer. What particularly appealed to him about urology was its diverse challenge as a discipline, the fact that it combined medicine and surgery with superb diagnostic techniques. "Where else" (as he put it in a feature profile that appeared in *Roche Medical Image* in 1968) "can you, in a single morning, relieve one patient from the agony of urinary obstruction, change the sexual characteristics of another, and arrest cancer in a third?"

Following graduation, Dr. Lattimer entered the surgical trenches, treating every conceivable kind of wound and trauma as a rotating (surgical) intern at Methodist-Episcopal Hospital in Brooklyn. He subsequently returned to Columbia to join the faculty as an assistant in urology (and resident at the Squier Urological Clinic), earning an ScD degree along with the prestigious Smith Prize Diploma in 1943. But trouble brewing overseas put a hold on his academic career and thrust him in history's pathway.

FROM NOTTINGHAM TO NORMANDY

Joining the Armed Forces, he originally selected the Air Force, until friends pointed out that they did not do any major surgery, whereupon he later got himself transferred to the Army (thanks to the intercession of a helpful young medical officer at the Pentagon named Dr. Michael DeBakey, who later made something of a name for himself in cardiac surgery). His six weeks of training at Carlisle Barracks were anything but basic. Realizing that the vast majority of fledgling medical officers had no experience whatsoever treating gunshot wounds, he pitched in to help fill in the blanks. An expert marksman, he also participated in Army wound ballistics experiments at the Anatomy Lab at P&S to establish what the Germans were doing to make their bullets tumble and tear into their human targets.

Sent overseas to Nottingham, England, he bided his time before the impending invasion by, among other endeavors, drill marching nurses, thereby attracting the attention of Winston Churchill, his picture making it (for the first of three times in his career) to the front page of the *New York Times*.

All fun and games came to a sudden and dramatic end on D-day. Dr. Lattimer recalls the experience of treating the enormous number of seriously wounded casualties of the Normandy Invasion at makeshift EVAC hospitals ashore and back in Great Britain as "a terrible, terrible time." With hundreds of evacuees suffering multiple life-threatening wounds to kidney, bladder, and genitals, and limited blood plasma available, he and his colleagues had to perform triage, operating on those most likely to survive. He worked fast and furiously and, on occasion, had to confront a pistol in the trembling hand of a GI whose buddy hadn't been picked.

When, at last, the Allies took the blood-soaked beachhead, Dr. Lattimer's unit went on to Antwerp, Kassel, Frankfurt, and finally, Munich, where a large German civilian hospital was retooled as the 98th U.S. Army General Hospital, and Dr. Lattimer took over as chief of Urology/Surgery.

"BOY, YOU GOT TO SEE THIS! THIS IS HISTORY!"

Pastor Henry Gerecke, the Lutheran chaplain of the 98th General Hospital and a friend of Dr. Lattimer's, was transferred to see to the spiritual needs of high-ranking Nazi prisoners, pending trial, and later walked the condemned to the gallows. Held at first at an old resort hotel in Mondorf-les-Bains, in Luxembourg (American code name "Ashcan"), the defendants were subsequently sent to a prison in Nuremberg to face the Tribunal. "Boy, you got to see this! This is history!" Chaplain Gerecke urged his friend on a return visit to the hospital.

While pursuing his duties at the General Hospital, Dr. Lattimer, on frequent occasions throughout the trial as one of several physicians, came to see to the prisoners' medical needs. In his compelling book *Hitler's Fatal Sickness and the Other Secrets of the Nazi Leaders*, published in 1999, the author taps his firsthand experience, as well as medical scholarship and speculation on the historical ramifications of Hitler's Parkinson disease, which, he believes, ultimately led Hitler to make the rash military judgments that cost Germany the war. Much of the book is devoted to Dr. Lattimer's impressions of the defendants from the point of view of a physician. While most elicited his unqualified contempt, Albert Speer, the only defendant to admit his guilt and take responsibility for the crimes committed under his watch, earned Dr. Lattimer's respect. Impressed by Speer's obvious intelligence and a willingness to face the truth, the author paraphrases the observation of a colleague on the American medical team, prison psychiatrist Dr. Douglas Kelley (a graduate of the New York State Psychiatric Institute) who compared Speer "to a young racehorse of great capability who was wearing blinders. He could see straight ahead and all he did was to run

to his greatest capacity without realizing the consequences." The highest rank-
ing and most notorious defendant, Reich Marshal Hermann Goering, earned
Lattimer's grudging avowal of a keen and wily intelligence. His wile served
Goering well in his final hour, managing as he did to cheat the hangman with
a hidden ampoule of cyanide. The ampoule container itself is now a part of
Dr. Lattimer's large collection of memorabilia from the trial.

WINNING THE WAR AGAINST RENAL TB
AND OTHER VICTORIES

Returning to the States, Dr. Lattimer rejoined the urology faculty at P&S
and the staff at Presbyterian (now New York-Presbyterian) and Babies (now
Morgan-Stanley Children's) Hospitals. Likewise serving as an attending consultant in urology at the Veterans Administration Hospital in the Bronx, he headed
up the Research Unit for Genitourinary Tuberculosis. Among the notable medical accomplishments of the postwar period, his team applied the then new drug,
streptomycin, later adding PAS and isoniazid, to help stamp out renal TB.

At P&S meanwhile, Dr. Lattimer, whose busy urological practice straddled
the line in the care of adults and children, began to gather and study the considerable body of data his pediatric service had amassed over the years. Pediatric urology was "a sleeping giant waiting to be awakened," he recalled in a
video-taped interview, conducted in 1982 by Emory Medical School Dean James
Glenn, in the AOA series "Leaders in American Medicine." Dr. Glenn acknowledges Dr. Lattimer as one of the field's founding fathers. And awaken it he did.
Combining his diverse talents at scholarship, administration, and spreading the
word, Dr. Lattimer stunned the old guard of the American Urological Association by filling a 2,500 seat auditorium at the annual meeting of the American
Academy of Pediatrics with urologists and other practitioners from around the
country eager to hear his findings. And so, almost overnight, the subspecialty
was born, first at P&S, then nationwide and worldwide.

Rapidly rising in academic ranks, in 1955, at age thirty-nine, he was named
professor and chair of the Department of Urology, and director of the Squier
Urological Clinic. In the course of his tenure, which lasted until his formal
retirement in 1980, Dr. Lattimer increased the number of medical students who
opted for what had previously been, in his words, "an underappreciated field"
and raised millions in endowments (including substantial personal contributions) to support departmental research. Stressing more imaginative teaching

methods, he urged urologists to think of themselves as "watchmakers, rather than plumbers." He helped awaken public awareness to the fact that prostate cancer was the leading cause of cancer deaths in men over sixty-five, thus helping urology to come into its own. The then newly created Office of Urology at the National Institutes of Health awarded his department its first training grant. As governor of the American College of Surgeons, he ran that distinguished body's educational and urological programs.

Dr. Lattimer likewise attracted the national and international spotlight in the field, appointed by President Lyndon B. Johnson as a consultant to the World Health Organization in 1968, rising to the presidency of the International Society of Urology in 1973, and the American Urological Association in 1975, the first person ever to hold both high offices simultaneously. He subsequently served as president of the Clinical Society of Genitourinary Surgeons and the Society of University Urologists.

A former medical consultant to *Time Magazine*, guest editor for the Medical Examiners *Gazette* and contributor to the *Encyclopedia Britannica*, his publications in peer review journals are numerous. His professional encomia have included the P&S Alumni Gold Medal in Clinical Medicine and the Dean's Distinguished Achievement Award, the Morgenstern Foundation Freedom Award for his role at Nuremberg, the Great Medal of the City of Paris, and a medal honoring his role in the liberation of Paris personally given to him by then Mayor of Paris, soon-to-be French President, Jacques Chirac. In 1987, he was the first recipient of the National Kidney Foundation's award for outstanding achievement in urology, and in 1996 he received the Keyes Medal, the top honor of the American Association of Genitourinary Surgeons. Named lectureships were established in his honor at five learned societies.

LATTIMER, THE COLLECTOR

While pursuing his multiple medical activities, Dr. Lattimer always found time to keep up his vast and diverse collection of historical objects, things, as he puts it, that "perpetuate your contact with the moment." An avid history buff, he made the front page of the *New York Times* a second time, when, dressed up as his ancestor Ethan Allen, he led a reenactment of the taking of Fort Ticonderoga. Dr. Lattimer has for many years helped coordinate the Medieval Festival at Fort Tryon Park, in New York, a public event complete with jousting and tilting, sponsored by the Metropolitan Museum of Art.

His collection includes, among many other items, the aforementioned early American swords on loan to the Metropolitan Museum of Art and the National Portrait Gallery; such World War II trinkets as German lugers, Goering's car armor, and original Hitler drawings; and memorabilia pertaining to the two assassinations that rocked American history, of presidents Lincoln and Kennedy.

LATTIMER, THE ASSASSINATION SLEUTH

Dr. Lattimer's extensive holdings relating to the Lincoln assassination (including a blood-stained collar, a glove and a cuff of the shirt Lincoln wore to Ford's Theatre on that fateful night), as well as his research and writing on the subject, made him perk up with a jolt on November 22, 1963, the day President John F. Kennedy was shot in Dallas. The parallels between the two events were astounding, as were the parallel legends of conspiracy. Tapping his own experience in ballistic research and his knowledge of firearms, Dr. Lattimer immediately got to work on a scientific forensic study of the circumstances of President Kennedy's death. Recognized for his knowledge in the field, he was the first nongovernment investigator granted access to the Kennedy autopsy materials, including x-rays, death photographs, and bloodied clothing. On January 9, 1972, Dr. Lattimer once again made the front page of the *New York Times*, with a photograph in which he demonstrates on his own head just where the bullets struck the president. Based on his tests with the rifle used by Lee Harvey Oswald and other findings, Dr. Lattimer backed the report of the Warren Commission and completely discounted the elaborate tales of conspiracy theorists. His book, *Kennedy and Lincoln, Medical and Ballistic Comparisons of Their Assassinations*, became a bestseller upon its publication in 1980.

In 1990, Dr. Lattimer published a third book, *This Was Early Englewood: From the Big Bang to the George Washington Bridge*, detailing the history of his longtime home town. He is currently working on a book on his silver swords.

While one of his ancestors, Bishop Hugh Latimer, was burned alive by Bloody Mary in 1550 for refusing to recant his Protestantism and another fell at the Battle of Lexington, kicking off the American Revolution, he and his wife, Jamie, live peaceably in Englewood, N.J. (in a grand old home that Dr. Lattimer laughingly labels "a urologist's paradise," complete with nine bathrooms). His daughter, Evan, followed in her mother's footsteps as an artist. His two sons, Jon K. '77 and Douglas G. '84, have taken after their dad—both are academic urologists.

A devoted alumnus and dedicated educator, Dr. Lattimer has guided the generosity of his patients toward upholding his legacy at P&S, where an endowed professorship-chairmanship in urology and a research fund bear his name. Having graciously declined a salary back in 1955 when he took over the reins of the Department of Urology, he discovered to his dismay upon his retirement that he had thereby, albeit unknowingly, forfeited a pension. Should push come to shove, he could always work the old family farm (all 400 acres worth) or sell off choice holdings, like his massive mastodon molar tooth, or objects from his Napoleonic collection, including a little item of urological and historical interest that attracted an Italian television news team to interview him in 1992, the emperor's penis, allegedly excised by the Corsican pathologist who did the autopsy. "Urologists are vital," Dr. Lattimer quipped to the visiting Italians, "but pathologists always have the final word."

YES, THERE IS A BALM IN GILEAD

MARGARET MORGAN LAWRENCE '40

Child psychiatrist Margaret Morgan Lawrence '40, a pioneer in mental health, among the first African American women to be admitted to P&S, and the first African American to complete a residency at the New York State Psychiatric Institute, enjoyed a successful career, despite the considerable hurdles of racial prejudice, and is alive and well, still beaming an infectious life-affirming smile.

———

THE GUEST SPEAKER at the 1987 Minority Student Recruitment Day Conference at P&S began with a song. As the overflow crowd of young people listened attentively, Margaret Morgan Lawrence '40 employed the lyrics of a black gospel hymn to convey her mandate to the would-be doctors in attendance. "Plenty good room in the Father's Kingdom," she sang, "Just take your seat, sit down!"

Dr. Lawrence is a distinguished child psychiatrist whose life and career in medicine are eloquently documented in *Balm in Gilead, Journey of a Healer*, a recently published biography by her daughter, Sara Lawrence Lightfoot.

Dr. Lawrence was the third black woman to attend P&S. She and her predecessors, Agnes O. Griffin '23, a retired ophthalmologist, and Vera Joseph '36, former director of the Smith College Health Service, helped open doors that had previously been closed to blacks, and in particular to black women.

Margaret Lawrence, née Morgan, was born August 19, 1914, at Sloane Hospital for Women in New York City, which was eventually incorporated into the Columbia-Presbyterian Medical Center (now New York-Presbyterian). Seventy years later, in 1984, Dr. Lawrence retired as associate clinical professor of

psychiatry at Columbia and director of the Developmental Psychiatry Service of the Division of Child Psychiatry, which she had helped found at Harlem Hospital Center (a Columbia affiliate). "So you see," she remarks today with a chuckle," I've been with Columbia a long, long time."

Hers is a truly extraordinary career, in the course of which she became the first child psychiatrist to practice in Rockland County, where she helped found the Community Mental Health Center; she was affiliated with the Child Development Center, the Northside Child Development Center, the City College Educational Clinic, and the Rockland County School Mental Health Unit. She has published two books, *Mental Health Teams in the School* (1971) and *Young Inner City Families* (1975), and is working on a third. She has also published countless articles in the field of child psychiatry.

At the same time, Dr. Lawrence succeeded against formidable odds in balancing family and professional life, creating a loving and supportive atmosphere for her three children (today a sociologist, a professor of law, and an educator). Throughout her career, she has labored tirelessly to identify and fortify the ego strength of children of all colors, creeds, and economic backgrounds.

EARLY DREAMS AND DISAPPOINTMENTS

It is in childhood that dreams, the harbinger of adult aspirations, take shape. Dr. Lawrence's lifelong "almost reverential" respect for children's feelings is rooted in a keen memory of her own childhood. Her decision to study medicine came early, at age nine, in response at least in part to the death of her infant brother. It was her good fortune to have supportive parents, her father an Episcopal minister who helped foster the dream, and her mother a school teacher, who inspired her daughter by her passion for education.

Though born in New York, she grew up in the small Mississippi town of Mound Bayou, and later moved to Vicksburg, Virginia, where educational opportunities for a young black woman were limited. Consequently, her parents sent her back to New York City to live with her grandmother and aunts. She enrolled in Wadleigh High School, an integrated elite classical public school for girls, where she thrived academically and graduated with honors in Greek. Cornell College accepted her on full scholarship, and she assumed, following the successful completion of her undergraduate studies with outstanding grades, that she would attend Cornell Medical School.

In those days, however, the "room" for minorities in medicine was less than "plenty good," and the "seat-taking" not merely a matter of talent and will. She was called in for what she believed would be a routine interview with the dean of the medical school, who began by telling her that she had done "very well" on a standardized examination, but proceeded thereafter to inform her that the Admissions Committee had regretfully decided not to accept her application. "Twenty-five years ago," the dean explained with dubious logic, "there was a Negro man admitted to Cornell Medical School and it didn't work out . . . He died of tuberculosis."

Friends urged her to apply to P&S and helped arrange for an interview. The members of Columbia's admissions committee, though not immune to the prejudicial climate of the period, interviewed the young woman. What would she do, they inquired, if in the course of her clinical training a white patient refused to see her? "I'd go back to my professor and ask for another patient!" she promptly replied, and was duly admitted.

Her medical school days were a happy time, Dr. Lawrence recalls. At P&S she found "the pleasures of disciplined retreat." And though throughout her four years here she was the only African American enrolled, her rapport with her fellow students was for the most part congenial, and she could be herself.

"There were ten women in a class of 104," Dr. Lawrence recalls. "That was an *interesting* population! I was proud to belong."

Women had first been admitted to P&S in 1917, in the wake of World War I, but until the late Sixties remained a small minority. "We knew we were fortunate to be there," Dr. Lawrence affirms, "and we intended to do well. There was a feeling among some of the professors: 'You're never going to use your degree! . . . Marriage, children, etc . . . You're just taking up room!' " All ten women fulfilled their promise, and went on to pursue active careers as clinicians, academicians, and researchers.

Another important source of spiritual support came from prominent professional women in the Harlem community, teachers like Drs. Lucille Spence and Melva Price, and the celebrated physician Dr. May Edward Chinn. The first black woman to graduate from Bellevue Hospital Medical Center and the first woman intern at Harlem Hospital, Dr. Chinn went on to become a leader in public health. She was awarded an Honorary Doctor of Science degree by Columbia on May 14, 1980. These women were mentors and formidable role models for the young medical student.

An encounter with a Columbia professor also left its stamp. Dr. Charles Drew (1904-1950), the noted medical researcher who helped develop techniques for blood banking, was at the time the only African American member of the faculty.

The student and the professor met one afternoon. Dr. Drew asked her about her experience at P&S. "I don't remember exactly what I told him," Dr. Lawrence said, "but I do remember his reaction: 'The only thing you have to do is your best work,' he said. 'You do your work and you will succeed, and race is not going to matter.' " Though questioning the professor's opinion, she appreciated his encouragement.

Another Columbia faculty member, Dr. Hattie Alexander, pediatrician and discoverer of the vaccine to combat influenza meningitis, proved an important influence, and inspired her promising student to pursue pediatrics.

But when Dr. Lawrence applied for an internship at Babies Hospital (now Morgan-Stanley Children's), she was rejected because there was no provision for women in the doctors' residence, and the only alternative, the nursing residence, refused to have her because of her color.

FINDING A PROFESSIONAL NICHE

Thereafter, she applied, and following a rigorous written examination, was accepted to a pediatric internship at Harlem Hospital. There she received a solid grounding in her primary specialty, "my beloved pediatrics," as she still refers to it. The lessons she learned were social as well as medical. She began to perceive "the connections between physical illness and community health," which inspired further study.

In 1943, she earned an MS in public health from the Columbia School of Public Health (now the Mailman School of Public Health), where one of her professors was the well-known pediatrician Benjamin Spock '29. Under his tutelage, she became aware of the interconnections between physical, social, and psychological health. "His exciting and well-integrated vision of the child, the family, the community, and society never left me," she recalls. And years before she was to pursue her formal psychiatric training, "it was Spock who gave me my first firm feeling of being a pediatrician and a child psychiatrist."

With her husband, the late Charles R. Lawrence, PhD, a distinguished sociologist, academic, and social activist, she moved back south, where he accepted an appointment to teach sociology at Fisk University and she joined the medical faculty of Meharry Medical College. It was here in the course of her teaching and clinical work that she became aware of the psychological dimension of physical illness: "My memory is of practicing a good bit of homespun child psychiatry with my patients and students . . . and realizing: Hey, you ought to be better trained in it if you're going to do it!"

However, the pre-Civil Rights Movement America of the late Forties could not conceive of a black psychiatrist, and traumatic encounters as a consequence of covert prejudice lay ahead.

The optimal place to train then, as it is now, was the New York State Psychiatric Institute. No blacks had ever been admitted as residents. However, a move to open the ranks of psychiatry to qualified black candidates was underway, led by, among others, Dr. Viola Bernard (clinical professor of psychiatry emeritus at P&S, and founder and former director of the Division of Community and Social Psychiatry at Columbia). Dr. Bernard interceded on Dr. Lawrence's behalf with the director of the Psychiatric Institute, Dr. Nolan Lewis, and in 1948, the first black resident was admitted to PI.

That same year she enrolled as the first black trainee at the Columbia Psychoanalytic Center. Having undergone psychoanalysis and fulfilled all the necessary requirements, Dr. Lawrence eagerly anticipated her certificate of graduation. It was not, however, readily forthcoming.

A false rumor had spread through a series of misunderstandings that Dr. Lawrence did not wish to work with black patients. Consequently, the director, Dr. Sandor Rado, called her in for an interview, at which he advised her, without ever telling her why, that he was withholding her certificate pending "further analysis."

This was the same experience of "depersonalization" she had gone through at the Cornell Medical School interview. Only this time, the racial sting was even more painful. She recalls the incident with anger. In heeding the rumor and never bothering to approach her directly to confirm or deny it, "these 'responsible' people were saying to me: You don't know who you are! You're nobody! You don't exist!"

But this time Dr. Lawrence persevered and, with the aid of influential supporters on the faculty, managed to resolve the matter and graduate.

Dr. Lawrence went on to do important work in child psychiatry, to propagate the cause of child mental health, and among other achievements, to develop some of the first child therapy programs in schools, day care centers, and hospital clinics.

For twenty years she served as director of the Developmental Psychiatry Clinic at Harlem Hospital, where a coworker, Dr. Denise Greene, said "she provided the rest of us with an incredible sense of calm when great chaos prevailed." Her unique contribution to psychiatry, suggests Dr. Greene, is "her emphasis on seeking out strengths in children and their families." Dr. Lawrence still feels most at home in the "playroom" she created in her office in Pomona, N.Y., where she continues to see a limited number of private patients.

Recipient of the Joseph R. Bernstein Mental Health Award, the Outstanding Women Practitioners in Medicine Award of the Susan Smith McKinney Steward Medical Society, and countless other honors, she has never lost sight of her goals.

A DOCTOR IN THE HOUSE—
THE *WHITE* HOUSE, THAT IS

BURTON J. LEE, III '56

*In 2005, twelve years after terminating his work as White House physician to
President George H. W. Bush, in an op-ed piece in the* Washington Post,
*Dr. Lee, a board member of Physicians for Human Rights, took a bold stand in
opposition to reported torture and abuse of prisoners in the war on terrorism
conducted under the administration of President George W. Bush. "It's precisely
because of my devotion to country, respect for our military, and commitment
to the ethics of the medical profession," he wrote, "that I speak out against
systematic, government-sanctioned torture and excessive abuse of prisoners
during our war on terrorism. I am also deeply disturbed by the reported
complicity in these abuses of military medical personnel. This extraordinary shift
in policy and values is alien to my concept of modern-day America and of my
government and profession." Dr. Lee died in 2016, at age eighty-six.*

———— ✿ ————

OTHERS MAY refer to the GNP and key economic indicators to measure the
health of the nation, but Burton J. Lee III '56 trusts his eyes and his ears. Every
morning he monitors the heartbeat of America, or more precisely, the beat that
currently sets the pace, that of George H. W. Bush, president of the United States.

What is it like to care for the health of the person at the top?

Dr. Lee, a veteran clinician, teacher, and medical researcher, affirms a special
sense of responsibility in his role as Physician to the President, yet cautions
against "some crazy sense of awe."

"After you get over the incredible experience of walking into the White
House the first few times, you soon get your feet on the ground," he insists,
"which is crucial if you're going to provide well-balanced care to somebody like

the president." A big problem in VIP medicine, in Dr. Lee's view, is that all too often a misplaced reverence for the patient blurs the physician's observations, and the consensus of a committee of experts replaces the common sense and sound judgment of an individual doctor. "Fortunately," he observes, "George Bush happens to be an old friend, and I can treat him the same way I've treated all my patients—I give him my best shot and refer to the best people I know for whatever the problem may be." It goes without saying that every medical decision involves a certain degree of risk, and when it comes to the health of the president of the United States, Dr. Lee is quick to add: "You can be sure I'm not going to have any problems with my decision before I make it, and if I don't know what the problem is, you can bet your life I'm going to get people in who do!"

AN INTERNIST IN THE P&S TRADITION

An internist in the P&S tradition of Drs. Robert Loeb and Franklin Hanger (whose dual influence he proudly acknowledges), Burton Lee applies the same sound clinical approach at the White House that he first learned at Columbia, sharpened in his two years of residency at Bellevue's First (Columbia) Medical Division, and further refined through the almost thirty years of his tenure in the Department of Medicine at Memorial Hospital (now Memorial Sloan Kettering) in New York.

"If somebody walks into my office, the president or anybody else," he says, "I will usually know the problem even before I've gotten to the physical by just looking and talking and getting the history."

As to his own personal history, doctoring runs in the family.

His great uncle, Hugh Auchincloss '42, associate clinical professor of surgery emeritus at P&S, started the breast surgery service at Columbia, and an uncle, Dr. Hugh Auchincloss, Jr., also a breast surgeon, followed suit. And Dr. Lee's grandfather on his father's side, also a surgeon, started the breast service at Memorial Hospital, where he served as the first medical director at its present address.

A graduate of Yale, Dr. Lee went on to P&S, where he spent "a most stimulating time," particularly enjoying the clinical years. Outstanding teachers like Drs. Robert Loeb and Franklin Hanger, among others "made a deep and lasting impression."

Following graduation, from 1956 to 1958, he served first as an intern then as a resident in the First Medical Division at Bellevue Hospital, a Columbia affiliate at the time. To the young doctor fresh out of medical school, it was "front-line service, just like being in the trenches." With countless patients in for a panoply of diverse emergency problems and one student nurse to help out through the night, "you really had to step up to bat and learn quickly! You just don't get that kind of experience in a white tower!" he recalls, relishing the memory. The two years he subsequently spent as a resident overseas in the U.S. Army Medical Corps, from 1958–1960, were almost a vacation in comparison.

Returning home, he intended to enter the field of ophthalmology but switched to medicine at the last minute. A residency, followed by a fellowship in cancer research at the Memorial Sloan Kettering Cancer Center, launched him on his life's work, researching therapies for the treatment of lymphoma and related cancers, a subject on which he has published extensively.

"I was really quite fascinated with the way they presented cancer to us in the pathology course at P&S," he recalls. "I was thrilled by the medical enigma of cells dividing and getting out of control, and nobody at the time had the foggiest idea why this was happening." Dr. Lee welcomed the challenge.

In 1962, he joined the faculty of Cornell University Medical College (now Weil Cornell) as a clinical instructor in medicine, simultaneously accepting a hospital appointment as clinical assistant physician in the Chemotherapy

Service at Memorial Hospital, where eventually he took charge of the Hematology-Lymphoma Service. "My proudest achievements to date," Dr. Lee said, "have involved the development of new, more effective ways to treat Hodgkin's lymphomas and myeloma."

Which brings us up to January 1, 1989, when the newly elected president of the United States, George H. W. Bush, asked Dr. Lee to set up practice in the White House. The last P&S alumnus to hold that office was Alexander Lambert, Class of 1888, personal physician to President Theodore Roosevelt.

"FIRST" FAMILY DOCTOR

"The president is in perfect condition—I should be so healthy!" the doctor observes of his patient, an avid jogger, known to outrun agile journalists half his age.

According to past procedure, the president's physician was with him at all times. Dr. Lee has chosen to leave mobile care to members of the military medical staff trained in strategic medicine, while he holds the fort at the White House. Caring for the president is only part of his duties. His office extends medical care and advice to members of the First Family, the vice president and his family, members of the Cabinet, the Supreme Court, the Federal Reserve, to a total of 1,800 people working in and around the White House. "We don't take care of them per se, except for the short haul," he explains. "But we make sure they end up in the right hands, whatever the problem may be."

"I am very lucky," he adds, "both George and Barbara Bush are level-headed realists and they are also very healthy, which definitely sets a standard for the staff."

Beyond his strictly clinical duties, Dr. Lee has chosen to address the public health policy side of his office. As physician to the First Family, he is in a certain sense the "First" Family Doctor in America, a public role he takes very seriously.

His views in medical matters have on occasion clashed with the official position of the Administration, most recently regarding the issue of abortion—Dr. Lee is pro-choice. He does not, however, see a conflict of interest here. As a doctor, he firmly believes that politics must inevitably come second: "You can't be an ideologue and practice medicine effectively."

A current policy matter of particular concern to him is the expense and public access to health care in the United States. His position on this sensitive issue has ruffled feathers in the medical community.

"The financial cost of health care delivery in this country is an express train that's coming down the fast track," Dr. Lee asserts. "We in the medical profession continue to deny the problem. Hey, I'm sorry, but it's costing too much and we're not delivering the product we should be delivering! If we doctors don't want other people coming in to solve the problem, then it's up to *us* to work with Congress and the executive branch and not fight them tooth and nail."

Dr. Lee is adamant about what he perceives as an imbalance of emphasis in the American health care delivery system. "We're the worst country in the industrialized world at taking care of our young, particularly our very young people." Meanwhile, he complains, "we are spending much too much doctor and hospital effort, too much time and money, on keeping people alive for the last month of their life."

He supports the monetary redistribution and relative value scale proposed by Dr. William Hsiao, professor of health systems economics at the Harvard School of Public Health. The plan would reapportion the level of remuneration among the various specialties, according a fairer share to primary care physicians. "It doesn't solve the problem, but I think it's a good start," Dr. Lee believes.

On his own initiative, he has also extended the purview of his office to embrace an active educational and advisory role. He conducts a postgraduate course at George Washington University Medical School, where he recently joined the staff, and supervises residents at the Walter Reed Army Medical Center. Concerned with the quality of health care in the District of Columbia, he has also become involved with local clinics and hospitals. Dr. Lee talks regularly to attendings at the Southeast Regional Medical Center, a facility that serves the inner city minority community.

His goal is to reach out medically to all segments of American society. "I try to get out there, and to let people know: "Hey, the president's doctor is interested in you!"

RECEPTIVE TO RECEPTORS

ROBERT J. LEFKOWITZ '66

In 2012, Dr. Lefkowitz shared the Nobel Prize in Chemistry with Brian K. Kobilka, for their groundbreaking work on G-protein-coupled receptors, helping to unlock the mystery of how the body's cells sense and respond to the environment.

———— ❀❀❀ ————

ROBERT J. LEFKOWITZ '66, the cardiologist-turned basic researcher who discovered the seven-membrane-spanning structure of adrenergic receptors, among other landmark findings, author or coauthor of more than 835 peer-reviewed papers, and the top-ranked scientist in citations in the field of biology and biochemistry in the 2002 ISI Essential Science Indicators, still had to face down his toughest critic, his mother. "Wistful at the fact that, in her view, I had abandoned my true calling, clinical medicine, for the lab, she asked, 'Well, you've been at this for so many years—don't you have the answer yet?'"

There were, of course, important "answers" along the way. In 1974, his research team developed a method for directly measuring the ß-adrenergic receptors by ligand binding, thus achieving a long-elusive goal. And in 1986, they succeeded in cloning and sequencing the gene coding for the human ß-2 adrenergic receptor and described its seven-membrane-spanning structure, a veritable molecular Rosetta stone that opened the way to our understanding of G-protein-coupled receptors. Pharmaceuticals that target these receptors—like beta-blockers, ulcer drugs, cortisone, antihistamines, antidepressants, estrogens, androgens, contraceptives, insulin sensitizers, to mention a few—"account for 60–70 percent of all the prescription drugs used in the world" (*in-cites*, 2002). But science continuously teases the receptive mind. As Dr. Lefkowitz put it in "Not Necessarily

about Receptors," a reflection on the scientific life published in the journal *Clinical Research*: "Each question we answered posed several new ones which seemed even more interesting."

Dr. Lefkowitz patiently fielded an interviewer's questions one afternoon in January 2008 at his office at the Duke Medical Center, in Durham, N.C.

"PEOPLE ARE MOST CREATIVE WHEN THEY'RE PLAYING."

At sixty-four, ever spry of body and mind, radiating an infectious Bronx-inflected enthusiasm, the James B. Duke Professor of Medicine and investigator at the Howard Hughes Medical Institute at Duke University Medical Center is clearly still having the time of his life. "At no time in my career—or careers, I should say, 'cause I've had two, initially as a 'real' physician and then as a scientist—at no point have I ever conceived or conceptualized myself as working for a living, I play. People are most creative when they're playing. I'm always playing," he smiles, "and I'm always serious."

BORN IN THE BRONX

The son of an accountant and a schoolteacher, Robert Lefkowitz was born in the Bronx. Among his idols were Yankee hitter Mickey Mantle, novelist Ian Fleming (of 007 fame), comic and filmmaker Woody Allen, and "our family physician, a hero closer to home, who always made me feel better. I wanted to be like him." Lefkowitz attended the highly selective Bronx High School of Science and Columbia College before following his dream of becoming a doctor.

At P&S, he came under the influence of Paul Marks '49, then a young faculty member whose erudite clinical lectures were infused with basic science. Dr. Marks subsequently served as dean of the medical school, before leaving to become president of Memorial Sloan Kettering Cancer Center. Lefkowitz rounded with another great physician-scientist, Nobel laureate Dickinson Richards '23, "a very colorful man," as he recalled. "If you really want to know what's going on, you put your ear on the patient's chest," Dr. Richards counseled.

Dr. Lefkowitz also relished his clinical medical clerkship with the late Dr. Donald F. Tapley. Like Dr. Marks, Dr. Tapley later served as a revered dean of the Medical School. His teaching style rubbed off on his young protégé. "He was so scholarly and so much fun. He had a certain way he would look down at you over his glasses . . . with a wink and a twinkle." Dr. Lefkowitz, who conducted rounds on the general medical service at Duke for some thirty years, modeled his own teaching style on that of Dr. Tapley.

Following graduation, Dr. Lefkowitz stayed on at Columbia-Presbyterian, where he interned and pursued a residency in the Department of Medicine. It was here on one fateful evening in the house-staff library that he first read a review article by future Nobel laureate Dr. Earl Sutherland, describing the hormone-sensitive enzyme system adenylate cyclase and its potential role in regulating the function of the cardiovascular system. Dr. Sutherland spoke of the concept of "hormone receptors, which he thought might represent the binding sites on the enzyme"—soon to become the object of Dr. Lefkowitz's lifelong quest.

BASIC SCIENCE AND CLINICAL MEDICINE:
TWO POINTS ON A CONTINUUM

In 1968, at the height of the Vietnam War, though still committed to a clinical career, he applied for and was accepted as a clinical and research associate at the

National Institute of Arthritis and Metabolic Diseases at the NIH, as an alternative to military service. His P&S classmate and friend, future Nobel laureate Harold Varmus '66, also joined the NIH—"It seemed like a much more attractive billet, if you will, than Vietnam." Neither knew quite what lay in store.

Lefkowitz lauds "the quality of the scientists there, our mentors who ignited the research spark in us." He worked under Drs. Jesse Roth and Ira Pastan. Varmus pursued one of Pastan's research interests at the time, which eventually led to his Nobel-prize-winning work on oncogenes. Lefkowitz pursued Pastan's other interest, the study of receptors, which would later lead to his own Nobel Prize.

But infused as he was with a clinician's expectations of "quick results and rapid feedback," and lacking basic lab techniques as well as the necessary patience and perspective, his fledgling attempts at research met with "unremitting failure." He went home for Thanksgiving, bemoaning his failure to his father. "'Chalk it up to experience! Run out the clock! You have a two-year assignment, then you'll go back to your clinical training and become the consummate clinician you always wanted to be," his father counseled. The plan seemed sound enough. Three weeks later his beloved father died from his fourth heart attack, at age sixty-three.

Devastated by the loss, Dr. Lefkowitz buried his grief in the lab. And "by the next year, the research was starting to work." The bench bug had bit, but he had already committed to pursue his clinical training as a senior resident in medicine at the Harvard affiliate Massachusetts General Hospital.

In Boston, where he subsequently pursued a fellowship in cardiology, he enjoyed treating patients but began to miss the lab. "I was like a junkie who needed a fix. For the first time in two years I had no data." So on top of his house staff duties—in addition to night shifts in various emergency rooms around town, insurance physicals, and a stint as team physician for the football squad at a local high school to make ends meet for his growing family—the data-deprived doc sought scientific solace in the Harvard lab of another illustrious P&S alumnus, the late Edgar Haber '56. Working on problems related to the catecholamine-sensitive adenylate cyclase system, the young researcher was fascinated "by the question of how a receptor could activate its effector counterpart, thus altering cellular metabolism or activity."

Receptors, Dr. Lefkowitz explains, "are specific molecules on, or in, a cell, with which a drug, hormone, neurotransmitter, or a stimulus interact, much in the lock-and-key analogy, triggering a cascade of events inside the cell, which make the cell change its physiology."

He chose to focus on adrenalin-sensitive receptors, specifically ß-adrenergic receptors, as his working model. The potential clinical implications for the cardiovascular system, the system that had failed in his father, were hardly lost on him—"What's more cardiovascular than adrenalin?" But as a clinical cardiologist by day and a basic researcher by night, he was riding an intellectual seesaw. "On some days I pictured myself as the consummate clinician-teacher, on others as a prominent investigator making notable scientific contributions." Something had to give.

In 1973, he accepted an invitation to join the faculty in the Department of Medicine at Duke University, moving to Durham, N.C., which for his Bronx relatives "might as well have been Tierra del Fuego." But Lefkowitz thrived and put down roots, eventually marrying a local. He has five children. "Sure, I always tell people, I'm a Southerner, I'm from the South Bronx!" And though he continued to round, the investigator in him eventually won out. Still, to this day he remains a firm believer that "basic science and clinical medicine are merely two points on a continuum."

"THE *CHUTZPAH* OF YOUTH"

There was considerable doubt at the time in the scientific community as to the feasibility of studying receptors: "The number of these receptors, if they existed at all, might be so small, people thought, that the kinds of techniques that were being bandied about to study them might not be up to the job.

"And yet—and this is the *chutzpah* of youth," his eyes twinkle in the telling, "for me, it was always a matter of *when*, not *if*—what self-delusion! I was not a trained biochemist by any stretch, much less a molecular biologist. And yet I had this unvarnished faith that it would all work. Would I have the guts today to go after what I went after then, given the background that I had? The answer is: No way!"

"Do they know from *chutzpah* in North Carolina?" an interviewer interrupts.

"I've educated them," Dr. Lefkowitz chuckles, pulling out his dog-eared copy of the *Joys of Yiddish* by Leo Rosten. "You gotta have *chutzpah*! You gotta be able to think out of the box!

"There are two completely antithetical ways to fail in science," he says. "One is to choose problems, which, while doable and answerable and publishable, are effectively trivial. The other way is to choose grand, wonderful problems, which, if you could solve them, would be huge accomplishments. The only problem is, you can't. To succeed in science, judgment is the key. You've got to be able to recognize an important, but doable, problem."

Successfully isolating and cloning the ß-2 adrenergic receptor in his lab, he used his understanding of its structure as a "basis for the discovery that all G-protein-coupled receptors have a characteristic seven-membrane-spanning domain arrangement." This discovery would later win Dr. Lefkowitz the prestigious Albany Medical Center Prize in Medicine and Biomedical Research. In the words of Albany Medical Center president and CEO Dr. James J. Barba, as quoted in the online publication *Inside*, this discovery "allowed researchers to develop drugs which parodied the effects of the body's hormones and transmitters."

The distinctive seven-span structure is immortalized by a metal sculpture, a gift from his wife for his sixtieth birthday, which he keeps on a window ledge. Hoisting it in the air, he grins: "Looks like a Chanukah menorah, doesn't it?!"

STUDYING RECEPTOR DESENSITIZATION

Parallel to their study of the structure and function of ß-2 adrenergic receptors, Dr. Lefkowitz and his lab mates examined the problem of receptor desensitization, whereby, "in seconds to minutes, depending on what system you're talking about, the response wanes, even though the stimulus is kept constant . . . The mechanisms for that desensitization were completely unknown." As physiological problems go, "nothing seemed to me more fundamental to the concept of biological regulation than that. So, right from the beginning of my career at Duke, I worked in two directions: What are receptors and how can I study them? But at the same time, I wanted to understand: How are they regulated? How do they get turned off?"

Lefkowitz and his Duke team found that G-protein-coupled receptors actually set two chains of events in motion. One initiates a signal cascade, engendering a specific response inside and on the surface of the cell. The other spurs a feedback signal in the cell, by means of a molecule, beta arrestin, effectively desensitizing the receptor and turning it off.

His lab subsequently discovered that beta arrestin can function as an independent signaling agent, a finding with profound implications for the simultaneous regulation and strengthening of heart function. Dr. Lefkowitz recently founded a biotech company to translate this and related findings into a new class of pharmaceuticals: "It's a real culmination for me, reaffirming the continuum from bench to bedside."

INHERITED TRAITS—OF THE FAMILIAL
AND SCIENTIFIC KIND

To Lefkowitz, his lifelong inquiry is not just an intellectual quest, it's literally *heart*felt. Like his father, who died of a heart attack, and his mother, who suffered angina, though she lived to be almost eighty-nine, he, too, inherited heart problems, undergoing quadruple bypass surgery at age fifty-one. A serious jogger until orthopedic issues caused him to restrict his exercise to a basement gym, where he works out daily, he takes two cholesterol-lowering medications and carefully restricts his diet.

But as any scientist worth his salt will tell you, inheritance comes from influence as well as genetics.

Dr. Lefkowitz is a firm believer in the importance of what he calls "scientific lineages" promulgated through the mentor-mentee relationship. Among the many awards he has received in his career, he is perhaps proudest of the 2006 Eugene Braunwald Academic Mentorship Award of the American Heart Association. Just as he learned the ropes by observing his own mentors in action, so an important part of his life's work over the years has been demonstrating how it's done: "In research, nobody can write down the rules. You can't explain it. You can only show it."

To illustrate the point, he plucks a metaphor from his medical school experience. "I remember sitting in my room at Bard Hall studying for exams with a beat-up old microscope and an atlas of what things were supposed to look like. I'd put the slide in, get it in focus, and then turn to the atlas to see exactly how that cell or tumor was supposed to look. But by the time I looked back, it had fallen out of focus . . . So I learned by trial and error how to put just enough torque on the fine-tuning knob so that I could look away, come back, and it would still be in focus, 'cause I was holding the knob. And I feel that's what I do in the lab. I put just enough pressure on these guys to keep them focused, but not too much, because you don't want to completely shut off the opportunity for inquiry."

The proof of the pudding is the success and devotion of his 200 plus mentees, the ongoing links in his "scientific lineage," many of whom have gone on to do outstanding work in receptor biology and related fields.

Dr. Lefkowitz's honors and awards fill three pages on his CV. He has served on countless editorial boards of scientific journals and held high office in scientific societies, including the presidency of the American Society for Clinical Investigation and the Association of American Physicians. He has delivered named lectureships around the country, including the 2007 Inaugural Clyde and Helen Wu Distinguished Lecture at P&S. He has coedited several books, notably the seventh edition of the *Principles of Biochemistry* (the third edition of which he himself had used in medical school). A member of the National Academy of Sciences, the Institute of Medicine, and the American Academy of Arts and Sciences, his encomia include the P&S Alumni Gold Medal for Distinguished Achievements in Medicine and honorary doctorates from the Medical University of South Carolina and Mt. Sinai School of Medicine.

A picture snapped at a reunion of his trainees, with which he is fond of concluding his guest lectures, eloquently (and spontaneously) evokes another kind of honor: "Once the formal group shot had been taken, the photographer asked, 'Is there anything else we can do?' And the next thing I know I'm up." The roomful of young researchers whose careers he helped launch had hoisted him into the air and turned him into a living trophy. The laughter and love were palpable in every face.

ADVENTURES IN VIROLOGY

JAY LEVY '65

Dr. Levy is presently engaged in the study of a new antiviral protein with potentially profound implications for the control of HIV/AIDS and other viral diseases.

—∞—

THE LABORATORY—all 80 square feet of it—in which Jay Levy '65, codiscoverer of the AIDS virus, identified the infamous microbe in 1983, is now literally a part of history, dismantled (bioassay hood, lab coat, notebooks, Bunsen burner and all) and stored for posterity at the Smithsonian Institute's National Museum of American History in Washington, D.C. Dr. Levy, professor of medicine at the University of California, San Francisco (UCSF), who half-jokingly dubbed his old "micro"-nook "The Center for Human Tumor Virus Research," likes to tell the story of a site visit by former California governor George Deukmejian. Seeking state funding for a new building, the University administration wanted to show him how crowded things were. But when the famously stern-faced governor stepped inside he broke into a smile: "You found the virus here?!" The virologist nodded. "You see," said the governor, "great things can happen in small spaces."

A KEY PLAYER IN HIV/AIDS RESEARCH

One of three scientific groups (along with those of Luc Montagnier and Robert Gallo) credited with discovering the AIDS virus—which he originally called the

AIDS-associated retrovirus (ARV)–Dr. Levy and his UCSF team remain key players in HIV/AIDS research. The first to clone the virus, in conjunction with Chiron Corporation, his group subsequently pioneered heat-treatment studies to inactivate HIV in clotting factor preparations, assuring the safety of blood products for hemophiliacs. Among other findings, he first reported the presence of the virus in cells of the brain and bowel, relating HIV infection to diseases in these tissues. He also showed the ability of a novel CD8+ cell antiviral factor (CAF) naturally secreted by T lymphocytes from healthy infected individuals to suppress viral infection without killing the infected cell. The latter discovery has profound implications for the development of a vaccine and immune-based therapies, and is a major focus of his ongoing studies.

Levy's current research program in the Department of Medicine and the Cancer Research Institute at UCSF comprises a small office hardly large enough to fit a desk and chair and a few filing cabinets. But the office, like the small size of his original human virus lab, does not appear to have crimped his style or hampered his productivity. Dr. Levy's warm smile is that of a man in his element. The filing cabinets are bursting and the floor is heaped high with mountains of papers on various research projects in progress. The walls are covered with his own impressionistic painted landscapes and a few photographs, including one taken of him in Paris with his twin brother, Dr. Stuart Levy, and the late Nobel Prize-winning author Samuel Beckett, best known for his play "Waiting for Godot."

A lab assistant was on duty bowed over the bioassay hood in an adjoining laboratory when Dr. Levy welcomed this writer in for an interview one morning in January 2009.

AN OUT-OF-THE-BOX THINKER

A double major in biology and French at Wesleyan University, where he earned his BA with high honors in 1960, Dr. Levy's intellectual horizons have remained wide open and his interests wide-ranging. His curriculum vitae runs to fifty-six pages at last count, with close to 500 scientific articles and reviews, the fourteen books he has authored or edited, including *HIV and the Pathogenesis of AIDS*, the seminal sole-authored work on the subject, and his classic four-volume series *The Retroviridae*. It also includes an in-memoriam tribute, "Conversations with Samuel Beckett," published in *The American Scholar*. The virologist first met the famously hermetic author while on a Fulbright Fellowship prior to medical school at the Laboratoire de Biologie Animale at the Université de Paris. The two of them remained fast friends until Beckett's death in 1989. "He [Beckett] said that the laboratory was like the theater," Dr. Levy recalled in the aforementioned text. "The scientist is the director and the test tubes are the players. You may predict what will happen, but you do not know exactly how it is going to turn out."

Outside of the laboratory, the versatile Dr. Levy is also an accomplished pianist, avid golfer and skier, impassioned botanist, antique car buff with his 1931 Citroen, and a respected painter whose work includes one of the painted ceramic hearts for San Francisco General Hospital's "Hearts in San Francisco" campaign. This installation series features painted hearts by local artists in public places to help raise funds for the San Francisco General Hospital Foundation.

"Does all this detract from my ability to do science? Absolutely not, it adds to it!" he insists. "The arts and sciences work together and with both you can appreciate the overall value of medicine. A person is a total being: the psychology and the nature and the ethics and all the feelings and emotions, this is more than biochemical reactions."

The son of a physician father in family practice and an artist mother, Dr. Levy grew up in Wilmington, Del., in a household that fostered investigation and cultivated the imagination. "We lived in the country and we liked to go into the forest and discover animals, biology was all around us." He and his twin brother, Stuart, and his sister, Ellen, all achieved successful careers in medical research.

THE INTELLECTUAL LURE OF VIRUSES AND OTHER MICROBIAL CHALLENGES

His interest in viruses dates back to his college days when Dr. Levy happened on a now classic article by the French virologist Dr. Raymond Latarjet suggesting that viruses could cause human cancer. This idea sparked his imagination and set him on a lifelong quest.

At P&S, he and a group of his classmates, including David Miller '65, Larry Ng '65, and Fred Siegal '65 (who remain close friends) formed a basic science discussion group to hash over recent research findings. Working in the laboratory of Dr. Herb Rosenkrantz, during his second and third years, Dr. Levy coauthored the discovery that a new compound, hydroxyurea, blocks DNA division in bacteria, the subject of his third published paper. That drug is now used in cancer therapy.

Through medical school, he pursued his passion for science and foreign experiences, also participating in Columbia's International Fellows Program. During his summers, he conducted research in Israel, Sweden, Kenya, and Uganda—the latter stint was devoted to the search for the viral etiology of Burkitt lymphoma. In his fourth year, following his return from Africa, he learned many aspects of clinical virology from virologist Dr. Eru Tanabe in Dr. E. C. Curnen's laboratory. This training was useful particularly for evaluating the viral cause of Burkitt lymphoma. It was obvious to him in medical school that he enjoyed the human contact of clinical medicine, but from the start he knew he was headed for a life in the laboratory studying the cause of human diseases.

At the University of Pennsylvania, where he did his internship and a first year of residency training in internal medicine, Dr. Levy balanced a heavy clinical caseload with bench work at nights and on weekends. He assessed the role of Epstein-Barr virus (EBV) in Burkitt lymphoma in the laboratory of Drs. Werner and Brigitta Henle at Children's Hospital, a UPenn affiliate. Their studies helped prove the association of a high-level immune response to EBV with development of the tumor. At the same time, Levy conducted research on human T lymphocytes at the Wistar Institute with Dr. Vittorio Defendi. Those scientific experiences helped prepare him for the challenge of AIDS later in his career.

With the war in Vietnam raging overseas, he was pleased to be accepted as a staff associate at the National Cancer Institute at the NIH, where he studied DNA and RNA oncogenic viruses in the laboratory directed by Dr. Robert J. Huebner. Like his classmate Keith Brodie '65, and other illustrious P&S alumni of his generation, Harold Varmus '66 and Robert Lefkowitz '66, he found an intellectual oasis in Bethesda: "It was highly competitive to get into the NIH, and if you were lucky enough to be there, you worked with some wonderful scientists." His mentor, the iconic virologist Dr. Huebner, was an imaginative thinker who fostered curiosity and calculated risk-taking in his young protégé. "Everyone said, 'Bob Huebner, 50 percent unbelievable, great ideas, and 50 percent crazy ones,' but he was very often right."

XENOTROPIC VIRUSES AND OTHER ENIGMAS

It was at the NIH, in studies of viruses found in the so-called New Zealand Black mouse—"the most published mouse in history, next to Mickey!"—that Dr. Levy made an important discovery that would some years later put him on the map. In the cells from these mice that developed autoimmune disease and lymphoma, Dr. Levy found and managed to grow retroviruses with unique characteristics. They came out of one species, the mouse, but could only infect and grow in cells from other species, like human, rat, or duck. For this reason, he called them "xenotropic" viruses, based on the Greek word *xenos* for "foreign."

Dr. Levy would apply his taxonomical talent and knowledge of Greek to name two other types of inherited or endogenous mouse retroviruses discovered by colleagues at NIH: the "ecotropic" virus that "stayed within the mouse and could go back and infect other mice," and the "amphotropic" virus that "grows in both mouse and other species."

Reflecting on his serendipitous discovery of murine xenotropic retroviruses, a subject that continues to intrigue him, Dr. Levy observes: "Imagination helps you to realize that there are things out there that we don't expect or fully understand. And I think embracing the arts, literature, and music opens your mind to other ways of thinking."

In the course of his early research, he had what he calls "another unconventional idea," namely that "maybe viruses aren't all harmful." The discovery of viruses in mice that cannot reinfect those mice led him to wonder what then they were doing in the mouse? He could find them expressed in normal tissues including placentas. In subsequent studies of human placentas he found evidence of endogenous retroviruses that he felt played a positive role in enabling the placenta to interact well with the uterine wall via cell—cell fusion or syncytia formation. That observation was supported by his later finding of "a blocking protein" in placentas of women with multiple miscarriages that prevented the biochemical activity of these viruses [. . .]." This posed a very interesting hypothesis, that "just like we inherit bacteria for a benefit, we might also inherit viruses for a benefit [. . .]"

A RECEPTIVITY TO THE UNEXPECTED AND FONDNESS FOR THE FOREIGN

Throughout his career, Dr. Levy has continued to seek out international research experiences. In 1970 on a return trip to Uganda, he helped capture wild chimpanzees and test their blood for Epstein-Barr virus and infectious hepatitis B virus.

In 1971, as a visiting scientist on a NATO fellowship, he studied human T cell transformation by murine RNA tumor viruses at the Hôpital St. Louis in Paris. In Paris he also collaborated on experiments involving the infection of mammalian cells with DNA from RNA virus-transformed rodent cells. On two subsequent leaves of absence he worked as a visiting scientist with Dr. Nechama Haran-Ghera at the Weizmann Institute of Science in Rehovot, Israel: first in 1978, on an Eleanor Roosevelt Fellowship, to study T cell differentiation and viruses in radiation-induced mouse tumors; and then in 1982, on an International Cancer Technology Transfer Fellowship, to research dual-tropic type C viruses in mouse T cell leukemia.

In 1979, he spent eight months with Nobel Prize winner François Jacob at the Pasteur Institute, studying the potential role of retroviruses in normal embryogenesis, which rekindled his interest in showing that inherited viruses could be beneficial. These international experiences not only exposed him to different scientific approaches and research techniques but also made him more aware of the global reach of disease, an insight that would prove invaluable in his later work on the AIDS pandemic.

A NEW DISEASE HITS SAN FRANCISCO

In 1971 he completed a second-year residency in medicine at the University of California, School of Medicine at San Francisco, and the following year joined the faculty as assistant clinical professor in the Department of Medicine and research associate at the Cancer Research Institute at UCSF School of Medicine, rising to the rank of professor of medicine in 1985.

Having come to the West Coast to continue his pursuit of a viral trigger for cancer using studies of mice, it was his ultimate dream to elucidate viral mechanisms in such human diseases as multiple sclerosis, Crohn's disease, autoimmunity, and others. One process intrigued him, called "hit and run," Dr. Levy explains. "The virus comes in, activates the immune system, gets eliminated, but the system may remain too overly programmed to fight the virus. That type of reaction could be responsible for those diseases."

His research focus, however, changed dramatically in 1981 when one of his former postdoctoral fellows, Dr. Paul Volberding, now head of medicine at the V.A. Hospital in San Francisco, called to discuss the case of a patient with Kaposi sarcoma. Because of the possible viral origin of this particular cancer, Dr. Levy decided to take a closer look. He hoped that he would establish the cause, and did not realize that this investigation would lead him to identify, and, thereafter, devote years to the study of a deadly new agent and disease: the AIDS virus, which he and members of the subcommittee of the International Committee on the Taxonomy of Viruses, chaired by Harold Varmus '66, named the human immunodeficiency virus (HIV).

The tenor of the time and the attitude of the university were hardly supportive of his AIDS investigations, given the character of the infected patient population, comprising mostly gay men and intravenous drug users. But working closely together with little or no support, Dr. Levy and a small group of UCSF researchers persevered. Independently discovering the virus, he and his team were the first to clone it in collaboration with Chiron Corporation. He also showed that heating clotting factor preparations would protect hemophiliacs from HIV infection. It took six months for his recommendation to pull all blood products from the market to be heeded, during which time more transfused hemophiliacs were infected. "What could I have done!" he recalls with much regret. "I was relatively young then and did not know how to have our work influence the decision of industry." His pioneering approach to heat treatment of clotting factor preparations, for which he was honored with the Murray

Thailan Award from the National Hemophilia Foundation, subsequently pro-tected countless hemophiliacs from HIV infection.

Dr. Levy likewise encountered skepticism when he reported finding the virus in biopsies of brain and bowel tissue, where, according to the then-current line of thinking, it was not supposed to be.

FOLLOWING LONG-TERM SURVIVORS:
A POSSIBLE CLUE TO A CURE

In 1986 he had another "*Oh! Ah!* Experience," based on his studies of long-term survivors of HIV infection. His lab was the first to show that a small number of otherwise healthy infected individuals secrete a CD8+ cell antiviral factor (CAF) as an innate immune system function. CAF controls HIV replication without killing the infected cell, thereby blocking the onset of AIDS. This was the first indication that CD8+ lymphocytes can have an antiviral function that is not the classic cytotoxic one.

"We then learned that there were some ways in which we could increase the function of the CD8+ cells by making them interact with certain antibod-ies to the cell surface." In ongoing research, in collaboration with a group at U.C. Davis, Dr. Levy's team is trying to "induce this type of innate immunity with a vaccine that alerts and gets other components of the immune system working better."

GRAPPLING WITH ALL SIDES OF THE DISEASE

Interested from the start in the epidemiology of the disease, as well as its patho-genesis, Dr. Levy traveled to Haiti as early as 1982, and to the Dominican Repub-lic, where his sister, Dr. Ellen Koenig, a respected virologist, now runs a major clinic for HIV infection and infectious diseases. Together they collected blood samples in gay bars and hotels, a project that helped trace the entry of the dis-ease into that country through tourists and Haitian sugarcane workers. In Haiti he attended and photographed a voodoo ceremony, pursuing and disproving the hypothesis that the virus might have come from chickens, whose blood many initiates drink.

In his lively lectures on AIDS to medical students and health profession-als, one of which is featured on YouTube, Dr. Levy tackles all aspects of the disease, including its etiology. "The virus that causes human AIDS probably came into the animal kingdom hundreds and perhaps thousands of years ago, and evolved with the species," he maintains. As to its passage into humans, "work with infected chimpanzees is becoming more and more compelling as the source of HIV. But don't tell me that it happened in the last 100 years. I think the virus had been in human populations in Africa for a long time, but was just never recognized."

SALUTED IN SAN FRANCISCO

In 1998 Dr. Levy was featured in the *San Francisco Chronicle*, along with for-mer San Francisco Mayor Willie Brown and filmmaker George Lucas, as one of the ten individuals who most affected Bay Area life. A fellow in the American Academy of Arts and Sciences, the American Association for the Advancement of Science, and the American Academy of Microbiology, his countless other encomia include a Distinguished Alumnus Award and Honorary Degree in Sci-ence from Wesleyan University, the first UCSF/ARI George Sarlo Award for Excellence in Mentoring, an Award of Distinction from the American Founda-tion for AIDS Research (AmFar), the Abbott Award for Outstanding Research in Immunology, and the 2008 Gold Medal of the P&S Alumni Association for Outstanding Achievements in Medical Research.

A member of the World Affairs Council and the Council on Foreign Rela-tions, Levy is also an adviser to France, India, Italy, China, Thailand, Mexico, Ethiopia, and the Dominican Republic on HIV/AIDS. He is editor-in-chief of the journal *AIDS*.

At the conclusion of the interview this writer was treated to a glimpse of human lymphocytes, clumped together like cobblestones, magnified under the microscope. "These are the CD4+ cells that are susceptible to HIV, the major targets of the virus," Dr. Levy explained. "They're social beings like us. See those projections bringing the cells together? They really benefit from one another."

It is tempting to reflect back on Dr. Levy's recollection of Samuel Beck-ett. In the tiny spotlight, the cellular protagonists mime the drama of disease under the watchful eye of the director-scientist. Godot never showed up, but Dr. Levy is hopeful that this tiny circle of light will hold the key to the scien-tific puzzle of AIDS.

A DIGITAL PIONEER AT THE NATIONAL LIBRARY OF MEDICINE

DONALD A. B. LINDBERG '58

Stepping down in 2015 as director of the National Library of Medicine, Dr. Lindberg remains a leader in the Federal Networking and Information Technology Research and Development initiative to improve health and health care. His encomia have included honorary doctorates from Amherst College, the State University of New York at Syracuse, the University of Missouri-Columbia, and the University for Health Sciences, Medical Informatics and Technology, Innsbruck, Austria, and Old Dominion University.

———❦———

A VINTAGE documentary film clip from 1966 shows an introverted young researcher at the University of Missouri taking pains to contain his excitement. Having devised the world's first automated laboratory system before the field he helped create had a name, Donald A. B. Lindberg '58 proceeded to announce that it was now "possible for the computer itself to discover new patterns and new syndromes in the information about patients." The age of medical informatics had begun and medicine would never be the same.

PREDICTED "A ROMANCE BETWEEN PHYSICIANS AND COMPUTERS"

Two years earlier, in a visionary paper entitled "A Computer in Medicine," Dr. Lindberg predicted "the development of a romance between physicians and computers which will rival that seen with stethoscopes and electrocardiography.

It will be a great but pleasant challenge," he added, "to see that this latest affair of the heart makes a significant contribution to medical knowledge and wisdom."

The romance Dr. Lindberg predicted and fomented has indeed blossomed into a virtual marriage between PCs and MDs, putting the latest findings and data at physicians' fingertips. The new frontier of molecular research would be unthinkable without computers to store and process genetic data. Automated laboratories, hospital diagnostic facilities like PET and MRI, high-tech classrooms, lecture halls, and libraries have fundamentally changed the teaching and practice of medicine in our time.

In an astounding career that took him from Columbia, Missouri, where for more than two decades he straddled the disciplines of pathology and information science, to Washington, D.C., where he has served since 1984 as director of the National Library of Medicine, and where from 1992 to 1995 he helped create and run the National Coordination Office for High Performance Computing and Communications (the folks that gave us the Internet), Donald Lindberg has ridden the tidal wave of change he helped stir up.

A tall man, still trim and energetic, his youthful enthusiasm unabated at sixty-five, Dr. Lindberg exudes the earnest charm of a Jimmy Stewart in *Mr. Smith Goes to Washington*. The difference, of course, is that he isn't just acting. "I was warned about the federal government," Dr. Lindberg likes to joke, "but I correctly suspected that twenty years in a state university was adequate training for any amount of bureaucracy they could muster around here!"

Ably and eloquently communicating his dynamic vision of the National Library of Medicine to the U.S. Congress, the keepers of the purse strings of progress, he has managed in a decade and a half at the helm, in effect, to oversee the Library's transformation from a distinguished, albeit dusty, repository of medical books and papers to a cutting-edge electronic clearing house of biomedical knowledge.

Housed in a fittingly modernist complex on the campus of the National Institutes of Health in Bethesda, Md., the Library is Dr. Lindberg's laboratory where he and his dedicated team maintain among their vast holdings, GenBank, the NIH database of DNA sequences, the very existence of which explodes our notion of a library. His object, as he put it in the 1993 Dainton Lecture at the British Library, aptly entitled "High Performance Libraries," is to "remove barriers that stand between library users and the information and knowledge they need." To that end, he has been busy building and improving technical, organizational, and conceptual bridges between the Library, health professionals, and the public.

Programs devised and refined under his direction include, among others: Grateful Med and its updated Internet version, access interfaces to MEDLINE (electronic heir to the famous Index Medicus, the world's largest collection of published medical information); and Unified Medical Language Systems, an electronic thesaurus to medical terminology; not to mention the diverse databases in such specialty areas as toxicology, cancer, bioethics, and health care administration. Another startling innovation is the Visible Human, a human database comprising a 3-D set of submillimeter resolution points of an adult male and female with countless potential applications, including virtual reality teaching and remote telesurgery.

"The medical profession just needs a little bit of a chance to get used to some of these new tools and be ready to make use of them," smiles the laconic Dr. Lindberg.

But get him talking about the computer's potential as a humanizing force for good in the world and a wizard's twinkle sallies forth from behind staid spectacles, exploding his modest Midwestern demeanor. The question, according to Dr. Lindberg, is not, as some asked in the past: "Can the computer do better than the human? It is rather: Can the computer and the person do better than the person alone?"

A PATHOLOGIST WITH A BINARY BENT

Earning his BA in biology (magna cum laude) from Amherst in 1954, back in the high-tech dark ages when "business machines" were still big bulky monsters of little practical use, Donald Lindberg gobbled up every subject in his path at P&S. "I fell in love with every medical specialty," he recalls. "I was going to become the world's greatest surgeon, internist, obstetrician, psychiatrist, you name it, but I ultimately decided that there were probably more answers in pathology, and I was after answers!"

Among the P&S faculty, he benefitted from the encouragement and support of Drs. Harry Rose and Yale Kneeland, who graciously invited him to join them on their daily infectious disease rounds, and the then chair of pathology, Dr. Harry Pratt Smith, who provided him with the laboratory space and funding to launch his study of gram-negative pneumonia, later to be awarded NIH research grant support. "The challenge of a good medical school," he believes, "is to provide an atmosphere in which the student who wants to learn everything can come pretty close to that but not become so stressed as to squelch his or her own creative juices."

Another profound intellectual influence at P&S was Dr. Robert Loeb: "He could take a seemingly very ordinary patient with a very common ailment and make that individual the world's most fascinating creature, whose every electrolyte value was alarming and amazing." While diagnostic artificial intelligence programs based on an encyclopedic approach have been developed, Dr. Lindberg set as his ultimate and as yet unfulfilled challenge to create "an electronic model of medical diagnosis that reasons from basic principles, the way Loeb did."

Columbia also did him "the ultimate favor"—it was here that he met his wife-to-be, Mary Musick, RN, then in the pediatric service of the Vanderbilt Clinic.

Pursuing an internship and residency in pathology at Presbyterian Hospital (now New York-Presbyterian), Dr. Lindberg took an NIH research grant along with him to the University of Missouri in 1960, where he started as a resident, and soon thereafter joined the pathology faculty, and in addition, took on the direction of the Medical Center Diagnostic Microbiology Laboratory.

The bucolic serenity of Columbia, Mo., where his three sons were born, and where he and his family liked to ride horses in their spare time, proved fertile ground for intellectual inquiry. While continuing his research (rising in the academic ranks to professor of pathology in 1969), he found it increasingly difficult to balance his time, between running the Microbiology Lab, teaching, and the pursuit of his own NIH-funded research. "Then one day, I finally figured out that information access was at the root of it all," he says.

A COMPUTER EPIPHANY

It was, as he likes to put it, "an idea born of bourbon and branch water." Actually, the idea emerged in the course of a social engagement with a physics student and his wife, a lab technician: "Before the evening was over, we saw no reason why we couldn't build a machine to look at the antibiotic sensitivity of bacteria growing in liquid media. It took us a couple of years, but we did it."

His early prototype displayed results by lighting up numbers on a vacuum tube. At first he wrote down the results by hand. He later graduated to using a Victor adding machine, pasting up the strips of tape. Finally, "we discovered that there was a thing called a computer that would save all the time and trouble of cutting and pasting." The computer, a Burroughs 205 located in the Math Department, to which he was allowed access for a quarter hour a night, between midnight and 12:15, permitted him to "actually make mathematical models of bacterial growth.

"And once I realized that the problem I was having with this lab was soluble by an information processing system," he recalls, "it suddenly dawned on me that, heck, a lot of other problems would be soluble in the same way. Then I finally fathomed that you could follow a single patient, use the computer to store and recap all that information on his workup. I was off and running! I wanted the patient record to be the subject of research and to get the computer to do it." The result was the first automated lab system in the world. "It was one of those things that couldn't be done, and certainly not in Missouri," Lindberg chuckles, "and, by George, we showed 'em we could!"

Subsequently asked to join an NIH study section on computers and biomathematics, he was quickly disabused of any incipient hubris. "It was the equivalent of a four-year postdoc fellowship with people who knew much more than I did about computing, mathematics, and engineering."

At the University of Missouri, he went on to develop an automated patient history acquisition system and an automated system for interpreting electrocardiograms, among many other medical applications for the computer.

Meanwhile, Dr. Lindberg began publishing articles in a field that would come to be called medical informatics. By the mid-Sixties, he had developed an international reputation. In 1967, he became director of the Missouri Regional Medical Program Information Systems. In 1969, he was named professor and chair of the Department of Information Science in the School of Library and Information Science.

Then in 1984 came the call to the Capitol. Despite the difficulty of pulling up roots from a town he and his family had come to dearly love, he quickly took to Washington ways.

Lindberg credits the sound political assistance and counsel of farsighted politicians, like Senator (and later Congressman) Claude Pepper, in helping to communicate the Library's message to Congress. It became quite clear in preparing for Congressional hearings "that if we went and talked about how far behind we were in cataloguing books and articles or shelving dusty memoirs, we wouldn't get anywhere. But we could—and did!—produce a string of patients who had been treated successfully with drugs produced by the recombinant DNA process, thanks to the NLM." He managed to convince Congress that the Library was a conduit to information essential in the decision-making process of scientists and pharmaceutical firms, and that the ultimate beneficiary of such information access was the patient and the general public.

HIGH-PERFORMANCE COMPUTING

In 1991, then Senator Albert Gore wrote and shepherded a bill that, with bipartisan support, was to become the "High Performance Computing Act." Dr. Lindberg's informatics credentials and experience came to the attention of the executive branch. In 1992, when a call came inviting him to lunch at the White House, he remembers remarking to an associate: "We're really in trouble now! Something has gone sour. They're hauling me in for a dressing down at the Oval Office!" President Bush appointed him director of the newly created National Coordination Office for High Performance Computing and Communications (HPCC).

Within two and a half years the HPCC Program had developed the powerful computers and the test bed to launch what would become the Internet. Completing his tenure in 1995, he looks back on a job well done: "It was a lot of fun and I learned a lot. It had nothing per se to do with medicine, and that's why I agreed to take on the challenge. I realized that unless somebody with some understanding of biomedical concerns was heavily involved right at the outset, medicine would be simply bypassed."

In 1996, Dr. Lindberg was named U.S. National Coordinator for the G7 Global Healthcare Applications Projects, a post he still holds along with his Library responsibilities.

A member of the Institute of Medicine of the National Academy of Sciences, he has been showered with honors and awards, including the Surgeon General's Medallion of the U.S. Public Health Service, the Presidential Rank Award of Meritorious Executive in the Senior Executive Service, and the prestigious Morris F. Collen, M.D. Award of Excellence of the American College of Medical Informatics.

Dr. Lindberg holds honorary degrees from Amherst, the State University of New York Health Science Center at Syracuse, and the University of Missouri. He has lectured worldwide.

A proponent of Thomas West's view of the computer as a tool to help foster a new generation of "visual thinkers"–"Apparently Einstein would first see the answer, then he would find words and numbers to express it."–Lindberg posits: "Is it not a delightful thought to imagine such a master with a modern computer!" And why not, one might well add, imagine a generation of biomedical wizards first picturing and then unlocking the mysteries of the human genome, thanks in part to the pioneering work of Donald Lindberg!

OUT OF ANGUISH *INTO* AFRICA

MARTHA M. MACGUFFIE '49

In 1950, the dean of students of P&S gave the following assessment of Martha M. MacGuffie '49 in a letter of recommendation: "This woman is large, powerful, and tireless." The words proved prescient. For the next half century, until her death on March 8, 2011, at age eighty-seven, this plastic surgeon and humanitarian extraordinaire gave of herself body and soul to assuage the suffering of burn victims and AIDS orphans in Africa.

———⁂———

TO ALLAY the fears of little patients in the OR, Martha "Bobby" MacGuffie '49 wears a specially designed, child-friendly shirt with a jungle animal print. Around her neck dangles a bullet removed from the hip of an infant she and a colleague literally saved from the jaws of death in a refugee camp in Zaire. The apparent paradox of two such disparate symbols, one gentle, one fierce, both worn against her skin, tells much about the wearer. Founder, president, and prime mover of the Society for Hospital and Resource Exchange (SHARE), a nonprofit organization she created in 1988 to bring U.S. medical technology and manpower to people who need it most, the respected plastic and reconstructive surgeon divides her time between a busy practice in Rockland County, N.Y., and an even busier practice in the bush of western Kenya, tending to the diverse medical needs of AIDS orphans and anyone else who needs help. Other medical missions undertaken on a moment's notice have included the treatment of African victims of the 1998 terrorist bomb at the American Embassy in Nairobi and the emergency care of survivors of Rwanda's bloodbath at a refugee camp in Goma, Zaire. "We'll go where conditions are worst and where we're needed most!" says the seventy-six-year-old surgeon without batting a lash.

"HUMANITARIAN WARRIOR-WOMAN OF THE DECADE"

Featured on the network television program "48 Hours" for her work with the children of Kenya, she was saluted as the 1980 *Harper's Bazaar* Super Woman of the Year and the 1986 Red Cross Citizen of the Year. In 1996, Rotary International honored her with their Service Above Self Award and Lions Club International followed in 1998 with their prestigious Humanitarian Award, the latter formerly given to Mother Theresa. But perhaps the tribute that best bespeaks her true temperament is the 1996 "Humanitarian Warrior-Woman of the Decade" Award of the Martin Luther King Foundation. For Dr. MacGuffie has been a lifelong fighter for causes close to her heart. "The fierceness is in the blood," she likes to joke, a gift from her Scottish warrior ancestors.

The first woman to train in plastic and reconstructive surgery at P&S under the legendary Dr. Jerome Webster (who had publically stated that he would *never* train a woman—that is, until "Bobby" MacGuffie came along!), she was the first woman surgeon to serve on the staff of a major suburban hospital, Nyack Hospital, in Nyack, N.Y. There she established the first burn unit (which she still runs), and for more than twenty-seven years, has officiated as surgical chief of the plastic surgery service. But the fight that cost her most dearly in anguish was the one she waged to try and save the lives of her two young sons, Rob and Reid. Both suffering from a rare blood disorder, they died following repeated blood transfusions, in 1978 and 1976, respectively, the cause, unknown at the time, only later identified as AIDS. An older son, Scott, was so distraught by the death of his brothers that he turned to drugs and disappeared. She believes he is dead. That was the fight that drove her to the brink of despair but which she ultimately turned to mankind's advantage when she created SHARE.

A SELF-PROCLAIMED "MISFIT" MAKES LIFE FIT HER MEASURE

Sadness and spunk wrestle for dominion of her deep-set blue eyes. The wrinkles may be battle scars, but the inextinguishable twinkle belies an indomitable jack-in-the box who keeps springing back up, no matter what. Lean, lanky, and spry, Dr. MacGuffie admits she is still a tomboy at heart. Just watch her with a pet wild ferret wrapped around her neck—"My little fur piece!" she laughs—or shaking hands with a baby raccoon she saved from hunters, and you can well imagine the wild child she once was.

Born in 1924 in Passaic, N.J., she and her family spent summers in Maine, where the young MacGuffie, a self-proclaimed "misfit," ran wild with her dogs in the woods. "They literally had to drag me home in the fall," she recalls. She got her nickname "Bobby" from the unruly tuft of hair that perennially stuck up like the feathered crest of the bobolink. Following a reluctant and dismal educational beginning, she leapt from all failing grades to high school valedictorian, and went on to study zoology as a premed at Cornell, where she attended classes with beagle puppies in her knapsack and a crow perched on her shoulder.

Having from an early age tagged along on house calls with her physician father and watched him perform surgery, she had no doubt about her future calling—"It was just a matter of getting a license to legitimize my interest!" she chuckles with hindsight. "Medicine interests me because it has to do with people," she put it succinctly in her P&S application, inadvertently writing her future credo: "Through my father's work . . . I can see that this field, though indisputably hard, has a noble and human purpose." At P&S, she earned the respect of the faculty, including associate dean Dr. Aura Severinghaus, who wholeheartedly supported her application for an internship at Presbyterian

Hospital, citing her academic prowess and clinical skills and praising her as a "large, powerful and tireless individual with unbounded energy and a devotion to her patients."

She was drawn to surgery, because of its ability to "put things back together and fix whatever's wrong." Undaunted by the ingrained antifeminine prejudice of the field, strictly a man's domain at the time, she sought out and studied with such legendary figures as Drs. Frank Melaney in surgical bacteriology, Cushman Hagensen in Halstedian surgery, and Arthur Purdy Stout in surgical pathology. A general internship and a surgical residency at Presbyterian Hospital were followed by training there in orthopedic surgery and by a chief residency in general surgery at Delafield Hospital. Her unquestionable expertise and the quality of care she gave to one particular Presbyterian patient (a man who, by chance, happened to be one of Jerome Webster's close friends) so impressed the illustrious plastic surgeon, an outspoken opponent of "wasting" training on women, that he ate his words and offered her the very last residency slot of his career. Dr. MacGuffie went on to pursue a fellowship from the National Cancer Institute, collaborating with her second husband, Dr. Perry Hudson, then a member of the P&S faculty at Delafield, on research concerning tobacco condensates. At the same time, she took on the tobacco lobby and launched an antismoking campaign saluted by the National PTA as the best of its kind.

On the home front, meanwhile, with two daughters from an earlier marriage, five more with Hudson, and a child from his first marriage to help raise, Dr. MacGuffie had her hands full. The memory of juggling family and profession still makes her shake her head with a gasp and a smile. "Those years were a blur," she was quoted in a 1994 profile in the *Denver Post*, "there doesn't seem anything that was as much work as those kids." As in all her pursuits, she thrived on the daunting dual challenge of super-surgeon and super-Mom. She relished the absolute focus and meditative calm of surgery. To this day, she considers the OR a safe haven from the demands of everyday life.

FROM BURNS TO WATERBEDS AND SCAR CREAM

Setting up a private practice in New City, N.Y., she treated patients suffering from skin cancer, breast cancer, and congenital defects, also specializing in reconstructive surgery for burn victims. At Nyack Hospital she developed the first burn unit. Once while operating on a patient who had suffered multiple burns, she wondered aloud to a colleague in the OR: "Wouldn't it be nice if he could float?" The idea bore fruit. "We got a huge polystyrene block, hollowed it out, and filled it with water laced with copper sulfate. . . . And we floated him." That first prototype of the waterbed, later commercialized and marketed by others and popularized in the youth culture of the Sixties, eased the pain of countless patients. Another byproduct of her scientific savvy and ever-active imagination, Dr. MacGuffie's Scar Cream, proved an effective and popular postop healing aid. This time, she decided to manufacture and sell it herself. Her company, Narwhale of High Tor, produces scar cream, sunblock, and moisturizers considered the finest on the market. Most of the proceeds go to SHARE.

FROM ANGUISH TO AFRICA

Tragedy disrupted her busy regimen when two of her three boys were diagnosed with a rare congenital blood disease, Fanconi anemia. Though she and the boys decided that they would live active lives—both became accomplished young athletes—frequent blood transfusions inexplicably caused them to waste away. Somewhere along the line they had contracted AIDS, an as yet unidentified disease at the time.

Her sons' deaths changed the ground rules of her life. Their loss was cataclysmic. Unable to cope with their passing, her husband left. "I could've either blown my brains out," she calmly reflects back, "or put the pain to good use. There's a point at which you're still salvageable to yourself and others." As she said in the aforementioned *Denver Post* profile, "I went from a full house to nothing and I headed for Africa."

Ever since childhood, inspired by the stories of the returning missionaries whom her father treated, she had dreamed of going to Africa. Many a time in later years, she would playfully tell her kids to buck up, or "I'm going to take a one-way flight to Kenya!" When her youngest daughter left for college, the moment had finally come to follow her dream.

What began as a veterinary safari to Kenya to try and take her mind off the loss of her sons evolved into a lifelong mission. While ostensibly there to look at veterinary conditions, she could not turn a blind eye to the human condition. Appalled by the absence of basic facilities and medicines and the generally abysmal state of the government clinics she visited, as she recalls, "I came back home to the States and saw them throwing all the hospital stuff away here." A subsequent trip to the U.N. and a fateful meeting with the Kenyan ambassador made her put two and two together. She pinpointed her target in the Nyanza province, a disease-ravaged region of western Kenya on the shore of Lake Victoria. The region has one of the world's highest birth rates, infant mortality rates, and incidence of infectious diseases. One in three has HIV, and 90 percent of the children suffer from malaria and/or schistosomiasis. It is here on an island in Lake Victoria that paleontologists Louis and Mary Leakey had discovered the earliest dated remains of human life on earth and here that Dr. MacGuffie saw human life fading.

The odds notwithstanding, she decided to take a stand, to invest the pain of the loss of her sons by "helping the most disadvantaged children in the world." The help has been unstinting. In a little over a decade, SHARE (which Dr. MacGuffie cofounded in 1987 with Dr. Renee M. Brilliant, a pediatric hematologist who had treated her sons) has built clinics, donated millions of dollars' worth of medical equipment and drugs, educated local residents on how to avoid disease, and organized a program whereby American paramedics help train their African counterparts. In addition, the organization has helped in the expansion of the Homa Bay District Hospital "from a grimy, run-down, poorly functioning unit to a clean, well-run facility" and helped establish and run the Double Joy C. Farm, where Kenyan AIDS orphans are reunited with surviving siblings and cousins into family units and given the wherewithal and training to learn and thrive.

AFRICAN AND AMERICAN CHILDREN PULL TOGETHER

SHARE's newsletter, "HARAMBE!" takes its name from a word in the Luo dialect that means "Pull together!" From the very start, Dr. MacGuffie has sought to create lasting links between America and Africa. Her goal has been to educate, sensitize, and thereby empower American children to make a difference in their own lives as well as the lives of those less fortunate. Lecturing on AIDS awareness to American schoolchildren, she shows them vivid photographs of immeasurable suffering, stirring their conscience and rallying their support. Children, whom she calls "one of the world's most powerful forces for good," have responded with boundless enthusiasm. One group of young schoolchildren in California started a successful program by contributing hundreds of teddy bears. Dubbed "SHARE BEARS," these stuffed animals are dressed up by volunteers to be sold and promoted as a source of support and a symbol of caring.

Dr. MacGuffie has been eminently successful at gently twisting adult arms too. Celebrity friends like comedian Bill Murray and dancer Mikhail

Baryshnikov have lent their talents to fundraisers. A retired former comptroller of Texaco now does SHARE's bookkeeping. Pharmaceutical giants like Lederle and Bristol-Myers have contributed life-saving drugs, including tetracycline and cytoxan, the latter now delivered four times a year to treat the disfiguring, albeit reversible, scourge of Burkitt lymphoma. The drugs are shipped free of charge, compliments of Federal Express. Transamerica Leasing provides the containers. AmeriCares, a Connecticut-based relief organization, has provided aid and funded many of her emergency missions. AARP funded an emergency mission to Somalia to care for the survivors of terrible tribal clashes. Rotary funded a custom-made jeep built to her specifications, designed for every kind of road condition or the absence thereof.

In a television special, "Stephen's Story," CBS News documented one of her most successful human linkups. On an island in Lake Victoria, Dr. MacGuffie came upon a young boy, Stephen Oyugi, who hadn't walked in 11 years and was about to have his legs amputated. Stephen had been the best student in the village. She took his case to a colleague, orthopedic surgeon Ohannes A. Nercessian '81, and arranged for Stephen's trip. Columbia Presbyterian covered the expenses of the operation and hospitalization. Unofficially adopting Stephen, she arranged for his acceptance at Rust College, in Holly Springs, Miss., whose president, it so happens, is also a Luo, Stephen's tribe. Completing the four-year course of study in two and a half years, Stephen has gone on to pursue a master's in computer science and another in biology. He wants to become a doctor. "Stephen came along at a time when I was most upset about the disappearance of [her third son] Scott. We've helped each other," she allows.

A HUMANITARIAN WILLING TO RISK HER OWN SKIN

She has risked typhoons, tribal clashes, a cholera epidemic, and the ever-present threat of a deadly strain of malaria from which one colleague died. Attacked and beaten by bandits on one occasion, she climbed back into her jeep to complete her mission. Not immune to the suffering she faces on each mission and the terrible specter of death, she manages to put the pain on hold. Asked about fear, she promptly replies: "I'm afraid of everything, but usually if something needs to be done, I'll let myself get afraid afterwards."

Dr. MacGuffie distinguishes between the role of the philanthropist, who helps but from afar, and that of the humanitarian, who gets involved at considerable personal risk, both physical and emotional. While reticent to compare herself with a hero of her youth, Dr. Albert Schweitzer, she modestly acknowledges his influence: " 'I do not know what your future will be, but this much I know, the only ones amongst you who will be truly happy are those who have learned how to serve.'—that's Schweitzer!" she nods. And while happiness may not be her lot in life, she exudes a profound, if restless, satisfaction.

Colleagues say her face lights up whenever she gets to Africa. "It's very energizing!" she admits. "It has something to do with being alive, I guess. . . . If you have an aching joint, you forget it, there's no time for the pain."

THE LIGHT ON LAKE VICTORIA

Peering at a photograph of the shimmering surface of Lake Victoria, Dr. Mac-Guffie shakes her head: "That's the direct sunlight on the lake, it's like silver once you see it, a magical light, but it also causes blindness!" Severe iritis, a frequent problem of local children, leads to panophthalmitis, which, if untreated, can make you go blind. "That's Africa, the beauty and the tragedy!" she affirms.

Keenly conscious of the link between nature and disease, she has played an active role in various environmental efforts. Working in conjunction with the International Center for Insect Physiology and Ecology, she raised the necessary funds to develop tsetse fly traps at Ruma National Park to help eradicate sleeping sickness in the area. The park is run by her friend, the paleontologist and conservationist Richard Leakey. She is currently engaged in an effort to build a bridge in place of a causeway that currently links the mainland to Rusinga Island. The causeway blocked a natural current, thus leading to the growth of a weed that chokes the wildlife and poisons the water and fosters the infestation of snails that carry schistosomiasis, a disease that kills thousands of children every year.

"THE ANSWER TO AIDS IS OUT THERE!"

AIDS is what first brought her to Africa and it is still her primary focus. In addition to her ongoing support of AIDS orphans at the Double Joy Children's Farm, she recently launched a new program back home in the States, SHARE Orphan Sponsorship, whereby American sponsors "adopt" an AIDS orphan, assuming the modest expense of his/her care and education. "The answer to

AIDS is here," she firmly believes. "These orphans are survivors, they don't have the disease." Can it be that they developed an immunity? Dr. MacGuffie nods. She also suspects that, contrary to conventional wisdom, mosquitoes may carry the HIV virus through their proboscis, which is basically similar to a hypodermic needle.

"IT'S TOO LATE TO RETIRE!"

Dr. MacGuffie's beloved home base is a manor house built by an admiralty lawyer in imitation of a thirteenth-century Norman castle, on a thirty-one-acre estate in New City, N.Y. Home and office, family reserve and private retreat, the compound includes a Skin Care Center for patients and a former stable redesigned as digs for one daughter, who is an artist and teacher. Two other daughters are physicians and two are teachers. Nine grandchildren return every chance they get. Her extended family includes five raccoons, two ferrets, two large dogs, six cats, three horses, not to mention the wild turkeys, deer, and woodchucks that also share her grounds. Itinerant artists have workshops on the upper floors of the manor, the only rent paid in art, like the OR shirt with the jungle animal theme designed by a tenant. And when she's not hosting her annual Scare Fair, a gala Halloween fund-raising event for SHARE, she lets other worthy organizations, like Children's Rescue, borrow the digs to raise funds of their own.

Miraculously, Dr. MacGuffie manages to find time for it all. As if there were ever any question of slowing down or, heaven help her, retiring, she grins: "I'm afraid it's too late now!"

BATTLING INVISIBILITY—A PRIMARY
CARE CLINICIAN AND SPOKESPERSON
FOR THE CARE OF LESBIANS, GAYS,
BISEXUALS, AND TRANSGENDER PEOPLE

HARVEY J. MAKADON '77

HARVEY J. MAKADON '77, clinical professor of medicine at Harvard Medical School and director of the National LGBT Education Center, a division of the Fenway Institute, Fenway Health, in Boston, is committed to a simple, seemingly self-evident truth: "Most doctors see LGBT people, but they don't know it. Yet in order to provide good care you need to know whether your patients are lesbian, gay, bisexual, or transgender." He has devoted his professional life not only to providing care but also to ending health care disparities. "The disparities are not due to complex biomedical issues," he adds, "they're really the result of stigma, discrimination, and ignorance." Dr. Makadon is the lead editor of *The Fenway Guide to LGBT Health*, published by the American College of Physicians in 2008, the first textbook on LGBT health for clinicians.

In October 2012, Dr. Makadon made time for an interview at his office in the National LGBT Education Center in the Fenway Institute, on one of two floors devoted to LGBT research, education, and policy development at the headquarters of Fenway Health, in Boston's West Fen's neighborhood.

"IN MUCH THE SAME WAY THE VIETNAM WAR
CHANGED A GENERATION'S SOCIAL THINKING,
AIDS ACTIVATED PEOPLE."

After earning his BA from Cornell University, Dr. Makadon briefly attended the University of Pennsylvania Law School, before deciding that law was not for him. While figuring out what to do next, he took a job with the Health Law

Project, and did work for the National Welfare Rights Organization, lobbying for Medicaid reform, and worked on a book on the history of Medicare. "I liked the work a lot," he says, "but I realized that what I really wanted was to be a doctor, a *real* doctor, i.e., primary care. [. . .] I was drawn to primary care because I felt like it was a way of beginning to improve the quality of care and access to care for poor people."

He relished his time at P&S, in particular the experience of his clinical years, under such "compassionate, tough, and thorough" attendings as Thomas Q. Morris '58, then course director of the third-year medical clerkship, who would go on to become president and CEO of Presbyterian Hospital, and the late Glenda Garvey '69, a revered specialist in infectious diseases who took over the clerkship and ran it for some twenty years. Dr. Makadon thought that P&S "was an amazing place to learn how to be a doctor," yet he faults the school for discouraging his interest in primary care and what he perceived as the institution's lack of social commitment. "Even though the medical school was located in the middle of one of the poorest parts of New York, social issues in medicine, such as disparities in American health care, were never really embraced at Columbia."

The Sixties and Seventies were a turbulent time of change on campuses across the country, and some might argue that Columbia was no more or less responsive than other major universities. And whereas specialization was then, and is still, held in high esteem at academic medical centers like Columbia, initiatives like the Columbia-Bassett Program (in which students divide their time between classes at the Health Sciences Campus in Washington Heights and a rich primary care and rural medicine clinical experience at Bassett Healthcare System campus in Cooperstown, N.Y.), the Center for Family and Community Medicine, and the Daniel Noyes Brown '32 Primary Care Scholars Program have reaffirmed an institutional commitment to primary care.

One of the most pressing social issues in medicine in recent times, the care of people suffering from AIDS, would become a catalyst for a profound shift of attitude in America and a focal point of Dr. Makadon's own professional life. It was, as he recalled in an article "Legacy of AIDS" (*Harvard Medical Alumni Bulletin*, Spring 1997), "an enormous catalyst in the renegotiation of the gay-straight social contract." Looking back, Dr. Makadon reaffirmed: "In much the same way that the Vietnam War changed a generation's social thinking, AIDS activated people in the LGBT community, and for many of us that commitment still exists. I see it every day here at the Fenway Institute, where young people who could be very successful hedge fund managers are doing research and learning more about the health care needs of homosexual and transgender people." The scourge of AIDS also prompted Dr. Makadon to address an unresolved issue in his personal life—coming out.

"I REALIZED I HAD AN ISSUE I HAD TO RESOLVE."

After training at Beth Israel Hospital in Boston, Dr. Makadon became a member of the clinical faculty in the Department of Medicine at Harvard Medical School, and joined Beth Israel's faculty primary care practice. In 1981, as he recalls in the aforementioned article, "we began receiving disturbing reports of strange illnesses occurring mostly in gay men." Although engaged in social issues and committed to caring for the underserved, he admits, "I was avoiding dealing with AIDS patients, because I felt like I did not want to be associated with the disease. I had internalized my own homophobia. It was a fear of being identified as what I was and am: a gay physician working in a world where at that time I could not imagine acceptance."

At institutions of higher learning, like Columbia and Harvard, and in particular at medical schools, the sexual orientation of faculty and students had long been a deep dark secret, addressed by a tacit "don't ask, don't tell" policy. As Lee Shapiro '77, a rheumatologist based in Saratoga Springs, N.Y., and a classmate of Dr. Makadon's recalls, "I had at least five gay classmates in medical school, but I knew none of them to be gay, nor did I have a strong sense of self-identity. Three of those classmates died within a few years of HIV. We had no network or support system of any sort. We were each in a state of insecure isolation, each believing we might be the only gay student there." The Lambda Health Alliance, under the umbrella of the P&S Club, presently provides a supportive space for gay, lesbian, bisexual, transsexual, and queer (GLBTQ) people at the Health Sciences campus and works to increase visibility of GLBTQ issues in medicine.

Dr. Makadon likewise kept his sexual orientation a secret at P&S, and then at Harvard, until, one day, a medical student actually said to him: " 'Why don't you come out? Because other medical students know you're gay, and it would be much better if they knew you were comfortable with it.' That student helped me to come out," Dr. Makadon, who was in his mid-thirties at the time, recalls.

The self-realization led to a personal and professional turnaround: "That's when I decided I needed to get myself reoriented, come out and deal with my sexuality. [. . .] Within a very short period of time I went from total avoidance to totally embracing the issues."

THE FIRST HOSPITAL-BASED HIV
PROGRAM ZIN THE COUNTRY

At Beth Israel Dr. Makadon set up the first hospital-based HIV program in the country integrated into a primary care practice. He helped establish a city-wide consortium, the Boston AIDS Consortium, to help people get AIDS services in the Boston area, and he founded the New England AIDS Education and Training Center. In addition to caring for and coordinating the care of countless people suffering the scourge of AIDS, Dr. Makadon became an outspoken health activist, not only in the battle to beat the disease but also in the resistance to the social stigmas faced by gays, lesbians, bisexuals, and transgender people restricting their access to care. Combatting the invisibility of the LGBT population became and remains a major thrust of his work.

Since 1985 Dr. Makadon has been active in various capacities, including fourteen years as a member of the board of directors, two as chair, with Fenway Health. Founded in 1971 by students from Northeastern University as a nonprofit ("50 cents or whatever you can afford to pay") neighborhood health center for seniors, gays, low-income residents, and students, Fenway, in collaboration with Harvard Medical School, became one of the first medical facilities in the United States to culture HIV from blood and semen samples. In 1986, Fenway's mission statement was revised to reflect a commitment to the health care needs of the gay and lesbian community. In 1990, it expanded its focus to include the care of transgender individuals. Dr. Makadon was one of the founding members of the Fenway Institute, an arm of Fenway Health devoted to research and evaluation, education and training and public health advocacy on behalf of lesbian, gay, bisexual, and transgender people living with HIV/AIDS, and the larger community. The Institute is supported by government and foundation grants. He serves as director of the Fenway Institute's National LGBT Health Education Center, which provides educational outreach and consultation for health care organizations throughout the country and around the world.

"DOCTORS AREN'T TAUGHT TO TALK
TO PATIENTS ABOUT INTIMATE ISSUES."

While providing quality primary care to patients was always and remains his primary concern, he has come to feel comfortable with his public role as a spokesperson for the health and wellness of LGBT people. "I always connected with people as patients, now I am working to create change in how others care for LGBT people," he says. "It's a new role, but an important one as we enter the era of population health and meeting the needs of the underserved."

At Harvard Medical School he was responsible for updating the HIV curriculum and for addressing intimate issues in the patient-doctor interview. He taught a section of the course on taking a sexual history. "Doctors aren't taught to talk to patients about intimate issues. Often when they take a sexual history they don't talk about sexual orientation," he points out. Furthermore, Dr. Makadon cites a study of doctors talking to people with HIV: "84 percent of the time they talked about whether patients were taking their medications, and only 14 percent of the time they talked to them about whether they were engaging in safer sex." Last year, Dr. Makadon helped organize a meeting at the Institute of Medicine to discuss whether or not sexual orientation and gender identity should become standard issues asked about when people go see a doctor.

Dr. Makadon believes that patients should routinely be asked about their sexual orientation, just as they are asked to identify their race and ethnicity, in hospital intake questionnaires: "A hospital can verify whether different racial and ethnic groups are getting the same standard of care, but they can't say that about LGBT people," because they aren't registered as such. "We can't say, for instance, whether lesbians are getting pap smears to the same extent that heterosexual women are. In fact, a lot of doctors feel that lesbians don't need pap smears, because they don't think they have ever had sex with men. That's just not true."

Physicians, he believes, can help LGBT individuals feel comfortable by having educational brochures that relate to issues they identify with prominently displayed in their waiting rooms. But brochures are not enough. In his own search for a primary care physician some years ago, Dr. Makadon was dismayed, to say the least, when, after telling the doctor that he was gay, information he considered relevant to his care, the doctor simply glossed over it and asked no follow-up questions. All health care professionals, including nurses and social workers, Dr. Makadon insists, need to be trained to be sensitive to issues of sexual orientation and gender identity: "It isn't that complicated really. It just requires leadership and commitment to diversity."

His educational outreach efforts have included a videotaped presentation on "Meeting the Healthcare Needs of Lesbian, Gay, Bisexual and Transgender People" on the website of the American Medical Association. He has been invited to address issues relating to LGBT care around the country and around the world, most recently to the Primary Care Association in San Juan, PR, and the

University of Arkansas for Medical Sciences, at Little Rock, Ark., where his remarks were well received. His grand rounds presentation on LGBT health at the Mayo Clinic in Rochester, Minn., drew an overflow crowd.

"I think that there is a real sense of awakening. The world has changed, but that doesn't mean that everybody has changed," Dr. Makadon cautions. "There are always going to be people who are biased, just like there are people who are racially biased. [. . .] Society and the medical profession were biased against black people too, but we got over it. Or at least we got over it to the extent that doctors realize that they need to take care of everybody who comes to see them. And I think the same thing is true of lesbians, gays, bisexuals, and transgender people."

HOMELESS YOUTH AND AGING SENIORS

Society, Dr. Makadon insists, has a duty to care for everyone. One of the groups he collaborates with is the National Healthcare for the Homeless Council. Some 30 to 40 percent of homeless youth are thought to be LGBT. Either rejected by their families or in some cases not wanting to live at home, they are not always accepted into homeless shelters, and are by the nature of their homeless status at greater health risk and less likely to find care.

Dr. Makadon has also addressed the needs of an aging population. "As Baby Boomers age there's going to be a big increase in the number of seniors and there's going to be a big increase in the number of gay, bisexual and transgender seniors," he said in an interview published on the website of the National Center for Health in Public Housing. "These seniors are of a generation that has been living openly. But some fear that, in order to get care and be accepted in nursing homes and other facilities, they may have to actually go back into the closet."

"THIS ISN'T ABOUT *ME!*"

In a write-up in the *Los Angeles Times* some years ago of an episode of the PBS special "The AIDS Quarterly" devoted to Dr. Makadon and his practice at Beth Israel, he was cited as "the real article," and lauded for "his genuine concern for patients, his optimism in the face of merciless sickness, and his faultless bedside manner." But when the camera crew that had followed him all day for several days in his consultations with patients wanted to film him in his garden at home, he said: "No! This isn't about me working in my garden at home. This is about me taking care of patients, what it's like to care for AIDS patients."

A private man, Dr. Makadon shuns the limelight: "I don't see my work as being about me. It's important for me to feel fulfilled in what I do and to feel that I might also serve as a support for others of the sort I didn't have when I was a medical student."

He is married to a fellow physician, Dr. Ray Powrie, an obstetric internist, associate professor of medicine at the Warren Alpert Medical School of Brown University, and senior vice president for quality and clinical effectiveness at Women & Infants Hospital, in Providence, R.I. "We're involved in what we do. We both work very hard and are deeply committed to our work."

AT THE CANCER COMMAND

PAUL MARKS '49

Now president emeritus of Memorial Sloan Kettering Cancer Center, an institution over which he presided for close to two decades, and where a prize for cancer research was named in his honor, Dr. Marks continues to pursue research in cell biology and cancer genetics.

———&&&———

HIS PIERCING blue eyes encased in steel-rimmed glasses flash the message: MIND AT WORK! His powerful frame (once used effectively to plough through the opposition back in the days when he played right tackle on Columbia's junior-varsity football team) is no less daunting now at age seventy. For close to half a century, as research scientist, teacher, medical administrator, and national health policy advisor, Paul Marks '49 has been a leading player and tactician in the war against cancer.

From his current command headquarters at Memorial Sloan Kettering Cancer Center on New York's Upper East Side, the nation's oldest and largest private institution devoted to prevention, patient care, research, and education in cancer, Dr. Marks's influence in the field of cancer research reaches around the country and the world. Recruited by MSKCC Honorary Board Co-chair Laurance Rockefeller in 1980 to the then newly created position of president and CEO, Dr. Marks has applied his combined talents as a world-class scientist and a strong administrator to reinvigorate research at the molecular level and refocus clinical care to encompass noninvasive alternatives to surgery.

A LIFELONG LOVE AFFAIR WITH BIOMEDICAL SCIENCE

A man accustomed to being at the top, who graduated first in his class at P&S in 1949 and twenty-one years later rose to the rank of dean of the faculty, Paul Marks is uncharacteristically humble when it comes to talking about the rigors of biomedical science. "In research, you've got to learn that the number of really exciting, satisfying experiments you do will be few and far between," he admits. "But hopefully, if you're working on something that's important, and you keep at it, its impact will be broad."

An abiding passion for the intellectual challenge of biomedical science buoys any doubt. "There is no answer which doesn't raise more questions," Dr. Marks reflects. "My life is a continuing love affair, if you will, with the whole potential of exploring the unknown."

The seeds of such passion were evident early on. "There is no doubt in my mind," he wrote in his student application to P&S, "that my greatest happiness lies in the pursuit and practice of medical knowledge to the best of my ability." Inspired by a high school English teacher to pursue medicine, Paul Marks took his BA at Columbia College and subsequently enrolled in P&S on a Navy scholarship as part of the V12 program.

At P&S, the biochemistry bug bit him and he has never been the same since. A student research project with Dr. Hans Stetten on the blood-brain barrier wet his appetite for more. And though in the course of an elective in biochemistry with another P&S legend, Dr. Erwin Chargaff, Marks failed to accomplish his ambitious goal of solving the problem of the biochemical defect of Gaucher disease, "the experience was thrilling, I got hooked on research."

After graduation, Dr. Marks spent a year as a research fellow at Cornell, where he worked under Dr. Ephraim Shorr on the biochemistry of cartilage and bone formation. He subsequently returned to Presbyterian Hospital to pursue his house staff training under Dr. Robert Loeb and a medical fellowship on problems related to the physiology of blood volume under Dr. Stan Bradley, himself a veteran associate of Nobel Prize laureates André Cournand '65 HON and Dickinson Richards '23 '66 HON.

Dr. Marks remembers with a smile Dr. Loeb's famous "Sunrise Serenades," those often grueling, but always enlightening, early morning consultations with house staff and fellows, six days a week, seven if you were on call. In the course of one such consult, Dr. Loeb, who had just returned from a visit to the NIH, discussed the exciting work being done there on the synthesis of nucleotides by Dr. Arthur Kornberg (later to win the Nobel Prize for his discoveries related to DNA synthesis). Loeb urged his promising young protégé to apply for a position in Kornberg's lab, for which he was accepted. Marks's experience at the NIH, where he also worked with Dr. Bernard Horecker at the National Institute of Arthritis and Metabolic Diseases, gave him "a real insight into and a taste for rigorous biochemistry at its best."

Recruited back to Columbia P&S as an instructor in medicine in 1955, Dr. Marks sought to apply his newly acquired biochemical expertise to a clinical problem. Setting up a laboratory in the basement of the old Delafield Hospital, he began to study the pathway by which blood cells metabolize sugar. Delafield was a cancer hospital and, consequently, the blood samples Marks studied came from cancer patients. He noticed a curious phenomenon. All cancer patients proved to have an elevated level of the enzyme G-6-P dehydrogenase and a slight hemolytic anemia, destroying their red blood cells faster than normal. This led to Marks's trailblazing discovery of two genetic blood disorders, G6PD deficiency and thalassemia, and his development of a molecular basis for red blood cell aging.

For the next two decades, Dr. Marks pursued his research at Columbia—with the exception of a sabbatical leave from 1961 to 1962, as a visiting scientist at the Pasteur Institute in Paris, where he worked with Drs. Jacques Monod and François Gros at the moment they discovered messenger RNA. He went on to study the mechanism of protein synthesis in cells and did seminal work on a class of cytodifferentiation agents, chemicals that have the capacity to induce cancer cells to resume normal growth and development.

In collaboration with Drs. Richard A. Rifkind '55 (now chair of the Sloan Kettering Institute) and Arthur Bank, Dr. Marks studied the effect of hexamethylene bisacetamide (HMBA) on murine erythroleukemia cells in the mouse. Rather than destroy cancerous cells, as do classical chemotherapeutic agents, treatment with HMBA, they found, altered the expression of certain genes, causing the cells to cease malignant growth and assume more normal characteristics. Clinical studies demonstrated the ability of such agents to induce remission in patients with certain cancers. Dr. Marks and his colleagues are still working today with a variety of agents in an attempt to optimize the results of cytodifferentiation therapy.

Rapidly rising in the academic ranks at P&S, Dr. Marks proved as superb a teacher and administrator as he was a scientist. Named director of the Hematology Training Program and director of Clinical Hematology at Presbyterian Hospital in 1960, he was instrumental in rethinking pedagogical methods in those areas that later served as a precedent for the important curricular reforms of 1968–70. In 1967 he was appointed professor of medicine, and in 1969 professor and first chair of the newly created Department of Human Genetics and Development. In 1970, he became dean of the Faculty of Medicine and vice president in charge of medical affairs. In that capacity, Dr. Marks reorganized the administrative structure at P&S, bolstered funding, and embarked on an ambitious recruitment of scientific talent from around the country. Illustrious faculty members he recruited included future Nobel laureate Dr. Eric Kandel, and Drs. Sol Spiegelman and Isidore Edelman.

In 1973, Columbia decided to separate the deanship and the vice presidency at P&S. Dr. Marks was appointed to the new title of vice president for health sciences and simultaneously assumed the responsibilities as director of the Cancer Research Institute, which he helped found. In 1974, he was named Frode Jensen Professor of Medicine.

Alas for P&S, Sloan Kettering managed to woo him crosstown in 1980.

Parallel to his research and administrative careers, Dr. Marks has answered repeated calls to public service at the highest levels. A member of the President's Biomedical Research Panel (1975–76), the President's Cancer Panel (1976–79), and the President's Commission on the Accident at Three Mile Island (1979), he subsequently served on an advisory committee to the director of the National Institutes of Health to help overhaul its intramural research program.

At the international level, he has served in various capacities as a kind of biomedical diplomat, helping to foster a cooperative atmosphere of scientific interchange of knowledge. While dean of P&S, he helped open a scientific dialogue with China. P&S was among the first American medical schools to welcome a group of Chinese physicians and scientists. In 1980, with the financial support and sponsorship of fellow P&S alumnus Armand Hammer '23, Dr. Marks organized the first bilateral Conference on Cancer Research in the People's Republic of China and the Unites States at P&S. He was also a member of the organizing committee of the International School of Developmental Biology, and a founding member of the Committee of the Radiation Effects Research Foundation in Japan.

He is the author or coauthor of more than 300 hundred scientific articles, nine book chapters, and some sixty articles on medical subjects of general interest. His editorial contributions include tenures as editor-in-chief of the *Journal of Clinical Investigation* (1967–71) and *Blood* (1978–82).

Such a prodigious achievement has earned him a garland of laurels, including honorary degrees from the University of Urbino, Italy, The Hebrew University of Jerusalem, and the University of Tel Aviv; the Centenary Medal of the Institut Pasteur; the President's National Medal of Science; and Columbia's Alumni Gold Medal for Distinguished Achievements in Medicine. He is a member of the American Academy of Arts and Sciences and the Institute of Medicine of the National Academy of Sciences.

Testifying over the years before various government organs, including the Senate Finance Committee on Health Care Reform, Dr. Marks has been an eloquent spokesman on behalf of America's great academic medical centers. "I believe that institutions such as Columbia and Memorial Sloan Kettering are vital to the health of our society!" he asserts. Acknowledging the crisis in funding for biomedical research, he argues against the dangers of short-sighted budget cuts. In cancer research, he insists, "the public's investment has paid off marvelously. Twenty years ago, about a third of all cancers were curable. Today, well over 50 percent are curable, and for those that aren't, we can control the disease for much longer periods of time, permitting even the afflicted a useful and valuable life experience."

The most exciting area of progress in current cancer research, according to Dr. Marks, is taking place at the genetic level. "The detection of genes that place individuals at increased risk," he points out, "gives rise to a whole new concept: presymptomatic diagnosis. The Human Genome Project has markedly accelerated the identification of these genes and the development of practical probes to detect them." Major challenges remain, however, notably "just how to intervene once you diagnose a presymptomatic cancer stage."

While the battle against cancer is by no means won, the disease is no longer the invincible bogeyman of old. "Yet we still have a way to go," he insists, "for while fifty percent of all cancers may be curable, fifty percent are not, and that's simply not acceptable!"

At a time of life when most people begin to consider retirement, Dr. Marks continues to put in thirteen-hour days at his desk and lunch hours in the lab. (His only other avowed ambition: "To be able to play tennis till I'm eighty-five!") "Biomedical research and health care is what I'm good at," he shrugs. "I'll be at it as long as I'm productive." From all appearances, that is likely to be for a good many years to come.

A PIVOTAL PLAYER AT P&S
AND PRESBYTERIAN HOSPITAL
THROWS IN THE WHITE COAT
(AND LOOKS BACK WITH PRIDE)

THOMAS Q. MORRIS '58

Upon his official retirement from P&S in 2003, Thomas Q. Morris '58 took up residence as a gentleman farmer, harvesting hay, herding cattle, and building walls in Upstate New York. But medicine remains an essential part of the picture. He continues to officiate in various capacities, including as chair of the editorial board of the journal Columbia Medicine, *board member of the Bassett Hospital in Cooperstown, N.Y., and vice chair of the board of the American University of Beirut, in Lebanon. He was saluted by his peers as P&S Honorary Alumni Day Chair in 2015.*

—————◦◦◦◦◦—————

"THIS IS my uniform, my way of life," Thomas Q. Morris '58 affirmed with a twinkle in his eyes, fingering the lapels of a spotless starched white coat. No mere garment to him, it's clearly more like a second skin. The genial curl of his lips and the pockets under his eyes attest to his joy in and tireless commitment to the medical way of life. "That's the way it began when I first added an MD to my name," he said, "so that's the way I want it to finish." After fifty years in various top leadership roles at New York-Columbia Presbyterian Medical Center—notably as acting chair of the Department of Medicine, interim dean of the faculty at P&S, and president and CEO of Presbyterian Hospital—he finally threw in the white coat in September 2003.

AN MD WITH MEDICINE IN THE GUT

He and his wife, Jacqueline, are giving up their home in Westchester County and moving full time to a farm they've owned for years in Delaware County, Upstate New York. It is well-nigh impossible for his many friends and associates at P&S to imagine the dapper, urbane Dr. Morris forsaking that spotless white coat for muddy overalls, but such is his intention—for the moment at least—to tend and till the vegetable garden and build stone walls, two of his long-time avocations. He will, in any case, be keeping several fingers—if not all ten—in the medical pie, as chair of the editorial board of *Columbia Medicine* (formerly P&S), active board member of the Bassett Hospital in Cooperstown, N.Y., and vice chair of the board of the American University of Beirut, in Lebanon, whose campus he visits several times a year.

"When you've got medicine in the gut, there's no leaving it behind," he readily admitted in the course of an interview over lunch at the P&S Faculty Club. The tangible fruits of his career as a key player at one of America's most respected medical centers include the construction of the Milstein Hospital Building and the Allen Pavilion. The intangibles are manifold just about everywhere you look, in the friendships he made and the medical legacy he leaves behind. As one long-time friend and supporter, Henry King, former chair of the Columbia Presbyterian Health Sciences Advisory Council, put it: "It is and has always been a delight to deal with Tom Morris, a man of consummate wit, intelligence, medical knowledge, dedication to Columbia, and, I might add, considerable charm. His door was always open."

"A lot of people have been at Columbia a lot longer than I have," Dr. Morris avowed, "but most of them have stayed in a particular department or area. I don't think they've had half as much fun as I have experiencing it all firsthand."

Consider the span and reach of that experience, 1954-2003: medical student; intern and chief resident at the famous affiliate, the First (Columbia) Medical Division at Bellevue; research trainee, faculty member, course director of the third-year clerkship, and acting chair of the Department of Medicine, vice dean and interim dean for clinical and educational affairs of the Faculty of Medicine at P&S; president and CEO of Presbyterian Hospital. From the insidious rise of HMOs to the fortuitous advent of medical informatics, to the diabolical first appearance of AIDS, there are few challenges affecting American academic medicine that Dr. Morris hasn't tackled.

FROM YONKERS TO WASHINGTON HEIGHTS
(WITH A DETOUR TO NOTRE DAME)

"Growing up in Yonkers, N.Y., just north of the City, Columbia-Presbyterian was the only place to go if you were really in major trouble," Dr. Morris recalled. And though he himself did not experience any major illnesses or accidents, the idea took seed early on that "medicine might be a useful and fun way to spend a life" and that "Columbia was *the* place to do it."

Premed from the start at Notre Dame University, in South Bend, Ind., he set his sights on P&S. While he focused mainly on his studies in college, graduating magna cum laude, he did manage to play a little football—"Only touch!" he winked, "but I still follow Notre Dame football very avidly, as most people around here know. Go to three or four games a year, just to make sure they're still doing it right!"

At P&S, he found a host of dedicated medical mentors: "The faculty in general had great concern for and devotion to the welfare of students, as they do to this day." Take Calvin Plimpton MSD '51 as a case in point, his third-year preceptor in medicine: "The interplay between and among everybody in his group was constant. His critical eye was on all of us all the time, but also his supportive eye."

During the time Dr. Morris pursued his internship and residency in medicine at the illustrious First (Columbia) Medical Division at Bellevue Hospital, the shining lights there were Dickinson W. Richards, Jr. '23, chief of the service, and André F. Cournand '65 HON CU, who shared the 1956 Nobel Prize in Physiology or Medicine for their pioneering work in heart catheterization. Dr. Morris recalled with unconcealed excitement, as if it were yesterday, the experience of working with and learning from such medical giants who always remained accessible to the house staff: "For us to be able to meet with a Nobel Prize winner every week and see someone who had such an in-depth understanding of science conduct rounds with us in, not only the most humane, but also the most informed way, clinically, that was really something." A firm believer in the mentoring principle, Dr. Morris has, in turn, performed that vital function for generations of P&S students. "Your instructors mold you. You may not realize it at the time, but they set the standard and all you want to do is meet or exceed that standard," he said.

Dr. Richards paid his protégé the ultimate compliment and mark of confidence, naming him chief resident the year he himself was due to retire. "That year of my chief residency turned out to be another wonderful time," Dr. Morris remembered, "because Dr. Charlie Ragan, who had been up at P&S, came down to Bellevue as the new chief of medicine." The young chief resident helped the new chief of medicine get acclimatized to the ways of a public hospital, and the two got along famously.

At Bellevue, Dr. Morris likewise interacted with another P&S giant, Dr. Robert Loeb, who came down regularly to make rounds. He also worked with dedicated members of the voluntary faculty, notably Dr. George Carden, "who practiced midtown and gave enormous amounts of free time."

"Overall, my experience at Bellevue," Dr. Morris said, "opened up a whole new range of medical opportunities for me."

UPTOWN TO HARLEM AND BACK HOME
TO WASHINGTON HEIGHTS

Following two years of military service at the U.S. Air Force Hospital, Scott Air Force Base, in Belleville, Ill., a large facility devoted to the care of patients with pulmonary disease (where, among other duties, he ran the cardiopulmonary lab), Dr. Morris returned to P&S as a research trainee in the laboratory of Dr. Stan Bradley, then chair of medicine. Dr. Bradley focused on renal and hepatic research, and Dr. Morris took advantage of the opportunity to study and publish on bile formation in experimental animals. At P&S, he also joined the medical faculty as an instructor.

Meanwhile, the NYC administration had decided to discontinue the First (Columbia) Division at Bellevue and to transfer Columbia's academic "allegiance" to Harlem Hospital. Dr. Ragan, who moved the service uptown, asked Dr. Morris to "come help me out." Maintaining his faculty appointment at P&S, in 1968 Dr. Morris followed the call to Harlem, where he began to make rounds as an associate visiting physician. "Among the accomplishments of the Columbia team," he said, "was to help raise the quality of care, introduce educational programs, put in a whole cadre of residents—in short, we shook things up and turned the institution upside down."

Then, in 1972, Dr. Ragan was asked to return to P&S as the new chair of medicine. "Don't spend so much time at Harlem," he strongly advised Dr. Morris, "come help me out here."

A TALENT FOR ORGANIZATION

Back at P&S that same year, Dr. Morris took over the administrative reins of the Third Year Clerkship in Medicine from his able predecessor, the late Donald Tapley HON '85. Though Dr. Morris had shouldered considerable responsibilities as chief resident at Bellevue, running the clerkship was his first major academic administrative test, which he passed with flying colors. He realized and relished a heretofore budding talent for institutional administration and began a long friendship with Dr. Tapley, another rising star at P&S. "I always told him I was straightening out all the things he did wrong," Dr. Morris chuckled, "and Don, in turn, was appropriately free with his advice."

In 1976, Dr. Morris was appointed chair of the Curriculum Committee. "The most important thing we did," he said, "was to foster communication among the course directors." Also instituting student evaluations and encouraging the active participation of students on the committee, he promoted well-advised suggestions, while cautioning against "change for the sake of change."

"The biggest challenge, not only in medicine, but it's glaring in medicine," he reflected, looking back, "is to be able to anticipate, think about and respond to change, rather than wait for it to happen and then catch up. Not easy!"

Dr. Morris has always managed to keep a steady course on the rapids of change. Named associate chair of the Department of Medicine in 1977, he was asked to step in as acting chair following the sudden death of Dr. Dan Kimberg. Taking the helm for what he thought would be a brief watch of several months, he ably steered the department for the next four years, never expecting the clinical hurricane that was about to hit American medicine.

THE CLINICAL EMERGENCE OF A NEW KILLER

"During the years of my tenure as acting chair, 1978–82, the house staff and I had a unique experience," he recalled. "A lot of seriously ill young men, primarily gay, came in and ultimately died of fulminating pulmonary infection. Initially, we didn't know what it was. As I told the resident group at our end-of-year dinner in 1982, we had witnessed the emergence of a new disorder about which we were then at the very initial stage of learning and that would affect our medical careers for the rest of our lives." His prognosis proved portentous. That disorder, of course, came to be called AIDS.

"It's a very humbling learning experience," Dr. Morris admitted, in hindsight, "when you don't know what you're dealing with or what to do about it and it's fatal. I had very frank conversations with the house staff concerning our medical and ethical responsibilities under these dire circumstances."

Among his accomplishments as acting chair of medicine, the one of which he is proudest is the pivotal role he played in recruiting and cultivating a cadre of clinically based full-time faculty who were both expert clinicians and wonderful teachers. Many of them are still here today.

Parallel to his leadership in the Department of Medicine, in 1979 he accepted the additional responsibilities of associate dean for academic affairs, overseeing, among other areas, academic promotions and appointments. From this vantage point, as he remembered in an interview that appeared in the newsletter *In Vivo* (9/15/03), "I was able to get a broader overview of [. . .] the institution and understand its mission more fully."

PRESIDENT OF PRESBYTERIAN HOSPITAL

Inevitably, his administrative talents came to the attention of the trustees of Presbyterian Hospital. It was the 1980s, and the old hospital, built in 1928, was wholly inadequate to the clinical needs of a new era. As acting chair of medicine and associate dean, Dr. Morris had already been involved in discussions and preliminary planning for a new building. In 1985, he was the natural in-house talent to tap for the top position of president and CEO.

Having closed a number of local community hospitals in Upper Manhattan, New York State called for the construction of a new community facility at the northern tip of Manhattan Island. Dr. Morris oversaw the planning, building, and opening of the Allen Pavilion in 1988, today a vital clinical and teaching arm of the hospital and a rich resource to the community.

Recommending that the university and the hospital combine their fundraising efforts to meet a heretofore unprecedented goal of $100 million toward a new building, Dr. Morris took a lead role in the development effort. "I ate a lot of lunches and dinners with prospective donors in those days," he said. A major gift of $25 million from the Milstein family, long-time friends and supporters of Columbia University, helped the hospital trustees realize their goal and Presbyterian's state-of-the-art new home, the Milstein Hospital, opened its doors to considerable fanfare in 1989.

IMPROVING ON HIGH SCHOOL SPANISH
AND OTHER PRIORITIES

As president, Dr. Morris was personally "committed to a tangible outreach to the community." That included, in his case, "rekindling my high school Spanish." He also took the senior hospital administrative staff on several Spanish immersion retreats. Following one speech he delivered in proficient Spanish, one local politician was so moved, "she gave me a great big hug." Needless to say, she listened closely to his recommendations.

If one had to characterize Dr. Morris's management style, it is one based on dialogue, collaboration, and cooperation. He treasured the extraordinary rapport he enjoyed with the late Dr. Henrik Bendixen, then dean of P&S. "We had complete respect for one another and very open communication." The Office of Clinical Trials, arguably one of the most effective and successful endeavors of its kind, was the result of a two-day retreat the two co-organized on basic and clinical research. Under their joint sponsorship, with a grant from the National Library of Medicine, the hospital and medical school teamed up to develop the Center for Informatics at the university and an integrated information system that has stood the test of time.

In another pioneering venture, this time in conjunction with the Greater New York Hospital Association, of which he served as a director, Dr. Morris participated in one of the first clinical care quality assurance efforts.

Does an institution take on the character of the individual at the helm?

"I used to wonder about that," Dr. Morris paused to ponder the interviewer's question. "At the time, you know," he pointed out, "we had between five and six thousand employees. It's a little like a very, very large flower pot. You can water it on top but you can never be sure how much gets to the bottom. Finally, all you can do is pick the right people and trust them to get the job done."

He stepped down in 1990, following a five-year tenure at the helm, but continued to lend his advice as a consultant to the hospital board of trustees.

INTERNATIONAL MEDICAL EXPERIENCE

From the early days of his medical career, Dr. Morris was always interested in the big picture at home and abroad. He had enjoyed working closely with fellows from around the world at P&S and Harlem Hospital. And when in the mid-Seventies, a former fellow from Iran invited him to come over as a visiting professor at the University of Shiraz, he and his family leapt at the opportunity. "The important thing about international experiences in medicine, I think," he suggested, "is not so much to see diseases you don't ordinarily see, but to take care of patients with disorders with which you are familiar, and yet to see them managed in a different way, usually with far less resources. That's a learning experience! It reinforces just how important it is to take a thorough history and do a good physical exam."

Dr. Morris was involved in a joint effort by the New York Academy of Medicine and the American Association of Medical Colleges to develop curricular innovations at American medical schools to enhance the clinical interaction. "The trick," he believes, "is to try and preserve those fundamental clinical skills in the face of what I would call overwhelming technology and data."

In 1981, during his tenure as associate dean of medicine, he embarked on yet another international adventure. "I received a call from the New York State Department of Education asking if I were willing to evaluate an offshore medical school. It was a school they hadn't visited in a while, way offshore, they said—the American University of Beirut, in Lebanon." Leading an academic evaluation team in the midst of a civil war, he found "a vibrant center of learning with very bright students and a dedicated faculty." So began a lasting association with the institution. A member of the American University of Beirut's board of trustees since 1985, he subsequently served as vice chair and visits the school at least three or four times a year.

HELPING TO REVIVE AND SUSTAIN TWO VINTAGE NEW YORK INSTITUTIONS

In 1990, Dr. Morris pitched in to reinvigorate the New York Academy of Medicine as its newly appointed vice president for programs. Once a pivotal advisory body to the New York City Commissioner of Health, the Academy had waned in importance over time. Dr. Morris helped dust off the Academy's reputation and bring it back into the main arena of public health policy, notably in extramurally funded epidemiological research. He still remains a senior advisor there.

Like his old friend the late Dr. Tapley, he also took an abiding interest in another historic New York institution, serving a tenure as president, 1993–1999, of the Morris Jumel Mansion, a colonial residence-turned museum, located within walking distance of the Medical Center. "It's an American jewel that just happens to be practically next door. I was proud," he said, "to play a role in its preservation and in its ongoing effort to educate the young people in the community."

BACK TO THE FUTURE II AT P&S

In 1993, Dr. Mike Weisfeldt, then chair of the Department of Medicine at P&S, asked if Dr. Morris would "help him for a year" as associate chair. The year ended, and he full well intended to return to the Academy, when Dr. Herbert Pardes, then dean of the faculty, called him back to the Dean's Office—"You can't leave now!"—reappointing Dr. Morris vice dean of the faculty, a position he had already held with distinction a decade before.

When Dr. Pardes followed Dr. Morris's lead, moving from the leadership of the medical school to that of the hospital, as president and CEO of the newly merged New York-Presbyterian Hospital, Dr. Morris stepped in to hold the fort as interim dean for clinical and education affairs (teaming up with Dr. David Hirsh, interim dean for research). And finally, when Dr. Gerald Fischbach took office as vice president and dean of the faculty, Dr. Morris resumed his role as vice dean.

His many honors have included the Dean's Distinguished Award for Teaching in 1997, the P&S Alumni Association Special Recognition Award in 1986, the Academy Plaque of the New York Academy of Medicine in 1997, the Columbia University Alumni Federation Medal for Outstanding Contributions to the School and to American Health Care in 2000, and the Gold Medal for Meritorious Service to P&S and its Alumni in 2002.

Aside from harvesting "the best hay in Delaware County" and spending more time with his wife, Jacqueline, and children, Amy, Mary Anne, and Tom, Dr. Morris will hardly be able to catch his breath, between shuttling back and forth to the Bassett Hospital in Cooperstown, American University of Beirut, and P&S, where, among other things, as chair of the editorial board of *Columbia Medicine*, he'll still don his white coat and wield his blue pencil "to make sure you get it right."

A SURGEON IN SPACE

STORY MUSGRAVE '64

At last count, Dr. Musgrave, age eighty-four, earned seven graduate degrees, flew on six NASA space missions, was awarded twenty honorary doctorates, operates a palm farm and a production company, serves as a landscape architect and concept artist with Walt Disney Imagineering, and also breathes when he gets a chance.

⸺⸺⸻

NASA, HOUSTON. Saturn-5, the mighty rocket that flew ten manned missions into space now lies flat on its side, an arcane metal dinosaur in a patch of grass. In a nearby field, a couple of Texas Longhorn cattle languorously chew their cud, oblivious to the pace of human enterprise. The juxtaposition is striking. Here at the hub of the great adventure of space travel, where rocket scientists hone humanity's wildest dreams, aerospace engineers give them shape, and a handpicked cadre of astronauts train to ride those dreams into history, the future flies by in a flash.

Most astronauts sign on for a limited hitch. But when you're in it for the long haul, like Story Musgrave '64, you can't get space out of your system. In 1997, at age sixty-one, following thirty years at NASA, and after flying all five space shuttles (Challenger in 1983 and 1985, Discovery in 1989, Atlantis in 1991, Endeavor in 1993, and Columbia in 1996), raring as always to go up again, the oldest space traveler reluctantly accepted retirement. Biting the bullet, he's shifted his focus to space education, to "communicate the heart and soul of what human spaceflight is about."

"NOW LIFE IS LEAPING OFF THE PLANET."

Lithely leaping over a wall to open the locked door of a test module at NASA, the ideal setting for an interview, the septuagenarian spaceman showed he still had the right stuff.

Best known to the general public as payload commander and lead repairman on STS-61, the first Hubble Space Telescope servicing and repair mission in 1993 (a stunningly successful effort that helped reveal distant reaches of the universe never before visible to the human eye), he communicated his impressions live from space.

Asked by ABC Nightline's Ted Koppel if the effort was worth the risk and cost, his unswerving, eloquent reply will surely go down in history: "We have no choice, Sir. It's the nature of humanity. . . . And maybe I'm not just a human up here, you know, now life is leaping off the planet. It's heading for other parts of the solar system, other parts of the universe. . . . It isn't simply politics. It isn't simply technology. . . . You could look at it as maybe the essence of life." Speaking on behalf of the human species, Story Musgrave was also espousing his own personal credo.

Massachusetts born, Kentucky bred, Dr. Musgrave's Southern-inflected speech and sinewy build may make him seem laid-back. In informal conversation, he tends to take his time, carefully selecting his words with the precision of an engineer and the conceptual lyricism of a philosopher-poet. (The author of twenty-five scientific papers, he also writes poetry. His voracious reading ranges freely across disciplines from aerodynamics to transcendentalism, from mathematics to theology, from physiology to Freud.)

But get him on the subject of space and you perceive a striking metamorphosis. His steel-blue eyes dilate with laser-like intensity. His shaven head suddenly takes on the contour of a helmet. Thought furrows his otherwise smooth brow. The Kentucky twang accelerates into astronaut high drive. Story Musgrave is ready for takeoff.

FROM DAIRY FARM TO DISCOVERY:
A LIFE IN HIGH DRIVE

Growing up on a dairy farm in Stockbridge, Mass., the son of an abusive alcoholic father and a loving but acquiescent mother, he found salvation in the care of livestock and the mastery of farm machinery. Young Story could run and repair anything on wheels. He started flying airplanes at age sixteen, "in a very informal kind of way: I drove them like I drove tractors, and then one day just leaped off!"

The next leap was to the U.S. Marines, which he entered in 1953, dropping out of high school to do so. Training at first as an aviation electrician and instrument technician, his love of aircraft and the need to get a license in order to fly them propelled him to pursue his studies. The reading of jet engine manuals ultimately led to an appreciation of books. An early flicker of intellectual curiosity rapidly burst into flame and has been roaring ever since.

Leaving the Marines to study mathematics and statistics at Syracuse, where he earned a BS in 1958, he interned as a mathematician and operations analyst at Eastman Kodak before attending UCLA and completing an MBA in operations analysis and computer programming in 1959. His interest in computers led, in turn, to a fascination with the human brain. ("I always keep coming back in my interests to the human dimension!")

Subsequently earning a BA in chemistry from Marietta College in 1960, and thereby fulfilling his pre-medical course requirements, he applied and was accepted at P&S. "I think I was taken on as an oddball," he reflects back.

"They must have reserved a few slots for people they perceive may develop in strange ways."

In fact, Dr. Musgrave comes from a distinguished medical lineage—nine straight generations of doctors on his mother's side, including his maternal great-grandfather and great uncle, who were both professors of surgery at Harvard, and his paternal grandfather, a noted physician and researcher on the effects of exposure to gas during World War I.

In New York, the erstwhile farm boy's eyes were opened to a wide world of possibilities. He fondly remembers his P&S peers, "bright, talented, great learners, all broad and diverse in their interests."

Pursuing his own research interests in the nervous system at the Neurological Institute under Dr. Donald Purpura (now dean of Albert Einstein College of Medicine), Dr. Musgrave decided to become a surgeon—"not," he is quick to explain, "because I wanted to help people, but because of a curiosity of what a human is and what it means to be human!"

Next stop, the University of Kentucky, in Lexington, where, while pursuing his surgical residency, he added to his academic credentials an MS in physiology and biophysics in 1966.

The seemingly diverse strands of his wide-ranging intellectual search all came together in 1967, when NASA opened its doors to scientist-astronauts, and Dr. Musgrave decided to link his destiny to the Space Program. The decision proved a personal epiphany: "Everything I'd ever done, I realized, every crooked path I took was leading me to this!"

EXPERIENCING SPACE

He spent the initial sixteen years of his involvement with NASA on the ground (as backup science-pilot and capsule communicator on various missions), aiding in the design and development of the Skylab Program, America's first space station, as well as various parts of the space shuttle program, including the space suit.

Learning how to work with a space suit, he says, is like putting on a second skin, "forcing you to reflect on anthropology, anthropometrics, and kinesthetic motion. That's why," he suggests, "being a physician and a physiologist proved a particular asset which I brought to space walking."

First hurled into the heavens in April 1983 aboard STS-6, the maiden voyage of Space Shuttle Challenger, he and a colleague conducted the first extra vehicular activity (E.V.A.), more commonly known as space walking, to test, among other things, the very space suit he'd helped design. He is considered today one of the world's authorities on space walking.

A perfectionist attuned to the tiniest detail, NASA colleagues, in fact, refer to him as "Dr. Detail." For each of his missions, he carefully choreographed every move in months of dry runs, so that once he stepped out of the spaceship, he could perform his duties "with the grace and ease of a ballet dancer."

In his second flight aboard Challenger in 1985, Dr. Musgrave served as systems engineer during launch and entry and pilot during orbital operations, also participating in major experiments in the life sciences.

Watching aghast from Mission Control, as Challenger exploded during take-off on its third voyage on January 28, 1986, Dr. Musgrave felt a profound personal loss at the death of the crew and the destruction of the craft he'd flown twice. "I went back to my office," he confessed to *American Medical News*, "stared out the window, and cried like a baby."

"The Challenger explosion," he says, "was a wake-up call to the Space Agency and a lot of other people, but not to me. I helped build this system, I knew what we were biting off." There was not the slightest doubt in his mind that he'd go up again the next chance he got.

Risk is a regrettable factor he can live with. "I do my best to control it, to minimize it. It's ironic," he chuckles, "I don't like the risk because I want to get to do it again." Unlike other astronauts, he is willing to openly acknowledge fear, particularly his fear during a launch: "When that thing goes, it goes! And you go where it goes! You can't affect the outcome!"

In 1989, he flew again aboard the Space Shuttle Discovery, a classified mission operating payloads for the Department of Defense.

Two years later, he went up again, this time on the Space Shuttle Atlantis, whose primary mission was to deploy a Defense Support Program satellite. On that flight, Dr. Musgrave also helped monitor numerous medical tests to support longer-duration Shuttle flights.

Then in 1993, as payload commander aboard Space Shuttle Endeavour, Dr. Musgrave performed three of the mission's five scheduled space walks, working in tandem with his fellow crew members to service and repair the Hubble Space Telescope.

"I told everyone that I did not know if we were going to pull it off," he recalls. "I said to the media, the only thing I can tell you is that we are ready to go forward. It's a drama, enjoy it! Stand by and let it unfold!"

Unfold it did, before millions of television viewers the world over who watched spellbound as Dr. Musgrave and his colleagues performed delicate space surgery on a floating mechanical eye.

And while Hubble's $1.5 billion technology and the very credibility of NASA were riding on that mission, Dr. Musgrave kept his cool. "I had worked the details down to every thread on every screw, every finger position for five days and 300 tools," he insists. "But I never felt any pressure, because I never thought about the result. Sure, I want a good result, but when I'm out there working in space, I focus on my task, to do a perfect turn on every single bolt."

He believes that the impact of the Hubble Repair Mission transcends science and technology. Hubble touches people of all ages, he suggests, "because it's about finding our place in the universe!"

While his sixth and final flight aboard Space Shuttle Columbia in 1996 was accompanied by far less fanfare than the prior mission, Dr. Musgrave considers it his most successful. His criteria are both professional and personal. The crew deployed and retrieved the Wake Shield Facility, technology vital to the development of thin film wafers in semiconductors for the electronics industry. And Story Musgrave experienced "a perfect night pass."

He lay blankets across the inter-deck access and turned off all the lights to "dark adapt" before peering out the portal. "You see lightning flash. You catch aurora, this silken curtain dancing over hundreds of thousands of miles." And best of all, he experienced flying under the earth and the thrill of free fall at zero-g.

"Talk about ecstasy!" he closes his eyes in the telling, savoring the memory. "To fall through the dark forever, that's the essence of space!"

"It's my philosophy," he says, "that you can't understand anything unless you've surrendered to it. That's why the idea of conquering space was so abhorrent to me from the very beginning. You'll never know it if your idea is to go out and vanquish it. If you bring in the big bulldozers, you are never going to understand the environment you're coming into, you're just going to level it and put up a cosmic parking lot!"

TOTAL IMMERSION

For Story Musgrave, the intellectual engine of course keeps running in retirement. He believes in being "a total participant" in whatever he does.

Leaving Houston, he will move to a house he recently purchased in Florida, not far from Cape Canaveral. And just as he did on the night prior to each flight, he will lie in the surf staring up at the heavens. He has had offers from various media, newspapers, TV, and film to write about space. The physical memory, he trusts, will help him translate his experience and tell what he knows.

"It's humanity's destiny to explore the universe," he firmly believes. "When we start thinking and working on that cosmic level, we will transcend our parochial differences and tribal natures and become global creatures, solar system creatures. Then we'll figure out where we fit in."

Meanwhile, Dr. Musgrave is pursuing his studies in psychology, history, sociology, and literature to round out his knowledge and bring the lessons of space down to earth.

A MILITARY NEUROLOGIST ON THE FRONT AGAINST CHEMICAL ATTACK

COL. JONATHAN NEWMARK, MC, USAR '78

Retired from the U.S. Army Medical Corps in 2013, Jonathan Newmark '78 has since pursued his abiding passion for music, earning a master's degree in composition from the College-Conservatory of Music, University of Cincinnati. His compositions have included a trombone sextet, each movement inspired by a different skeletal bone, entitled "Six Bones for Six Bones."

THE STANDARD red, pocket-sized *Medical Management of Chemical Casualties Handbook*, issued by the U.S. Army Medical Research Institute of Chemical Defense (USAMRICD) begins: "Chemical warfare is not a popular topic, and most military health care providers do not willingly become familiar with it." One notable exception is Col. Jonathan Newmark, MC, USAR '78, chief of operations of chemical casualty care at USAMRICD, at Aberdeen Proving Ground, Md., and clinical associate professor of neurology at the Uniformed Services University of the Health Sciences in Bethesda, Md. Col. Newmark wears multiple hats, as an expert and educator in the medical response to nerve agent attack; a consultant and advisor to defense and investigatory organizations, both domestic and foreign; and coordinator of research in neuroprotection and medical response to chemical attack.

Since transferring to Aberdeen in 1997 from his prior posting as staff neurologist at the Madigan Army Medical Center in Tacoma, Wash., he has functioned, for the most part, behind the scenes, in the relative obscurity of the military medical research and training community—that is, until 9/11.

BATTLE LINES SHIFT TO INCLUDE THE HOME FRONT

Not many civilians, let alone health professionals, had ever pondered the possibility of chemical or biological attack back home. Then came the unsettling news that the late Mohamed Atta, alleged ringleader of the terrorist attack on the World Trade Center, had previously shopped around for crop dusters ordinarily used for the aerial spraying of insecticides (the manufacture and dissemination of which dovetails that of chemical munitions). Next came reports of mysterious anthrax outbreaks in Florida, New York, New Jersey, and Washington, D.C. Gas masks and the antibiotic ciprofloxacin (brand name Cipro) entered popular parlance, and the public has been scrambling for accurate information ever since.

Needless to say, Col. Newmark's calendar filled up pretty fast. He and his team at USAMRICD have been on regular call to the FBI, the White House, and other government entities on questions of domestic preparedness. Nerve agents are now on the agenda at American Association of Neurology national meetings and other educational forums.

"You civilians have just woken up to a risk and reality that we in the military live with daily," the colonel laconically observed in the course of an interview at his base of operations at Aberdeen Proving Ground, on a peninsula of flatland jutting out into the Chesapeake Bay. It was here that the U.S. Army established and built up its offensive chemical weapons program immediately prior to America's entry into World War I. Until its disman-tling, in fulfillment of the terms of the chemical armaments ban signed by President Carter, this had been the largest chemical weapons manufactur-ing facility in the world. While stockpiles of old chemical munitions await safe destruction, an environmental headache and security risk, the installa-tion has since changed its mission to treaty verification, surveillance, and defensive research.

A HAVEN OF TOXIC TRANQUILITY

The impressions of a first-time visitor to Aberdeen Proving Ground are dis-concerting, to say the least. The architecture is military modern, straight out of some Sixties Grade-B sci-fi clunker. Vintage Cold War era warning signs would ordinarily seem arcane, were it not for the heightened national state of alert in the wake of September 11. But just beyond the cement blocks of the security clearance checkpoint, where one might expect a giant mutant alien to appear, a buck peaks out from behind a tree and shakes its antlers at a troop of soldiers jogging along in full gear. Overhead, meanwhile, a bald eagle circles low, com-peting for airspace with an Army chopper.

"One of the pleasant peculiarities of this place," Col. Newmark points out, "is that restricted access and the absence of predators have made it a prime wildlife habitat. We have 100 nesting bald eagle pairs, the largest number in the Northeast corridor."

Wildlife notwithstanding, the barbed wire surrounding certain restricted facilities dispels any illusions of bucolic tranquility. Though manned by a rela-tively small contingent of research personnel, USAMRICD, only one of several operations on base, is America's lead training facility and lab for countermea-sures against chemical warfare agents.

A MEDICAL MILITARY MAN FOR ALL SEASONS

"Welcome to our country. We have ways to make you enjoy your stay with us!" Col. Newmark captures the mood in a mock-Transylvanian accent. There is nothing Dracula-like about him, though his warm smile clashes with the sever-ity of a military crew cut, and his ebullient personality and boundless energy seem caged in khaki fatigues. Among his unusual mix of qualities and talents, Col. Newmark, a clinical neurologist by training, is also an accomplished musician, conductor, and composer, a master oarsman (1987 Kentucky State Single Sculling Champion) and the genial talk show host and costar of three satellite CME programs on Medical Response to Chemical Warfare and Terrorism. Responding to an interviewer's question as to his preferred title, Doctor, Colonel or Maestro, he grins, "Right!"—a nod to all three.

FROM CLINICAL NEUROLOGIST TO COLONEL

As Col. Newmark wryly remarked in a prescient talk entitled "Chemical Warfare Agents: A Primer," presented at a military medical conference, "The Operational Impact of Psychological Casualties from Weapons of Mass Destruction," in July 2000: "Terrorism follows its own dynamic." While the stakes may have changed for civilians since September 11, militarily speaking, it's still the same old game.

Clicking around on his computer, he found and displayed for a visitor's benefit "The Sarin Fight Song" of the Japanese religious cult Aum Shinrikyo, the folks responsible for the 1994 release of the nerve agent sarin in Matsumoto, resulting in seven deaths, and the 1995 release on the Tokyo subway that killed thirteen, sickened thousands, and panicked a nation:

> In the peaceful night of Matsumoto City
> People can be killed, even with our own hands.
> The place is full of dead bodies all over.
> There! Inhale sarin, sarin!
> Prepare sarin! Prepare sarin!
> Immediately poisonous gas weapons will fill the place.
> Spray! Spray! Sarin the brave, sarin.

"Probably sounds better in the original Japanese," he concedes.

A walking encyclopedia on the history of chemical warfare, Col. Newmark's particular area of expertise is nerve agents, the deadly class of chemical weapons first developed (though never used) by the Germans during World War II, and first employed on the battlefield by Iraq against Iran in the late 1980s, costing thousands of lives. "One thing I like about the military," he stresses, "is that you don't deal with the way things ought to be, but the way things really are. And things aren't always nice."

His own shift from white coat to khaki is a tale unto itself with multiple divertimentos. Though a grandfather was drafted and completed his term of duty in the Czar's army before emigrating from Russia to Morristown, N.J., his parents' decidedly pacifist leanings hardly predisposed him to military aspirations. "Is this reaction formation or what?" he recalls asking a psychologist friend after joining the Medical Corps of the U.S. Army Reserve in 1989. "I always wanted to be a soldier," he shrugs.

A first deployment as solo task force physician with Operation Fuertes Caminos, a humanitarian mission to Belize, whetted his appetite for military life. His parents were less than pleased when a second planned deployment would have taken him to the combat zone of Somalia, had President Clinton not called home the troops in time. He finally did deploy in 1996 to Saudi Arabia, in the immediate wake of the terrorist attack on the U.S. Army barracks at the Khobar Towers. Deputy surgeon with TF 2-1 Air Defense Artillery and Army Forces Central Command in Riyadh, he was the ranking officer of his unit: "So by dumb luck, I became a mass casualty planner." Tending to the medical needs of his detachment, he also participated in Grand Rounds at King Saud University Hospital—"the first Jewish Grand Rounds speaker they've had for a while," he chuckles.

He had previously opted for active duty in 1993 and served as staff neurologist, chief of quality assurance, chief of the neurology clinic, and chief of readiness for neurology services at Madigan Army Medical Center, in Tacoma, Wash. It was at Madigan that he first experienced "the joys of military medical practice at a state-of-the-art facility with great patients, excellent residents, and a faculty appointment to boot at the University of Washington." An enthusiastic advocate of military medicine, Col. Newmark sees the system as "a bomb shelter against some of the detrimental changes going on in American medicine." As a clinician, he found it "profoundly liberating" to be able to "just do what I think the patient needs," with no bureaucrats second-guessing his medical decisions, because "no money changes hands."

"THE BRAIN HAS MORE INTERESTING THINGS TO SAY THAN 'LUB-DUB.'"

Clinical neurologist to the core, he was inspired to study and treat the ailments of the brain by such mentors as Dr. Linda Lewis at P&S: "You couldn't ask for a better clinical role model than Dr. Lewis. She just had that presence and authority that patients respect. And at the same time, she was very thorough and very caring." Another P&S mentor, Dr. William G. Johnson, a Parkinson researcher now at the University of Medicine and Dentistry of New Jersey—Robert Wood Johnson School of Medicine, in Piscataway, N.J., once remarked: "Neurologists get to talk to the brain and it says much more interesting things than lub-dub, lub-dub!"

Interning at Roosevelt Hospital, he pursued postgraduate training at the State University of New York Downstate Medical Center in Brooklyn and subsequently accepted a research fellowship in the Development and Metabolic Neurology Branch of the National Institute of Neurological and Communicative Disorders and Stroke at the NIH. Additional training took him to Boston City Hospital, New England Deaconess, and Massachusetts General Hospital, where he completed a coveted fellowship in neuro-oncology and occupational neurology. In 1985, he joined the faculty of the Department of Neurology at the School of Medicine of the University of Louisville, in Louisville, Kentucky.

"TELL US ABOUT NERVE AGENTS!"

A pivotal moment in his career path came in 1991, in the course of a fellowship in neuromuscular disease at the University of Pennsylvania. He had already joined the U.S. Army Reserve. One day, at a departmental meeting on the eve of Operation Desert Storm, called to discuss the hospital's responsibility to treat war casualties who might be evacuated to Philadelphia, his chair, Dr. Donald Silverberg, turned to him and said: "You're in the Army, tell us about nerve agents!"

That conversation impelled him to sign up for the course in Medical Management of Chemical and Biological Casualties at USAMRICD, Aberdeen Proving Ground, the same course that, since coming aboard, he has personally taught to more than 7,000 military and civilian health care professionals, including students from twenty foreign nations. That's not counting the global audiences of the interactive satellite CME programs in medical response to chemical warfare and terrorism, in which he thrice costarred and that he helped write and design.

Col. Newmark and his team also regularly take their expertise on the road, teaching the multiple dimensions of medical response to chemical attack at home and abroad. He has traveled to and taught in over fourteen countries, including a training mission to coach NATO troops in Kosovo. Two of his students later showed up in the pages of *Vanity Fair* magazine as members of the rescue team at the World Trade Center in New York. "We're the only people in the country doing the medical training in this field!" he points out. As a member of the faculty of the Uniformed Services University of the Health Sciences in Bethesda, he also supervises residents in neurology.

While training is his top priority, Col. Newmark's mission as chief of operations includes a significant consulting component. His short tactical deployments have included, among other missions, service on the Army Chem/Bio Rapid Response Team assigned to the pastoral visit of Pope John Paul II to Saint Louis, Missouri, in 1999; the Department of State Foreign Emergency Support Team assigned to security measures in Europe for the Millennium changeover 1999–2000; and the FBI Domestic Emergency Support Team sent to Salt Lake City in 2001 to engage in a dress rehearsal of security measures for the 2002 Winter Olympics.

In his capacity as research coordinator at USAMRICD, he built upon the work of Col. Edward Vedder, the head of the Army Biomedical Research Laboratory, at Aberdeen, who in the 1920s did landmark clinical descriptions of survivors of chemical attack. Col. Newmark's research protocols (all on animal models) include a behavioral study of the effects of nerve agent and a study of the primary mechanisms of neuroprotection, which may be similar in both stroke patients and in survivors of nerve agent attack. He also sponsors a study of huperzine-A, a Chinese dietary supplement, as a treatment for nerve agent poisoning.

The current recommended antidote to nerve agent exposure is the immediate administration of atropine and pralidoxime chloride, plus diazepam in severe cases, as well as ventilation and suction of airways.

One of his primary assets, as a clinician with contacts in the civilian medical community, is to "connect the lab a bit better than it had been to the clinic." The historic link between military and civilian medicine has in the past reaped some rich rewards. So, for instance, Drs. Goodman and Gilman, authors of the classic *Pharmacological Basis of Therapeutics*, studied nitrogen mustard as a vesicating agent. While it did not prove effective as a chemical weapon on the battlefield, they did stumble on the first chemotherapeutic agent in the war on cancer.

And though, he insists, "I was not recruited as a scientist, but rather to spread the gospel about nerve agent treatments to soldiers around the world," science, some with extra-military implications, is indeed being done under his watch. Nerve agents work on the cholinergic system. "Well, it turns out, in Alzheimer's disease, there is a deficiency of the neurotransmitter acetylcholine. So the Alzheimer's drugs are of interest to us."

MUSIC MAN

While he tackled the study of medicine straight out of college, and took to soldiering in midlife, music was there almost from the start. A violist and pianist, though he lacks a music degree, he has studied, albeit intermittently, at various institutions, including the Julliard School Preparatory Division, the University of Maryland, and the University of Louisville. For the past twenty-one years, he has been a regular participant at the Chamber Music Conference and Composer's Forum of the East at Bennington College, in Vermont. During his term of duty in Washington State, Col. Newmark played with the Tacoma Symphony Orchestra, the only active-duty Army officer in the country to serve in a professional symphony orchestra. Guest soloist over the years at various other venues, he has also tried his hand at the baton. Having studied conducting as a youth at the National Music Camp in Interlochen, Mich., and later at the University of Louisville, his recent gigs have included a stint as guest conductor with the Independence Sinfonia at Pennsylvania State University, Abington campus.

He launched into original musical composition in the early Nineties, and in 2000 entered a newly minted string trio and won the Southeastern Composers Symposium competition, sponsored by Old Dominion University, in Norfolk, Va. A member of the Baltimore Composers Forum, he is particularly proud of a Chaconne and Fugue for horn and piano in memoriam for John C. Wood, Jr. '76, a dear friend from P&S.

The Army has been most accommodating of Newmark's musical talent. Asked to perform for the Army's Surgeon General, he has also played as guest soloist and been named an honorary member of the 389th Army Band at Aberdeen. In addition, an Army woodwind quintet was put at his creative disposal.

Judging by the success of his ongoing balancing act of military chemical defense, medicine, and music, clearly the chemistry is right. "Wow, what a deal," Newmark waxes ecstatic, "the Army gives me top residents, they give me great patients, and now they're giving me this government-issue woodwind quintet! What's wrong with this picture?"

Col. Newmark recalls once asking a friend, Dr. Jim Nuzzo, then a resident in the Boston/Harvard/Longwood program, how long he planned to stick with neurology. "Until it stops making me giggle," his friend replied. Paraphrasing the response, Col. Newmark avows with a genial grin: "As long as the Army keeps making me giggle and treating me well, I plan to stick around."

IT TAKES HEART

SUZANNE OPARIL '65

A leading researcher in the study and treatment of hypertension committed to raising public awareness of its preventable causes, and an ardent proponent of exercise, Dr. Oparil reduced her own stress galloping on the back of a horse until a fall curtailed her jumping. In 2017, she was honored with the P&S Alumni Gold Medal for Outstanding Achievements in Medical Research.

———— ∞ ————

THE BAD NEWS is that cholesterol, salt, and a sedentary lifestyle have supplanted Cupid's arrows as the primary perils to the health of the human heart. The good news, thanks to decades of cardiovascular research, is that hypertension and many other previously life-threatening conditions are now treatable and, better yet, preventable. The best news is that Suzanne Oparil '65, one of the nation's leading clinical investigators in hypertension, and currently president of the American Heart Association, is leading the battle against heart disease from laboratory and lectern.

For three decades and counting, Dr. Oparil has been exploring the biochemistry, physiology, and molecular biology of the heart and its links to the circulatory system. Her early pioneering research at the Massachusetts General Hospital on the role of angiotensin-converting enzyme (ACE) inhibitors led to the development of one of the most important pharmaceutical agents for the treatment of high blood pressure and heart failure. In her subsequent work at the University of Chicago and at the University of Alabama at Birmingham, where she is director of the Vascular Biology and Hypertension Program and professor of medicine, physiology, and biophysics, she has focused on the neural control of the circulation and the role of electrolytes in regulating blood

pressure, among other areas. She was the first woman president of the American Federation for Clinical Research, the largest clinical research organization in the world, and is a member of the Institute of Medicine of the National Academy of Sciences. She is the author of more than 285 peer-reviewed papers in clinical cardiology and hypertension.

A vocal and committed advocate of heart health, Dr. Oparil has been equally active outside the laboratory.

As a longtime affiliate of the American Heart Association, the largest voluntary organization in the world dedicated to the prevention of and research in cardiovascular diseases and stroke, she has held various offices and served on numerous committees at the local and national level before ascending to the presidency.

FROM FARM FIELD TO LABORATORY

"The scientific seed was planted early in my life," says Dr. Oparil, who grew up on a farm in Upstate New York, where she "learned to appreciate the link with life and nature and a respect for circumstances that you can't control." She still retains all the vigor of her rural childhood, as if she's only just come in from the cold. Her farm background, she insists, likewise cultivated an independent streak and a stubborn endurance that she put to good use as a clinical investigator. An undergraduate sojourn at Cornell (which she attended as a National Merit Scholar, graduating in the top 2 percent with distinction in all subjects) helped sharpen an already formidable intellect and broaden the scope of her tireless curiosity. "People who function in my way are natural researchers," she says. "We're in the business of generating new knowledge."

At P&S, where she graduated first in her class, she enjoyed "the personal aspect of my medical education, a closeness between faculty and students, the like of which I haven't seen since in any other place I've been." Lecture classes with distinguished scientist-teachers like Dr. Elvin Kabat, Higgins Professor Emeritus of Microbiology, and the late Dr. Harry Rose were "both terrifying and electrifying." Another favorite professor was the late Yale Kneeland '26, who "could keep us absolutely on the edge of our chairs while inculcating the principles of physical diagnosis."

Following a medical residency at Presbyterian Hospital, she went on to pursue a fellowship in cardiology at Massachusetts General Hospital with another illustrious P&S alumnus, Edgar Haber '56, the individual, she insists, "who really changed my professional life." Impressed by his "intellectual forcefulness, rigor, and clarity," she welcomed his tendency to "take the emotion out of the medical equation." It was in Dr. Haber's laboratory that she made her seminal contributions to our understanding of the role of the ACE inhibitor in high blood pressure.

Dr. Haber, who has followed her subsequent work with great interest, delivered the keynote address at a celebration marking her presidency of the American Heart Association at the University of Alabama on March 30, 1995. "She was innovative and highly imaginative in the lab," he recalls of his former protégé, "and I don't expect she's gotten any worse since!" Dr. Haber credits her scientific sense of adventure: "She was very willing to take on problems that were uncertain in their outcome, difficult in their solutions, yet if brought to fruition, able to make a truly important impact on our knowledge."

Hypertension, a condition of elevated intravascular pressure in the arteries, appealed to her as a field of inquiry because "you can really practice preventive medicine, preventing clinical heart disease, and the practice goes hand in glove with research."

The study of hypertension, she is quick to point out, is very much linked to P&S. Early work in the field was done by two distinguished members of the faculty. Dr. Howard Breunn, an emeritus professor of medicine at P&S, was President Franklin Delano Roosevelt's personal physician toward the end of the president's life, when he was suffering from the complications of a malignant hypertension from which he later died. The condition had gone untreated because of his previous physician's mistaken notion that hypertension was benign. Dr. Breunn established an aggressive regimen, restricting salt, and prescribing the rudimentary drugs that were available at the time. And a few years later, George Perera '37, professor of medicine emeritus and former associate dean of P&S, published a milestone study, showing how serious a condition hypertension really is.

Following her seminal work with converting enzyme, Dr. Oparil became interested in the way the brain regulates blood pressure, a completely different area of investigation. "That's one of the nice things about academic research," she says. "If you can support yourself with grants you can change directions and work on anything you want." She discovered that the neuradrenalin pathways in the brain were very important in the pathogenesis of hypertension, and furthermore, that there were connections between the kidney and the brain that affected how blood pressure is generated. "This is a big issue in humans," she says, "although it's very hard to actually study the process in the living human brain." MRI and PET hold promise as noninvasive research tools. Other recent studies have involved the study of the effect of vasoactive peptides on the pulmonary artery, in which area she credits the important work done by two P&S professors and friends, Drs. Al Fishman and Gerard Turino '48.

AT THE HELM OF THE AMERICAN HEART ASSOCIATION

Another friend, fellow former resident at Presbyterian Hospital and cardiology fellow in Dr. Haber's lab at Mass General, Dr. Myron Weisfeldt, former Samuel Bard Professor and chair of the Department of Medicine at P&S, was also a past president of the American Heart Association (AHA). He credits Dr. Oparil for having done "a remarkable job of steering the Association, capitalizing on molecular biology, molecular medicine, and at the same time, leading the field toward concern about quality issues in the area of health care."

Dr. Oparil is staunchly committed to the public health and public policy aspect of her role as president of the AHA. "My number one priority is to try to raise the public awareness. If we could get everyone to stop smoking, control their blood pressure, lower cholesterol, control their weight, and exercise more," she insists, "we could probably prevent half of the heart attacks in this country!"

Prevention alone, however, is not enough.

Hypertension, a condition that, if unchecked, can have fatal repercussions, strikes some 50 million Americans. Heart and blood vessel diseases continue to kill more Americans than any other cause—particularly in her neck of the woods, the Southeast, a region also known as "The Stroke Belt." Cause, she urges, not for despair, but for tireless research and public education. Diet and a predisposition to hypertension and stroke among African Americans are significant factors in the South, and Dr. Oparil has directed part of her effort to advancing clinical investigation and treatment in cardiovascular medicine for minorities and women, two groups heretofore neglected in clinical studies.

Effective treatment calls for continuing study of the basic scientific as well as the behavioral aspects of the problem, and study demands funding.

In this era of growing fiscal austerity, she insists, Congress has to be convinced of the economic necessity of research. "The cost of cardiovascular health care was $128 billion in 1994," she estimates, "the lion's share of which went to nursing homes, hospital care for the very ill and disability and insurance payments for people who can't work anymore. Only $868 million went to government-funded research in heart disease and stroke." Yet it is only research, she argues, that can in the long run dramatically cut the cost of health care.

Under her leadership and that of such distinguished recent past presidents as Drs. Weisfeldt, Harriet Dustan, and others, the American Heart Association has done its best to help foster a research-friendly climate. The Association funds about $93 million annually in direct support of research, a large part of which is parceled out in seed grants to young investigators. As a young cardiology fellow at the University of Chicago, Dr. Oparil herself was the beneficiary of a five-year AHA grant that helped establish her research career. And she has been active in the AHA granting peer review process ever since.

Dr. Oparil and the AHA are adamant about the need to revise and update the influential Comroe-Dripps Report (first published in *Science* in 1976). The report presented convincing evidence, she says, "to show just how basic research—which seems to be tied to nothing—is necessary for major clinical advances.

"Government and the public need to understand and be more sympathetic to research." To that end, she adds, "I'll probably do a little jogging with the President."

Exercise is nothing new to Dr. Oparil.

As a farmer's daughter, she was always running around with the livestock. And as an avid horsewoman until a serious accident took her out of the saddle a few years ago, she ranked second in adult show hunting in the state of Alabama, and fifth in open hunter—no small feat, she points out, "competing with a bunch of seventeen-year-olds in ninety-five-degree heat!"

Her rural upbringing continues to inspire her to this day. "Research is like farming," she says. "It's a twenty-four-hour-a-day, seven-days-a-week job! The cells grow and you have to be there to tend them, and when the time is right, to harvest the results. It's like bringing in the hay!"

AN EDUCATOR NOT AFRAID TO STICK HIS NECK OUT

CALVIN H. PLIMPTON MSD '51

*Having lived his life as a great adventure, that included admitting women
and thereby shaking up the all-male bastion of Amherst College, of which he
served as president, facing down a would-be armed kidnapper when he was
president of the American University of Beirut, and paddling around Manhattan
Island to get the lay of the land before taking on the direction of SUNY
Downstate Medical Center, Calvin H. Plimpton died on January 30, 2007,
at age eighty-eight.*

—∞∞—

IN THE course of a long and distinguished career, in which he piloted three
great institutions of higher learning through turbulent times and played a
pivotal role in others, veteran educator Calvin H. Plimpton MSD '51 weathered many tight spots—none tighter than the night in 1984 he single-handedly
scared off prospective kidnappers, as the newly inducted president of
the American University of Beirut (AUB), following the assassination of
his predecessor: "A heavy screen door between us, I greeted them politely,
a semi-naked man with a large revolver in hand, which caught the light
beautifully.—'S-cuse! S-cuse, pliss!' Never had to fire a shot!" Less perilous perhaps, but no less peppery were his tangles with restive students and irate trustees
in his role as president of Amherst College in the explosive Sixties, and his
wrangles with Albany bureaucrats over the budget of SUNY Downstate Medical Center in Brooklyn, which he ran through the economic down-spin of
the Seventies. "Learning," he once said, "is the act of sticking one's neck out."
Educator to the bone, for five decades he has been stretching his neck out to
practice what he preaches.

A MASTER ORATOR DISPENSES WIT
AND WISDOM OFF THE TOP OF HIS HEAD

Whereas most academic and political leaders depend on professional speech writers to speak their minds, Dr. Plimpton has always minded his own. A volume entitled *The Spoken Word*, published in 1981, comprising the oratorical tour de force he wrote and delivered in his capacity as the thirteenth president of Amherst College, attests to his mastery of the art of public address. (Included is a talk entitled "Ask Not What Amherst Can Do for You" that inspired President Kennedy's famous inaugural remarks, as well as the stirring meditation "Four Weeks Ago He Was Here," written in the immediate wake of the President's assassination.) Anyone who has ever heard Dr. Plimpton at the lectern has come away enlightened and entranced.

Eighty-three years into the time of his life, his six-foot, four-inch frame folds with some difficulty into a chair, but he's still got the raconteur's knack for rubbing sparks off the flint of experience, and the twinkle in his eye is still wild as a dancing flame on the tip of a candle wick.

A PREMED CHILDHOOD DOWN ON THE FARM

Born into comfortable circumstances, his ancestral roots going back to an enterprising haberdasher on the Mayflower, Calvin Plimpton grew up on the family farm in Walpole, Mass., not far from the family owned mill. His father was a successful publisher of textbooks. His mother saw to the education of her offspring, including lessons in cow milking, counterpoint, fencing, horseback riding, good English, and poker, not to mention French and German. Family chamber music recitals, a serious affair directed by a visiting student from Julliard, were occasionally disrupted, he recalls, by sticky-fingered ginger ale fights amongst the little fiddlers. "It is the flavor of learning which makes any activity worthwhile," he later told Amherst undergraduates.

An early bout with asthma, successfully treated by a season on a cattle ranch in Arizona, gave him firsthand knowledge of medical matters and a practical attitude toward adversity. "Illness can be a very educational experience, and in recognizing this I am not pleading some masochistic perversion," he reflected in a talk entitled "The Advantages of Illness, the Benefits of Disease." "Even when we fight battles, we don't merely liquidate our enemy. We also learn from him." The would-be MD perfected his surgical skills on unsuspecting poultry and crystalized his aspirations under the strict, albeit loving, tutelage of the late Josephine Hopkins Norton (P&S '30), his nanny, working her way through medical school at the time, whom he credits with weaning him of pirate cutlass in exchange for Bard-Parker scalpels.

Graduating cum laude in English at Amherst, he took his MD, likewise cum laude, from Harvard Medical School. While at Harvard, he spent a memorable summer in the Andes studying and helping to develop a vaccine for verruga peruana (Oroya fever), a fatal illness borne by sand flies. He also acquired a speaking knowledge of Spanish. The experience wetted his taste for medicine in exotic climes.

But Dr. Plimpton really got his feet wet serving in the Third Army, 83rd Field Hospital during World War II, for which he later earned a Battle Star. "Doctor, you are now a surgeon!" he was told by his commanding officer. Based with his unit in the Rhineland, treating battle casualties on the spot, he learned to operate literally under fire and relished the high stakes challenge. Returning to Harvard after the war, he pursued an MA in biochemistry. While intrigued by the bench work, specifically his studies on hexokinase, an enzyme important in sugar transport, he sorely missed the human element of the hospital environment: "A test tube is fine, but it's people that are fun!"

AMONG MEDICAL THOROUGHBREDS AT P&S

Medicine to him has always been a profoundly human experience. "It should really be obvious," he mused in a talk entitled "Humanism and Medicine," "that part of the fun of medicine is teaching [. . .]. In medicine the positions of teacher-student, and doctor-patient are inextricably interwoven. At its very best, the doctor-patient relationship becomes a joint exploration into the meaning of life."

To pursue the clinical experience at its best, Dr. Plimpton came to Columbia, where he trained in medicine and earned an MSD degree under the tutelage of the legendary Dr. Robert Loeb. Other teachers who made a deep impression were Dr. "Big Bill" Palmer, then chair of medicine, and Dr. Dana Atchley. Dr. Plimpton describes the Department of Medicine of that day as a "stable of thoroughbred race horses on which Big Bill Palmer rode herd. P&S was definitely where the medical action was!" Among that memorable team, he fondly recalls "the ever elegant, ever eloquent Drs. Yale Kneeland . . . Randy West, a Shakespearean character who looked like Falstaff and mastered blood anemia," and many others. "You'd never go home on your night off, you just couldn't bear to leave the place!" he shakes his head. "That's when the children [a daughter and three sons] began saying, 'Daddy's the man who comes to lunch on Sundays—*sometimes!*' "

As chief resident, he had admitting privileges to Harkness Pavilion, and, sweeter still, got to call Dr. Loeb "Bob," at the daily "Sunrise Service." The experience, he reflects, "wasn't just a summary of who'd been admitted, it was Bob Loeb's review of everything medical under the sun, including the very latest findings." Among Dr. Plimpton's other duties, he enjoyed choosing case, speaker, and pathologist for the Clinical Pathological Conferences, a responsibility he later passed on to his colleague, the late Abbie I. Knowlton '42, with whom he worked for many years in the Endocrine Clinic and maintained a lifelong friendship. Dr. Plimpton later joined the "thoroughbred stable" of the faculty of medicine and for the better part of a decade pursued teaching and research along with a busy private practice at Presbyterian Hospital.

PLIMPTON OF ARABIA

Whether from the bite of a Peruvian sand fly, an insidious drop of water from the Hassayampa River in Arizona, or a bout of vertigo in the Tyrol, Dr. Plimpton contracted a serious case of Wanderlust, or what his wife, Ruth, a published author, diagnosed as "itching feet." He took a leave of absence from Columbia, accepting the invitation of Joe McDonald, then Dean of Medicine at the American University of Beirut (AUB), to become the chair of their Department of Medicine, assistant dean of medicine and chief of staff of University Hospital, positions he held from 1957 to 1959. "It was at the time unquestionably the best medical school in the Middle East," he says. Thrilled by the challenge, he and his family soon fell in love with the place and he added Arabic to his store of languages. "I had never been to that part of the world before and found everything so fascinating, the people and the diseases. The atmosphere was very intimate too with little stoves to heat the wards. Much later we built a modern medical center."

So began a lifelong commitment to AUB, founded in 1866 as an independent nonsectarian institution of higher learning by an Amherst man, the Reverend Dr. Daniel Bliss. Dr. Plimpton later joined the board of trustees of which he subsequently served an extended tenure as chair. Beirut, then known as "the Paris of the Middle East," had a unique cosmopolitan flavor with Sunni and Shiite Moslems living side by side in apparent harmony with Druze, Jews, and Maronite Christians. The tenuous idyll, alas, exploded in a civil war, and President Eisenhower sent in American troops in 1959. Summoned home by Dr. Loeb—"Either you come back here or you get off the faculty list!"—Dr. Plimpton reluctantly left Lebanon. But a new adventure in education was about to begin.

AT THE TILLER OF AMHERST IN THE TURBULENT SIXTIES

John Jay McCloy, chair of Chase Manhattan Bank and of the Amherst board of trustees, had gotten wind of Dr. Plimpton's administrative talents and leadership skills. Inviting him down to his office to discuss the search for the next president of Amherst, the banker stunned the doctor by offering him the job. "Mr. McCloy, you should see your psychiatrist more often!" replied a flabbergasted Dr. Plimpton and promptly left the room. After thinking things over a bit, however, still suffering from the "itchy foot" syndrome and with his wife's blessing, he decided to take the job.

In the notes and comments to *The Spoken Word*, Edward S. Morse, an Amherst alumnus and trustee, wrote:

"There is no record that Dr. Plimpton actively practiced medicine at Amherst during his Presidency, but to many alumni he was the guiding College Physician, concerned with the students' pulse and temperature, guiding the health of body and mind, and preserving a spirit of sanity in the undergraduate community throughout his eleven, some of them tumultuous, years as President of the College."

"If you're crazy enough to be a college president, the 1960s was the time to be it!" Dr. Plimpton once quipped. He put it a bit more judiciously in his commencement address of 1968, a time when all hell was just beginning to break loose at college campuses around the country: "A college is a wonderful means for bringing the older and the younger together. Each group keeps the other curious, hence young and wise."

Like their peers at Berkeley, Columbia, and elsewhere, Amherst students demonstrated and took over buildings, submitting lists of "nonnegotiable" demands to a sympathetic, albeit ruffled, president. "The students were right, of course," he insists, looking back. "They wanted to call attention to injustices in this country and to what we were doing overseas. But it seemed to me that my main job was to keep the college running." Dr. Plimpton's inclination was to "keep talking, keep talking," despite disruptive student tactics and pressure from some of the trustees to "call in the cops and get rid of the bastards." His nephew, author and editor George Plimpton, recalls his uncle's upset at "spelling mistakes" in the list of demands, adding: "I've never met an Amherst graduate who didn't admire him enormously."

Fortunately, the president prevailed, peace was maintained, and change did come to Amherst and America.

But Dr. Plimpton prefers to remember other highlights of his tenure: "I could snap my fingers and have Robert Frost come down and talk to us as Simpson Lecturer." Poet and president became fast friends. "I would walk him over to the Lord Jeff Inn after dinner, and he said, 'Cal'-this would be about 11 o'clock—'You aren't tired, are you?' 'No.' 'Well, let's walk back again!' So we walked back and forth this way for a quite a while, during which we had a superb conversation. I wish I'd had a tape recorder." Frost felt right at home on campus, as he put it, "[pulling] ideas out of the boys' heads they didn't even know they had!"

Other memorable personalities met in the Amherst orbit include poet Archibald MacLeish, novelist Ralph Ellison, physicist Niels Bohr, mathematician Kurt Gödel , and President John F. Kennedy who flew in to deliver his last speech there before his assassination, one line of which Dr. Plimpton fondly recalls: "When power corrupts, poetry cleanses."

Another revered acquaintance made in the line of duty was the Reverend Dr. Martin Luther King. Both were to speak at a commencement ceremony at another college. Despite a bad cold, Dr. King thrilled the crowd. "Don't fall asleep during a revolution!" he declaimed from the podium before excusing himself: "I'm sorry I can't stay for this whole affair. I have to go to jail in Atlanta tomorrow morning."

Among his accomplishments while at Amherst, Dr. Plimpton takes particular pride in having recruited a number of fine professors, including the first women, and of helping to found the experimentally inclined Hampshire College.

ENNOBLED BY COMMITMENT

"We need an idea so big," he once said, "that we are willing to lose ourselves in it." To this end, education, and more specifically institutions of higher learning, have served him well as he served them. "Whenever you see something that's bigger than you, more valuable than you, more interesting than you, it has an ennobling effect."

The "big thing" for him has always been the university: "Universities are one of man's greatest and hardiest institutional inventions. They have the leisure to think instead of having to squeeze out a solution by the pressure of the moment." To protect and foster that intellectual leisure for others, he has been willing to face the moment's pressures head-on.

Next stop, Flatbush.

A BROBDINGNAGIAN IN BROOKLYN

Eager to get back to the nitty-gritty of medicine, in 1971 Dr. Plimpton ascended to the presidency of SUNY Downstate Medical Center in Brooklyn—but not before he took a five-day- and four-night-long journey by canoe around New York waterways, ostensibly to reconnoiter his new terrain, and incidentally, to call attention to an underappreciated resource in an hilarious account, "The Frontier Inside," published in the Harvard Medical Alumni Bulletin.

He spent the next decade in the presidential hot seat, doubling as dean of what was at the time the third-largest medical school in the United States, with seventeen affiliated hospitals to oversee and a sprawling inner-city community to serve to the best of his ability, despite a slumping national economy and a statewide budget crunch. "Brooklyn is a wonderful place very much like London," he claims, "a collection of small towns with every race under the sun represented. We needed good doctors in the worst way!"

Dr. Plimpton worked hard to bring in the medical talent. Among his "red-hot recruits" at Downstate was Dr. Samuel Koontz, a topnotch African American surgeon from Stanford, willing to trade in suburban comfort for the chance to make a difference in Brooklyn's simmering urban hot pot.

Following completion of his term of office at Downstate, Dr. Plimpton was named special consultant in international affairs to the National Library of Medicine, a brief scholarly interlude cut short by another call to service.

RETURN TO ARABIA

In 1982, things started to heat up again in the Middle East. Israel invaded Lebanon in June. AUB President David Dodge was kidnaped in July. This was followed in 1983 by attacks on U.S. Marines and an explosion at the U.S. Embassy in Kuwait. The mounting tension for AUB trustees, faculty, and students culminated on January 19, 1984, with the assassination of University President Malcolm Kerr.

At age sixty-six, when most people contemplate retirement, the self-styled "unemployed physician and untrained New England schoolmaster" took up the fallen baton as the tenth president of AUB. "Lots of people thought I was out of my mind," he allows.

On the way to Beirut, to bolster the spirits of the beleaguered faculty, he encountered Mother Theresa, who was herself headed there to preach peace. "Look, Mother," he cautioned, "there's a war going on, you ought to watch out!" "Oh no," she countered, a like-minded advocate of tight spots, "we always go where we're needed most!"

Dr. Plimpton had his hands full in Beirut, with the welfare of some 4,500 AUB students, 450 faculty members, and 12,000 campus workers to look after, while the bombs burst and war raged all around. Somebody needed to hold the fort of this "island of sanity, a sanctuary for intellectual development"—at least until the cavalry came. In fact, the fighting grew so fierce and the situation so risky, he was forced to run the school from Damascus, Cyprus, and the New York office, with short strategic hops to Beirut. "A lot of things are discouraging," he told a reporter for the *Cape Cod News* at the time. "Have you tried treating cancer lately? It's a very discouraging disease . . . but you don't give up."

His mission was clear. "We have to continue to do our business," he was quoted in the *Christian Science Monitor* at the time of his appointment. "That business," he said, "is educating people—not indoctrinating but educating them to think for themselves—and let the chips fall where they may." Like other institutions in an embattled Lebanon, the University, though spared heavy bombing, took a spiritual hit. Still, AUB survives today and continues to set a standard for higher education in the Middle East.

A RESTLESS RETIREE

People like Calvin Plimpton are not inclined to sit still. In 1990, he applied to the Peace Corps to teach English in Central Europe, but was turned down.

Still, his interest in things larger than himself continues unabated. Until recently a member of the Council on Foreign Relations, he spoke out against military action at the time of the war in the Persian Gulf. His numerous honors and awards have included the Order of Cedars, Commander rank, of the government of Lebanon; the Jane Award of the National Geographic Society; and honorary degrees from institutions of higher learning around the country and the world. He was saluted in 1998 as Distinguished Alumnus of the Year by the Society of the Alumni of Columbia-Presbyterian Medical Center.

"There will always be the frontiers between the old and the new, the past and the future, the known and the unknown," he once wrote. Averse to the idea of ever having "covered a field," at eighty-three, Calvin Plimpton is the living embodiment of a "médecin sans frontières," a doctor without borders, though the organization might turn him down if he applied.

NOTES OF A PIONEERING NEUROSURGEON

J. LAWRENCE POOL MD '32, MSD '40

Rounding out a memorable interview in 2000 at his home in Connecticut's scenic Litchfield County, the nonagenarian neurosurgeon sang French songs remembered from his service with the Ninth Evac in North Africa during World War II, and fondly recalled, among other vivid memories, directing the commander of one of Field Marshal Rommel's tank divisions and his captured troops to a prison camp, and dancing with the diva Marlene Dietrich. He died in 2007, at age ninety-seven.

—·⊶⊷·—

"THE BRAIN is a world consisting of a number of unexplored continents and great stretches of unknown territory," wrote Spanish neuroanatomist Dr. Ramon Y Cajal. Marble reliefs and scarred skulls found at the Temple of Luxor suggest that the ancient Egyptians took an early "crack" at it. Subsequent intracranial reconnaissance missions took a while to get underway, several millennia to be exact. The first significant inroads were made by neurosurgeons Sir Victor Horsley in England, Dr. Harvey Cushing in America, and Dr. Wilder Penfield in Canada, in the early days of the twentieth century. Notable among the next generation of neurosurgical trail blazers is J. Lawrence Pool MD '32, MSD '40. His multiple innovations, including the introduction of the microscope to operate on cerebral aneurysm and the development of the myeloscope to pinpoint problems of the lower spine, as well as his consummate skill in the OR, made him the second American ever to receive the prestigious Medal of Honor of the World Federation of Neurological Sciences.

At ninety-five, with arthritic spurs pinching his spine, the indomitable Dr. Pool still maneuvers his way around his West Cornwall, Conn., ranch house, nimbly alternating between a wheelchair, two canes, and a pusher. He may not move quite as swiftly as he once did on the squash courts as two-time National Squash Racquets Champion in 1929 and 1931, or with the agility of the ace fly fisherman and transatlantic Yankee skipper that he was in younger years. But everything's in tip-top shape upstairs in that part of the human anatomy he helped map out and mend.

A decade ago, deriding those content to sit on their laurels and "stick to their left or 'banker's' brain," he set out to "learn something brand new." Life's challenges continue to engage and stimulate the vigorous nonagenarian. The walls of his home are covered with his and his late wife's watercolors and pastel depictions of nature. The bookshelves are well stocked with books on a multitude of subjects, including the fifteen volumes authored by him to date. Having lost his beloved Angeline some years ago, he pretty much fends for himself. And while the years have chiseled away at his ruddy good looks, they have not robbed him of the gusto he continues to invest in everything he does, most recently in the writing of book number sixteen, observations on the antics of Connecticut wildlife. After more than three decades in rural Litchfield County, the self-proclaimed "newly planted rustic" is not averse to looking back on his years in the Big Apple, especially his time at P&S and The Neurological Institute [NI] of New York, where he trained and later served as chair of neurological surgery from 1949 to 1972.

OF BRIDGE CABLES AND CADAVERS

Born in a bygone era of gaslight and horse-drawn buggies, or as he puts it in his lively memoir, *Adventures and Ventures of a New York Neurosurgeon* (1988) "an age of cholesterol and coal," Dr. Pool likes to joke that "it [the Neurological Institute] was founded in 1909 and *I* was founded in 1906, which makes me the statelier institution!"—though he is quick to add that the NI is "my favorite hospital of all time."

Taking his BA from Harvard, he was a member of the first P&S class to attend medical school at the new medical center uptown. Among his classmates was anesthesiologist-to-be Virginia Apgar '32 (of the "Apgar Score" fame). From his first-year anatomy table, he dissected muscles and organs while watching out the window as construction crews strung the cables of the George Washington Bridge. He studied surgery under the eminent Dr. Allen Oldfather Whipple (of the "Whipple Operation") and became hooked on the intricacies of the human nervous system under the tutelage of Drs. Frederick Tilney and Harold Riley, the neurologists who coauthored the classic textbook of the day. Surgery, you might say, ran in the family. An ancestor, Dr. John Adams Pool, earned his degree from the old Queens College (later Rutgers) in 1824. His father, Dr. Eugene H. Pool, a past president of the American College of Surgeons, was one of the country's top general surgeons. His cousin John L. Pool '34 is a distinguished retired chest surgeon.

As a medical intern, Dr. Pool already made history, helping to inaugurate the new New York-Cornell Hospital in 1932. "I was the low man on the totem pole," he recalls with his trademark chuckle, "so I was privileged to admit the very first patient to the entire medical center. Nobody knows that, except me!"

Following a year of research on the circulation of the brain at Harvard, he returned to Presbyterian Hospital (now New York-Presbyterian) to pursue an internship in general surgery, followed by residencies in neurology and neurological surgery at the Neurological Institute. Thereafter working as an attending neurological surgeon at Bellevue Hospital, he simultaneously pursued research toward an MSD back at P&S, which he received in 1941. His postgraduate investigation, conducted with neuroanatomist Dr. Fred Mettler, tracing the path of nerve impulses in the wake of convulsive seizures in animal models, had seminal implications for paraplegics. He later tried without success to interest IBM in building a device that would electrically stimulate damaged neurons and enable rudimentary moves. The idea was picked up years later in the "Para-Step" system.

BRAIN SURGERY ON THE BATTLE LINES
(AND DANCING WITH DIETRICH)

World War II brought a sudden shift of focus and locale. Dr. Pool was shipped off to North Africa with a mobile tent hospital, the Ninth Evacuation Hospital, to treat the casualties of combat with Germany's fabled "Desert Fox," Field Marshal Erwin Rommel. His schedule vacillated from lengthy periods waiting for action to frenetic day and night stints in the makeshift OR. Following Rommel's defeat, Dr. Pool fondly recalls directing the commandant of a long column of German trucks and tanks straight to the prison camp. "God, were we ever glad to see them surrender!" Later transferred to Italy, in preparation for the Allied invasion of southern France, he was based in Naples. On one occasion, at a USO dance, he had the pleasure of dancing with Marlene Dietrich. Demobilized in 1946, Dr. Pool retired from the U.S. Army Medical Corps with the rank of Lieutenant Colonel.

A FLY IN THE OR AND OTHER EXPLOITS AT
THE TILLER OF THE NEUROSURGICAL SERVICE

Then in 1947, he returned to the Neurological Institute as a junior staff member. A mere two years later, to his amazement and delight, he was named professor and chair of neurological surgery and chief of the neurosurgical service, positions he held with great distinction for the next twenty-five years. His accomplishments in that capacity were both legion and legendary.

Former resident, colleague, and lifelong friend, the late Edgar Housepian '53 liked to tell of the time a fly got into somebody else's OR. Surgeon, resident, nurse, anesthesiologist—everyone was in a pickle, until Dr. Pool happened to peek in, spotted the winged intruder, thrust out his hand, grabbed it out of thin air, and walked out. "It was really spectacular! He was only there for several seconds, and he took the thing—swoosh!" His expertise on the squash court and as a fly fisherman came in handy.

Fly catching was not, of course, his only claim to fame.

Regarding his old friend's dynamic technique and 'on your feet' thinking, Dr. Housepian recalled, only half tongue in cheek, that "Dr. Pool had a thousand surgical ideas a month. Anyone who gets that many ideas, has 600 crackpot ideas, nobody else has 300 ideas that work—but he did."

DIFFUSING TIME BOMBS IN THE BRAIN

Among his most celebrated innovations, Dr. Pool introduced the use of the microscope in aneurysm surgery in 1963. "We were having so much trouble with aneurysms, which are little 'blood blisters' of a brain artery. The blood vessels were so tiny you could hardly see them. We had used jewelers' loops but they didn't magnify enough. I heard about binocular microscopes being used by ear surgeons," he recalls, "and figured, well here's the microscope, why not use it in the brain—so we did!"

Another path-breaking idea came, as many surgical innovations do, at a moment of crisis. In the midst of an aneurysm operation, the patient's heart suddenly stopped beating. Dr. Pool kept his cool, thinking "if she dies I might as well fix the aneurysm, if she lives she'll have it fixed and won't have to go through it all again." With lightning speed, he commanded the surgical resident on hand to "slash the chest open, put your gloved hand in and squeeze the heart." Which he did, until the head of the surgical cardiac arrest team, John Schullinger '55, came to the rescue. Unfortunately, the mechanical cardiopulmonary resuscitator malfunctioned and Dr. Schullinger had to take turns with the resident manually pumping the heart while Dr. Pool wrapped up the ruptured blood vessel and proceeded with the operation.

"I got that idea," he chuckles, "from reading sea stories and ocean racing. Columbus had no shipyards off the coast of Cuba. So they took an extra sail, swung it under the boat, and hooked it up like a diaper to keep the water from pouring into the hull. That's just what I did. I still remember the patient. She had seven children. I said to myself, 'I've got to save her!'" And he did. In less than twenty minutes the aneurysm was located and repaired. The success of the operation subsequently led surgeons to deliberately stop the heart under controlled conditions to cut off blood flow to the aneurysm and facilitate safe and speedy repair.

OTHER SURGICAL BRAINSTORMS

An acknowledged master at the art of doing spinal taps, Dr. Pool invented the myeloscope, a plastic tube combined with a tiny millet-seed-sized bulb invaluable in the detection of abnormalities in the lower spine. A symposium at Yale was devoted to this innovation.

Dr. Pool is also credited with the discovery of the ulnar adductor reflex of the ulnar (or "funny bone" nerve). As a young resident at the NI, he examined a young girl who complained of a funny feeling in the hand. While senior colleagues relegated the patient's problem to neurosis, Dr. Pool diagnosed an unspecified problem in the spinal cord. He was later proved right when the same patient presented a year later with a paralyzed arm, and tumors of the neck and cord were found to be the cause.

Other noteworthy accomplishments are the early diagnosis and surgery of acoustic nerve tumors, previously considered inoperable; the refinement of frontal lobotomies with a high record of success; establishing cerebral vasospasm as an observable phenomenon; and proving that prompt intracranial surgery was the optimal way to treat bleeding aneurysm during pregnancy.

Dr. Pool also lent his leadership skills to help create and run professional organizations in his chosen field. He was a founding member and the first president of the New York Neurosurgical Society, a past president of the American Academy of Neurological Surgery, and two-term treasurer of the World Federation of Neurosurgical Societies.

FROM SKILL WITH A SCALPEL TO
MASTERY OF PEN AND INK

Surgeons, as Dr. Pool readily admits, are not generally thought to be of a reflective bent. "My friends used to kid me on that score. 'Larry,' they said, 'you'd rather act than think!'" Man of action though he is, Dr. Pool has done more than his fair share of reflection too. The proof of the pudding is his more than 100 articles and fifteen books, including two celebrated textbooks, *The Early Diagnosis and Treatment of Acoustic Nerve Tumors* and *Aneurysms and Arteriovenous Malformations of the Brain*; a medical book for laymen, *Nature's Masterpiece, The Brain and How It Works*; a *History of the Neurological Institute of New York*; two memoirs; and other eminently readable volumes on everything from Izaak Walton and fly fishing to Valley Forge and the great fighting sloops of the American Revolution. Among his multiple benefactions to P&S, Dr. Pool established the J. Lawrence Pool Prize in Medical Writing given annually to a medical student author of the best paper published in the student-run P&S *Medical Review*.

UNABASHED DELIGHT IN MULTIPLE
EXTRA-MEDICAL PURSUITS

Dr. Pool prefaced the aforementioned memoir, *Adventures and Ventures of a New York Neurosurgeon*, with a tongue-in-cheek disclaimer: "For the fun that came my way as a would-be horseman, skier, and plane pilot I apologize to those who worked while I played. The ancient proverb 'all work and no play' is my feeble excuse. As a fisherman, more ardent than apt, I was granted happy intervals of freedom from research ventures and arduous hospital and teaching duties." Such "intervals" were spent on the squash court, the deck of a ship, and the bank of many a mountain stream, and with his family, wife Angeline, and three sons, at a camp in Maine. "I kept my weekends remarkably free for the family."

He likewise found time for his medical alma mater, serving as chair of the P&S Club Faculty Advisory Board and president of the P&S Alumni Association, and helping out in countless other official and unofficial capacities. A helpful advisor to generations of students, he and his wife would invite students and house staff out to their home at least once a month. His generosity has included the construction of a state-of-the-art squash court in Bard Hall and the endowment of a professorship in neurosurgery in his name.

Dr. Pool was honored both with the 1974 P&S Alumni Association's Gold Medal for Service to the School and its Alumni and the 1982 Gold Medal for Distinguished Service in Academic Medicine. Honorary Alumni Day chair in 1985, he received the 1992 Presbyterian Hospital Medical Excellence Tribute, and the aforementioned Medal of Honor of the World Federation of Neurological Sciences.

The "slowed-down" year of his ostensible retirement from practice and teaching, 1972, saw him sprinting round the globe, lecturing as visiting professor in Edinburgh, addressing an international meeting in Prague, salmon fishing in Iceland, and officiating at a Neurological Academy meeting in California. While the pace has slackened some in subsequent decades, the life gusto has not diminished one iota. "I'm pleased to be here with the buttons still working!" he winks, wheeling his way back to the typewriter.

FIRST WOMAN OF MEDICINE

HELEN RANNEY '47

Helen Ranney '47, a renowned hematologist best known for her pioneering work in sickle cell anemia, chose medicine as a career because, in her words, as opposed to other fields, "Medicine attempts to fix what it studies." Dr. Ranney died on April 5, 2010, at age eighty-nine.

FROM BENCH work to bedside, from teaching to administration, Helen Ranney '47, the quintessential physician-scientist, has covered all the bases with equal prowess. Academician-clinician-research scientist extraordinaire, noted for the major contributions she made to understanding the structure and function of human hemoglobin, she was the first woman to chair a department of medicine in the United States, at the University of California, San Diego, 1973–86. And though most of her research has been in biochemistry, there is no question about her primary identification: "I see myself as a physician, first and foremost, that's somebody who takes care of people!"

Dr. Ranney made her medical mark in the postwar period that Dr. Lewis Thomas has called the golden age of scientific medicine—or to use her own inimitable turn of phrase: "A time when fish flew and forests walked and figs grew upon the thorn.

"We were the group that was there in medicine when medicine became a science," she observes. "We were there when the antibiotics came out. We were there for the polio vaccines and the great contributions in infectious diseases and medical microbiology. We represent the beginning of the era of people who can see medicine as a series of scientific questions."

After half a century of scientific questioning, her vigor has not waned one iota. Her broad open face and the laser-like intensity of her bespectacled gaze still convey the curiosity of the tireless investigator, as though peering at life through a high-power microscope, while a ready smile and a hearty laugh attest to what former P&S colleague, the late Abbie Knowlton '42, described as "her evident delight in the humor of the human estate."

A "NATURAL" FOR MEDICINE

The mere mention of her name at P&S elicits a spontaneous outpouring of respect and affection from old colleagues, students, and friends, a sentiment put most succinctly by the late Dr. Aura Severinghaus, former associate dean of admissions, in a letter dated June 1, 1946, recommending Dr. Ranney for an internship at Bellevue:

> "There are only a few persons whom one admits to medical school with the conviction that here is a 'natural' for medicine. I had that feeling about her upon admission and it has proven correct. She is in my opinion, one of the best qualified students we have had at the College of Physicians and Surgeons during my twenty-year association with it."

The fact that, such praise and her outstanding academic record notwithstanding, Dr. Ranney was nevertheless refused at Bellevue reflects the tenor of the times in which a woman's chances for advancement in academic medicine were slim, to say the least. (Presbyterian Hospital had the wisdom and foresight to admit her for an internship and residency in medicine.) Asked about any discrimination she might have experienced as a woman, she replies with a shrug, "Well I never really thought much about it!"

A cum laude graduate of Barnard College, Helen Ranney set her sights on medicine from the start.

"Economists, sociologists and the like study things you can't fix, even if you could find out what was wrong," she insists, "medicine attempts to fix what it studies." The daughter of an Upstate New York farmer and avid "gadgeteer" and an independent-minded school teacher mother, she was reared with a roll-up-your-sleeves, hands-on attitude to life. "I used to operate a team of horses on the farm," Dr. Ranney proudly recalls.

Rejected when she first applied to P&S in 1941, she managed to turn that early disappointment to her later advantage. She took a job as a laboratory technician at Babies Hospital (now Morgan-Stanley Children's Hospital), where she proceeded to acquire and master the basic lab techniques that would come in handy in her future research in hematology. (To this day, she still lists her stint in the lab near the top of her curriculum vitae under the rubric "Education.") And when, on the encouragement and prompting of her superiors at Babies, she reapplied to P&S, history proved on her side.

With America's entry into World War II, the country needed doctors, and the new climate favored the acceptance of a small number of qualified women at top medical schools like P&S (which had been admitting a few women since 1917). And since most of the medical men now had their tuitions paid for by Uncle Sam, the availability of endowed scholarships enabled her to graduate with no debt.

Once accepted, Dr. Ranney experienced no marked prejudice.—"New York City has generally accepted minorities of any sort with a kind of: Well, if you can do it, show me! attitude."

And show them, she did!

Over the course of her association with P&S and Columbia Presbyterian Medical Center, as student, intern, resident, fellow, and finally, junior faculty member, she shone in the dual arena of bench and bedside medicine.

Under the tutelage of the late Dr. Robert Loeb, Dr. Ranney learned the art of patient care. Recalling his influence in a stirring tribute at the dedication ceremony of a portrait of Dr. Loeb in 1993, she saluted him as the "living example of the knowledgeable, confident, and compassionate physician, concerned about the patient and about the science." Above all else, by his own example, he taught her and generations of doctors how to listen. "I'm always amused nowadays when I get to the clinic and the young doctors tell me that neither the old chart nor this and that test result has come in," she chuckles. "'Why don't you just ask the patient?' I say. 'He'll tell you most of what you want to know!'"

While acknowledging a sometimes daunting side to Dr. Loeb's demeanor, her respect and affection overrode any upset, even though "he never much knew what to do with women in medicine." Despite her proven academic talent and inclination, he once tried to persuade her to take a job in student health, whereupon she laughed quite openly, and that was that.

Another P&S faculty member who exerted a profound influence on her own teaching style was the late Yale Kneeland '26, professor of medicine and her third-year preceptor, to whom, as she puts it, "the English language was a servant not a master," a mastery she would come to share.

Andrew Frantz '55, professor of medicine and chair of the Committee on Admissions at P&S (and incidentally, Dr. Kneeland's nephew), breaks into a broad smile remembering his own experience of Dr. Ranney as his third-year preceptor. In addition to her infectious enthusiasm, her ability to relate to patients and students as individuals, and her in-depth knowledge and painstaking attention to detail, it was her sparkling wit and her way with words that made her such an inspiring teacher. "To this day," he insists, "whenever I supervise a student or take a medical history from a patient, it's her way of doing it that I am conscious of and I can still feel her presence looking over my shoulder and saying: 'Andrew, I think you could sharpen that up a bit!'"

METABOLIC AND ACADEMIC PATHWAYS

It was during her postdoctoral training in the Department of Biochemistry at P&S that Dr. Ranney began clinical investigations in sickle cell disease as a sidelight of her hematological studies with Dr. Irving London. The department, then under the direction of Dr. Hans Thatcher Clarke, had an outstanding reputation, thanks in part to Dr. Clarke's recruitment of the cream of scientific exiles from Nazi Germany. "P&S had without a doubt the most exciting biochemistry department in the country," Dr. Ranney recalls. "They were one of the first groups to use isotopes to trace body elements; they knew about metabolic pathways."

Combining the technical laboratory expertise she got at Babies Hospital with her newly acquired biochemical know-how and clinical experience, she devised an experimental means of establishing precisely how the molecular structure of normal human hemoglobin differs from abnormal hemoglobin found in the red blood cells of individuals with sickle cell anemia, a disorder particularly common among African Americans.

Employing Presbyterian Hospital's clinic patient population, which at the time included a large African American population, she was able to study the normal and abnormal hemoglobin found in members of the same family, thus providing some of the first evidence of a genetic link. To Dr. Ranney, the science was never far removed from the person. "I've never liked the strictly abstract," she admits, "if you get to be very good at the biophysics of the thing, you become so theoretical you stop doing experiments and just calculate how they would come out if you did them."

Dr. London moved on to Albert Einstein Medical College, soon thereafter inviting Dr. Ranney to join him. There she pursued her study of abnormal hemoglobin and was named professor of medicine in 1965. In 1970, she left Einstein to accept an appointment as professor of medicine at the State University of New York at Buffalo. And then in 1973, when the University of California, at San Diego, went looking for a new chair of medicine, Dr. Ranney made history as the first woman to head a major department of medicine in the United States.

In recommending her for the position, Paul Marks '49, then dean of P&S, now president emeritus of Memorial Sloan Kettering Cancer Center, called her "one of the nation's outstanding investigators in the area of hemoglobinopathies and the structure and function of normal and abnormal hemoglobins." In addition to "her excellence in clinical investigation," Dr. Marks noted, "she is an outstanding clinician and a superb teacher . . . a person of the highest integrity and quality."

Her reputation has only risen over the years. Honors and achievements have followed in rapid succession. Recipient of the P&S Gold Medal for Medical Research and the Dr. Martin Luther King, Jr. Medical Achievement Award for Outstanding Contribution in the Field of Sickle Cell Anemia, among many other awards; fellow of the American Academy of Arts and Sciences and member of the National Academy of Sciences; coauthor of two noted textbooks and more than 100 papers in hematology; member of the board of directors of the Squibb Corporation; Distinguished Physician in the Department of Veteran Affairs, VAMC San Diego—Dr. Ranney's vitae documents an astounding range of accomplishments.

As to the comparative climate for women in academic medicine then and now, Dr. Ranney offers a sober appraisal. "When you think back, had I been a man at Columbia, I probably would have had a faculty appointment earlier rather than later. Things have definitely opened up a fair amount for women, but I still don't think that, by and large, they are nearly as well represented on the faculties as they are in the student bodies in medical schools."

A major problem she sees is women not being able to undertake the period of advanced scientific training they need. She has used the strength of her reputation to lobby at the NIH and elsewhere for the creation of academic support systems to help women assistant professors who take a leave of absence to have a family, to "get the essential scientific retooling without the pressure of grant hunting" upon their return to teaching and research.

As to the future of medicine, Dr. Ranney smiles as she wipes her glasses, and with her characteristic mix of irony and excitement says, "Clearly what we think now will appear amateurish in another twenty years, just as when I look back twenty or twenty-five years, I sometimes have to laugh at the things we took for granted."

MEDICINE BY BLUE PENCIL

ARNOLD RELMAN '46

Arnold "Bud" Relman '46, the academic internist-editor who helped shape the New England Journal of Medicine *into the gold standard of medical science, conscience, and care, died of melanoma in 2014, at age ninety-one. Though retired from the* Journal, *he remained committed to medicine to the end, correcting the galleys of his last article at the time of his death.*

———⟨oↄœↄo⟩———

MOST DOCTORS just call it "*The Journal.*" It is the oldest continuously published medical journal in the world, and the most quoted. Its weekly appearance is eagerly awaited in doctors' offices, clinics, laboratories, libraries, and committee rooms around the country. Its contents regularly make headlines and, on occasion, send shockwaves down Wall Street.

For the last fourteen years until his retirement in January 1991, a soft-spoken philosopher-physician, Arnold Relman '46, called the shots as editor-in-chief of the *New England Journal of Medicine.* An internationally respected nephrologist noted for his work in potassium metabolism, renal acidosis, and the regulation of acid-base balance, Dr. Relman is also an MD with a mission.

Grounded in the fundamental ethical tenets of the humanist tradition— he studied philosophy at Cornell before entering medical school—Arnold Relman is a firm believer in the doctor's social commitment to service, and he has been adamant about upholding that commitment in the face of economic and political pressures to the contrary. His outspoken views expressed in editorials devoted to the economic, ethical, legal, and social aspects of health care have stirred considerable controversy over the years.

Dr. Relman, currently a professor of medicine at Harvard with a dual appointment in the departments of medicine and social medicine, is a fellow of the American Academy of Arts and Sciences and a member of the Institute of Medicine of the National Academy of Sciences. He is also a master of the American College of Physicians and a fellow of the Royal College of Physicians in London. Among his many honors, he was awarded the 1981 Gold Medal for Outstanding Achievements in Medicine of the College of Physicians and Surgeons, where he maintains close ties as a member of the National Visiting Council.

The following interview was conducted in 1991. Dr. Relman's responses to an interviewer's questions were so succinct and so perfectly phrased, there was nothing more to add. It therefore seemed advisable to keep to the Q&A format.

> PW: *You began your editorship at the* New England Journal of Medicine *quite literally with a bang, taking on the volatile issue of violence and gun control in your first published editorial, "More Than Sutures and Transfusions," 9/8/77. Did you get any flak for this?*
>
> AR: Oh yeah! When I published this editorial, I received many, many very vitriolic rebuttals from the National Rifle Association and from people of that ilk, saying: Why are you meddling in issues that are not relevant to medicine? Why don't you stick to your knitting as editor of a clinical research journal! They accused me of all sorts of horrible liberal tendencies. As you know, murder with guns is the commonest cause of death among young black males in America!
>
> PW: *In your editorials over the years, you have chosen to focus on the social and ethical issues of medicine and leave the more technical medical subjects to others. Was this a matter of personal choice or the traditional role of the editor?*
>
> AR: As medicine has become more and more specialized, and as the science and technology of medicine have become more sophisticated, it is harder and harder for any editor, any one person, to be comfortably competent enough to comment on the scientific and the clinical issues of a technical order. You can write about the social, economic, and ethical impact—that's okay. But if you want to write a definitive authoritative editorial evaluating the state of the art in a certain field, you have to be an expert in that field.

UNIVERSITY WITHOUT WALLS

PW: *You once described the* Journal *as a "university without walls." What did you mean by that?*

AR: The *Journal* isn't just a publication, it's a medical institution. It has been part of American medicine almost from the beginning, since 1812. It's the oldest continuously published medical journal in the world. It has grown up with American medicine, it has reflected all the changes, it has given a pulpit to almost every eminent name in American medicine over the years. It has always played a role in the controversial social issues.

For example, during the Civil War, the *Journal's* editors carried on a vigorous campaign against inefficiency in the Union Army Medical Services. They also campaigned against the conditions in the insane asylums. Articles and editorials leading to the first awareness of the appalling health and biological consequences of nuclear warfare were published in the *Journal* editorials—this was under Dr. Joseph Garland's editorship, 1947-67—for the first time opening the eyes of the medical profession to the cataclysm that would happen if we used nuclear weapons in war.

The *Journal* has published important articles about developments in medical education, medical ethics, and legal issues relating to medicine, and also concerning some of the most important scientific developments in clinical medicine. It's basically a clinical, not a basic science, journal.

It was and is part of the literature of medicine. I remember when I was a medical student, when you became professionalized—that change that occurs toward the end of second year when you begin to learn how to examine each other and you examine patients, acquire a stethoscope and a white coat—that's when you took a subscription to the *New England Journal of Medicine*. On rounds, it was expected that students would know what was in that week's issue. It has always served as an evolving textbook and forum for everything current and important in medicine. Many, many physicians practicing today grew up on the *New England Journal of Medicine* and have subscribed ever since they were medical students.

PW: *You entered the ranks of medicine following the conclusion of the great cataclysm of World War II with its accompanying revelation of profound human calamity: Auschwitz, Hiroshima, Dresden. Did the moral tenor of the times*

and an awareness of recent history have an effect on your decision to study
medicine and on your view of yourself and your role as a doctor in society?

AR: I think so. Everyone, Jew, Gentile, Moslem—everyone with any
conscience—was profoundly shaken by the revelations of what happened. And I felt that a life in medicine would be for me one of the
few paths that one could chose in which one could find great personal satisfaction and reasonable practical rewards for doing good.
I couldn't think of anything bad about being a physician, and that
was very important to me.

PW:—*except the instance of the Nazi doctors—I'm thinking of say, a*
Dr. Mengele.

AR: Yes, but that was an aberration, a perversion. The essence of medicine, the thrust of medicine, its raison d'être is good. And there are
very few other pursuits that don't require taking advantage in some
fashion of other people, endeavors in which there aren't winners
and losers. Medicine practiced properly and ethically is a win-win
situation, everybody wins. And it is also so exciting scientifically.

When I went into medicine, science was just beginning to be applied to the
practice of medicine in a very real way. It was still possible to lead a life of science and be an active physician at the same time. And that was very appealing
to me.

Being a native New Yorker, I had a New Yorker's provincialism: I thought that
everything important happened here. So naturally I applied to P&S. And in those
simple, wonderful days, I remember my interview with Dr. Aura Severinghaus,
who was then dean of admissions. He had my college record there before him.
We chatted for a while, and he said: 'Okay, you're in. Welcome.' That was it.
I never applied anywhere else.

PW: *Did P&S live up to your expectations in terms of intellectual challenge?*

AR: It was a very heady, very exciting experience. There were brilliant
scientists here and brilliant clinicians. The dominant figure was
Dr. Robert Loeb. When he came on the wards there was a sort of
electricity in the air, and you were all fired up to do your best,
frightened that he would call on you and you would be stupid, but
excited at the same time. And there were lots of brilliant people in
medicine: Dr. Randolph West, who died prematurely, Drs. Frank
Hanger, Dana Atchley. You had the sense that you were at the center
of medical learning, and it was so thrilling. I remember coming here

and feeling that I was entering a kind of priesthood: I was seeing things and hearing things and learning things that would change me forever and would make me different from the people outside the walls of the medical center. And I lived and breathed and thought nothing but medicine in those days.

PW: *To recap your career path in brief: following an internship and residency at Yale, you joined the faculty of Boston University, where you rose in the ranks to become the Conrad Wesselhoeft Professor of Medicine, and from thence moved to chair the Department of Medicine at the University of Pennsylvania School of Medicine, all the while pursuing research in nephrology. At the same time, you began to be active in medical editing.*

AR: From 1962–67, while at Boston University, I served as editor of the *Journal of Clinical Investigation*. That's a rotating five-year appointment. You're supposed to do your regular academic work and be editor on the side, nights and weekends. I found that while doing clinical research and laboratory research, I also enjoyed my editorial duties, thus reawakening in myself a long-time latent interest. I had been one of the editors of my high school newspaper and of my college literary magazine. I had always been a very bookish kid. And so I jumped at the chance to combine interests in language and ideas with science. Then in 1968, I was offered the post of chair of medicine at U Penn, an offer I simply couldn't resist.

PW: *It was during a sabbatical as a visiting scientist at Oxford that you were "drafted" by the* New England Journal of Medicine—*is that right?*

AR: It was serendipity, I suppose. At Boston University, one of my closest friends and colleagues was Dr. Franz Ingelfinger, head of the gastroenterology unit at the Evans Memorial Hospital, a very distinguished diagnostician. Because of my editorial interest, I had been appointed by the Massachusetts Medical Society to be a member of the Committee on Publications of the Society, which is the supervisory board for the *New England Journal of Medicine*. I had published articles in the *Journal*, I had reviewed for them, and now I was on the Committee on Publications. And when the then editor, Dr. Joseph Garland, retired because of ill health and old age, I was asked whether I wanted to step down from the committee and be a candidate for the job. I was then much interested in academic medicine and I thought it wasn't the right time in my career. So I suggested Franz Ingelfinger, and it was an inspired suggestion, if I have to say so myself: he was just perfect for the job.

PW: *What made him a "perfect" editor?*

AR: First of all, an editor has to have a supple mind and be a quick study: you have to be capable of learning a new specialty language all the time. You have to have good judgment, you have to be very critical and very skeptical. You have to be tough but fair, and open-minded and open to all points of view. In an exposed controversial job like that, whatever decision you make you're going to make some people very angry at you. You can't blow with the wind. You have to know what you're doing, you have to be principled, you have to be consistent. You also have to know something about writing, to be attuned to what good writing is and what bad writing is, and be able to help people to write better. And Ingelfinger was all of those things. Tough, smart, fair, talented as a writer, a good judge of quality.

Whenever I'd see him, I'd ask: Do you enjoy your job at the *Journal*? He'd say: It's the best job I ever had, as a matter of fact, I think it's the best job in American medicine!—while you last!

So the *Journal* was under my skin by that time. And when I took a sabbatical at Oxford in '75–76, I'd been at Penn for eight years and I wasn't sure I wanted to serve another term as chair. I was tired of management and administration and the academic politics of running a huge department. So I took that sabbatical and I returned to hands-on basic research. And even as I was mulling over my options for the future, my friend, poor Franz, got cancer of the esophagus, and being himself an authority on diseases of the esophagus, he felt it didn't make any sense for him to continue, so he submitted his resignation, effective as soon as they could get a replacement. He recommended me. I subsequently got a call from Boston: Did I want to be a candidate? And then I realized: Yes, that's what I wanted. And everything fell into place.

PW: *You once admitted that when you first accepted the position as editor of the* New England Journal of Medicine, *you "thought the best anyone would say about my tenure was 'at least it didn't deteriorate.' " Clearly under your leadership, the* Journal *has not deteriorated. It has thrived and expanded in new directions. What do you see as the major changes and innovations under your tenure? What aspects of your editorship are you most proud of?*

AR: I would say that the greatest single change that occurred in the *Journal* under my editorship has been its entry into the public policy arena in a major way and its involvement in the important ethical, legal, political, and economic questions surrounding health care. While there have always been articles of this kind, over the past fourteen years that I've been editor the technical progress in medicine and the changes in the economic and political climate have generated problems and questions that were never that urgent before. I've taken pains to see to it that the *Journal* would provide a forum for these issues to be aired and debated in a responsible scholarly way.

There have also been other changes in the way we review articles with concern for—what shall I call it?—"Journalology," to coin a word. Medical editing used to be almost a marginal activity that busy clinicians and scientists did on the side. In the last decade or two, however, all sorts of questions have arisen—whether of conflicts of interest or fraud, plagiarism, duplicate publication, redundant publication, problems of authorship, ownership of data—you name it! I was one of the founders of an organization called the International Committee of Medical Journal Editors, which deals with these issues. Under by editorship, the *Journal* has also gained a much larger international readership, and, I think, a greater impact internationally.

> PW: *In an interview that appeared in* Second Opinion, *you said: "Medicine, after all, is an amalgam of science and human service. It is basically a serving profession. Without that moral element, it becomes mere technology and potentially dangerous. We do not want to encourage a whole generation of indifferent technicians. The moral component is essential." Could you elaborate on what you see as the moral component in medicine?*
>
> AR: Medicine, as distinguished from biological science, is not just concerned with understanding the nature of man, the machinery of man, but with helping people who are ill, in danger of becoming ill, or otherwise at risk. In order to do that, physicians have to make an ethical commitment to serve—not just a commitment to learn, to know, to understand—but to serve, to be helpful! It means you have to know what it means to be helpful and how to be helpful. It means you have to be concerned about people and their values and needs. Without that concern, medicine is lost.

I am very much worried lest we stray too far from the Samaritan tradition of medicine. In our profession, that's what empowers us. We have rights, very important and unique rights. We have a licensed monopoly—to put it in economic terms—and that's part of a contract we've made with society. Society after all subsidized our education, gave us autonomy and authority and a virtual guarantee of a good living. On an individual basis, our patients put their lives in our hands and reveal to us things about themselves that they might not tell anybody else, including their nearest and dearest. An enormous power has been put in our hands, in exchange for which that contract calls for a commitment to serve.

We're not doing medicine just because it's interesting and fun. We're not in it just to make a living or to get rich. Those things are secondary. We're in medicine to serve, to help, and if we forget that, our contract with society is going to be ruptured, with dire consequences for the profession and for the public.

> PW: *P&S, among other major medical schools, is currently in the process of reviewing and revising its curriculum. What can medical schools do to bring back the broad-minded doctor-humanist of old?*
>
> AR: We can't turn back the clock! There's no going back, there's only going forward! We will never be able to return to the "good old days" of the cultivated universalist, a master of everything concerning man. That's gone! There's just too much to know. What we can do, however, is make sure that every person who leaves medical school with a diploma and enters the medical profession understands the commitment to serve and understands that service is the essence, the key to being a medical professional.

We have to change our selection of medical students and we have to change the way we educate them. And no less important, perhaps even more so, we have to change the systems into which they go after they leave medical school. No matter what you teach them, when young physicians come out into the real world and find that the only way to survive is to compete like businessmen and put their own economic and personal interest first, then everything is lost.

Medical education should do its part. We've got to be much more catholic in our view of what makes a good medical student. The emphasis on quantitative science and biology shouldn't be so exclusive. We have to be much more open to people from other backgrounds. True, you can't be a doctor without a certain amount of scientific discipline. You can't just be all heart and emotion and not understand how the human body works. You have to have the capacity to learn, but that's not very hard. I would say that in recruiting and selecting medical students, we ought to be willing to take young people who have maybe not done so well in science but are clearly bright and want to be committed and understand what it means to be a doctor.

And I think we have to provide an environment in medical school in which students feel more comfortable with and more attracted to learning about the broader aspects of being a professional. You have to have faculty to demonstrate that. One of the big problems in medical education today is that most of the people who teach medicine are specialists themselves who have little interest in these larger issues concerning the social milieu in which health care is provided.

I think that key appointments of very strong people who exemplify the humane tradition can go a long way. It doesn't mean that you turn away from scholarship, that you value scholarship any the less; it means that you take a broader view of what scholarship is. The main business of a research university is research, but in medical school if you don't have faculty who exemplify and teach the human aspects of medicine, you produce a graduate who's socially crippled.

> PW: *Should this—can this—social dimension of medicine be addressed in the curriculum?*
>
> AR: I think so, yes, but it begins with people. You can design any curriculum you want—it may look great on paper, but if you don't have people to exemplify what it is you're talking about, then it won't work. You have to recruit and reward people who are the kinds of doctors that you want your students to become! Most good medical schools, like Columbia, are turning out young people who are technically competent; what they're not doing is making them into real doctors, real professionals!
>
> PW: *In speaking of the doctor's calling, you have distinguished between a career and a mission, opting for the latter—what is the difference?*
>
> AR: A career is any kind of vocational choice, any kind of vocational commitment that you make. Careers are morally neutral. You can have a career as a bank robber or a dope peddler or an arms dealer or a lawyer for the mob or whatever. A mission involves a moral commitment to be helpful—at least as applied to medicine: it's a commitment to make things better, to weigh in on the side of humanity. Life is very short. I believe it's one time around. And to make the most of it, to get any kind of comfort at the end, you have to be able to say to yourself: I did what I could! I tried to help!
>
> PW: *How has the way society views doctors and the way the doctor views him- or herself and the doctor's role in society changed over the years since you left medical school and first entered the profession in 1946?*

AR: When I entered medical school, doctors were dominant, deified, revered more than almost any other career professional. They were unchallenged, they were paternalistic, they were economically speaking, in a seller's market, unquestionably in command of the American health care system. And they were, in general, very widely respected. That has changed. The doctor's technical competence is greater now than ever before. and the doctor has the tools and the concepts to do things that were unimaginable a generation ago. And for the most part, people have confidence in the technical competence of their doctor. They expect miracles and sometimes they even get miracles. But the doctor's unchallenged dominance over the health care system is gone. Paternalism is out. Consumerism is in. Doctors have revealed that they have feet of clay. Doctors are seen more and more as simply vendors of health services, and unfortunately, many doctors think of themselves that way: they talk about the contract between doctor and patient as a kind of business contract. Patients sense that. Patients trust doctors less. They sue them more often.

In the last ten, twenty years, people have begun to talk about the health care industry, the business of medicine. And there are many, many doctors around who say: Yes, I'm a businessman. But just because you have to earn a living—and, of course, meet your expenses and show a profit at the end of the year if you're going to survive—that doesn't mean you're a businessman, any more than a judge is a businessman! The position of medicine as a profession trusted by the public, trusted by patients, is eroding, and doctors don't feel very good about that, and well they shouldn't.

PW: *When it comes to health care, do ethics and economics necessarily clash?*
AR: Yes, they do. The market is a pretty good mechanism for distributing most goods and services according to the ability to pay and desires of the consumer. And if you have an informed consumer, given the choice of many standard products, the market works to establish some kind of satisfactory steady state in which the products that the consumer wants and is willing to pay for are going to be made available at the price that they are willing to pay. That's totally inappropriate for medicine. Health care is just not that kind of thing. It's not packaged in standard units, it can't and shouldn't be marketed, because consumer demand is not the crucial thing—it's

consumer need! And in the ordinary marketplace, the vendor, the producer is trying to stimulate desire so that the consumer will want to buy the products of the vendor. That would be terrible in health care. Unfortunately, that's what's happening—and it *is* terrible!

The public knows that medicine is not an economic good, although they have to pay for it. And doctors, in their hearts, know that what they're supposed to be doing is not selling, marketing their services, but advising and counseling patients for what they need and only what they need—and then doing only what's necessary as efficiently and prudently as possible. Until we get the commercial virus out of the health care system's body, there's going to be more of the same: a continuing spiral toward uncontrollable inflation, less equity, less access, more inefficiency, more waste, and more unhappiness—and therefore, by necessity, more constriction of doctors' freedom.

> PW: *Let's discuss the remark, "Arnold Relman represents deep down inside what each individual doctor would like the world to be like—and isn't." (James Todd, Sr, MD, deputy executive vice president of the American Medical Association, as quoted in* Boston Business.*)*
>
> AR: I'm sure that Jim Todd, who is my friend, meant that to be kind and complimentary. I'd like to believe it was well-intended, but I'm saddened all the same to hear it. As a leader of the largest professional organization, for him to be willing to accept what has happened to the medical profession, to say we all wish it were different, but that's the way it is—that's an admission of defeat. We don't need to accept the status quo. Doctors have the power to change it.

That's what I'm going to try to do. Now that I've retired from the *Journal*, I plan to write and speak out. I will be talking to the medical profession as well as to the public, and I will be telling my colleagues in the profession—and I hope the public will listen!—that we doctors have the power to reverse the deprofessionalization of medicine. If we don't, everything that we value in medicine except the technology is going to slip from our grasp. We won't even be rich any more. We surely won't be successful businessmen. And medicine will end up as kind of public utility.

A DOCTOR TO THE WORLD

ALLAN ROSENFIELD '59

Another distinguished P&S alumnus, Thomas Frieden '86, at the time NYC
Commissioner of Health, and more recently outgoing director of the Centers
for Disease Control and Prevention, said of Dr. Rosenfield: "Allan is one of
a small number of people we can say has truly improved the world, especially
for women." Dr. Rosenfield died of ALS and myasthenia gravis in 2008.
He was seventy-five.

⸺∞⸺

WHEN ALLAN ROSENFIELD '59, a legend in the field of public health and the longest serving dean of any school of public health in the nation, announced plans to retire after twenty years at the helm of the Mailman School of Public Health of Columbia University, you could practically hear a global gasp from Bangkok to Broadway. The gasp was promptly followed by a global outpouring of love that is not likely to abate any time soon.

A REVERED ADVOCATE FOR REPRODUCTIVE HEALTH AND OTHER PRESSING CAUSES

Back home in Washington Heights, he is best known for building the School of Public Health from a small department within the medical school into one of the country's most prominent schools of public health, a major institutional player in the age of AIDS and the post-9/11 era. But to the international public health community, he is first and foremost the man who put the neglected M back into MCH (Maternal Child Health) and reminded the world of the forgotten M in MTCT (Mother-to-Child-Transmission of HIV). For more than half a century he has battled mightily for the cause of reproductive health and the empowerment of women to control their own bodies and destinies.

Geeta Rao Gupta, PhD, president of the International Center for Research on Women, summed up the sentiments of many at a Global Health Community Career Tribute held in Dr. Rosenfield's honor in New York on May 31, 2006: "A man who stands for women's rights and reminds the world that a woman must not be taken for granted is definitely a hero to be worshipped. Millions of women worldwide should know that they're better off today because of your efforts."

To others, like actor Richard Gere, founder of the Gere Foundation and Healing the Divide, an activist humanitarian in the battle against AIDS and other social causes, Allan Rosenfield's name is quite simply the gold standard in public health. "Wow! Wow! Wow!" the celebrated screen star enunciated three times, and then a fourth, overwhelmed by emotion at the podium of the World Leaders Forum: Taking a Stand: Challenges and Controversies in Reproductive Health, Maternal Mortality and HIV/AIDS. The two-day event honoring Dr. Rosenfield's leadership was held June 7–8, 2006, in two massive tents on the downtown Columbia campus. The roster of distinguished speakers included UN Secretary General Kofi Annan, New York Senator Hillary Clinton, and former U.S. President Bill Clinton. "I knew he was important; I had no idea—and the reality is, I just like the guy!" Mr. Gere confided to the overflow crowd.

"In addition to his passion," President Clinton said of Allan Rosenfield, "he has something I find quite useful in the nongovernmental world. He actually knows how to get things done."

Dr. Rosenfield's astounding efficacy in making good things happen is founded upon his extensive medical knowledge and experience, a profound belief in the access to health care as a universal right, a rare ability to think out of the box, seemingly limitless stamina, and not least of all, great personal charm. Diagnosed with amyotrophic lateral sclerosis (ALS), a debilitating and often deadly degenerative disease, he has resolved to wrestle with destiny. While stepping down as dean, he will retain his academic titles and continue to be active on the world arena in causes dear to his heart as long as his health permits.

HIS SECRET WEAPON: THE ROSENFIELD SMILE

And then there's the Rosenfield smile, a joyous affirmation of life that emanates straight from the heart and rebounds in the mind, where it melds with wit, welling up in the eyes and meeting the interlocutor pupil to pupil, immediately establishing a common bond of shared humanity and neutralizing all resistance.

Nobody can say no to Allan Rosenfield.

Not Claire Stein Rosenfield, his wife of more than forty years, who, weeks after meeting him, accepted his proposal of marriage and his proposition to join him on a "working honeymoon" in Lagos, Nigeria, where he'd been hired to teach ob/gyn at the University of Lagos Medical School.

Not Phyllis Mailman, president of the Joseph L. Mailman Foundation, whose family foundation made history with the largest naming gift ever bestowed on a school of public health, thereafter the Mailman School of Public Health. "The man is a skilled sorcerer," she declared, tongue in cheek, at the aforementioned Forum. "He managed almost single-handedly to bedazzle and bum-foozle three reasonably intelligent human beings—my daughter Jodi, my son Josh, and me, who, incidentally had absolutely no connection to Columbia or to public health. He then proceeded to separate us from a significant chunk of our Foundation resources. Allan does not practice sleight of hand, he practices sleight of mind, and we are eternally grateful that he is such a master at it."

Over more than a half century in the fray, Dr. Rosenfield has refined "can do" into a formidable martial (or rather, peaceable) art.

A longtime colleague and friend, the late Dr. Georgiana Jagiello, V. G. Damon Professor of Ob/Gyn Emeritus at P&S, vividly recalled their first encounter in the office of the late Dr. Raymond Vandewiele, former chair of the Department of Ob/Gyn. Both she and Dr. Rosenfield had been recruited to collaborate in a new departmental venture, the International Institute for the Study of Human Reproduction, she to run the basic science component, the Center for Reproductive Sciences, and he to direct its public-outreach arm, the Center for Population and Family Health. "We were blathering one afternoon, Raymond and I," Dr. Jagiello remembers, "and the door bursts open and in comes this dynamo of a guy in dirty loafers, with a slightly harried look, having just flown in from Thailand. He shook hands and said, 'May I use the phone?' "—she makes the sign and sound of frenzied dialing—" 'Hello,' he says, 'is Danny Kaye there?!' Pause. 'Hey, Danny, what about that money you said you'd donate to my Center?' After a while he hung up and smiled, "I got it!" That was my first encounter with Allan Rosenfield!

"I'm sure," Dr. Jagiello adds, "he must've rubbed some people the wrong way, but I never met them, and I've been here a very long time!"

A BOSTON OBSTETRICIAN'S SON TAKES
HIS MD ON THE ROAD

Born in the Boston suburb of Brookline and educated at Harvard College, Allan Rosenfield entered P&S intending to follow in the footsteps, and eventually inherit the practice, of his father, the late Dr. Harold Rosenfield, a respected Boston obstetrician/gynecologist.

But the Korean conflict intervened, and shortly after earning his MD, young Dr. Rosenfield was drafted and served as director of hospital services at a U.S. Air Force hospital in Osan, Korea. Volunteering after hours at a local civilian hospital, he got his first taste of medicine in the developing world. While the medical resources were sparse, the doctors few, and the conditions grim, he was impressed by what could be done and gripped by a desire to pitch in.

Returning to the States to complete his ob/gyn residency at the Boston Hospital for Women, a Harvard affiliate, he decided, with the consent of his then bride-to-be, to postpone his practice and accept an offer to teach ob/gyn at the University of Lagos Medical School in Nigeria. Accustomed to the care available in major medical centers in urban America, he was struck in Nigeria by the limited access, particularly in rural areas, to maternity care and family planning services, and the resultant staggering number of deaths of women in childbirth.

To his father's initial puzzlement and dismay, rather than return to Boston to take up practice following the end of his teaching contract, Dr. Rosenfield took another "temporary" stay of postponement to work with the Population Council in Thailand as an advisor to the Thai Ministry of Public Health. A one-year leave turned into a six-year commitment. Dr. Rosenfield helped the Ministry to develop a national family planning program. Assessing the scarcity of obstetrician/gynecologists outside the cities and the underutilization of auxiliary midwives, he took the bold step of recommending that the Ministry train midwives to provide prenatal and intrapartum care. In addition, he suggested that midwives be educated and licensed to prescribe oral contraceptives. His recommendations were accepted and, as a direct consequence, millions of Thai women and their families have lived healthier lives.

The Thai experience also had a profound personal effect. Realizing that he "could have a far greater impact on the health of individuals by addressing the health needs of populations," his perspective shifted conclusively from the micro-focus of an obstetrician to the macro-concerns of a doctor of public health with a keen interest in the health and welfare of women.

PUBLIC HEALTH BACK HOME IN THE HEIGHTS

In 1975, he returned to Columbia to accept a joint appointment as professor of ob/gyn and professor of public health and to take on the reins of the newly named Center for Population and Family Health. Considering the health problems in the Medical Center's own backyard, particularly in the largely low-income Dominican immigrant population in Washington Heights, he decided that "teenage issues were the key."

In 1977 he and a young recruit, Dr. Judith Jones, established the Young Adult Clinic, the first-ever evening family planning and reproductive health clinic for adolescent girls in the neighborhood. He subsequently opened another clinic for teenage boys and innovative school-based clinics in intermediate and high schools. These programs are still alive and thriving today and have served as statewide prototypes. Dr. Rosenfield helped revitalize the health of the neighborhood, also raising funds to build an ambulatory care facility across Broadway, and in the process, helped make the Medical Center more responsive to community needs.

And in 1985, when Columbia's School of Public Health sought a new dean, Dr. Rosenfield topped the list of candidates. He took office the following year, and, building on the efforts of his two immediate predecessors, Robert J. Weiss '51 and Jack Bryant '53, he proceeded over the course of two decades to revolutionize the school's administrative structure and institutional mission.

Another eminent Columbian, William Henry Welch (P&S 1875), the acknowledged father of academic public health in this country, had taken his talents to Johns Hopkins in Baltimore, where he served as dean of the medical faculty and, thereafter, as the first director of the School of Hygiene and Public Health, an independently governed body within the university structure.

Holding up as an example the successful Hopkins model, Dr. Rosenfield convinced the trustees of Columbia University to confer independent faculty status on the School of Public Health. This was the first step in the School's meteoric rise, under Dr. Rosenfield's visionary leadership. He helped strengthen existent departments, recruiting dynamic faculty to run them, and started new programs, like the Executive Master of Public Health in Health Services Management, a degree program geared to clinicians assuming managerial roles. Other notable academic initiatives launched under his watch include the National Center for the Study of Children in Poverty and the International Prevention of Maternal Mortality Program.

"WHERE IS THE M IN MCH?"

For Dr. Rosenfield, innovative administration and independent thinking have always gone hand in hand. In 1985, he and a colleague, epidemiologist Dr. Deborah Maine, challenged the public health establishment with a seminal paper they coauthored and published in the *Lancet*, "Where is the M in MCH (Maternal and Child Health)?"

"Although in recent years much attention has been given to 'maternal and child health'," wrote Rosenfield and Maine, "scrutiny of MCH programs shows that most of them will do little to reduce maternal mortality [. . .]. The world's obstetricians are particularly neglectful of their duty in this regard."

Subsequent meetings with the World Bank were followed a year later by the first-ever meeting on maternal mortality, held in Nairobi, Kenya, where the Safe Motherhood Initiative was born. Ever sensitive to social inequities, he argued, furthermore, for a focus on women in general, not just mothers, "because not all women necessarily want to be mothers. They are often at the mercy of a lot of sexually active men."

Meanwhile, back at the fort, with the seed support of the Carnegie Corporation of New York, Drs. Rosenfield and Maine established the Prevention of Maternal Mortality Program, an international interdisciplinary effort to promote greater access by women to emergency obstetric care. And when Carnegie funds ran out, never shy of promoting a worthy cause, Dr. Rosenfield brought maternal health to the attention of the then fledgling Bill & Melinda Gates Foundation. The Foundation came through with an initial grant of $10 million, and thereafter, in 1999, with a $50 million grant, at the time the largest grant in Columbia University history, to create and support the Averting Maternal Death and Disability Program. The Program has brought emergency obstetric care to women in more than fifty countries in sub-Saharan Africa and Asia.

"WHERE IS THE M IN PMTCT (PREVENTION OF MOTHER-TO-CHILD TRANSMISSION)?"

And then came the devastating scourge of AIDS, and women were once again forgotten victims lost in the medical shuffle. In another landmark paper, "Where is the M in pMTCT (Prevention of Mother-to-Child Transmission)?," coauthored with Dr. Emily Figdor, and delivered at the World AIDS Conference in Durban, South Africa, in 2000, and later published in the *American Journal of Public Health*, Dr. Rosenfield pointed out the unconscionable flaw in treatment regimens geared to prevent mother-to-child transmission in the unborn child, regimens administered through the mother that used her as a conduit and, thereafter, left her to die.

Galvanizing global attention, and with private foundation support, Dr. Rosenfield and colleagues launched the MTCT-Plus Initiative to extend AIDS care and treatment to mothers, as well as their children. U.N. Secretary General Kofi Annan summed up its effectiveness: "Among all the initiatives that have been taken in the struggle against HIV/AIDS, none has done more than MTCT-Plus to focus attention on the situation faced by women in the pandemic." Thanks to an additional $125 million grant from the President's Emergency Plan for AIDS Relief, the largest federal grant ever awarded Columbia University, Dr. Rosenfield subsequently oversaw the creation of the International Center for AIDS Care and Treatment Programs, under the direction of Dr. Wafaa El-Sadr. Over 100,000 individuals in sub-Saharan Africa have to date benefited from treatment.

A SCHOOL (AND A BUILDING) NAMED

The figures speak for themselves in the Mailman School's astounding administrative success story under Dr. Rosenfield's watch. He expanded the School's budget from $12 million to $161 million and bolstered its endowment from $2 million to $86 million. Sponsored research has grown to $136 million, student applications have more than doubled, and the student body has grown to 915 under his tenure. Dean Rosenfield made Columbia the hot place to study public health and to help change the world for the better.

Success proved infectious.

One day in casual conversation with the lawyer of a small family foundation looking to promote health in the City, Dr. Rosenfield let slip: "You know, if you really want to make a splash, why don't you think about naming the school!"

$33 million later, the Mailman School of Public Health was named to honor the memory of philanthropist Joseph L. Mailman. His widow, Mrs. Phyllis Mailman, called the result of the family's largesse "the inspiration of a lifetime."

"The combination of the Mailman gift and the Gates grant gave us a lot of visibility we didn't have before," Dr. Rosenfield allows. "More philanthropists," he adds, "are beginning to understand the important role of public health in society."

With its facilities, faculty, and staff heretofore scattered in various buildings all over the Health Sciences campus, Dr. Rosenfield pushed to realize his long-held dream of centralizing public health educational activities at Columbia under a single roof. And when construction of the new New York State Psychiatric Institute building on Haven Avenue was completed, the dean found a home for his school in PI's old digs, the splendid nineteen-story Beaux Arts building on 168th Street.

In June 2006, Columbia University's board of trustees resolved to name that building in honor of Allan Rosenfield. In addition, a Tribute Fund has been established in his honor dedicated to the building's renovation and to the search for a worthy successor.

There are few national and international public health organizations in which Dr. Rosenfield has not played a pivotal role. Former chair of the Association of Schools of Public Health; the Executive Board of the American Public Health Association; the Scientific and Technical Advisory Committee of WHO's Human Reproductive Programme; the boards of Planned Parenthood Federation of America, EngenderHealth, and the Guttmacher Institute; the New York State Department of Health AIDS Advisory Council; and amfAR's Program Board, he was a founder of Physicians for Reproductive Choice and Health.

His countless encomia include awards from the government of Thailand, the International Federation of Obstetricians and Gynecologists, the American College of Obstetricians and Gynecologists, the Jacobs Institute of Women's Health, the American Public Health Association, and a Special Recognition Award from the P&S Alumni Association. He was honored more recently with the New York Academy of Medicine's Stephen Smith Award for Lifetime Achievement in Public Health, the Doctors of the World (USA) Health and Human Rights Leadership Award, and Planned Parenthood Federation of America's Margaret Sanger Award. The list goes on and on.

In the course of a televised interview on PBS, Dr. Rosenfield came pretty close to summing up his public health credo: "If you empower women so that they're equal," he said, "it changes society, it changes their role, it changes the future." That future looks a little brighter for women and the global family, thanks to Allan Rosenfield.

KIDNEYS ARE COLOR-BLIND

VELMA SCANTLEBURY '81

In 2008, Velma Scantlebury '81 relocated to Delaware to serve as director of the Kidney Transplant Program of the Christiana Care Health System.

⸙

"IT HELPED, for one thing, to be stubborn," Velma Scantlebury '81 allows. The photographs of Sojourner Truth and Harriet Tubman that grace the wall of her office at The University of South Alabama, in Mobile, where she is professor of surgery and director of transplantation, epitomize the kind of stubbornness she means. Her smile is serene. Her hands, once deemed "too small for a surgeon," have cut and stitched their way through more than 200 living donor and more than 800 deceased donor kidney transplants in children and adults, as well as myriad other complicated organ transplants. "Small hands can be better than big hands in surgery, especially when you're working on kids," she affirms, from her extensive experience in pediatric transplantation. Stubborn indeed, Dr. Scantlebury, the first and for many years the only African American woman transplant surgeon in the country, graciously agreed to look back on her career in the course of an interview at her office in Mobile in November 2006.

UNDAUNTED BY EARLY EDUCATIONAL HURDLES

The untimely death of an older sister first sparked her desire to become a doctor. A native of Barbados, she came to the United States as a child and

settled in Brooklyn, N.Y., where her parents believed she would have a better educational opportunity to pursue that dream. But unexpected hurdles stood in the way.

"High school was terrible," Dr. Scantlebury recalls, "my potential did not come forth and I was viewed as a quiet nerd." And when she sought advice for college applications, a high school guidance counselor bluntly told her to forget about higher education and get a job at a hospital instead. Sticking to her guns, she applied and was accepted to Barnard College, with an offer of a one-year scholarship. Concerned by the financial burden for her family, she ultimately decided to attend the Brooklyn campus of Long Island University (LIU), which offered her a complete four-year scholarship. And though she made the dean's list with honors and thrived academically at LIU, one of her professors, no doubt disappointed that his hand-picked favorites hadn't made the grade, merely shrugged upon learning of her acceptance to Yale Medical School and P&S. The only reason she got into medical school, one of her college mates suggested, was "because they needed a token black."

SURGERY, LOVE AT FIRST CUT:
FROM P&S TO HARLEM HOSPITAL

At P&S, she welcomed the camaraderie of fellow students in the Black and Latino Student Organization and the support of Dr. Margaret Haynes, then director of the Minority Student Office. And from the start of her first-year gross anatomy class at P&S, she knew she wanted to become a surgeon. "While everybody else seemed eager to get out of the anatomy classroom, because of the smell, I was fascinated," she recalls, "by all the connections . . . the nerves and muscles and circulatory system . . . It was a really big turn-on for me to go from body to body and study the different functions and abnormalities."

In her senior year, she participated in research and coauthored a scientific paper on endoscopic polypectomy with Kenneth Forde '59, Jose M. Ferrer Professor of Clinical Surgery Emeritus and a newly elected Columbia University trustee, who, as an African American and fellow native of Barbados, was a powerful role model. But to her great dismay, though she enjoyed her surgical rotation, other members of the surgical faculty discouraged her from pursuing surgery, her preceptor going so far as to withhold his recommendation, offering, instead, to recommend her for pediatric training.

Part of her problem, she believes, as a woman of color discouraged from asserting herself, was that she lacked the aggressive manner needed to get ahead: "I grew up not talking a lot. I was always the one in the corner reading the book. But I had to force myself to be aggressive. This timid, quiet person was really working to my detriment." Observing the forthright behavior of some other medical students, she realized, especially in the interview process for residencies, "you had to show off, ask questions, and that was very difficult for me."

Despite the discouragement, she once again held her ground: "Well, I'm going to do this! I'm going to apply and I'm going to get in! Because they said I couldn't!" She ultimately went on to complete an internship and residency in general surgery at Harlem Hospital, where doors began to open.

There, for the first time, she found a woman surgeon to emulate, a true mentor in Dr. Barbara Barlow, then the director of pediatric surgery: "She was very encouraging. She led me, taught me, gave me advice, groomed me, and told me I needed to do research, and then she made the opportunity for me to spend time in transplantation surgery under Dr. Mark Hardy." Dr. Scantlebury spent six months in the lab with Dr. Hardy, assisting him in his research on renal flow experiments in kidney transplantation in animal models. And though, at the time, she viewed this research primarily as a prerequisite for a future career in pediatric surgery, it would prove to be a propitious experience.

TRANSPLANTATION IN PITTSBURGH

Dr. Mark Ravitch, then the director of the pediatric surgery program at the University of Pittsburgh, where she applied, advised her that additional research background would improve her chances of admittance to the highly competitive program, and recommended she pursue her interest in transplantation at Pittsburgh under the legendary transplant surgeon Dr. Thomas E. Starzl. Dr. Starzl interviewed and promptly admitted her for training. Her intense and challenging two-year fellowship in transplantation, 1986–1988, set her on the path of her life's work.

"There was such a need for clinical fellows to take care of transplant patients back then," she recalls, "that we never even had time to set foot in the lab." And, after the first year, she realized, "well, I've got another year to do and then perhaps two more years of pediatric surgery—I was inspired by all aspects of transplantation surgery, especially the ability to perform pediatric transplantation. And so I decided to stay with transplantation full time."

And while most of the other fellows found it too emotionally draining to transplant children, because of the high mortality rate at the time, though she, too, found it tough, she embraced the surgical and emotional challenge and ultimately focused on pediatric as well as adult transplants.

"I DON'T LIKE BEING BORED."

Once lovingly confronted by her mother, who suggested that she always appeared to pursue the most difficult tasks, Dr. Scantlebury conceded a fondness for challenges: "Maybe I chose to always be up against another hurdle, maybe that's what makes me thrive. I don't like being bored.

"It really was the boot camp of fellowships," she admits in retrospect of her training in Pittsburgh. With few compliments forthcoming, Dr. Starzl held his fellows to the same high standard to which he held himself: "No matter how much you busted your chops in the OR, there was always something that could have been done better." The fellows were expected to participate in the entire process, from harvesting the organs to conferring with the families, whatever the outcome.

She still remembers the emotional roller-coaster ride of her first transplant, an adult patient with a liver tumor who came in for a resection and was told that a transplant was his only hope of survival. The patient's family initially balked at her doing the transplant, but the senior attending held his ground. A liver was located and flown in, but even as Dr. Scantlebury performed the transplant, she sensed that something was wrong with that liver. "Oh, no, no, no, not my first case!" she said to herself. Still, she kept her cool. "I'm going to be upfront with you," she told the family, "I don't know whether this liver is going to work or not." As it turned out, the liver was damaged and needed to be replaced. She subsequently transplanted another liver and the patient survived: "I ended up being good friends with that family for years. My honesty paid off."

While kidneys and livers are color-blind, patients and their families are not. "In the beginning, yes, people felt uncomfortable, not only with a female, but a black female, doing the transplant; it was very humiliating, degrading," she remembers. There were times when a patient demanded: "Nurse, pass the bedpan!" Or: "I'm ready to go home and I have yet to see the real doctor!" " 'Well, who do you think I am?!' I wanted to scream."

But her stubborn streak helped her keep a stiff upper lip and a steady hand. "I remember one patient in Pittsburgh who didn't want to be transplanted by me. And I said, 'I'm okay with that.' I got to the point where I saw it as their loss, not mine, just ignorance on their part."

Dr. Scantlebury was invited to stay on at Pittsburgh following the conclusion of her fellowship and in 1988 joined the faculty in the Department of Surgery, rising to the rank of associate professor. She also helped launch a living kidney donor program and eventually specialized in performing live kidney transplants in pediatric and adult cases.

At Pittsburgh, she also conducted landmark research on transplantation and pregnancy. It had previously been the rule to discourage patients from getting pregnant, as the potential effect of the posttransplant drugs on the fetus was not known. But as it turned out, a number of patients were already pregnant prior to the transplant. Dr. Scantlebury conducted a study of the birth defects and prematurity in their offspring. Over time, with data in hand, she was able to advise patients of child-bearing age regarding the necessary precautions for healthy births: "Now we tell them, if you want to have a child, wait at least a twelve to fifteen months to make sure you're stable and outside the rejection period."

She is the coauthor of more than eighty-five peer-reviewed papers and ten monographs and book chapters

MOBILE BECKONS

In 1996, another former fellow and friend, Dr. Ferdinand Ukah, a native of Nigeria in Africa, established the University of South Alabama Regional Transplant Center, in Mobile. But Dr. Ukah met his untimely death that same year, and the program subsequently floundered. The program was later managed by Dr. Barry Brown, who left four years later.

Then in 2002, Dr. Scantlebury moved to Mobile to join the surgical faculty as a full professor and to put the program back on its feet: "I wanted to make it work, in part because this was my friend Ferdinand's dream, and in part, because it was a new challenge and time to move on." In addition, she relished the educational aspect of her new job, particularly the educational outreach to the African American community regarding the availability of and need for transplantation. Cognizant of Alabama's less-than-rosy history in regard to race relations, she hoped to help redress the staggering disparity, particularly in the South, between the low number of blacks being transplanted and that of whites. Roughly two-thirds of her patients are African American. They come from a wide perimeter that includes south Alabama, the neighboring gulf coast of Mississippi to the west, and the panhandle of Florida to the east.

"My passion," she was quoted in a recent profile in Ebony magazine, "is to educate the African American community and to empower dialysis patients with the knowledge and understanding that they too can have a better life through the gift of transplantation."

Balmy Mobile has proven a climatic relief from Pittsburgh's long, chilly winters. The proximity to the water, reminiscent of Barbados, was another plus. Her husband, Harvey White, PhD, is professor of public and international affairs at the University of Pittsburgh and president-elect of the National Association of Public Administrators. With two tight academic schedules and two teenage daughters, they have managed to survive and thrive despite the strains of a long-distance, frequent flyer marriage.

Dr. Scantlebury maintains a tight daily regimen. Up at 5:30, she drops her daughters off at school and scrubs in at the OR by 7:30. If no new cases are scheduled, she proceeds to her clinic visits, seeing posttransplant patients on Mondays and Thursdays, doing pretransplant evaluation on Tuesdays and Wednesdays. But the contingencies of transplant surgery demand her being on call at all times, whenever kidneys become available. She currently performs about thirty-five kidney transplants a year.

Outside the OR, the biggest challenge, she says, is maintaining longevity. The average survival time for a kidney is ten to fifteen years for a living donor kidney transplant and eight years for a deceased organ transplant. "We're good at controlling acute rejection early on, but we still don't have a good handle on controlling the chronic destruction that occurs over time."

Another challenge, particularly in caring for the economically hard-hit population of south Alabama, is finding the funds to pay for essential post-transplant drugs. Medicare covers 80 percent of the cost of medications for the first three years after transplantation. Beyond that, as Dr. Scantlebury bluntly puts it: "You're on your own, honey! Medicare expects people to get a job and go back to work, but not everybody is able to do that." Many of her patients are either uninsured or underinsured. With Medicare copays sometimes running as high as $500–$800 a month, family budgets are strained beyond the limit. Consequently, patients stretch their medications to make them last, kidneys fail, and they return to dialysis. "It's a medical Catch 22," Dr. Scantlebury concedes. She and a social worker do their best to squeeze the government and the pharmaceutical companies to try and help her patients remain compliant.

GETTING THE WORD OUT

A fellow of the American College of Surgeons, Dr. Scantlebury is a member of the American Society of Transplant Surgeons and the American Society of Minority Health and Transplant Professionals, among other organizations. She also sits on numerous boards and committees, including Donate Life America, the National Minority Organ and Tissue Transplant Education Program, and the United Network for Organ Sharing.

Listed in Who's Who of American Women, she was twice voted among the Best Doctors in America by Pittsburgh Magazine, and was the recipient of the Outstanding Young Women of America Annual Award, the Black Achievers Award, and the Lifetime Achievement Award of the American Society of Minority Health and Transplant Professionals, as well as honorary doctor of science degrees from Seton Hill College in Pennsylvania and from her undergraduate alma mater LIU.

She has given countless lectures and presentations at professional meetings and public forums and has frequently been interviewed in documentaries and on radio and TV.

Of equal importance, she takes every opportunity to speak to students and their parents, urging young people not to "let the negative perceptions of others sink into you to become your own perception of who you are," and urging parents to "encourage your young ones, whatever their dreams and aspirations."

Though wanting at this point in her career to slow down some and spend a bit more quality time with her family, she remains passionately committed to her work. "I've always said that I would not retire till there are at least ten other African American women in transplantation." Currently there is one other African American female transplant surgeon active in Los Angeles. With nine more to go, Dr. Scantlebury will still have her hands full for a while.

THE HANDS-ON SURGEON-IN-CHIEF OF THE HOSPITAL FOR SPECIAL SURGERY

THOMAS P. SCULCO '69

In 2014, Thomas P. Sculco '69 stepped down as surgeon-in-chief of the Hospital for Special Surgery, a position he held with great distinction for eleven years, returning to full-time clinical practice.

—⊶∘∘⊷—

THOMAS P. SCULCO '69, surgeon-in-chief and medical director of the Hospital for Special Surgery (HSS), the institutional gold standard in orthopedic care, and himself a world-renowned orthopedic surgeon specializing in hip and knee replacement, likes to recount a conversation he had with one of his most famous patients, the late, great Vladimir Horowitz. Dr. Sculco first treated the maestro's wife, Wanda, and subsequently attended to a knee problem Horowitz was having. When on their first meeting the piano virtuoso, well into his eighties at the time, extended his hand to shake, the orthopedist asked: "Mr. Horowitz, aren't you concerned that I might crush your fingers by shaking your hand?" "Well, Dr. Sculco, you're a surgeon, aren't you?" the pianist replied with a wink. "You have as much respect for your hands as I have for mine, so I have no problem shaking yours."

After more than 10,000 total hip replacements and countless replaced knees, those expert hands are still going strong. Dr. Sculco graciously agreed to an interview at his office at the Hospital for Special Surgery, in New York, in September 2013.

Founded in 1863, the Hospital for Special Surgery, the biggest and arguably the preeminent musculoskeletal center in the world, has been described as a highly tertiary medical center in a community hospital setting. With a staff of some 100 orthopedic surgeons that conduct some 28,000 orthopedic operations a year, HSS has, amazingly enough, in the view of its surgeon-in-chief, "retained its relatively collegial family kind of feel. [. . .] Everybody knows everybody. Everybody cares about everybody."

Much like the institution over which he presides, and at which he has spent his entire professional career, Dr. Sculco manages to perform at the top of his game while maintaining a down-to-earth, unassuming manner. A native of Westerly, R.I., where his grandfather had migrated as a stone cutter from Italy, and where his father, a Julliard-trained jazz trumpeter who played with big band legends Tommy Dorsey, Harry James, and Benny Goodman, retired from the limelight to teach music at the local schools, Dr. Sculco still retains a healthy helping of small town civility. His open smile and seemingly easygoing way belie a fierce commitment to his calling, to the people in his care, and to those who report to him. Benjamin Bjerke-Kroll '09, a third-year surgical resident, calls him "a model mentor. A caring and compassionate surgeon and hard-working leader, Dr. Sculco manages to strike a rare balance of personability and professionalism with his patients and those lucky enough to train with him. He makes himself available to his residents whenever possible. You just want to be like him."

FROM THE CLASSICS TO ORTHOPEDICS

His was not a typical path to medicine and orthopedic surgery. A classics major at Brown University, Thomas Sculco originally aspired to become an archeologist. He was also intrigued by and did extremely well in biology, zoology, and comparative anatomy, but did not take the full complement of premed classes. Impressed by his academic performance and his potential, the chair of the Department of Biology at Brown asked him, "Did you ever think about medical school?" Which got young Sculco thinking. A beloved uncle was a neurosurgeon. On a whim he applied to just one medical school, P&S, figuring if it didn't work out he'd head off to Athens for a dig at the ancient Agora, in which he was scheduled to participate. In an admissions interview with the legendary P&S professor of medicine, Yale Kneeland '26, "your classic wise old internist," who likewise came to medicine from a background in the humanities, they mostly discussed the virtues of studying Latin. And to the applicant's great surprise and delight, shortly thereafter he received an acceptance letter. The beneficiary of a generous scholarship, Dr. Sculco returned the favor many years later by endowing a named scholarship at P&S.

Dr. Sculco fondly recalls Dr. Kneeland's eloquence and wit in his class on physical diagnosis, his presentations always replete with memorable and mnemonic bon mots, including a description that leapt to mind of one particular heart murmur as "sounding like a humming bird flapping its wings." Other favorite P&S faculty members were Drs. Malcolm Carpenter in neuroanatomy and P. R. Srinivasan in biochemistry.

Readily acknowledging that he has to date never met another classics major in orthopedic surgery, Dr. Sculco nevertheless believes that a background in the classics, and the humanities in general, "allows you to approach the patient in a holistic way." Given the clear sentence structure, Latin, he also firmly believes, teaches intellectual problem solving. "Medicine is problem solving. You take all the data, the history, the physical, the x-rays, the lab work, you put it together and synthesize it, and you come up with a solution. Latin helps you organize your thought process into a problem-solving mode. Taking the data, namely taking apart the sentence, and putting the pieces back together, proved a great mental discipline [. . .] ideally suited to the practice of medicine."

While he did have to buckle down and study extra hard in the basic sciences in the first two years to catch up on classes he had not taken, he hit his stride in the clinical experience: "The interaction with patients is what really grabbed me and made me love medicine."

Another dedicated mentor at P&S, Dr. Keith McElroy, a Canadian orthopedic surgeon on the clinical faculty, his preceptor for his orthopedics rotation, inspired him to enter the field: "He got me very excited about all the amazing things you could do. Total hip replacements had just been introduced. You could see people who came in crippled and walked out with a smile. It seemed like a very uplifting specialty."

Pursuing an internship and residency in general surgery at Roosevelt Hospital, he followed up with a three-year residency in orthopedic surgery at the Hospital for Special Surgery. After winning a prestigious Bowen-Brooks Scholarship from the New York Academy of Medicine that took him abroad to study orthopedic practice in several countries, he fulfilled his military service as an orthopedic surgeon at Andrews Air Force Base, in Maryland. He then returned to New York to join the clinical faculty in the Department of Surgery (orthopedics) at Cornell University Medical College and the staff at the Hospital for Special Surgery. He was named professor of clinical surgery (orthopedics) in 1991 and professor of orthopaedic surgery at Cornell in 2002, and appointed director of Orthopedic Surgery and chief of the Surgical Arthritic Service at HSS in 1993, and surgeon-in-chief and medical director in 2003.

THE ART AND CRAFT OF HIP AND KNEE REPLACEMENT, ACCORDING TO DR. SCULCO

Dr. Sculco likes to listen to classical music to aid concentration as he directs his surgical team through the three "movements" of an operation: "The beginning part of an operation, essentially the exposure, is usually pretty routine, how you get into the hip. But then you get into the guts of the operation, and it becomes more intense. Now you've got to create a new socket, a new femur. Everything gets relatively quiet until you get the hip or knee in. The next, and last, part of the operation is the closure, and that's more relaxed. The hard work is done, you're happy with what you've accomplished.

"As a rule, you want it all to be fairly routine. It's when it slips out of the routine that problems occur!" Dr. Sculco cautions. Ten thousand total hip replacements and innumerable knees into the game, the seasoned orthopedic surgeon teaches his residents to respect the creative challenge. "Every hip is a little different. You are, after all, taking something that's abnormal, and you've got to create something that is as normal as you can get it once you've replaced it. There's a great deal of creativity involved, particularly in the more complex cases. It calls for problem solving skills, some engineering, some sculpting, and of course a cool hand."

He still recalls one of his first cases, that of an elderly lady with a severely malformed hip: "I'd been in practice for maybe two weeks, three at the most. The hip was completely dislocated, an arthritic and old congenital hip problem, the worst I'd ever seen. I showed the x-ray to my old mentor, Philip D. Wilson, Jr. '44. I said: 'I know I can do this case, but would you mind scrubbing in with me?' It all went beautifully, absolutely no problem. I did the whole operation myself. [. . .] But I always tell young surgeons: Beware of surgical hubris! Never be too proud to ask for help and advice! You can risk bruising your ego. Always remember it's the patient that matters most."

AN INNOVATOR IN THE OR

Ever an innovator in surgical technique, Dr. Sculco helped develop less-invasive approaches. "In the past," he says, "we were more radical than we needed to be with our incisions and our exposures. That increased blood loss and interfered with recovery. Bottom line, the function was delayed." In the course of streamlining the operation, Dr. Sculco developed a series of instruments: "A few of them are patented, but all are out there for other surgeons to use. I'm happy to say that a lot of people, a lot of companies have copied them."

Also interested in anesthetic technique, he championed the use of regional anesthesia: "It's safer than total anesthesia, particularly in older patients. There's much less morbidity, they bleed less. So hospital stay is reduced and they're out and on their feet, and back to their normal life in less time."

Dr. Sculco's interest in successful outcomes also extends to the lab. He has been engaged for a number of years in basic scientific research trying to mitigate the effects of osteolysis, a reaction to wear of implants that produces inflammation and breaks down the bond between the implant and the bone. "We are trying to define the cellular mechanisms triggered by wear debris or reaction to wear debris, causing an inflammation that activates the osteoclast, a cell that can resorb bone and break down the bond between implant and bone," he says. He has published extensively on this and other basic scientific and clinical issues relating to joint replacement surgery.

THE HSS SURGEON-IN-CHIEF KEEPS ONE FOOT IN THE OR

His work week is carved out and carefully paced. Monday is reserved for administrative meetings, often from 6:45 A.M. until after 8 P.M. Tuesdays he schedules meetings in the morning, then sees patients. Wednesdays he operates. Thursdays he mostly takes care of institutional business, meeting with departmental heads at Cornell Medical College, chiefs at New York Hospital, and often also with members of the board of directors of HSS. Fridays he operates. He also operates one Saturday a month.

"In a lot of orthopedic departments when somebody becomes chair oftentimes they stop being clinically active. At this institution that doesn't work very well, because you need to be in the trenches," he points out. "I'm in the OR several times a week, where I'm walking around, talking to the different nurses, and talking to the technicians, so I get a good feel of how the place is running. Plus, I'm a surgeon, I like doing surgery. I don't want to be sitting behind a desk in my office all day."

For Dr. Sculco, postoperative interaction with patients is not just a professional responsibility, it also satisfies a personal need: "You can be down. Say something didn't go well, you're down about it. You keep telling yourself: I wish I had done it *this* way! Then you see patients for follow-up appointments.

A patient will tell you: 'Your surgery really changed my life!' And it just rejuvenates you. And all of a sudden you find that the issues you were fretting about seem to go away. That's what makes medicine what it is. Despite all the headaches and the bureaucracy we have to deal with, nothing can take away from the fact that you have a unique relationship with another human being. It's a special bond. That's why I love what I do."

His office is filled with treasured tokens of appreciation from grateful patients, including artworks by sculptors Mark Di Suvero and Donald Gummer, calligraphy from China, a ritual bejeweled dagger from a Saudi Arabian princess, and a bronze representation of a pair of healthy knees.

"I'M A GLOBALIST. I LIKE TO KNOW HOW THINGS ARE DONE ELSEWHERE."

The aforementioned Bowen-Brooks Scholarship from the New York Academy of Medicine, which took him to top specialty hospitals in Finland, Switzerland, Holland, Italy, and Great Britain, not only gave him a privileged first-hand look at orthopedic practice abroad but also instilled a lifelong passion for intellectual border crossings.

"I'm a globalist," he says, "I've been a globalist all my life. I want to know how things are done in other countries, learn from and borrow the best, and bring the knowledge back home."

Years later he would apply the same eagerness to engage in international dialogue to help found and direct the Bone and Joint Seminars in Salzburg, Austria, to train orthopedic surgeons from Eastern and Central Europe. The program has since evolved into an educational forum for young surgeons from all over the world. In recognition of his pivotal role, in 2013 he was awarded the Austrian Cross of Honor, First Class, for Science and Art. Dr. Sculco has been saluted with innumerable other honors in the course of his career, including the 1991 Hip Society's Otto Aufranc Award and its 1995 Charnley Award, the 1999 Arthritis Foundation Lifetime Achievement Award, and the 2005 P&S Alumni Gold Medal for Outstanding Achievements in Clinical Medicine. A member of the Hip Society and founding member and president of the Knee Society, he has served on the board of directors of the American Academy of Orthopedic Surgeons and is currently on the board of directors of the Arthritis Foundation.

As if he did not already have enough on his agenda, he was the driving force in 2005 in the establishment of the International Society of Orthopedic

Centers, of which he is executive director. Now comprising some seventeen member institutions on four continents, the Society brings together musculoskeletal specialists from the top academic institutions to share cutting-edge research findings and innovations in patient care. The format, according to an article in the journal *Medical Meetings* (Sept./Oct. 2010), "is designed to foster idea generation and collaboration rather than simply disseminate knowledge." In Dr. Sculco's words: "Here you have the biggest players [in orthopedic surgery] around the table, a group of very talented and very experienced people trying to resolve the issues we share and to learn from each other." Every meeting also includes a cultural program, often a concert. It helps with the harmony.

Dr. Sculco also has established an exchange program with China and travels there once or twice a year to teach and on occasion perform surgery. He has established a symposium run by HSS on hip and knee replacement that has been featured at the Chinese Orthopedic Association meeting in Beijing for the past three years. He regularly has a Chinese research fellow working with him. Aside from the clinical and research aspects of his Chinese connection, he enjoys trying to speak the few words of Mandarin that he knows and especially eating Peking Duck.

Outside the OR and the committee room, music remains for him an abiding passion. His favorite way to unwind is to attend a concert with his wife, Cynthia. A member of the faculty of the College of Nursing at NYU, Mrs. Sculco received her MEd and EdD from Columbia Teachers College. They have two children, daughter, Sarah Jane, a college guidance counselor at Millennium High School in Brooklyn, and son, Peter '09, an orthopedic senior resident at HSS. Dr. Sculco also serves on the board of directors of Carnegie Hall. "Some colleagues like to play golf or go to the beach, some like skiing," he says. "The ideal vacation for me is to travel with my wife to Salzburg and in a week's time take in five operas and maybe three or four concerts."

In a memorable appearance as a guest on "Mad About Music," Gilbert Kaplan's popular radio show on WQXR, Dr. Sculco recounted how once, upon hearing Herbert von Karajan direct the Vienna Philharmonic in a performance of Bruckner's Eighth Symphony at Carnegie Hall, he leaned over to his wife and whispered, "If they're playing music in heaven, this is what they're playing."

Back home on the planet Earth in the meantime, Dr. Sculco devotes most of his waking moments to conducting the affairs, setting the tempo, maintaining harmony, and ensuring optimal outcomes at the Hospital for Special Surgery, where he recently completed a second term at the helm.

THE ASSISTANT SECRETARY FOR HEALTH
IS A DOCTOR FIRST AND FOREMOST

EVE SLATER '71

Since stepping down as U.S. Assistant Secretary for Health, Eve Slater '71 has returned to teaching at P&S as a member of the clinical faculty in the Department of Medicine and serves on a number of boards of foundations and biotech companies.

⸻

IT'S A HOP, skip, and a jump from her office in the Hubert Humphrey Building, headquarters of the U.S. Department of Health and Human Services, where the nation's health policy is shaped, to the Capitol building, where health-related bills await their turn to be debated, before, politics willing, passing into law. The proximity is both exhilarating and daunting to Eve Slater '71, Assistant Secretary for Health, whose job description includes oversight of the U.S. Public Health Service. "Every once in a while," Dr. Slater admits, "you pinch yourself and say, this is me, I'm really here." Not that she's had much time to sit back and enjoy the view!

SOS ANTHRAX: A PUBLIC HEALTH CALL TO ACTION

Officially confirmed on January 25, 2002, though she put in time well before that, the new Assistant Secretary of Health and helmswoman of the Office of Public Health and Science hit the ground running. At 9 A.M. sharp, on the very first day she reported to work, the telephone rang and the first report came through of a postal worker admitted to the Washington Hospital

Center with anthrax infection. "So, literally, my first few months in office were spent with daily—three or four times a day—meetings and briefings and huddles," she says. In a coordinated effort under the aegis of the Department of Health and Human Services, the Public Health Service, the Centers for Disease Control and Prevention, and the Food and Drug Administration leapt into action, opening lines of communication with health officials, hospitals, and law enforcement in the affected areas, recommending precautionary measures and appropriate treatment, ultimately controlling the problem and helping to curtail the widespread panic—though the culprit(s) have not been nabbed to date.

And while the nation was shaken to the core and is still suffering the ramifications of 9/11, the anthrax attack, and the protracted war on terror, Dr. Slater takes some solace in the heightened public awareness. "One of the few positive things that came out of all this," she says, "is a rekindled interest in public health. We had been in a heyday of wealth and prosperity and what I term 'designer medicine.' You got new hips, you got new hearts, you got new genes—maybe. And sure it was expensive, but the entrepreneurs were basically going full speed ahead, assuming there was going to be a market. In the meantime, for all intents and purposes, people forgot about public health."

In the wake of 9/11, Dr. Slater believes, "America has awakened to the common good, that we *do* need a public health infrastructure. We need to worry about the kids in the inner cities who aren't getting immunized. We need to worry about our senior citizens in nursing homes who are being overmedicated on the wrong medicines. I think, ultimately, we've come to realize that we're all in this together."

SORROW'S SILVER LINING: THE WILL TO REBUILD THE PUBLIC HEALTH ADMINISTRATION

Bristling at some critics' suggestions that in focusing on bioterrorism and homeland security Washington may be neglecting other pressing public health concerns—"That would be a cheap accusation!"—Dr. Slater is convinced that the new precautionary measures being set in place will ultimately benefit the entire system.

"Under the Bio-terrorism Bill, yes, the first priority is to make sure our citizens are not exposed to undue risk from bio-threats, and to make sure that the states can respond to a nuclear, biological or chemical attack. But in so doing," she points out, "we're rebuilding the public health system. This is the money that we've so desperately needed to put back into the states to rebuild the infrastructure. So just because they develop a list of the elderly invalids in nursing homes who might need a smallpox vaccination, that same list can be used for flu immunization." The same electronic communications system and administrative infrastructure now being installed in various states to facilitate rapid response in case of attack, she adds, will likewise facilitate response to AIDS, "an enemy in some ways far worse than Mr. Bin Laden, obesity and other pressing public health needs."

"Clearly, one can never deny the power of money," the Assistant Secretary acknowledged in the Charles Leighton Memorial Lecture that she delivered October 19, 2002, at the Leonard Davis Institute of Health Economics of the University of Pennsylvania. Her talk, entitled "Fostering Innovation in Medicine and Research," stressed the government's role as a facilitator of private initiative and referee of quality control. While crediting the importance of a strong federal commitment to biomedical research, she underlined the substantial investment of funds and brainpower of the private sector. As the former senior vice president of Merck Research Laboratories (the first woman to attain this rank in the company), Dr. Slater herself helped harvest the fruits of innovation.

In the course of her close to eighteen-year tenure at Merck, she was responsible for, among other notable accomplishments, the rapid approval of Crixivan to treat HIV infection, and helped hasten the approval of major medicines to treat hypertension, cardiovascular disease, osteoporosis, asthma, arthritis, prostate disease, and vaccines for chicken pox and *Haemophilus influenzae*.

Her erstwhile boss and fellow P&S alumnus, P. Roy Vagelos '54, retired chair and CEO of Merck & Co, salutes her appointment. "As head of regulatory functions at Merck," Dr. Vagelos recalls, "Eve was a superb spokeswoman because she understood the science so well, therefore bridging the gap between what is accomplished in the lab and what will have an impact on humans and human disease. The Department of Health and Human Services is an important new challenge and another place where she will, I'm quite sure, make important contributions to human health."

Dr. Herbert Pardes, president of New York-Presbyterian Hospital and former dean of P&S, likewise sings her praises. "She's so smart, so articulate, so astute about all aspects of health policy," Dr. Pardes reports. "It's wonderful to have such a talented physician—and a P&S graduate to boot—in a top leadership position in health policy making."

FROM ACADEMIC MEDICINE TO MERCK TO WASHINGTON

Dr. Slater has long been a leader, mastering multiple professional challenges in the course of her career, and in the process knocking down a gender barrier or two. In 1976, she became the first woman to be appointed chief resident in medicine at the Massachusetts General Hospital—"I was just the natural person to pick as I love to teach." She subsequently served there as chief of the Hypertension Unit and joined the faculty of Harvard Medical School, rising to the rank of assistant professor of medicine in 1979. Directing laboratory research funded by the National Institutes of Health and the American Heart Association, she published widely on biochemical mechanisms in blood pressure control and diseases of the aorta while simultaneously devoting much of her time to teaching and patient care.

Recognition was not slow in coming. In 1977, she was one of the recipients of the Ten Outstanding Young Leaders of Boston Award and the following year made *Who's Who of American Women*. In 1981, *Boston Magazine* included her in its list of "Boston's 100 New Female Leaders," *Next Magazine* ranked her among the "100 Most Powerful People for the Eighties," and the *Journal of the American Med-*

ical Women's Association wrote up her accomplishments in its "Profile of a Young Achiever." Among her more recent honors, Dr. Slater was the recipient of the 2003 Virginia Kneeland Frantz '22 Distinguished Woman in Medicine Award at P&S.

OF MUSIC, MEDICINE, AND MOTHERHOOD

Her extra-medical achievements hardly lagged behind. A talented flutist, Dr. Slater appeared in 1975 as a soloist with Arthur Fiedler and the Boston Pops. Having started playing the flute early in life, she studied with some of America's foremost flutists, including Murray Panitz of the Philadelphia Orchestra and Julius Baker, first flutist of the New York Philharmonic.

Harmonic skills would come in handy in raising her two sons, Peter and James, now both college students. In the commencement speech she gave at James's graduation from the Newark Academy on June 9, 2002, a speech that eloquently linked the needs of science, society, and the soul, she noted that being a mother is "my most distinguished title."

But the balancing act of family and professional life was not always easy. "I think it's harder on women because of conflicting expectations," she maintains. "Women invest so much in their careers and then, all of a sudden, oops, you've got kids, and as you know, parenting is a 100 percent full-time job unto itself. And then you've got to get very good at juggling your time."

Fortunately, she says, "medicine has loosened up a little. They've allowed more flex time, larger group practices, half-time jobs for women with families, all of which is moving in the right direction."

"THE WHOLE EDUCATIONAL EXPERIENCE AT P&S REALLY SOLD ME ON MEDICINE."

As a Vassar undergraduate, though intrigued by biology, Eve Slater initially contemplated a professional career in music. Then one day, out of the blue, her father, an MIT-trained theoretical mathematician-turned actuary, suggested: "Well, what about medicine?" "Who *me*?! I hate the sight of blood!" was her knee-jerk response. "And plus," she added, "I would never want the responsibility." Whereupon her father replied, "Well, if you don't take the responsibility, who will?" His words hit home.

Her first choice of medical school was P&S. "If I don't like it," she figured, "I can always drop out and go to Julliard." At P&S, she played with the Bard Hall Orchestra and managed to squeeze in musical lessons on the side with master flutist Julius Baker, still a dear friend. But it was the art of medicine that really captured her imagination: "Once I arrived on the wards and actually started taking care of patients, the decision was very clear. The whole educational experience at P&S really sold me on medicine."

Dr. Slater credits the influence of such "truly inspiring teachers" as Drs. Paul Marks, John Loeb, the late Andy Frantz, Henry Azar, and the late Sven Kister and Arthur Wertheim, among many others: "They were all just so good at what they did and, clearly, so happy in their professional lives."

Women in medicine were still a distinct minority at the time. She has stayed in touch with several other women in her class, all of whom are in active practice today. Though she cannot recall any overt gender-related hostility in medical school, she acknowledges, in hindsight, that "over the years, women have had to evolve their own personal style of expressing themselves. Many of us have struggled with an identity issue of how aggressive or unaggressive to be. Since there were fewer of us back then than there are now, people were kind of looking at us with microscopes. It was a fine balance to figure out how to come across." Unfazed by such close attention, it was only a matter of time before Dr. Slater turned the lens around and began to look outwards at the big picture.

THE CALL TO PUBLIC SERVICE

"I had no political background at all," she recalls. "But gradually, I came to realize the importance to the practice of medicine of the health debates that occur on the floor of the Congress. So, increasingly, I became more involved, I read and learned. And actually, my last year at Merck—though I didn't know then it was going to be my last—I switched into a position concerned with external policy that put me right at the interface between the private sector, academic medicine, and government."

The fact that another high-profile MD, the then newly elected Senate Majority Leader, Senator Bill Frist from Tennessee, a surgeon by training, was making waves in Washington, prompted the question: Should more M.D.s get involved in government?

Dr. Slater is careful in her response. "The simple answer is, of course, yes. The more you're aware of what's going on, the more you can have a say in what's going on, instead of just simply letting it all happen." She cautions, however, against the dangers of information overload. "I guess the trick—depending on your capacity and how many hours of sleep you need—is to really hone in on just a few topics or issues in which you can make a difference. I do think," she allows, "that it's increasingly important for medical schools to teach courses on health policy."

"THE HUMAN ELEMENT" IN TRANSLATING INFORMATION AND PUTTING POLICY INTO ACTION

In a talk entitled "Attack on America: Rebuilding the U.S. Public Health Infrastructure," which she delivered on April 23, 2002, to the Commissioned Officers Association in Atlanta, Dr. Slater saluted her "troops," the 6,000 officers of the Public Health Service, as "the human element in translating scientific information and policy into action at the state and local level . . . [working] . . . to bring the message of healthy life styles and education about behavior modification to our fellow Americans." The focus of public health has evolved, she said in the speech, "always [. . .] embracing a new frontier, from health of seamen, quarantining of travelers, the improvement of workers' safety, or dealing with natural disasters, or man-made events such as the tragedies of September 11 and anthrax." While mourning the tragic loss of human life from terrorist attack, she reminded her colleagues of the pressing need to address and control preventable diseases. High on her list of public health priorities is grappling with "the epidemic of behaviors that place Americans at risk."

"In the United States today, among other pressing problems, we have a growing epidemic of our own making. We are literally eating ourselves to death," she declared in the aforementioned commencement speech at Newark Academy. "There are no magic bullets," she warned, proposing a national agenda to modify eating habits. Elsewhere, she has argued, that "chronic conditions such as cardiovascular disease and diabetes are among the most prevalent, costly and preventable of all health problems."

Dr. Slater oversees the functions of twelve offices, including those in charge of the National Vaccine Program, Disease Prevention and Health Promotion, Minority Health, Women's Health, and the President's Council on Physical Fitness. The Office of the Surgeon General is also under her watch, as are Human Research Protection, Research Integrity, and Population Affairs. As if that weren't enough for one plate, Dr. Slater adds, "I also drive some special projects for Secretary Tommy Thompson on public health. He's particularly interested right now in improving the system of health care practice in this country." To that end, Dr. Slater has launched the Best Practice Initiative, an ongoing effort to establish and address key factors, including substance abuse and tobacco abuse that affect the health of the American family.

HEALTH AND THE INFORMATION HIGHWAY

"Gathering medical knowledge, data, and know-how is vital," she maintains, but no less important is the need to get that information into the hands of those who can use it to make a difference. "I share the Secretary's view that one of the keys to changing the health system—and improving care, reducing errors and, over the long term, saving money—is to fully incorporate information technology into the health care delivery system," she said on October 29, 2002, in a speech to the Third Annual Health Legacy Partnership Conference at the National Press Club.

She put the problem succinctly: "An explosion of new knowledge resulting from biomedical and health research has surpassed the ability of individual practitioners to absorb and apply it during the normal course of delivering care."

To redress this information gap, Dr. Slater advocates the creation of electronic medical records for the general public of the kind that military personnel already carry throughout their careers and into veteran status. With the proven popularity and effectiveness of health websites, she argues, "we still have a lot further to go to give people control over their own personal health information." In the same speech, she lauded the new bar-coding technology, which Secretary Thompson has instructed the Food and Drug Administration to begin using in prescription drugs in an effort to reduce preventable medication errors.

ALWAYS A DOCTOR FIRST AND FOREMOST

While much of her day is taken up directing the smooth running of a massive federal bureaucracy, there is nothing the least bit bureaucratic about Dr. Slater. Forthright and plain spoken, she's still in the business of healing. "I have always, throughout my career, considered myself a doctor first and foremost," she insists. "Even though I did other things—I taught, I did research, I ran regulatory affairs at Merck—underlying it all, I have just tried to practice good medicine." And as in every stage of her career, so too in Washington, she hopes "to have a hand in something that'll be lasting, to help make America a little healthier."

REBEL DOCTOR *WITH* A CAUSE

BENJAMIN SPOCK '29

The interview on which the following profile was based was conducted in 1993 at the home of the legendary baby doctor on the island of Tortola, in the British Virgin Islands. Ever committed to the welfare of children, in A Better World for Our Children: Rebuilding American Family Values, *a book published in 1994, he fretted: "When I look at our society and think of the millions of children exposed every day to its harmful effects, I am near despair." Still, he took heart: "Our greatest hope is to bring up children inspired by their opportunities for being helpful and loving." Dr. Spock died in 1998, at age ninety-four.*

⎯⎯⎯⎯◦◦◦◦⎯⎯

A DETERMINED high jumper as a boy, Benjamin Spock '29 practiced daily by leaping over a slender bar, and in a sense, he has been vaulting ever since—only the hurdles have changed. At ninety, the celebrated and often controversial baby doctor still won't take life sitting down.

As he rises and extends a hand of welcome, there are three things you immediately notice: the length of his legs, the size of his hands, and the warmth of his smile—"Hi, I'm Ben."

He speaks in soft, measured tones, the inflection pure Connecticut Yankee. And while a gravelly undertone hints at a certain seniority, a jaunty tilt to the shoulders, a twinkle in the eye, and a ready laugh gives age the lie. He wears his years like a suit of clothes that he hasn't yet quite grown into and, likely, never will.

"It's one of the most characteristic things about my life," says Dr. Spock, "that I thought of myself as a timid boy who couldn't measure up to the other fellas!"

That from the athlete who helped row the Yale Crew to win a Gold Medal at the Paris Olympics of 1924; the pediatrician who challenged the traditional

split between physical and mental health, and first slipped Freud in with the booster shots; the author who's classic, *Baby and Child Care*, returned the ultimate authority in child rearing from the doctor to the parent; the tireless political activist who has repeatedly staked his reputation on the inseparability of pediatrics and peace.

Timidity indeed!

"Trust Yourself," reads the first chapter heading of *Baby and Child Care*, followed by the famous words: "You know more than you think you do."

So where did the confidence come from?

AN AFFINITY WITH CHILDREN

The story begins in New Haven, Conn., just after the turn of the century, where a fiercely independent-minded mother instilled in her first-born son a stubborn conviction to always stick to his guns (though Dr. Spock, an opponent of war toys, would likely discount such a bellicose metaphor). She also passed on to him a love of babies. More like a parent than an older brother to the other siblings, the boy soon developed a knack for child care. A summer job as counselor at the Newington Crippled Children's Home in New Haven reaffirmed his affinity with children and sparked a lifelong desire to ease their aches and ailments.

Whereas most medical students take four years to decide what kind of doctor they want to become, Spock went to medical school with the firm resolve to become a pediatrician. And whereas premeds (then as now) often tend to immerse themselves in the sciences, Spock opted for a broad-based college education, majoring in English and history at Yale. "I certainly feel," he says, looking back, "that the undergraduate years ought to be used to broaden your perspective and to find out about the world outside the hospital and the doctor's office."

He attended Yale medical school for the first two years, and thereafter transferred to P&S, where he graduated in 1929, first in his class. It was in the course of a two-year internship and residency at Presbyterian Hospital (one year in internal medicine and one year in pediatrics) that he conceived the then unheard of idea that a pediatrician ought to have psychological training. "It's the only original notion for which I really claim credit!" he insists today. To that end, he took a one-year residency in psychiatry at Payne Whitney, and thereafter, while pursuing additional part-time training at the New York Psychoanalytic Institute, opened a private pediatric practice with a special interest in psychological aspects.

The year was 1933, and the country was in the throes of the Great Depression—not exactly a fortuitous time to attract patients—particularly since none of the obstetricians who would ordinarily have sent him referrals could quite figure out exactly what kind of doctor he was.

"I had," Dr. Spock recalls—with a chuckle at the choice of adjective—"a *minute* practice. It took me three years to make enough to pay my office rent, which was only $125 a month." In time, however, patients started coming, and except for two years of service in the Navy during World War II, he continued in private practice through 1947, when he was invited to join the teaching staffs of the Mayo Clinic and the Rochester (Minnesota) Child Health Institute.

In retrospect, he would come to view his fourteen years of private practice as one long elaborate experiment, in which "I was trying to take the psychoanalytic concepts I was studying and somehow fit them together with what mothers were telling me about their babies." He learned from observing the interaction between parent and child. "It was mothers and babies," he candidly admits, "who contributed the substance of the book." While other pediatricians of his day dwelled on "the interesting case," Dr. Spock was more interested in the ordinary. And while supervising his little patients' healthy development through oral and anal stages, from thumb sucking to toilet training, he tried to understand them and sought sensible solutions to their everyday problems. Avoiding medical jargon, he dished out advice to their parents in plain English.

Word spread of Dr. Spock's uncommon concern for common concerns.

When Doubleday first approached him five years into his practice to write down what he knew, he refused, saying he didn't yet know enough. Five years after that, Pocket Books repeated the proposal, adding: "The book we want doesn't have to be very good—at twenty-five cents a copy, we can sell 10,000 a year!"

The book that finally appeared in 1947 exceeded all expectations. It even passed muster with his severest critic, his mother, a woman not given to compliments—"Benny, I think it's quite sensible," she said.

At 40 million copies and counting, *Dr. Spock's Baby and Child Care* (first published in plain English and subsequently translated into some twenty-seven languages) has become the bestselling book of all time, outranked only by the Bible. To the parents of the postwar baby boom generation, in fact, the book *was* their bible—as it still is to the grown-up baby boomers and their babies. Now in its sixth edition, it is the single most popular childrearing manual of all time.

And *manual* it is. Compact enough to be held in the palm of one hand while grasping a screaming infant in the other, the book offers reassurance and sound advice in an encyclopedic array of indexed concerns from blisters to botulism, from diet to divorce—bold type indicating emergency information. Its most unique feature is its readability.

Dr. Michael Rothenberg (collaborator and coauthor of the sixth edition) links the book's lasting appeal to the fact that "it makes parents feel that Dr. Spock is speaking directly to them, and that he (and I) see them as sensible people." The secret of its success, he believes, "is Ben's deep and abiding love of children and genuine concern and respect for parents, a quality that comes through in every word."

Even the "competitors" on the baby book shelf concur.

British psychologist Dr. Penelope Leach, the author of another widely read parental guide to the perplexed (who raised her own children according to Dr. Spock) credits him as a pioneer, "the first person who seemed to understand parents' feelings and children's feelings." And fellow P&S-trained pediatrician, T. Berry Brazelton '43D, one of America's leading authorities on child development, readily acknowledges Dr. Spock as "a hero." Says Dr. Brazelton, "He certainly changed parenting by giving choice back to parents, choice about what they did with their children and a chance to understand the child's side, as well as the parents'."

THE ACADEMIC AND CLINICAL SPOCK

"Not many people realize, with all the things he's done," Dr. Brazelton reminds, "that he was a brilliant teacher too! He had such a powerful influence on so many people." Dr. Spock's academic career included faculty appointments at the University of Pittsburgh, where he organized a teaching program in child psychiatry and child development, and Western Reserve University (now Case Western Reserve) in Cleveland, Ohio, where he taught as professor of child development from 1955 to 1967.

One of the people he influenced was future *Baby and Child Care* collaborator, Dr. Michael Rothenberg, who vividly remembers rounds with Dr. Spock at Western Reserve.

"You never felt you were being patronized," Rothenberg, a pediatric resident at the time, recalls. "He never played those games all too frequent in academia of asking questions designed to try to make a fool of the student. Ben really wanted to share what he knew and what he felt about children and families."

"He was a fabulous clinician!" says Rothenberg. "He had a marvelous way of interacting with children. I will never forget the image of Ben picking up a very young baby in one hand—his hands are enormous!—a fussy, crying baby, and making this little clucking sound that worked like magic. That's the clinical feel that you can't teach; you can role model it but you can't put it where it isn't!"

THE POLITICAL SPOCK

Benjamin Spock's role modeling extends beyond the purview of medicine. By word and example, he teaches self-reliance in the grand old New England tradition of Emerson and Thoreau. And like the latter, he believes in civil disobedience if the cause is right. Which brings us to the political Spock.

"I could scarcely avoid having a political attitude after the Depression set in," he recalls in his memoir *Spock on Spock* (coauthored with his second wife, Mary Morgan).

Yet aside from "New Deal" liberal sympathies, the active political dimension of his life remained largely dormant until his (and the century's) sixties, *The* Sixties, when the youth of America, the baby boomers he helped raise, rose up and dared criticize their elders and the order they had wrought. At a time in life when many consider retirement, Benjamin Spock had a second wind, entering the fray as a peace activist. He spoke up against nuclear proliferation and came out against the war in Vietnam and even went to jail for acts of civil disobedience. In 1972 he ran for president on the People's Party ticket, traveling around the country and lecturing at over 800 college campuses to promote a platform of social justice.

"Some people challenged me: Why have you deserted children?" Spock recounts. "And my answer has always been: I'm ashamed to say that it took me so long to realize that politics is a crucial part of pediatrics. How else are we going to get better schools, health care for our children, and housing for their families, if not by political activity!?"

At ninety, he avows, "I'm still a rabble-rouser, though I don't get nearly as many invitations to climb fences." With another book in the works (his thirteenth to date), a regular child care column to write for *Redbook*, and a busy schedule of interviews and appearances, he can hardly be said to be taking it easy.

He and his wife live within eye- and earshot of the ocean, summers in Maine and winters on Tortola in the British Virgin Islands, where he still rows daily— and where, in the course of a recent interview, pelicans and ospreys dove for their breakfast, and an old-fashioned clipper ship hugged the horizon, having sailed in from another century.

"From the beginning of the species, old geezers have viewed with alarm what's going on in the present," Dr. Spock laughs, "which doesn't keep them from wanting to correct the mess."

A VETERAN NIH INVESTIGATOR TAKES ON COMPLEMENTARY AND ALTERNATIVE MEDICINE

STEPHEN E. STRAUS '72

Stephen E. Straus '72 succumbed to brain cancer in 2007.

—⬩⬩⬩—

YOU'RE NOT likely to find Stephen E. Straus '72 seated in a lotus position, fingers curled, chanting "*OM!*" or popping *Echinacea* pills at the first signs of a sniffle. But the sunny glass-walled National Center for Complementary and Alternative Medicine (NCCAM), his base of operations in Building 31 at the National Institutes of Health, the nation's medical research Mecca in Bethesda, Md., emits good vibrations—of the scientific kind.

"I'M A SKEPTIC, BUT NOT A NIHILIST."

"I'm a skeptic, but not a nihilist," Dr. Straus said of himself in the course of an interview at his office in March 2006. "There's an important difference," he added. "Skepticism is essential to science, you have to scrutinize your own observations. Nihilism is a corrosive force. The belief that nothing could be true really negates an opportunity for inquiry and rational thought."

Granted that opportunity for inquiry by former NIH director Harold Varmus '66, who appointed him first director of NCCAM in 1999, Dr. Straus and the Center have made waves in the vast and complex field of complementary and alternative medicine. One controversial study displeased some in the CAM community, failing to confirm the effectiveness of St. John's Wort, a popular herb, in treating depression. But two other ongoing studies hold great promise.

One that he wrote up in the *Annals of Internal Medicine* showed that acupuncture is an effective adjunctive therapy, along with conventional therapy, for the treatment of patients with osteoarthritis of the knee. And another, the largest herbal study ever done, suggested that the herbal remedy Gingko biloba may have some efficacy in preventing the onset of Alzheimer's disease. If the findings are confirmed in subsequent follow-up studies, "it would be spectacular," said Dr. Straus, "and even if Gingko biloba turns out not to be effective, the study will teach us much more about the natural history of the onset of dementia in otherwise healthy individuals than we currently know."

NCCAM has funded 1,200 projects to date, many in collaboration with other institutes at the NIH. And while some in the medical establishment may have questioned the decision to put the considerable clout of the NIH and a start-off budget of $105 million behind the study of modalities of care outside the mainstream, and others in the alternative and complementary medical community may have been wary at first of Dr. Straus's Western medical bias, by most accounts the Center has been effective under his watch in testing and weeding out the potentially beneficial from the bunk.

"THIS ISN'T ABOUT MAGIC"

Dr. Straus's excitement in his work is palpable. You can sense it in the smile that slips past a skeptical caution and the balance of passion and reserve evident in his voice. "This isn't about magic," he is careful to point out. "If things are going to work in the body, it's because they have some physiological, pharmacological effect."

In the rarefied scientific atmosphere of the NIH, Dr. Straus is a heavy hitter with a proven track record of discovery. A veteran NIH investigator and internationally renowned virologist, he concurrently holds the title of chief of the Laboratory of Clinical Investigation of the National Institute of Allergy and Infectious Diseases (NIAID). He is best known for having demonstrated the effectiveness of acyclovir in suppressing recurrent genital and oral herpes and for first characterizing autoimmune lymphoproliferative syndrome, a heretofore unrecognized genetically determined disease, among other notable accomplishments.

And while his skepticism has not diminished one iota, he has brought scientific rigor, open-mindedness, and a zest for discovery to the study of therapies and modalities outside the medical mainstream.

"As a scientist for the past thirty years [twenty-seven of which were spent at the NIH] I can tell you that a lot of my hypotheses in the lab and the clinic are proven wrong. It's the nature of biomedical research," Dr. Straus insists. "But if you are open to the process and accept the results, the scientific method sets things right over time." A staunch adherent of the basic premises of the Western tradition of medicine, he nevertheless remains cognizant and respectful of other medical traditions and open to their potential provable benefits.

ANCIENT MEDICAL MODALITIES AND MODERN METHODS PUT UNDER THE MICROSCOPE

"The notion that complementary and alternative medicine is new, or that people are just newly attracted to it, is preposterous," Dr. Straus contends. "People have been constantly building their own health care theories and practice philosophies in all societies at all times."

Among other areas of interest, NCCAM is examining ancient non-Western medical traditions from China, India (Ayurveda), Tibet, Africa, the Middle East, as well as Native American remedies. The growing number of recent immigrants from Asia has heightened interest in the medical practices they brought with them. Acupuncture, in particular, is an increasingly popular regimen.

But the use of herbal remedies and other natural products, common in non-Western traditions, is hardly anathema to Occidental practice.

"Western medicine never gave up on natural products," Dr. Straus said. "They are the basis of some seventy-five prescribed drugs today for many different conditions." Taxol, quinine, and penicillin are just three examples. "There are still people out there mining our natural kingdom, looking for new treatments," he added.

In one noteworthy instance, a Chinese herbal product called quinghaosu or artemisinin, traditionally used in Southeast Asia for the treatment of recurrent fevers, was studied and has since been accepted as a standard remedy, used in conjunction with another drug, mefloquine, for otherwise drug-resistant malaria.

In addition, old treatments once thought to be a lot of hokum have been shown to have a new utility. Dr. Straus cited, for example, the use by microvascular surgeons of leeches, and specifically a protein they secrete called hirudin (reproduced in the lab by recombinant technology), as a potent anticoagulant to sustain viable blood circulation after reimplanting an amputated finger.

Another "rediscovered" natural product with promising prospects is cranberry juice. "People have long believed that cranberry juice is good for preventing recurring urinary tract infections," he said. And while medical science tended to pooh-pooh its benefits as a function of "extra fluid . . . to flush out the bladder," Dr. Straus noted, "the data now suggests otherwise. There is a chemical constituent in cranberry that seems to block the ability of certain bacteria to adhere to the epithelial cells lining the bladder, and adhesion is necessary for the infection to take hold." NCCAM is currently engaged in ongoing clinical studies with a standardized cranberry product.

Still, Dr. Straus cautions against a misguided blind faith in the benefits of everything natural: "There is a tension between that long and venerable history and the assumption that because it's natural, and really potent drugs have been found in nature, it's necessarily going to be good for you."

NEW IMMIGRANTS AND A GROWING
SENSE OF MEDICAL EMPOWERMENT

According to NCAAM's five-year strategic plan, "Expanding Horizons in Healthcare," CAM is in ever wider use in the United States. Between 1990 and 1997, the estimated number of Americans who tried health care modalities outside the mainstream increased from 427 to 629 million.

And whereas Dr. Straus credits the influence of immigrant cultures, he traces the growing interest in the population at large to "a larger sociological phenomenon. Over the past decades, Americans have felt increasingly empowered to make decisions about their own health and lifestyle. Some of these decisions, like eating less meat and exercising more, have proven to be very good." This self-empowerment, he allows, was, in part, a response to "an authoritarian medical system. The doctor was right a lot of the time. But the patients' ability to participate in the decision-making about their care was very attractive."

The aforementioned NCCAM strategic plan makes the point that, given the "dramatic gains in the health and well-being of Americans and a remarkable increase in average life expectancy," today's informed adults hope to live better lives, and consequently turn to CAM to treat the symptoms of chronic disease, which conventional Western medicine has done less well at alleviating, and to lessen the noxious side effects of some Western remedies.

STANDARDIZATION OF DOSES AND QUALITY

Given the public's documented use of herbal products and dietary supplements and some alternative treatments, the Center's research priorities initially differed from those of most other institutes at the NIH, whose primary focus, Dr. Straus said, is the "study of things that people haven't used yet. At NCCAM, we went backwards. We started with clinical studies and then moved back towards earlier phase and mechanistic studies."

More recently, however, the Center changed course. "Our original assumption actually proved a bit naïve," Dr. Straus acknowledged. "Lots of things are easy on the blackboard but when you get to the bench they get difficult. The huge variability in the quality of products already in wide use compelled the Center, in many cases, to start from scratch and recreate a standardized product."

FROM BROOKLYN TO BETHESDA

Dr. Straus's own blackboard training began in his native Brooklyn. He honed his mental faculties at MIT, where he earned a BS in life sciences. Initially headed for a career in chemical research, an eye-opening experience as a counselor to disadvantaged neighborhood adolescents at MIT's Science Day Camp led him to pivot to premed.

At P&S, he relished "the process of engaging with patients," while never leaving the lab far behind. One of his mentors was the late Dr. Harold Neu, whom he credits with kindling his interest in infectious diseases. In medical school, he also learned "about the privilege of insinuating myself into the lives of my patients. I saw birth. I saw death. I'm very proud of what I've been permitted to do. It all started at P&S."

Following an internship at Barnes Hospital in St. Louis, he got his first taste of NIH science as a research associate in the Laboratory of the Biology of Viruses at NIAID. And after returning to Barnes Hospital to complete his residency in medicine, Dr. Straus came back to Bethesda, as head of the Medical Virology Section of the Laboratory of Clinical Investigation at NIAID.

There he conducted landmark clinical studies, treating some of the first patients in the United States with the drug acyclovir and demonstrating that it suppressed recurrent genital and oral herpes.

In the course of these early phase human studies, he was obliged to ask questions that touched upon potentially sensitive areas: "When I saw a young woman who had come in with genital herpes, I was seeing a person in crisis at many levels."

Writing up his findings for the *New England Journal of Medicine*, he was the first to prove the existence of asymptomatic shedding and transmission of genital herpes, showing that a person could transmit the disease while shedding the virus, not knowing that he or she had the infection. In human terms, the study helped to eliminate the shame associated with the disease.

In addition, he identified autoimmune lymphoproliferative syndrome, a rare, albeit debilitating, disease of children born, as a consequence of genetic error, with lymphocytes that proliferate wildly, thus greatly increasing the risk of lymphoma.

He also studied a variety of conditions, some of which were considered controversial at the time, such as chronic fatigue syndrome. "I was confronted by individuals who believed they were sick and sought answers," he said.

"It was in treating patients with chronic and complicated viral diseases," Dr. Straus recalled in an online interview for the Damon Runyon Cancer Research Foundation, "that I began to see the larger clinical dimension of these illnesses . . . [Some of his patients] . . . were also some of the first to seek complementary and alternative approaches, so I welcomed the opportunity to bring my research background to the discipline of CAM."

A HEIGHTENED AWARENESS OF THE HUMAN EXPERIENCE IN CAM RESEARCH

More than in many other fields, Dr. Straus believes that "working in complementary and alternative medicine reveals the nature of being human and what people want and what they're seeking and what they're willing to do to get it. Whether or not I agree with it, whether it's scientifically proven or not, it's all about the human experience."

Ever the caring physician, he is willing to entertain questions that transcend the traditional strictures of medical science and touch upon the way people derive meaning in life. "Maybe it's not so important whether you can prove that a person will be more likely to survive a certain procedure or a certain disease better with a prayer," he conjectures, "and more important to ask whether he or she can traverse that difficult time in their life more comfortably. These are questions that can be studied."

Elected to a number of prestigious professional societies, including the Association of American Physicians and the American Society for Clinical Investigation, Dr. Straus was the recipient of five medals and several commendations from the U.S. Public Health Service, notably the Distinguished Service Medal for innovative clinical research and the Health and Human Services Secretary's Distinguished Service Award. He is the author of more than 400 research papers and editor of several textbooks.

If NCCAM's director can be said to have a scientific mantra, it is this: "The plural of anecdote is not evidence." At a lecture in 2002 at the University of California at San Francisco, he characterized complementary and alternative medicine as "a controversial area that holds promise and lacks proof." Seven years and counting into his mission, he is mining the promise and amassing the proof.

A PIONEERING AFRICAN AMERICAN
PERINATOLOGIST LOOKS BACK WITH PRIDE

YVONNE THORNTON MD '73, MPH '96

BEST KNOWN for her instrumental role in refining and helping win FDA approval for the practice of chorionic villus sampling (CVS), an alternative form of prenatal diagnostic testing that can be performed safely and with minimal discomfort to the mother much earlier than amniocentesis, pioneering perinatologist Yvonne S. Thornton MD '73, MPH '96 broke two glass ceilings. She is the first African American woman in the United States to be board certified in high-risk obstetrics and the first to be accepted into the highly selective New York Obstetrical Society. Having risen from modest means and surmounted obstacles of race and gender prejudice to reach the leading ranks of her specialty, it is a particular point of pride to her to have fulfilled her father's dream that his daughters become doctors. Personally delivering more than 5,000 babies and overseeing or supervising more than 12,000 high-risk deliveries in the course of her career, and pursuing landmark clinical research on weight gain prevention intervention in obese pregnant women, she managed, moreover, to do it all while raising a family of her own. Her son, Shearwood, III (Woody), and daughter, Kimberly, are both MDs.

Dr. Thornton chronicled her experiences in two bestselling memoirs, *The Ditchdigger's Daughters*, subsequently made into an award-winning movie and recently optioned for a Broadway musical, and *Something to Prove*, the grand prize winner in the 2011 New York Book Festival.

In September 2017, she revisited her medical alma mater to talk about her life and career.

"I WANT TO BE AROUND WHEN ONE PERSON BECOMES TWO PEOPLE!"

Dr. Thornton's calling in life became clear to her early on. At eight years old, on a visit to the hospital with her aunt, a registered nurse, upon witnessing a woman give birth in an elevator she resolved: "I want to be around when one person becomes two people!"

One of five daughters, and a sixth adoptive daughter, of the late Donald and Itasker Thornton, her parents worked tirelessly, her father held down two and sometimes three jobs at a time, and her mother cleaned other people's houses as well as her own to put food on the table, clothes on their backs, and move the family from the projects to a real home that Mr. Thornton built from scratch in Long Branch, N.J. Her mother, who had always regretted interrupting her studies at an historically black college, Bluefield State Teacher's College (now Bluefield State College), in Bluefield, W.V., because she didn't have the money to pay the tuition, framed and treasured every diploma her daughters earned. Given to reciting Keats's and Wordsworth's verse while scrubbing floors, she convinced her husband, himself a high school dropout with a sharp mind, that education was a top priority.

Some people are content to dream. Others do everything in their power to realize their dreams. Bucking the odds against a black, working class family in the 1950s, notwithstanding the ridicule of neighbors and coworkers, Donald Thornton decided that his daughters would become doctors. A homespun philosopher, he imbued in his children his own single-minded determination to achieve a better life for them. "If the front door isn't open," he said, "go around to the back and climb through the window. If the window is closed, try to get in through the cellar. If that's locked, go up on the roof and see if you can get in though the chimney. There is always a way to get in if you keep trying." As to the challenges ahead, he laid it on the line: "You're black and you're girls, and the world has already written you off." A realist with a dogged optimistic streak and a can-do attitude, he nevertheless insisted: "This country gives blacks a lot of grief. But it gives them a lot of opportunities too. Work hard and people will help you, doors will open."

The stethoscope, or what he liked to refer to as "that scripperscrap," was more than a mere medical device to him. A symbol of care, it also leveled the playing field. "When someone's in need of healing," Mr. Thornton reasoned, "he won't care about the color of the doctor's skin."

After earning a BS with distinction in 1969 from Monmouth College (now Monmouth University), in West Long Branch, N.J., the door did indeed open for his middle daughter, Yvonne, at Columbia P&S. Two other sisters would later follow suit in the medical and dental fields.

Dr. Thornton still vividly recalls her interview with then Dean of Admissions, George Perera '37. Based on her glowing undergraduate faculty letters of recommendation, Dr. Perera joked, "I thought I would see somebody with a halo on her head!" And when he asked her if she thought she could keep up with classmates from Yale and Stanford, she looked him in the eye and calmly replied, "I may come from a small college, but nobody can out-study me!"

True to her word, she hit the books every weekday waking hour. And come weekends she joined her siblings in the family band "The Thornton Sisters," another brainchild of her ever-dynamic father to help fund his daughters' studies. Winning six consecutive appearances at the legendary Apollo Theater Amateur Night, the band, in which Yvonne played alto saxophone and her mother played fretless bass and designed costumes, went on to play the northeast college circuit and was voted Princeton's favorite band.

She did well academically at P&S and made time to pursue research in sickle cell disease at The Rockefeller University, coauthoring her first paper, "Pharmacology of cyanate, II. Effects on the endocrine system," in the *Journal of Pharmacology and Experimental Therapeutics*.

With little time left over for socializing, her sole exception was a friendship that would later turn into a budding romance with an equally committed and determined fellow medical student, Shearwood J. McClelland '74 MD '96 MPH, whom she married in 1974. Associate professor of clinical orthopedic surgery at P&S, Dr. McClelland is the director of the Department of Orthopedic Surgery at Harlem Hospital Medical Center. (A short profile on him appeared in Winter 2004 in P&S, the precursor of Columbia Medicine.) Glad to become Mrs. McClelland, his wife-to-be insisted: "My parents worked too hard to help put me here at P&S, and if I'm going to be a doctor it's going to be Dr. Thornton!"— in honor of her father.

Donald Thornton lived to see his dream come true. Visiting his daughter one day at Roosevelt Hospital, where she trained in ob/gyn from 1973-1977, the sweet sound of "Paging Dr. Thornton!" emanating from the P.A. system was music to his ears.

At Roosevelt Hospital, where she was named chief resident, Dr. Thornton thrived under the guidance of Dr. Thomas F. Dillon, her departmental chair, and Dr. Abraham Risk, head of the residency program. Given its location on 59th Street and 10th Avenue, the hospital attracted a diverse patient population that included the working poor of Hell's Kitchen and the upper crust of Central Park South. Often putting in 110–120-hour work weeks, as she recalls, "I just lived and breathed ob/gyn, soaking up as much knowledge as I could. I really blossomed there."

In 1977, Dr. Thornton returned to Columbia to pursue a postdoctoral fellowship in maternal-fetal medicine at the Babies Hospital and the Sloane Hospital for Women (now The Morgan Stanley Children's Hospital) at Columbia-Presbyterian Medical Center. She would go on to receive double board certification, in obstetrics and gynecology, in 1979, and special competency in maternal-fetal medicine in 1981, the first black woman certified in the field.

From 1979 to 1982, on the urging of her husband, who felt that it was time "to give back to our country," she and Dr. McClelland voluntarily served in the U.S. Navy. Commissioned as Lieutenant Commander of the Medical Corps, Dr. Thornton joined the staff in the Department of Ob/Gyn at the National Naval Medical Center, in Bethesda, Md.

OF HIGH-RISK PREGNANCY AND PROFESSIONAL PREJUDICE

In 1982, based on her stellar CV and a glowing professional assessment from Dr. Roy Petrie, her Columbia mentor, his counterpart, the then chair of the

Department of Obstetrics and Gynecology at Cornell Medical Center (now New York-Presbyterian Hospital Weill Cornell Medical Center), accepted her, sight unseen, as an assistant professor and fulltime member of the academic staff. There had never been a fulltime academic person of color on staff in the Department of Ob/Gyn at Cornell (also known at the time as the New York Lying-in Hospital). But as soon as she walked through the door and he set eyes on her, his enthusiasm cooled. "It wasn't verbalized, the furrow in the middle of the forehead, the quick glances, I just knew I wasn't welcome."

"We don't have room for you on this floor," she remembers him saying, "you'll have to work in the sub-basement."

Gritting her teeth, following a pep talk from her father who reminded her: "You're not there to be liked, you're there to practice medicine!"—she rolled up her sleeves and got to work caring for her patients as director of clinical services of Cornell's ob/gyn clinic, in the sub-basement. She remembered, "Find your opportunities in the castaway areas of life."

It's the patients that mattered most. As she recalled in *Something to Prove*: "I always thanked my patients for keeping me a very happy person. Because with every high-risk delivery, I knew I had a bit of immortality in my hands." Elaborating on the special bond between obstetrician, mother, and baby, especially in maternal-fetal medicine, she explained: "This baby can have another baby, and that baby can have another, and well, I feel like I'm promulgating life, helping the human species survive." She has remained friendly with many patients and their children whom she sees as an extended family. "There is nothing more satisfying than hearing from a former patient many years later that her baby, who, but for a quick intervention and a lot of luck, would have been lost, just made the fifth grade honor roll!"

Dr. Thornton earned the ultimate approval of her professional peers when she was accepted into the ranks of prestigious New York Obstetrical Society, the first African American woman to become a member.

CVS, AN EARLY DIAGNOSTIC ALTERNATIVE
TO AMNIOCENTESIS

First developed in Denmark and finding its way to the United States via China, Italy, and London, chorionic villus sampling is a prenatal technique for obtaining genetic diagnostic information about the developing fetus by sampling the chorionic villus, the growing placenta, that can be performed as early as the eighth postmenstrual week of pregnancy. After the method was introduced in the United States as an alternative to amniocentesis, her director, who was initially skeptical of its viability, still wanted someone on staff to give it a go. That designated doctor was Dr. Thornton, whom he selected as the lead investigator in CVS trials at Cornell. The first institution to introduce the technique in New York was Mt. Sinai, but Sinai faculty proved protective of their newfound knowhow. So Dr. Thornton went to Thomas Jefferson University, in Philadelphia, to learn it from Drs. Laird Jackson and Ronald Wapner, who were more than happy to pass on the knowledge.

"The learning curve in CVS, fine tuning the manipulation of the thin plastic catheter to insert it in the growing placenta to get the chorionic villi out, is very difficult," she recalled. "The tube is malleable, you have to shape it to reach where you think the growing placenta is going to be. Some doctors just couldn't get it right, but I took to it like a duck in water." But after other practitioners' faulty application of the procedure, and a consequent string of infections often leading to loss of the fetus or removal of the uterus, the FDA put a hold on the technique pending further investigation at selected academic medical centers around the country for its efficacy and safety. Following extensive clinical trials, in a paper she coauthored, "Effect of chorionic villus sampling on maternal serum alpha fetoprotein levels," published in the *American Journal of Perinatology*," Dr. Thornton was among those who helped convince the FDA of the viability of CVS.

The welfare and comfort of her patients and felicitous pregnancy outcomes were always her first priorities.

Then in the early Eighties, she and colleagues at Cornell faced another daunting challenge—how to care for pregnant women with AIDS. "The general mindset was that these patients came from another planet," she recalls. "Women, many of them illicit drug users—there was a social overlay and the unspoken sense of: Good riddance!" Panicked physicians and nurses resorted to triple gloving in the OR. "But after a while, a common consensus kicked in. Look, we're health care professionals. The patient needs to be cared for. Let's do this."

FACING THE TRAUMA OF MALPRACTICE
SUIT AND OTHER CHALLENGES

"The body is a wonderful thing," she wrote in *Something to Prove*. "If you can fend off the attacks from the hundreds of billions of microbes that conspire to undermine its every organ, if you can determine the right treatments, then the body will take it from there and heal itself."

But sometimes a physician is faced with hard choices. In a gut-wrenching passage in her memoir, she describes the emotional toll of a malpractice suit from a patient whose life she had saved. After she opted in one high-risk case to terminate a pregnancy, and ultimately to remove an infected uterus to save the mother's life, the patient later sued her for malpractice. "It's like being shot in the chest. The jagged edges may have healed but the hole is still there," she still winces at the memory. "That somebody whose life I'd saved would do that to me!"

Again her father's wisdom helped attenuate the pain and helped her move on. "You can't hate a person," he said. "You can hate the things they do or the ideas they have, but not the person himself."

Soon thereafter she faced a professional frustration. After being overlooked for the position of director of Maternal-Fetal Medicine at Cornell, bypassed for a younger colleague who lacked her clinical training and experience who just happened to be a white male, she decided to seek opportunities elsewhere.

Following a brief stint at running a freestanding perinatal clinic in New Jersey, in 1992 Dr. Thornton accepted the invitation of her old residency program director at Roosevelt Hospital, Dr. Abraham Risk, then recently named chair of ob/gyn at Morristown Memorial Hospital, in Morristown, N.J., to join him as director of the hospital's first center for perinatal diagnostic medicine. Local community doctors were initially reluctant to refer their patients. But they were finally swayed by the decision of insurance companies to restrict reimbursement for any perinatal diagnostic testing and care to certified perinatal centers.

At Morristown she was reacquainted with the unique roll of midwives. "Midwives introduced me to an entirely different approach to pregnancy," she wrote in *Something to Prove*, "encouraging me to think about obstetrics as part of the natural order, not as pathology. [. . .] The midwives at Roosevelt Hospital instilled in us the understanding that [. . .] our empathy and humanity were every bit as important as our medical training. [. . .] They lived the true definition of 'obstetrics,' which means 'to stand by.' They were there not to interfere but to assist, and to make sure that the mothers were as comfortable and warm as possible."

Opting to understand the changing dynamic of American medicine from an administrative perspective, in 1996 Dr. Thornton and her husband both earned Master of Public Health degrees in Health Policy and Management in the Executive Masters' Program at the Columbia School of Public Health (now the Mailman School of Public Health). And after returning to join the Division of Maternal-Fetal Medicine at St. Luke's-Roosevelt Hospital Center, where she had trained, she decided to apply her newly acquired knowledge, accepting the position of vice chair and director of Maternal-Fetal Medicine in the Department of Obstetrics and Gynecology at Jamaica Hospital Medical Center, a public hospital serving a predominantly minority and immigrant population in Jamaica, Queens, a position she held for three years.

But wearying of the long commute from her home in New Jersey, often being obliged to wake up in the middle of the night to rush to oversee difficult pregnancies, in 2007 she joined the faculty of New York Medical College as clinical professor of obstetrics and gynecology and the staff of Westchester Medical Center, as a senior perinatologist and preceptor at the high-risk obstetrical clinic.

While at New York Medical College, she published the first-ever randomized clinical trial on perinatal outcomes in nutritionally monitored obese women. She had also published a suspension technique she developed for delivering morbidly obese patients that was subsequently dubbed "Thornton Suspenders."

PRACTICING MEDICINE FROM THE PRINTED PAGE, TV SCREEN, AND LECTURE PODIUM

Meanwhile, another vocation beckoned. Recalling the thrill of her early stint performing and singing in the family band, and eager to reconnect with an audience, Dr. Thornton found her voice again. "When that spotlight shines on you it changes your whole molecular structure," she avows, only half tongue in cheek.

In addition to the two aforementioned memoirs, she is the author of a widely read medical textbook, *Primary Care for the Obstetrician and Gynecologist*, and two women's health books for a general readership, *Woman to Woman* and *Inside Information for Women*. Also having produced three instructional videos, she is a consultant and contributor to numerous lay journals and electronic media, including the *Huffington Post*, MSNBC, *Ladies' Home Journal*, and *Essence* magazine.

Having appeared to promote her books and address women's health issues on the *Oprah Winfrey Show*, the *Today Show*, *Good Morning, America*, and other broadcast venues, and for a time as host of her own TV show and radio program, Dr. Thornton hit the public speaking circuit, becoming a spokesperson for the March of Dimes. She was the first woman in the 165-year history of the International Platform Association to win the Daniel Webster Oratorical Competition.

Among the highlights of her career at the lectern was a keynote address she delivered in 2003 at the commencement ceremonies at Tuskegee University, the historic African American institution of higher learning in Tuskegee, Ala., at which she was also awarded an Honorary Doctor of Science Degree.

Other encomia include a Distinguished Alumni Award and an Honorary Doctor of Humane Letters degree from her undergraduate alma mater, Monmouth University. In 2013, she was honored as a "Living Legend" by the National Medical Association. And in 2017, P&S saluted her achievements with the Virginia Kneeland Frantz '23 Award for Distinguished Women in Medicine. Included among The Best Doctors–New York Metropolitan Area, she was also listed in *New York Magazine* as One of the Top-Ten Maternal-Fetal Medical Specialists in New York City.

She had experienced another high point in her public speaking career in 1995 when she was asked to deliver the keynote remarks at the commencement of Bluefield State College, in West Virginia, her mother's alma mater, on the occasion of the school's conferring on her mother, the late Itasker Frances Edmonds Thornton, a posthumous doctor of humane letters degree. "Oh, Lordy, do I remember that moment! She finally got her sheepskin!"

SETTING THE RECORD STRAIGHT AND OTHER PHILANTHROPIC GOALS

Herself the recipient while in medical school of a generous scholarship from the National Medical Fellowships, in 2014 Dr. Thornton returned the favor and sought to set straight the historical record when she established the Anarcha, Betsy, and Lucy Memorial Scholarship, to be awarded to an African American female medical student enrolled at an accredited U.S. medical school who is a known descendant of American slaves. The scholarship is named in honor of three slaves who, as involuntary subjects of experimentation, helped shape advances in current clinical and surgical knowledge. Dr. James Marion Sims, the nineteenth-century doctor from South Carolina who was dubbed "The Father of Modern Gynecology," honed his surgical skills on enslaved black women without their consent and without anesthesia. His statue still stands in Central Park across the street from the New York Academy of Medicine.

Twenty years earlier, in 1994, Dr. Thornton established the Donald E. and Itasker F. Thornton Memorial Scholarship at P&S to honor her parents' memory and support deserving medical students.

"I remember those who helped me. It brings me full circle," she reflects. "When you give back in the form of a scholarship, the recipient remembers who was there for them when they needed it. Like delivering babies, being there when one person becomes two people, it's another form of immortality, which is why I became a doctor to begin with."

MERCK'S MD AT THE TOP

P. ROY VAGELOS '54

After reaching the compulsory retirement age and stepping down in 1994 as President, CEO and chair of Merck & Co., the pharmaceutical giant he helped steer to new heights, Dr. Vagelos took the reins as chair of the board of the astoundingly successful biotech firm Regeneron Pharmaceuticals, and also invested his leadership skills as chair of Columbia University Medical Center's Board of Visitors, and chair of the P&S capital campaign Defining the Future. In 2017, pursuant to a generous gift totaling $450 million from Dr. Vagelos and his wife Diana, the medical school was renamed the Vagelos College of Physicians and Surgeons.

———⊗⊗⊗———

ASK P. ROY VAGELOS '54, President chair and CEO of Merck & Co., to talk about himself and he deftly shifts the conversation to the renowned pharmaceutical concern he heads. In an era of high-profile head honchos whose names and faces are sometimes even better known than their company products, Dr. Vagelos prefers to step back and let the products and the company's record for successful drug development take the spotlight.

"The excitement here is drug discovery," says Dr. Vagelos, who is universally credited with the remarkable success of Merck, dubbed "King of the Medical Molecule Makers" by *Fortune* magazine and for four consecutive years voted "America's most admired corporation" in that magazine's annual surveys.

"This place lights up when we hit on a new molecule that will make an important impact on health," he says. "The excitement affects everybody—secretaries, janitors, scientists, engineers, the sales staff, the marketing staff.

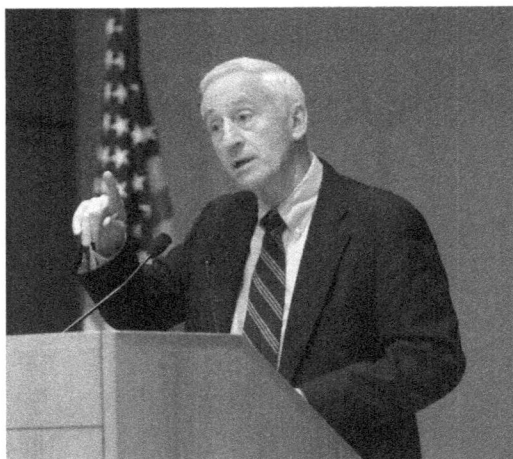

I take great satisfaction in the accomplishments of the people of Merck. I've gotten to the point where I think they can almost do magic."

(Among their recent feats of scientific "magic:" *Mevacor* and *Zocor*, cholesterol-lowering agents; *Vasotec*, an angiotensin-converting enzyme inhibitor for high blood pressure, and the promising *Proscar*, a prostate-shrinking agent currently showing favorable results in clinical tests.)

To hear Dr. Vagelos speak of drug discovery is to hear a chess master take you through his winning moves—making them sound deceptively simple.

"You start with very simple molecules and put them together in an interesting way, and if you get the right ones under the right conditions they combine to form different molecules with different properties," he says. "In the life process, of course, enzymes catalyze chemical reactions. If you can block the enzyme that's involved in a particular disease with another molecule—which is a drug—then you can interfere with the disease process."

Dr. Vagelos is that rare corporate instance of a medical scientist in charge, and he sees this as giving him a clear edge. As he puts it, "The beauty of Merck is that the head of the company can talk to the head of research and we speak the same language."

A renowned enzymologist, he had been a senior scientist at the NIH and founder and director of the Division of Biology and Biomedical Sciences at Washington University in St. Louis when he was recruited by Merck as senior vice president for research in 1975.

Before then, pharmaceutical research had been carried on as a costly, time consuming, trial-and-error process with haphazard results at best. Applying a medical man's understanding of the relationship between disease and body chemistry, Dr. Vagelos put the horse before the cart, where it belongs. He instructed his researchers to target biochemical reactions triggered by a disease and come up with chemical bullets to stop them.

Promoted to the presidency of Merck Sharp & Dohme Research Laboratories in 1976, he took on the additional responsibilities of senior vice president in charge of strategic planning at the parent company in 1982. Two years later, he was elected executive vice president of Merck & Co. In 1985, he became president and chief executive officer, and the following year, chair of the board of directors, on which he had served since 1984.

His direction in the laboratory as well as the boardroom have earned impressive profits and global encomia for the company. In addition to the *Fortune* magazine accolades, Merck has been cited by *Business Week* as one of the country's best-managed and most-innovative companies and by the *Wall Street Journal* as one of the "select few companies poised to lead business in the 90s."

Under Dr. Vagelos's leadership, the firm has also attracted favorable attention for its work environment. There is no executive dining room. Dr. Vagelos eats in the canteen with everyone else; he runs in corporate competition with the company team, the Merck Striders, and his opponents on the tennis court are as likely to be salesmen as research scientists.

The latter, wooed away from some of the nation's top academic institutions, liken the well-equipped facilities in Rahway, N. J., to a "college campus in heaven." Merck avidly seeks out and promotes talent. It is "one of the best places for blacks to work," according to *Black Enterprise* magazine; and among the best U.S. companies for working mothers, according to *Working Mother* magazine. And in 1989, the company was honored by the National Organization for Women Legal Defense and Education Fund "in recognition of its vigorous programs to recruit, develop and promote women and minorities—especially those with potential to move into senior management."

"One of my greatest contributions is recruiting and developing the best and brightest people in the world," Dr. Vagelos says. "And I work at it all the time."

The CEO himself speaks to promising prospects on college campuses around the country. Merck hosts an annual program of summer student interns, and Dr. Vagelos takes a particular delight in meeting them personally. "Maybe in thirty years, one of you will be addressing this group," he told the latest crop—no doubt mindful of the summer of 1951, following his first year at P&S, when he was an intern in the same Merck lab he came to direct three and a half decades later.

Even earlier he had an indirect relationship with Merck, when his parents ran a luncheonette just outside the company gates, and young P. Roy Vagelos, helping out after school, absorbed the conversation of company chemists who stopped by for coffee.

Pindaros Roy Vagelos is the son of Greek immigrants; his paternal grandfather earned his MD at the University of Athens. Dr. Vagelos earned his AB degree in chemistry in 1950 from the University of Pennsylvania before attending P&S, where, to quote his classical namesake, the poet Pindar, he was "perfected in the healing of sickness that brings many pains to men." (His son, Randall Vagelos '83, is a cardiologist at Stanford.)

"My training in medicine was superb," he reflects, recalling the influence of such teachers as Helen Ranney '47, Dr. Irving London, George Melcher '46, and George Humphreys, II MSD '35.

He went on to an internship and residency at Massachusetts General Hospital, where, thanks to his clinical background at Columbia, he felt better prepared than most of his colleagues: "I was just more comfortable dealing with patients."

Though intrigued by internal medicine, Dr. Vagelos finally turned to a career in research. His broad grounding in basic sciences and medicine at P&S, he believes, gave him "enormous flexibility" in his choice of direction, enabling him to go from clinical work to pure basic research and finally to the kind of applied research he mastered at Merck.

The move to industry did not mean a distancing from academia. Quite the contrary, as Dr. Vagelos has maintained strong ties with such institutions as Rockefeller University and the University of Pennsylvania, where he is a trustee, and P&S, where he serves on the National Visiting Council. He has received honorary Doctor of Science degrees from Washington University, Brown, the University of Medicine and Dentistry of New Jersey, New York University, and most recently, Columbia.

Admitting that he sometimes misses the joy of teaching and hands-on lab work, he feels his chief executive role enables him to gain an overview, to monitor a wide range of results, "to do many things simultaneously," and thus to "learn more, faster" and "magnify my impact on health care."

Under his direction, Merck's longstanding commitment to educational programs in the biomedical sciences has expanded to include grants to young faculty and postdoctoral fellows, and more recently, to predoctoral students at various institutions. The company also gives generously to academic research programs.

He sees academia and industry as having a common ultimate goal—the health of the public—but very different immediate purposes.

"Universities do pure basic research and train people. Industry principally does applied research and produces products, picking up both people and ideas from the universities," he says. In his view, it would be futile and self-defeating to encourage universities "to turn more to product discovery and thereby attract more public attention," as some critics have suggested. Nor should industry be expected to invest more in pure basic research. Dr. Vagelos argues that this would result in fewer new ideas and fewer new products.

With his broad-ranging experience at Merck, Dr. Vagelos—a classical music enthusiast—has been likened to the conductor of a symphony orchestra who started as a violinist and moved through the brass, woodwind, and percussion sections before finally taking up the baton.

"When I walk around the production plants I feel that I understand the chemistry and the engineering, because I came through the laboratories," he says. "It's wonderful to have played all the instruments."

NOBEL LAUREATE AT THE NIH

HAROLD VARMUS '66

Since stepping down as director of the National Institutes of Health in 1999, Dr. Varmus served for ten years as president of Memorial Sloan Kettering Cancer Center, and five years as director of the National Cancer Institute, returning in 2015 to fulltime active research as Lewis Thomas University Professor of Medicine at Weill Cornell Medical College and the New York Genome Center. Among his extra-biomedical research activities, he and his son, Jacob Varmus, a jazz trumpeter and composer, presented a series of concerts entitled "Genes and Jazz: The Music of Cell Biology," at such venues as the Guggenheim Museum, the Smithsonian Institution, the Boston Museum of Science, and the Kennedy Center for the Performing Arts.

IT'S A 12-mile drive from his home in downtown D.C. to his office in Building One on the Bethesda campus of the National Institutes of Health but the new director easily eludes traffic, navigating the Beltway, or rather eluding its traffic tangle on side roads, by racing bike. To Harold Varmus '66, shifting gears is a way of life.

At fifty-four, the limber Nobel Prize–winning bench scientist-turned biomedical administrator has covered more territory than most of us can dream of in the course of a single career. "I thought it was time to put scientific perspective in this office," he explains his decision to accept President Bill Clinton's nomination, confirmed by the Senate in November 1993, "and while I wasn't my own first choice, I thought I would give it a try. For my part, I wanted a change of pace; it has something to do with the biological clock ticking inside me."

Lest anyone suppose he is leaving bench work behind—he now keeps two laboratories running, one at the NIH and one back at the University of California, San Francisco (UCSF), where he maintains his academic affiliation—Harold Varmus has merely diversified his intellectual portfolio, extending his line of inquiry from genetics to the big picture of science and society.

When President Clinton nominated the 1989 Nobel Laureate in Physiology or Medicine to head up the largest biomedical research enterprise in the world, he was sending a clear message that America is committed to the future of basic scientific research. In the words of the late Senator Edward Kennedy of Massachusetts, who helped champion the nomination in the Senate, "Dr. Varmus has the vision and skill to lead this nation's biomedical research into the twenty-first century."

The NIH, which began as a modest hygienic laboratory in 1891, has mushroomed under successive federal administrations to an $11 billion enterprise. Today encompassing eighteen intramural research institutes, the National Library of Medicine (the world's largest repository of medical literature), a clinical center, a new National Center for Genome Research, and an extensive program of funding for extramural research, the NIH calls the shots at the cutting edge of medical science. Yet given the current climate of budgetary constraint and the public clamor for cures to such pressing health concerns as AIDS and breast cancer, among others, it has been suggested that "the NIH . . . must now face some fundamental ambiguities in its mission" (*Science*, September 24, 1993). Whether the new director choses to tinker with or, as the *New York Times* put it, to "reinvent the organization that is the life blood of the nation's biomedical enterprise," the stage is set for confrontation and discovery. Enter Harold Varmus!

A DIRECTOR FROM THE SCIENTIFIC TRENCHES

"My preparation for this job has been unusual," Dr. Varmus readily admitted to the Senate. The selection of a renowned bench scientist, as opposed to a clinical administrator, to sit in the NIH director's chair dissolved any lingering perception of a split between central administration and research. As Dr. Varmus put it in an interview shortly after his confirmation, it signaled a welcome to "the geeks out there in the [research] trenches," and that "I'm a geek, too!" (*Science*, November 26, 1993).

In the Nobel lecture delivered in Stockholm, December 8, 1989, Dr. Varmus prefaced a discussion of his (and corecipient Dr. Mike Bishop's) path-breaking work on retroviruses and oncogenes with a personal biographical note.

He recalled, tongue in cheek, how his "commitment to experimental science occurred, by today's standards, dangerously late in a prolonged adolescence." An English major at Amherst College, he studied Dickens and wrote and edited antiestablishment journalism while fulfilling his premedical requirements. Disillusioned with letters, however, following a short detour into English graduate studies at Harvard, he applied to P&S, initially intending to pursue psychiatry, before succumbing to the lure of the molecular and the thrill of serious hard science in the making. He credits the influence of such challenging teachers as Drs. Elvin Kabat, Malcolm Carpenter, and Paul Marks, among others. Subsequently, he pursued an internship and residency in internal medicine at Presbyterian Hospital.

The Vietnam War interrupted his immediate plans for an academic career in internal medicine. In part to avoid the draft, he applied for and was accepted for a research training position at the NIH. There, in the course of his training, Dr. Varmus underwent the further transformation from a clinical investigator to a full-fledged basic scientist.

"Science has such a magnetic draw to anybody associated with health," he insists, "and biomedical science is surely one of the most exciting intellectual pursuits of our time!" A broad smile belies an air of cool dispassion—this is a man who clearly loves what he does! "Are the intellectual frontiers any greater in law or business or in any of the humanities!?" he asks rhetorically, as if science itself were on trial, and he its most ardent defender. "When the history of this age is written, we'll see that the twentieth century is the century—of Picasso, of course!—but also of the atom, the computer, and the gene! And we're in the phase of the gene right now. It's riveting, I can tell you!"

Working as a clinical associate at the National Institute of Arthritis and Metabolic Diseases, in the laboratory of Dr. Ira Pasten, a thyroid-oriented biochemist interested in bacterial gene expression, Dr. Varmus bit the bullet of basic research, and eagerly pursued additional scientific training offered in evening courses. "The NIH at that point was a real mecca for people like myself," he recalls, "doctors who had been trained at good medical schools but lacked the background in the basic sciences."

In related studies, he learned about tumor viruses and decided to enter the field as a postdoctoral fellow under Dr. Mike Bishop in the Department of Microbiology at USCF, where he was rapidly promoted from lecturer to full professor. He currently holds simultaneous professorships there in microbiology and immunology, biochemistry and biophysics, and is American Cancer Society Professor of Molecular Virology.

His and Bishop's collaborative work on retroviruses in the early 1970s demonstrated that cancer genes (oncogenes) can evolve from normal cellular genes, called proto-oncogenes, the discovery for which they shared the 1989 Nobel Prize in Physiology or Medicine.

Experimenting with the Rous sarcoma virus, which causes cancer in chickens, Drs. Bishop and Varmus tested a then-accepted notion, "the oncogene hypothesis" of cancer causation, which held that the source of the cancer was genetic material from the virus inserted long ago into normal cells. What they found, to their surprise, was that the cancer-causing agent was not the viral gene but a normal cellular gene gone awry, which the virus picked up from the cell. The implications of their findings not only overturned the oncogene hypothesis, but also led to the discovery of a cluster of some forty genes crucial to normal cellular functioning, which established a common causal pathway for cancer, and offered a way to plug into the circuitry of the cell.

A SPOKESMAN FOR THE SCIENTIFIC COMMUNITY

Thrust into the spotlight of public acclaim, Dr. Varmus was frequently called upon to speak out on behalf of the scientific community, a role he came to embrace, and which eventually brought him to the attention of advisers to the White House. A member of the Institute of Medicine and the National

Academy of Sciences, and a fellow of the American Academy of Arts and Sciences, he served as chair of the Board of Biology for the National Research Council, an adviser to the Congressional Caucus for Biomedical Research, and cochair of the New Delegation for Biomedical Research. In 1986, he chaired the subcommittee of the International Committee on the Taxonomy of Viruses that gave the AIDS virus its name HIV.

An impassioned defender of free-ranging basic research, and an outspoken opponent of any imposed "roadmap to major discoveries," he has, nevertheless, come to recognize the political expediency of "strategic thinking."

"Actually, Maryland Senator Barbara Mikulski put it very nicely," he credits. "She said she knows that science is not a motorboat, you don't just get out on the bay and buzz to the next port. It's more like sailing, you need to know where you're headed, in general, but you have to tack where the wind's opportune. A boat loaded with fuel and waving the banner 'Breast Cancer' will just run aground!"

Arguing for the need to accumulate knowledge about the life and death of the cell, he insists "you will either gather so much information that, finally, you can put it all together, or more likely, somebody will make an outstanding discovery that cuts through to a new insight and may lead to a major new therapy or manner of detection."

Varmus takes a realistic view of his role at the helm of the NIH: "The best I can do is to help foster a good atmosphere in which to do science."

Among his top priorities, he sees the need to reactivate the educational function of the NIH, thanks to which his own scientific inclinations were nurtured. He favors a recruitment focus on young investigators. "Our big opportunity," he says, "the niche I seek to have the NIH fulfill in the intramural program is to bring in the very best young postdoc candidates from the external community, particularly those lacking research credentials, and especially MDs from the minority population who have been underrepresented in science."

Other priorities include the institution of more rigorous standards for the intramural program and a reform of the often cumbersome extramural peer review process for grants.

To accomplish all this, Dr. Varmus will, inevitably, have to ruffle a few feathers.

Some have questioned his abilities to maneuver effectively in Beltway politics. Varmus sees it differently: "I'm an impatient, fast-talking guy who wouldn't be thought of as your optimal bureaucrat. But I believe you don't have to be a consummate master of protocol, but a person who speaks his mind and has a certain amount of integrity. That's more important in Washington than suavity and unctuousness."

Time will tell if Varmus succeeds. He has in any case set his own time limit on his tenure, three to ten years, after which he plans to return to fulltime research.

What would it please him to accomplish?

"Certainly I'd feel good if, while I'm here, our work led to major discoveries that transformed our ability to treat diseases like AIDS and cancer, but I can't make that happen. I'd be happy if I brought in good people. I'd like to see an increased number of women and minorities in this game rising to the top of their profession. I'd like to see the NIH more involved in coordinating educational programs at all levels."

His own most recent book, *Genes and the Biology of Cancer* (coauthored with Robert Weinberg), published by the Scientific American Library, is geared to a general readership. His bibliography includes three prior books and some 300 scientific papers.

Meanwhile, Dr. Varmus wrestles with such hot issues as the legal patenting of DNA sequences and the ethics of fetal research, and battles what he calls "the mighty paper flow of government bureaucracy."

"Science as a culture is fundamentally chaotic, ought to be chaotic," he avows. "And, of course, government runs exactly the opposite way: it's all ordered." The paradox makes for a compelling challenge, something to dwell on in traffic, while training for—why not?—the Tour de France.

ADVOCATE FOR WOMEN'S HEALTH

LILA WALLIS '51

Lila Wallis, founding president of the National Council on Women's Health, was cited on the website of the National Library of Medicine in its celebration of America's women physicians among those individuals who helped change the face of medicine.

───⊙⊙⊙───

IN THE more than four decades of her medical career to date, Lila Wallis '51, a soft-spoken academic-activist who has been called "the godmother of women's health," has witnessed "a modest improvement in the scant attention paid to medical concerns and research specific to women," an improvement hastened in no small part by her tireless efforts. Clinical professor of medicine at Cornell, master of the American College of Physicians, past president of the American Medical Women's Association, founder and first president of the National Council on Women's Health, she has labored from consultation couch, clinic, lab, and lectern to help put women's health on the medical map.

An internationally recognized authority on osteoporosis, estrogen replacement therapy and menopause, she is also an inspired educator. The Teaching Associates Program that she instituted at the New York Hospital-Cornell Medical Center in 1979 revolutionized the teaching of sensitive and competent breast, genital, and rectal examinations. Her landmark *Textbook of Women's Health*, published in December 1997, has been hailed as the first of its kind. "It fills in some of the gaps," Dr. Wallis allows with a smile and a sigh, conveying an inkling of the distance traversed and the distance still to go.

VISIBLE SYMPTOMS, UNEXPLAINED CAUSES

Back in 1955 when she launched her practice, following a residency in internal medicine and a fellowship in hematology at Cornell/New York Hospital Medical Center (now Weill Cornell), Dr. Wallis was baffled by certain medical problems she'd never encountered in the course of her study and postgraduate training.

Some of her women patients, for instance, presented with recurrent bouts of cystitis followed by yeast infection, and whereas the male urinary tract had been taught as the standard, conditions unique to the female tract had never been addressed in lecture or text.

The only physician in the United States, male or female, to have acquired board certifications in internal medicine and hematology, as well as endocrinology and metabolism, Dr. Wallis decided to pursue her own independent course of "post-postgraduate" training, with the expert advice of urologists and gynecologists of her acquaintance. At that early date she evolved her own guidelines of diagnosis and care for recurrent urinary tract infections, such as culturing urine, establishing antibiotic sensitivity, preventing yeast super-infection, and explaining precautionary measures to her patients.

Women also came to see her with suspicious bruises. These women were often accompanied by their spouses or partners. After taking the patient aside and risking indelicate questions, she established the truth and confronted the heretofore taboo issue of domestic violence. And while colleagues urged her to back off and mind her own business—"You're a doctor, not a social worker!"—she concluded that the physical and mental trauma of her patients was indeed her medical business. No shelters for battered women existed at the time. "It's my patients who have always guided me and taught me much of what I needed to learn," she insists.

A NECESSARY OCCUPATION

Lila Amdurska Wallis, born in Grodno, Poland, briefly considered becoming an astronomer before World War II abruptly brought her back down to earth. Having had her medical and scientific studies at the University of Stefan Batory, in Wilno, cut short by the German invasion and occupation, she first delivered care clandestinely nursing the wounds of underground partisans at a cousin's country home. She also taught Polish to the local children, since the Germans had closed down the schools.

The brutal realities of war convinced her of the importance of medicine: "I realized that there were four necessary occupations, no matter what: medicine, teaching, the priesthood, and farming. I'd tried teaching, and well, I couldn't be a priest, and while I loved gardening, and still do, I wasn't about to devote my life to it. That left medicine."

Immigrating to the United States after the War, she attended Barnard College, graduating with a BA in chemistry, summa cum laude, in 1947. A Columbia scholarship and grants from outside foundations enabled her to attend P&S, where she made Alpha Omega Alpha in her junior year. Delighting in "the sheer pleasure of discovering knowledge and learning new skills," she made lifelong friends among her classmates and "felt privileged to be learning my chosen calling from famous teacher/physicians."

She did, however, experience occasional snubs from a few of the more immature male students who could not fathom a serious young woman, already married and determined above all to pursue her studies—"After losing so many years during the War, my job was to gather education, not to socialize!" Misogynist attitudes were unfortunately condoned, if not fostered, by certain members of the faculty who still saw the education of women medical students as a wasted investment, as they would probably get married and leave medicine.

But she also found staunch supporters on the faculty, inspiring professors like Yale Kneeland '26, who brought "great elegance to the teaching of physical diagnosis" and his sister, Virginia Kneeland Frantz '22, who "made surgical pathology come alive." Her outstanding academic record notwithstanding, when Dr. Wallis confessed to Dr. Frantz a certain anxiety about learning the ropes at Cornell, where she had been accepted for training, the latter assured her young protégé that P&S had prepared her to meet any challenge.

Cornell/New York Hospital Medical Center, in fact, became Dr. Wallis's home base where she has taught and practiced ever since. Following her training, she joined the faculty as an instructor in medicine and rose in the ranks to her current title of clinical professor and attending physician.

Her early research, performed in conjunction with her mentor, Dr. Ralph Engel, focused on multiple myeloma. Together they published a book on immunoglobinopathies. They also coauthored a series of important papers on the combination of adult Franconi syndrome and multiple myeloma that appeared in the *American Journal of Medicine*. (She is the author or coauthor of over fifty peer-reviewed publications.) Lecturing on her findings to the Department of Endocrinology, in which field she subsequently attained board certification,

Dr. Wallis shifted her research focus to osteoporosis and developed a proneness index based on patient history.

In 1974 she instituted the "Update Your Medicine" program at Cornell, one of the earliest, longest running, and most successful continuing medical education programs in the country.

While relishing the research, she was all too aware of the absence of women principal investigators at the time: "I would always have been second fiddle, and I didn't want that." Given her facility with patients and enjoyment of the "intellectual challenge of differential diagnosis," she opted for the clinical track.

In addition to her private practice, she saw patients in New York Hospital's endocrine and hematology clinics. Yet despite her obvious qualifications, she was excluded as a woman from practicing in the Vincent Astor Clinic, which was devoted to the care of corporate VIPs. Dr. Wallis's practice has always included both men and women. She fondly recalls a patient she'd seen when still a student, a male hemophiliac, who told her she'd make a fine doctor, "because I had a gentle touch."

TEACHING THE GENTLE TOUCH

Two women in medicine had a profound influence on the course of her career. Dr. Connie Guion, the first woman named clinical professor of medicine at Cornell, offered encouragement and more importantly, referred patients. And Dr. May Edward Chinn, the first African American woman to graduate from Bellevue Hospital Medical Center and the first woman intern at Harlem Hospital, taught her the art of the competent and painless pelvic exam. Dr. Chinn, who went on to an important career in public health, saw patients at the Strang Cancer Prevention Clinic then located in Memorial Hospital (now Memorial Sloan Kettering Cancer Center).

Honing her skills over years of practice, Dr. Wallis sought to promulgate the practical wisdom she'd picked up from peers and patients through the Teaching Associates Program that she instituted at Cornell in 1979 and directed for eleven years. Inspired by an experiment conducted by Dr. Robert Kretschmar at the University of Iowa, in which nonmedical women served as demonstrators and subjects for the teaching of pelvic exams to medical students and residents, and with the input and advice of members of the Boston Women's Health Book Collective, Dr. Wallis fine-tuned the concept into a workable pedagogical model that has since been adopted by medical schools around the country.

Until then, pelvic exams had been demonstrated upon clinic patients who were often sedated. The procedure was not only degrading to patients but also flawed, in that the students were left more or less in the dark, never knowing if they were inflicting pain or even palpating the right structure.

Alternating as subject and examiner in teams of two, the teaching associates demonstrated that pelvic exams never need be painful, unless there is pathology or the examiner is rough or untrained. A major portion of the discomfort felt by patients, it turned out, had been due to the inadequacy of training of the examiner. Student trainees at Cornell got top grades from their toughest referees, the clinic patients, and needless to say, the program caught on. With the help of the Teaching Associates Program, Dr. Wallis documented the painlessness of downward (as opposed to painful upward) pressure on the uterus, and emphasized the importance of language. Instead of frightening the patient by talk of speculum "blades," she called them "bills" and preferred the term "footrests" to "stirrups." Taking pains to warm the instrument before inserting it in the cervix, she acknowledged anxiety and discomfort and discounted the tendency some doctors have of "distracting" the patient with extraneous conversation during breast and pelvic exam. Most importantly, she taught that "ovaries are just as sensitive as testes: nobody squeezes the testes, so why squeeze the ovaries!" At the request of male medical students, Dr. Wallis later added the teaching of male genital and rectal exams.

"Education works both ways," Dr. Wallis firmly believes, "doctors learn from patients and patients learn from doctors."

AN ACADEMIC-ACTIVIST

Increasingly aware of the politics of health care, Dr. Wallis became active with the Women's Medical Association of New York City (WMANYC), ascending to the presidency in 1974. Much to her amazement and delight, she discovered that "I could speak in public without too much trouble and grief." In 1979, she helped found and became the first president of the National Council on Women's Health, an advocacy group whose goal is to foster a working partnership between women health professionals and women patients. And in 1988, she was elected president of the American Medical Women's Association (AMWA). Founded in 1915, AMWA is a professional organization devoted to the professional and personal development of women doctors and medical students. Working on behalf of AMWA, Dr. Wallis became a high-profile spokesperson on women's health, often interviewed in the media.

In 1989, following her tenure as president, she chaired AMWA's Task Force on Women's Health Curriculum. In that capacity, she developed an "Advanced Curriculum in Women's Health" for physicians who take care of women, and helped found the National Academy of Women's Health Medical Education to oversee the infusion of the basic principles she had helped develop into medical school and postgraduate education. The curriculum targets the health challenges of women at different life phases from a multidisciplinary viewpoint.

WHY WOMEN'S HEALTH?

"Differences between women's and men's health," as Dr. Wallis pointed out in an article in the *Journal of Women's Health*, "go beyond the reproductive tract and affect every system." Hormonal balance and socioeconomic circumstances also affect the course and treatment of disease, as do documented gender differences in the metabolism of pharmacological agents. Women's social role as the "distribution vehicle," acting on behalf of spouses and children, makes them pivotal links in the health delivery system. Yet gender bias has skewed biomedical research with clinical trials that focus on "the 70 kg male" as the universal model. And women tend by and large to receive care fragmented between gynecologists, internists, family practitioners, and other specialists.

Case in point. Intending to include a model form for physical exams in her *Textbook of Women's Health*, Dr. Wallis discovered that the outline of the body currently used in hospital charts is a man's body. "I had to re-do the curves," she smiles.

The differences are more than cosmetic. "Pain patterns of heart disease are frequently different in women," Dr. Wallis points out, but classic cardiology has only been concerned with "the heart problems of the businessman in the prime of his life."

While promoting the advancement of women's health on the clinical and research front, she is opposed to the establishment of an independent specialty in the field. This, she believes, "would marginalize women's care, drawing all those interested away from other specialties and allowing other physicians to leave it to the women's health specialists . . . and not themselves feel the need to learn anything about women! I definitely don't want women to receive second-class treatment."

SUPPORT AND TRIBUTE

Next to her patients and students who "helped make me more effective as a physician and teacher," Dr. Wallis credits the "tremendous support" of her husband of more than fifty-six years, Dr. Benedict Wallis, a retired chemical engineer, and their two sons, James and Jeffrey, both physicians.

Encomia have come from many quarters. In 1986, with the financial support of grateful patients, Cornell established the Dr. Lila Wallis Distinguished Visiting Professorship in Women's Health, the first of its kind in the country. AMWA saluted her in 1990 with its highest honor, the Elizabeth Blackwell Medal, and more recently, established an annual Lila Wallis Award in Women's Health. She was the recipient in 1994 of the Georgeanna Seegar Jones Lifetime Achievement Award from the Society for Advancement of Women's Health Research, the Warner-Lambert Company, and the National Health Council. That same year she received the Woman of the Century Award from WMANYC and was elevated to mastership in the American College of Physicians. The keynote address at the annual Women's Health Program of the National Council on Women's Health was named in her honor.

She is currently putting the finishing touches on a mass market book for a general readership on women's health over various life phases. Her goal is "to educate women to become their own doctors and to use physicians as their consultant." When that's done she will turn her attention to a variety of other book projects, including a fifth edition of *The Modern Breast & Pelvic Examinations, A Handbook for Health Professionals*.

Dr. Wallis continues to lecture worldwide, and though officially retired from private practice, still sees some of her old patients—"Teaching the patient how to take care of herself is one of my greatest joys!" Not one to stand still for long, she reflects on her life's journey: "It's not what happens to you that matters, but what you do with it!"

A MATTER OF HEART

CLYDE Y. C. WU '56

Cardiologist-educator-philanthropist Clyde Y.C. Wu '56, the Columbia University trustee who, with his wife, Helen, reestablished a scientific and educational dialogue between his beloved medical alma mater and his native country, China, culminating in the creation of the Wu Family China Center for Health Initiatives, died in 2015, at age eighty-four.

<hr>

AT SEVENTY-NINE and counting, most people would be content to kick up their heels and count their blessings. Not so Clyde Y.C. Wu '56, who maintains a tireless schedule sharing those blessings with the world.

Officially retired from his clinical faculty position in the Department of Medicine of the School of Medicine at Wayne State University, in Detroit, and from his practice as a cardiopulmonary specialist at Oakwood Hospital, in Dearborn, Mich., he recently stepped down following thirteen years as a member of the Board of Trustees of Columbia University, ten years of which he served as chair of the Health Sciences Committee, overseeing the affairs of the Medical Center.

"Once a doctor always a doctor," he observes. Having changed medical specialties from cardiac to philanthropic care, it's still for him a matter of heart. Among other vital "interventions," he and his wife Helen endowed the Clyde and Helen Wu Center for Molecular Cardiology, as well as five professorships at P&S. In addition, they sponsored the Clyde and Helen Wu Distinguished Lecture Series and support medical student life, having funded musical, theatrical, and social activities and installed a music room in their names at Bard Hall, among countless other kindnesses.

Perhaps their proudest accomplishment is the reestablishment of the historic relationship between P&S and Peking Union Medical College (PUMC) in Beijing, and through their support of the Sino-American Exchange Program, fostering of a vigorous exchange of clinical knowledge and expertise between Columbia P&S and major medical schools in China.

A MEDICAL ODYSSEY

Born in Hong Kong in 1931, one of nine siblings, Dr. Wu's personal and medical odyssey took him from the hardships and challenges of rural life in the Chinese heartland, where the family fled the Japanese occupation during World War II, and where, as a young man, he first felt the calling to medicine, to P&S, where, as one of only two Asian students in his class, he fulfilled his boyhood dream of becoming a doctor.

"It was not exactly a travelogue type of experience, not like Pearl Buck's *The Good Earth*," he says with a bittersweet intensity, pinching his eyes and pursing his lips as he reflects back on the four and a half years he spent with his family in Guangdong. Conditions were hard, food and medicine scarce, doctors a rarity. Still, the resilience of simple people in the countryside made a profound impression on him. During that time period, he attended eight different high schools. But education was a priority for his mother, who had not herself finished school. And whereas he had been a fair student in Hong Kong, the tough times and the ethics inculcated in him by the missionary schools in the Chinese hinterland helped hone his discipline and develop his sense of commitment and his desire to serve the community.

Back in Hong Kong again after the War in 1946, young Clyde helped his father, Chung Wu, rebuild his taxi business. The elder Mr. Wu would later be known as the "Taxi King" of Hong Kong. He subsequently invested in real estate, and together with Clyde's younger brother, Gordon, who earned a degree in civil engineering from Princeton University, founded Hopewell Holdings, today one of Hong Kong's and Asia's leading real estate and construction concerns. But whereas his brothers all went into business, encouraged by his mother, Clyde Wu decided to pursue the study of medicine.

On July 13, 1949, with tears in his eyes and a fierce determination, he boarded the U.S.S. *President Cleveland* for California. "Of course, at that time there were not too many Chinese students coming to America. I was one of the very few of what you might call pioneers. But I was willing to take the chance." Failure was no option. Seeing him off, his older brother, James, told him, "If you don't succeed, you may as well forget about coming back."

In Hong Kong, still a British protectorate at the time, students went straight from high school to medical school. So Clyde Wu was puzzled to find all his American applications rejected. But after one year in a small community college in Stockton, Cal., he applied to and was admitted as an undergraduate at Johns Hopkins University. His English was far from perfect. "However," he shrugs, "you can compensate by working harder and working longer, and that's exactly what I did." Earning a BA in three years, he applied to and was accepted at several medical schools, including Columbia P&S.

The lone Chinese member, and one of only two Asians, in the Class of 1956, Dr. Wu takes note of the 30 Asians out of 150 admitted students in the Class of 2014.

"Do you feel a sense of gratification at having helped open the door?" an interviewer cannot help but inquire.

"I would not claim such an important accomplishment," he demurs, "but I cherish the school that admits people regardless of race or religion, based only on qualifications and promise."

His P&S interview with the then dean of students Dr. Aura Severinghaus still sticks out in his mind. The interviewer showed a sensitivity and keen interest in the applicant. As a young man, it turned out, Dr. Severinghaus had been one of a select group of promising medical academics to teach and pursue research on the faculty at PUMC in Beijing. The school had been founded in 1921 by the China Medical Board of the Rockefeller Foundation. Dr. Severinghaus pursued vital research there on the sexual cycle of *Schistosoma japonicum*, a parasitic worm that afflicted the rural China population.

The PUMC faculty attracted other rising stars, a number of whom, like Dr. Severinghaus, later taught at P&S, including surgical bacteriologist Dr. Frank Meleney, who discovered anaerobic micro-streptococci and introduced the use of hydrogen peroxide as an antiseptic agent; pioneering pharmacologist, Dr. Harry Van Dyke; and surgeon, Dr. Jerome B. Webster, the founding father of plastic surgery. But the institution fell on hard times. Seized by the Japanese, it was subsequently closed for the duration of the War, nationalized in the wake of the revolution, downsized, and during the Cultural Revolution, underwent a brain drain, hemorrhaging a lost generation of teachers to forced "re-education." PUMC went through multiple name changes and became a shadow of its former self. But Dr. Wu never forgot Dr. Severinghaus's account of the school's glory days as China's (and Asia's) most respected and influential medical school.

At P&S, Dr. Wu stayed in touch with Dr. Severinghaus and also got to know Dr. Meleney, profoundly impressed, not only by the latter's brilliance in the lab but also by his compassion at the bedside. "At P&S, I learned that a good doctor should have true empathy with his patients." Other teachers who taught by example were Drs. Randal Bailey, Hamilton Southwirth, Dana Atchley, and the legendary Robert Loeb. "From them I learned that clinical medicine, teaching, and research are the Holy Trinity of American medical education."

His eyes still light up at the memory of the day he first put on a white coat in physical diagnosis in the spring term of his second year. "I felt great. I said, 'Oh, this is what I've been waiting for! And putting the stethoscope to my ear, the thump of the human heart was music to my ears, oh my!'"

Music, as it turns out, would later take on a paramount role for him in matters of the heart, after meeting and marrying the pianist and musical educator Helen Tseng.

BACK TO HONG KONG AND ONWARDS TO DETROIT

Opting for internal medicine, Dr. Wu interned at the University of Rochester and pursued a medical residency and a fellowship in cardiology at Boston City Hospital, where he engaged in research on the biochemical changes caused by cardiac failure, dividing his time between the clinic and the lab.

In 1961, he was elected a member of the Royal College of Physicians in Great Britain and returned to Hong Kong as a lecturer in cardiology at Hong Kong University Medical School, where he helped start up one of the first cardiac catheterization labs. As a medical student he had rotated through Bellevue, where, at the time Drs. André Cournand HON '65 and Dickinson Richards '23, who shared a Nobel Prize for their development of heart catheterization, ran the Pulmonary Division.

Though gratified to have fulfilled his dream of practicing medicine and using his knowledge to help the Chinese, the experience of practicing medicine in Hong Kong proved something of a shock when, midway through a blood transfusion, the metric pressure gauge suddenly malfunctioned. The equipment had to be shipped back to the United States for repair. "That meant the lab being six weeks to two months out of commission," he says. "It suddenly dawned on me that I couldn't count on the comforts of American medicine. It was then that I realized that I had better hone my clinical skills."

Returning to the States, he joined the faculty in the Department of Medicine at Wayne State University in Detroit, where he taught and pursued research on cardiac metabolism under Dr. Richard Bing. He also joined, and subsequently became chief of, the Pulmonary Division at Oakwood Hospital in Dearborn, and served as a principal member of the Cardiac Catheterization Unit at Detroit General Hospital. Following several years of teaching and research, he ultimately decided to devote himself to fulltime clinical practice.

It was a time of great change in cardiology. When Dr. Wu entered the field many people were still dying from heart attacks and rheumatic heart disease was still a serious, and often fatal, condition. Dr. Wu was among the clinicians who benefited from and helped to implement the revolutionary life-saving advances, including the introduction of bypass surgery, the development of statins to reduce cholesterol, and such behavioral changes as regular exercise and smoking cessation. The clinical cardiologists of his generation saw a sea change in the longevity and quality of life of their patients.

In 1973, he became a fellow of the American College of Cardiology and in 1981 achieved the distinction of fellowship in the Royal College of Physicians.

THE GROWING WU FAMILY AND EXTENDED "FAMILY" OF WU FELLOWS

There were many satisfying years of practice. Meanwhile, the family grew. He and his wife Helen had two sons, who both grew up to became doctors, Roger, a child psychiatrist, and David, a chest specialist. Then came four grandchildren. Fearing that China was "a remote and hazy place" to the second generation, Dr. and Mrs. Wu took their children and grandchildren on a trip to China to reconnect with their roots.

In 1992, the China Medical Board decided that they would no longer be able to support the postdoc fellows from Beijing and Hong Kong that they regularly sent to America to pursue advanced training. On the urging of the dean of Hong Kong University Medical School, Professor Ma, Dr. Wu's sister-in-law, Lady Ivy Wu, agreed to step in and lend her support, but with the stipulation that Clyde Wu would act as an adviser. With the help of his wife, Helen, Dr. Wu enthusiastically participated in the selection process.

While in China, Dr. Wu remembered Dean Severinghaus's stories and asked to visit the PUMC campus in Beijing. "My emotion," he recalls, "was very mixed. This was *the* PUMC, the school I'd heard so much about, but it was sadly dilapidated . . . the building itself, as well as the spirit of the place. The old were getting older and the young were not really well trained." The Cultural Revolution had purged a missing generation of teachers. So, in addition to participating in the selection of Ivy Wu Fellows, Dr. Wu volunteered to help PUMC.

He decided to select fellows from the ranks of junior faculty in the Department of Medicine at PUMC and support their training for a year at P&S. A number of the former Clyde and Helen Wu Fellows have since risen to positions of leadership in China, notably Dr. Chen Zhu HON '16, China's former Minister of Health.

As with the original educational mission of PUMC, not just to educate doctors but to educate teachers of medicine, and thereby to have a broader influence, the Wu Fellows Program has an ambitious goal. "The whole idea," says Dr. Wu, "is that if you train one teacher, hundreds of students and society in general will benefit. Helen and I have not deviated from that idea."

Dr. and Mrs. Wu were actively involved in the selection process: "You may say that is our paternal and maternal instinct. They are in a sense 'our children.' We are invested in their future and in what they will do for society."

The Wus have also supported senior P&S faculty on educational missions to China. A number of collaborative studies have resulted, including an ongoing international comparative clinical study of osteoporosis in China, Hong Kong, and the United States, whose lead investigator, John Bilezikian '69, professor of medicine and pharmacology at P&S, and chief of the Division of Endocrinology at Presbyterian Hospital, was one of the first P&S faculty members to lecture in China with Dr. Wu's support.

"You cannot do everything in life," says Dr. Wu, "but if you choose the things that you like, and do the things that you like, and do the things that have meaning for you, and know that you have done your best, you can be happy."

In this effort and so many others, Dr. Wu has gone far above and beyond the call of duty as two-term plus trustee of Columbia University.

"Whether our efforts have done any good in the long run, only history will tell," he reflects, "but both sides, Columbia and China, have benefited, and this has brought Helen and myself great joy."

THE SCIENTIFIC WUNDERKIND OF BIOTECH
MAKES PROTEINS DO THE RIGHT THING

GEORGE D. YANCOPOULOS PHD '86, MD'87

*Regeneron, the company to which George D. Yancopoulos PhD '86, MD '87
hitched his intellectual wagon, has since grown into a biotech powerhouse.
The former Wunderkind, now a scientific superstar, a principal inventor and
developer of Regeneron's six FDA-approved drugs, as well as its foundational
technologies, including the Trap technology, VelociGene® and VelocImmune®,
succeeded beyond his wildest dreams, leading the company's discovery and in
the process becoming pharma's first billionaire. A talk titled "Building a Better
Biotech: The Story of Regeneron," in 2018, drew a standing room crowd to the
Clyde and Helen Wu Auditorium in the Roy and Diana Vagelos Education
Building at P&S.*

———— ∞∞∞ ————

GEORGE D. YANCOPOULOS PHD '86, MD'87, the physician-scientist whose lab
first shed light on one of biomedical science's holy grails, the nerve-muscle interface, among other fundamental discoveries, defies conventional thinking. Age
forty-four, the author of more than 200 peer-reviewed papers in multiple fields,
Dr. Yancopoulos keeps leapfrogging freely between disciplines and domains.
Listed in a 1997 survey of the Institute for Scientific Information as one of the
eleven most highly cited scientists in the world, he is a molecular biologist with
a structural biological background and an immunological focus, a basic scientist
actively involved in clinical applications. Further befuddling all expectations,
Dr. Yancopoulos comfortably straddles the divide between academe and industry on an intellectual footbridge of his own devising. He is a bench worker in
a business suit—actually, he prefers jeans!—a scientific thinker devoted to the
development and production of therapeutic agents.

President of Regeneron Research Laboratories, and chief scientific officer and founding scientist of Regeneron Pharmaceuticals, Inc., a cutting-edge biotechnology firm committed to science-based discovery, Dr. Yancopoulos simultaneously maintains strong academic ties as adjunct professor of microbiology at both Columbia P&S and New York Medical College. Much sought after as a lecturer and scientific collaborator, he organized and cochaired a P&S Biomedical Symposium on angiogenesis at Columbia's Arden House in Harriman, N.Y., in July 2001.

Perhaps most surprising of all, leaders of both academia and industry concur in their estimation of the man and his qualities.

Saul J. Silverstein, MD, professor and chair of the Department of Microbiology at P&S, who first knew Yancopoulos as a PhD candidate and postdoc and subsequently offered him a coveted junior faculty position, only to have his offer respectfully declined, waves off with a smile any suggestion of his erstwhile protégé's (and continuing collaborator's) defection from the ranks of academe: "I don't think George has ever actually left anything; he keeps ten feet in this university alone, and ten hands in teaching institutions across the country." Silverstein, who nominated Yancopoulos for Columbia University's Medal of Excellence, lauds the latter's "uncommon ability to conceptualize scientific problems and use information from many disciplines to discover how molecules work." In a nominating letter, Silverstein characterized Yancopoulos's "research daring [as varying] from the procedural to the profound."

P. Roy Vagelos '54, the retired chair and CEO of the pharmaceutical giant Merck & Co., another academic scientist who has crisscrossed the academic-industrial divide, a man not ordinarily given to superlatives, considers Yancopoulos "one of the smartest and most gifted research people in all of the biosciences today and perhaps the strongest scientist in the combined biotech-pharmaceutical industry"—high praise indeed from the trailblazer of science-based discovery, who's peerless reputation landed him on the cover of *Fortune* magazine! Vagelos was, in fact, so impressed with Yancopoulos that, upon his retirement from Merck, he joined Regeneron as chair of the board (a notable body that includes, among other scientific heavy hitters, Nobel laureates Michael S. Brown, MD; Alfred G. Gilman, MD, PhD; and Joseph Goldstein, MD). Asked what he considered so remarkable about the company, Dr. Vagelos replied without hesitation: "Mostly, George!"

A PASSION FOR SCIENCE

At first sight, the nondescript gray metal shelf covered with red labels resembles a pharmacy cabinet stocked with the ingredients of prescriptions waiting to be filled. A closer look reveals a wall full of neatly ordered published papers. The white board at his back is messy with equations and calculations, an arsenal of felt tips ready for takeoff. Yet lest you be taken in by the apparent nonchalance of his open collar and blue jeans, the laser-like intensity of his dark gaze will instantly set you straight. Yancopoulos means business and that business is science!

Of medium height, with the open face and the lean and sinewy build of a former college athlete (he rowed on the crew and played baseball for Columbia College), George Yancopoulos lives and breathes biology. Notwithstanding what he perceives as a certain degree of hype spun off by the Genome Project, Yancopoulos insists that "sophisticated biology still requires an all-encompassing approach that is almost as rare and challenging today as it was decades ago." Figuratively wed to his work, his biography reveals a single-minded commitment, with time off for family.

"Day-to-day science, I have to say, and even what happens over a period of years is a little bit boring," he claims. "Actually, I'm a boring guy, I have my family and Regeneron!"

Boring indeed! Quiet waters run deep. George Yancopoulos is a man on a quest. His hydra-headed, fire-breathing dragon is/are human immunologic disorders. His weapon of choice is/are the body's own naturally occurring proteins replicated, redirected, blocked, or enhanced by his team at Regeneron to repair processes gone awry.

MENTORS, MYTHIC AND MORTAL

The American-born son of Greek immigrants, he was nurtured on tales of the ancient Greek sages, Archimedes, Euclid, Plato, and on the exploits of his own paternal grandfather and namesake, George Damis Yancopoulos, an electrical engineer who built Greece's first electrical power plants. "So I was primed from the start," he asserts, only half joking, "like I was some sort of biological experiment. All these stories made me think, if my ancestors and my own grandfather, whose name I bear, could do great things, then maybe I could too!"

Graduating as class valedictorian in 1976 at New York's prestigious Bronx High School of Science and winging it again in 1980 at Columbia College, where he earned a BA summa cum laude in biochemistry, Yancopoulos was named Outstanding Chemistry Student and Dwight D. Eisenhower Top Scholar-Athlete. He continued to shine at P&S, garnering the Alfred Steiner Award for Medical Student Research in 1984 and the Louis Gibofsky Award for Research in Immunology in 1987. Earning his PhD in biochemistry and molecular biophysics in 1986 from the Columbia University Graduate School of Arts and Sciences, he was selected, based on an outstanding thesis, to speak at commencement, and subsequently won the prestigious Lucille P. Markey Award in Biomedical Sciences.

And just as the ancient Greek sages had fed the dreams of his childhood, contemporary Columbia scientists inspired him, by their example, to bring those dreams to fruition. He considers the time he spent at Columbia, as undergraduate, medical student, PhD candidate, and postdoc, as "the most formative period in my life."

"I do think," says Yancopoulos, "that young people need inspiration and a lot of role models who excite them and make them say, 'Hey, that's what I want to be doing!'" The P&S faculty comprised a rich panoply of such mentors. "When you have truly top-tier people, like Drs. Elvin Kabet, Argis Stradiatis, Fred Alt, Richard Axel, Erik Kandel, to name only a few, people who lecture you and with whom you interact socially, talk science, and joke around, people who themselves have done incredible things, it makes you believe that you can be like them!"

As an undergraduate at Columbia College, he had focused on x-ray crystallography and the structure of proteins, and more specifically, the mechanism of the shape changes hemoglobin molecules undergo in the transport of oxygen. At P&S, under the influence of Dr. Argis Stradiatis, Yancopoulos shifted his focus to the genetic encoding that predisposed the action of protein molecules.

Entranced by the new study of single nucleotide polymorphisms, Yancopoulos now zeroed in on the microbiological phenomena that "coded for and led to production of these tiny little protein machines."

Under the influence of another P&S mentor, Dr. Fred Alt, then a member of the faculty, Yancopoulos applied this newfound focus on DNA technology to the field of immunology. A precocious student, he got involved in his teacher's pathbreaking study of just how the body mounts an immune response to foreign microbes, and coauthored the published results.

A PIVOT, *NOT* A DEPARTURE, FROM ACADEMIA

Twenty years and multiple publications later, Yancopoulos and his scientific team at Regeneron Pharmaceuticals, Inc., the firm he helped found (with president and CEO Leonard Schleifer, MD PhD) in 1989, are still engaged in studying disease situations in which the body needs to fight off or make more of various endogenous proteins.

Despite the intense lobbying not to "jump ship" by friends and well-wishers in academe, including Nobel laureate Dr. David Baltimore, Yancopoulos felt it was time for an intellectual adventure. Having operated primarily in a university setting for all of his adult life, he felt "if I was going to do something totally risky, totally zany, this was the time in my life to do it." Intrigued (and inspired) by a call from Schleifer, Yancopoulos took the leap of his life, climbing aboard as senior staff scientist of the fledgling firm in 1989. In 1992 he was promoted to vice president of discovery, in 1997 to chief scientific officer, and in 2001 to president of Regeneron Research Laboratories and a member of the board of directors. Engrossed in his research and the nuts and bolts of helping to lead a company, Yancopoulos has never had time to look back.

He and his scientific team at Regeneron have published fundamental findings in diverse fields, including, early on, the discovery and characterization of novel neurotrophic factors in the regulation of neuronal survival and function. Among the subsequent outcroppings of his multiple research interests were the initial descriptions of paradigm multicomponent cytokine receptor systems and identification of the in vivo trigger in the formation of the neuromuscular interface between nerve and muscle. More recently, he and his team successfully identified a new set of angiogenic factors involved in mediating normal and pathological blood vessel growth. They also hit upon fundamental factors in the mechanism of muscle growth and degeneration. And they hit virtual pay dirt with the realization that a neurotrophic factor that they had previously studied in another context had the potential to address the problem of obesity.

And while all this research regularly made it into such leading medical and scientific journals as *Science, Cell,* and *Nature,* it also led to human clinical studies and the development of promising products on the drug pipeline.

Among the therapeutic agents closest to making a splash is Axokine, a drug to regulate obesity, currently in the final stages of testing in humans, which appears to far outperform any other agent on the market. Other agents developed by Yancopoulos and his team at Regeneron are also making news. Cytokine antagonists or Traps, now in human trials, hold great promise for the regulation of such immunologic disorders as asthma and rheumatoid arthritis. The team has also developed promising angiogenic regulators in cancer and vascular disease.

THE VAGELOS FACTOR

Regeneron has recruited other P&S alumni, but the company's greatest coup was landing pharmaceutical legend P. Roy Vagelos '54.

As scientifically successful as Regeneron was, says Yancopoulos, "it took Roy Vagelos to take us to the next step and say, 'Hey, great technologies, but while you started out trying to address neurodegenerative diseases, none of us will be around to see the fruits of your labor!'" Vagelos convinced Yancopoulos and company president Schleifer to apply the same revolutionary scientific technologies they'd developed to more tractable disease situations. "Take those same micro-genetic approaches," said Vagelos, "and apply them to obesity, to diabetes, to rheumatoid arthritis, to allergy and asthma!" Says Yancopoulos: "That's just what we did! We're really on the verge of making a difference, coming up with whole new ways of attacking old diseases!"

Yancopoulos recalls the fortuitous irony of the fact that when, as a young man, he first expressed a serious interest in science as a career, his encouraging, albeit cautious, Greek parents pointed to Vagelos. Having followed with interest the astronomical rise of the senior biomedical scientist with Hellenic roots, they said, "Son, if you're going to become a scientist, at least be one like Roy Vagelos!" "Funny," reflects Yancopoulos with a smile, "that after all these years, our paths converged!"

YANKEE CENTER FIELD OR BUST

Just like his old hero and role model, Roy Vagelos, who did it all at Merck, George Yancopoulos enjoys the manifold and varied responsibilities of his corporate role: "I can't imagine a more challenging and fun job! One minute I'm at a basic science meeting trying to understand a biological mechanism, the next minute I'm talking with our clinical people about our upcoming human trials, and the next minute I'm engaged in a business discussion. I get to do it all!"

Are there any regrets?

"The only other thing I could imagine wanting to do, maybe, would be to play center field for the New York Yankees! But only," he stresses with a wink, "if I were an all-star caliber player, maybe that would do it!"

For the moment, at least, the frustrated athlete will just have to stick to coaching his daughter's soccer team and to the more rarefied pursuit of pitching proteins!

AUTHOR'S BIO

ALUMNI NEWS Writer and Managing Editor of Alumni Publications of the Columbia University College of Physicians and Surgeons from 1987 to 2018, and from 2016 to 2018, director of communications of the Wu Family China Center for Health Initiatives, Peter Wortsman is the author of work in multiple modes, including fiction (*A Modern Way to Die*, 1991, *Cold Earth Wanderers*, 2014, and *Footprints in West Cement*, 2017), stage plays (*The Tattooed Man Tells All*, 2000 and *Burning Words*, 2006), poetry (*it-t=i*, 2004), and travel memoir (*Ghost Dance in Berlin: A Rhapsody in Gray*, 2013). Also a critically acclaimed translator from the German, his many English takes on German classics include: *Posthumous Papers of a Living Author*, by Robert Musil (now in its third edition: 1986, 1995, 2006), an anthology, *Tales of the German Imagination: From the Brothers Grimm to Ingeborg Bachmann*, which he also compiled and edited (2013), and *Konundrum, Selected Prose of Franz Kafka* (2016). His plays have been produced in the U.S. and Europe. His articles have appeared in the *New York Times*, the *Los Angeles Times*, the *Boston Globe*, *Die Zeit, Die Welt, Cicero*, the *Paris Review*, and other major newspapers, journals and websites in the U.S. and abroad. His travel reflections were included for five years in a row, 2008–12, and again in 2016, in *The Best Travel Writing*. Recipient of the 1985 Beard's Fund Short Story Award, the 2008 Gertje

Potash-Suhr Prosapreis of the Society for Contemporary American Literature in German, the 2012 Gold Grand Prize for Best Travel Story of the Year in the Solas Awards Competition, and a 2014 Independent Publishers Book Award (IPPY), Wortsman was a Fulbright Fellow in 1973, a Thomas J. Watson Foundation Fellow in 1974, and a Holtzbrinck Fellow at the American Academy in Berlin in 2010. He is a member of PEN, the Authors Guild, and the Fulbright Association.

PHOTO CREDITS

Samuel Bard
Milstein Division, The New York Public Library

Karen Antman '74
Photograph by Peter Wortsman

Mary T. Bassett '79
Photograph courtesy of Mary T. Bassett

Baruch Blumberg '51
Photograph by Peter Wortsman

T. Berry Brazelton '43
Photograph courtesy of the estate of
T. Berry Brazelton

Keith Brodie '65
Photograph by Peter Wortsman

Stanley Chang '74
Photograph courtesy of the office
of Stanley Chang

Davida Coady '65
Photograph by Peter Wortsman

**Ron Cohen '81, Paul Maddon MD, PhD '88,
George Yancopoulos PhD '86, MD '87**
Photograph by Chris Ware

Robert Coles '54
Photograph by Peter Wortsman

Robin Cook '66
Photograph by Peter Wortsman

Abdul El-Sayed '14
Photograph by Peter Wortsman

Ephraim P. Engleman '37
Photograph courtesy of the estate of Ephraim P. Engleman

Kenneth Forde '59
Photograph courtesy of Kenneth Forde

Thomas R. Frieden MD/MPH '86
Photograph by Peter Wortsman

Jerome Groopman '76
Photograph courtesy of Jerome Groopman

Karen Hein '70
Photograph courtesy of Karen Hein

Charles S. Houston'39
Photograph by Anne-Marie W. Littenberg
https://commons.wikimedia.org/wiki/File:Charles_S
_Houston_2008.jpg

Michael Iseman '65
Photograph courtesy of Michael Iseman

Fadlo R. Khuri '89
Photograph by Peter Wortsman

Karen Kinsell '93
Photograph by Peter Wortsman

Margaret Morgan Lawrence '40
Courtesy of the National Institutes
of Health (NIH) photo archives

Burton J. Lee, III '56
Photograph courtesy of the estate of Burton J. Lee

Robert J. Lefkowitz '66
Photograph by Peter Wortsman

Jay Levy '65
Photograph by Peter Wortsman

Martha M. MacGuffie '49
Photograph by Peter Wortsman

Paul Marks '49
Photograph courtesy of the National Cancer Institute

Story Musgrave '64
Photograph courtesy of NASA

Col. Jonathan Newmark, MC, USAR '78
Photograph by Peter Wortsman

Suzanne Oparil '65
Photograph courtesy of Suzanne Oparil

Calvin H. Plimpton MSD '51
Photograph by Peter Wortsman

Velma Scantlebury '81
Photograph by Peter Wortsman

Eve Slater '71
Photograph courtesy of Eve Slater

Benjamin Spock '29
Photograph by Peter Wortsman

Yvonne Thornton MD '73, MPH '96
Photograph courtesy of Yvonne Thornton

P. Roy Vagelos '54
Photograph courtesy of the Science History Institute.
https://commons.wikimedia.org/wiki/File:P._Roy
_Vagelos_JPS_2005_03_10_crop.TIF.

Harold Varmus '66
Photograph courtesy of the Memorial Sloan-Kettering
Cancer Center and the National Cancer Institute

Clyde Y.C. Wu '56
Photograph courtesy of the estate of Clyde Y.C. Wu

George D. Yancopoulos PhD '86 MD '87
Photograph courtesy of George D. Yancopoulos

Peter Wortsman
Photo by Jean-Luc Fievet

GPSR Authorized Representative: Easy Access System Europe, Mustamäe tee 50, 10621 Tallinn, Estonia, gpsr.requests@easproject.com

www.ingramcontent.com/pod-product-compliance
Lightning Source LLC
Chambersburg PA
CBHW031940090426

42811CB00002B/253